Alice Schultz

Reflective Planning, Teaching, and Evaluation

K–12

Third Edition

Judy Eby
San Diego State University

Adrienne L. Herrell
California State University, Fresno

James L. Hicks
Barrington Unified School District
Barrington, Illinois

Merrill
Prentice Hall

Upper Saddle River, New Jersey
Columbus, Ohio

Library of Congress Cataloging in Publication Data

Reflective planing, treaching, and evaluation, K-12/Judy W. Eby, Arienne Herrell, James L. Hicks.—3rd ed

p. cm.

Includes bibliographical references and index.

ISBN 0-13-029296-6

1. Effective Teaching. 2. Thought and thinking. 3. Educational tests and measurements.   I. Herrell, Adreienne L. II. Hicks, James L. III. Title

LB1025.3 .E28 2002
371.102—dc21   00-066448

Vice President and Publisher: Jeffery W. Johnston
Managing Editor: Debra A. Stollenwerk
Assistant Editor: Daniel J. Parker
Production Editor: Kimberly J. Lundy
Design Coordinator: Diane C. Lorenzo
Cover Designer: Thomas Mack
Cover Image: Eyewire
Production Manager: Pamela D. Bennett
Electronic Text Management: Karen L. Bretz, Melanie N. Ortega, Marilyn Wilson Phelps
Director of Marketing: Kevin Flanagan
Marketing Manager: Krista Groshong
Marketing Services Manager: Barbara Koontz

This book was set in Transitional 511 by Prentice Hall. It was printed and bound by R. R. Donnelley & Sons Company. The cover was printed by The Lehigh Press, Inc.

Photo credits: Scott Cunningham/Merrill, pp. 107, 133, 169, 191, 263; Anthony Magnacca/ Merrill, pp. 1, 21, 237, 293; Anne Vega/Merrill, p. 215; Tom Watson/Merrill, p. 49.

Pearson Education Ltd., London
Pearson Education Australia Pty. Limited, Sydney
Pearson Education Singapore Pte. Ltd.
Pearson Education North Asia Ltd., Hong Kong
Pearson Education Canada, Ltd., Toronto
Pearson Educación de Mexico, S.A. de C.V.
Pearson Education-Japan, Tokyo
Pearson Education Malaysia Pte. Ltd.
Pearson Education, Upper Saddle River, New Jersey

10 9 8 7 6 5 4 3 2 1
ISBN 0-13-029296-6

preface

We all have a powerful desire to be successful in any educational venture we undertake throughout our lives. Nowhere is this more true than in the elementary classrooms of schools around the world. Each morning that a new school term begins, children wake up, brush their teeth, put on their clothes, eat their breakfasts, and walk out the door with the same hopeful longing: "I hope I get a good teacher."

What does the child mean by a good teacher? We believe that a good teacher is one who uses what Kounin (1977) calls *withitness* to perceive the needs of the varied students who come into our classrooms. But, after the many and varied needs of students have been perceived, then what?

We offer you some answers to "then what" in this textbook. Here is our combined experience as both learners and teachers and our analysis of the best practices in research that can enable you to approach your new role as teacher with confidence that you and your students can succeed. We offer you our original model of how caring, reflective teachers think and feel on the job. We call it *reflective action.* You will find it highlighted in Chapter 1, and then referred to again and again throughout the book. Essentially, it is a proactive teaching/learning process that prepares you to combine and alternate perceptiveness of your students' needs with periods of reflection, getting support and feedback from trusted colleagues, making plans, predicting possible outcomes of your plans, taking action, reflecting on your action, and acting again, each time with more care and precision than the time before.

Features of This Edition

We're excited about this concept. We hope that you are, too. But we recognize that you are entering the teaching profession at a time when there is more to think about every day. This edition has been redesigned to respond to the new challenges in education that have grown out of the change in demographics in all areas of the country.

We have redesigned this text to ensure that it is current and up to date in regard to both federal guidelines and state standards for teacher credentialling programs.

CLAD

The planning, teaching, and evaluation strategies we describe throughout this book are well suited for use in Crosscultural, Language, and Academic Development (CLAD) credential programs that prepare teachers to meet the needs of culturally diverse students. Our reflective action model prepares teachers to become more adept at considering the needs of culturally diverse learners. Suggestions for scaffolding language, adapting lessons for the language acquisition stages of students, and actively involving nonfluent speakers of English are incorporated into Chapter 3. Assessment strategies which allow students to demonstrate their knowledge and understanding in a variety of ways are included in Chapter 11.

TECHNOLOGICAL INNOVATIONS IN THE CLASSROOM

We're also well aware of the greatly changing educational landscape due to the growth in technological innovations available to teachers and students at home and in school. Chapter 10 is devoted entirely to using technology in your teaching. It includes descriptions of school districts that have pioneered in technology-based education. There are many specific descriptions of how teachers use computers, video cameras, scanners, photocopiers, and compact and laser disks to stimulate and motivate their students to learn. There are many stories of students doing research on the Internet and networking with people around the globe to gather and share information.

PROFESSIONAL PORTFOLIO FOR TEACHERS

At the end of each chapter in this book, we include learning experiences that will stimulate beginning teachers to become proactive in their classroom visitations. As they visit other teachers' classrooms and complete the end-of-chapter assignments, they will have the opportunity to reflect deeply on their own philosophies, priorities, and values in education. They will be prompted to use the steps of the reflective action model as they begin to document their own best practices, strengths, and talents. The end result can be a professional portfolio filled with curriculum plans and classroom management strategies that a beginning teacher can show with pride at employment interviews.

Companion Website

Technology is a constantly growing and changing aspect of our field that, creating a need for new content and resources. To address this emerging need, Prentice Hall has developed an online learning environment for students and professors alike—Companion Websites—to support our textbooks.

The content for each user-friendly website is organized by topic and provides professors and students with a variety of meaningful resources.

FOR THE PROFESSOR—

Every Companion Website integrates **Syllabus Manager**™, an online syllabus creation and management utility. **Syllabus Manager**™ provides you, the instructor, with an easy, step-by-step process to create and revise syllabi with direct links into Companion Website and other online content without having to learn HTML.

- Students may log on to your syllabus during any study session. All they need to know is the web address for the Companion Website and the password you've assigned to your syllabus.
- After you have created a syllabus using **Syllabus Manager**™, students may enter the syllabus for their course section from any point in the Companion Website.
- Clicking on a date, the student is shown the list of activities for the assignment. The activities for each assignment are linked directly to actual content, saving time for students.
- Adding assignments consists of clicking on the desired due date, then filling in the details of the assignment—name of the assignment, instructions, and whether or not it is a one-time or repeating assignment.
- In addition, links to other activities can be created easily. If the activity is online, a URL can be entered in the space provided, and it will be linked automatically in the final syllabus.
- Your completed syllabus is hosted on our servers, allowing convenient updates from any computer on the Internet. Changes you make to your syllabus are immediately available to your students at their next logon.

FOR THE STUDENT—

Every Companion Website also includes content and features designed specifically for students.

- **Topic Overviews**—outline key concepts in topic areas
- **Web Links**—a wide range of websites that provide useful and current information related to each topic area
- **Lesson Plans**—links to lesson plans for appropriate topic areas
- **Projects on the Web**—links to projects and activities on the web for appropriate topic areas
- **Education Resources**—links to schools, online journals, government sites, departments of education, professional organizations, regional information, and more

- **Electronic Bluebook**—send homework or essays directly to your instructor's email with this paperless form
- **Message Board**—serves as a virtual bulletin board to post—or respond to—questions or comments to/from a national audience
- **Chat**—real-time chat with anyone who is using the text anywhere in the country—ideal for discussion and study groups, class projects, etc.

To take advantage of these and other resources, please visit the Companion Website for *Reflective Planning, Teaching, and Evaluation: K–12*, Third Edition, at

www.prenhall.com/eby

References

Kounin, J. (1977). *Discipline and group management in classrooms.* New York: Holt, Rinehart and Winston.

brief contents

contents

CHAPTER 9   TEACHING STRATEGIES THAT INCREASE AUTHENTIC LEARNING   215

CHAPTER 10   INTEGRATING TECHNOLOGY INTO THE CURRICULUM   237

**CHAPTER 11   ASSESSING AND REPORTING STUDENT
ACCOMPLISHMENTS   263**

introduction to the third edition
by jim hicks

Judy Eby asked me to co-author this edition of this textbook for beginning teachers because she knows that although I have been a classroom teacher for many years, I am still as passionate about my profession as I was when I began teaching.

As I thought about what I wanted to contribute to this book, I realized one of the issues I most wanted to address is the question of why some new teachers thrive and others don't. Many new teachers have been successful students, have passed their teacher education courses with flying colors, and yet, they seem to lose their bearings in their first few years of classroom teaching, lose heart and motivation to continue, and leave the profession early. Some people call this "teacher burnout." I want to share my suggestions for how to avoid teacher burnout and develop into a successful teacher who thrives on the daily interactions with students, other faculty, and parents that are a hallmark of our profession.

Teaching can be one of the most rewarding career paths, and in my view, is also one of the most influential professions that you can choose. The joy associated with inspiring students to learn and achieve is very satisfying. The potential for making strides in our own personal growth develops out of learning and sharing new ideas with colleagues. Words of appreciation and other forms of positive feedback from students and parents are very fulfilling. Most of all, the realization that as a teacher you can make a huge impact on society gives you a sense of noble purpose in your life.

There is a dark side to teaching, however, that also needs to be addressed. If you take it seriously, teaching is one of the most demanding and time-consuming careers available. At times, beginning (and experienced) teachers can experience a roller coaster of emotions that may shock and dismay even the most tolerant personality. One day you experience sheer excitement over your contributions in the classroom and the next day everything seems to go wrong and you may begin perceive yourself to be totally ineffective.

I have occasionally hit lows that cause me to think about retiring early and going into some other profession that is not nearly so demanding, and I have sadly watched as other colleagues give up, burn out, and leave teaching forever. From my experience, I have concluded that there are many contributions to teacher burnout. Some of the potential conditions that cause teachers to become dissatisfied include the following:

1. Demanding schedules: Teachers may be on duty for many hours a day without a break. A teacher can't be late for class; in fact, teacher tardiness may have liability consequences.
2. Seemingly endless paperwork: We have assignments to create, homework to evaluate, and administrivia to complete and return to the office before lunch.
3. Constantly being on stage: Every class period we are expected to present new information, use withitness to perceive the needs of every student, patiently review and reteach, make split-second decisions, and change course whenever it seems necessary.
4. Excuses, excuses: Another problem for seasoned teachers is hearing or witnessing the same excuse from students for the nth time. It is hard to treat each case as fresh and not become jaded. It can appear at times that we have turned into a nation of excuses, especially in the field of education.
5. Unexpected interruptions: Right in the middle of an important lesson, the fire drill rings, an administrator comes to observe your class, or a student gets sick.

However, even though you may not be in control of your day, you can learn to control your emotional reactions to these and many other disturbing events. If you are hoping to become a "lifer," like me, just surviving is not very appealing when looking toward the future. You want to be able to thrive, not just survive. Why do some teachers flourish while others wilt and go to seed? There is no precise rubric for success. A lot depends on knowing yourself. It is important that you consciously reflect on how you will handle the stresses of teaching. You know from your own experience as a student that many adults do not have the patience and positive attitudes needed for success. Do you? Look inside and learn more about your own personality and your reasons for becoming a teacher.

One important thing to reflect on is why you want to become a teacher. It is hoped that you are entering teaching because you like working with young adults, you know your subject matter well, and you are interested in learning a variety of teaching techniques.

Another important factor is to be willing to allow your students to know that you are a human being with feelings, too. Be open with your students. Ask for feedback and they'll be more willing to accept the feedback you give them.

Find a way to demonstrate your passion for teaching and for your subject matter. Keep trying new techniques; keep learning more about your subject and bring in the latest and most up-to-date examples to share with your students. Your passion and enthusiasm for your subject will awaken a similar passion and motivation in your students. Use the summer recess or other planning times to bring yourself up to date about technology and curriculum ideas and to do research in your field so you have something fresh to offer each year.

Don't just accept the first teaching job you are offered. Look for a good match between you and the other faculty members at the school you select. Join a good team or initiate a collegial group where you can discuss the daily rigors of teaching, and get feedback you can trust. Knowing that you are not the only teacher facing difficulties and having the opportunity to discuss viable solutions to problems is an important way to prevent teacher burnout.

Get parents on your side from the first week. Communicate the good news as well as bad news through notes or phone calls. Invite parents to visit or, even better, come in and volunteer. Being a "sage-on-stage" all the time can be tiring. Develop a variety of teaching styles and approaches that allow you to be the guide-on-the-side sometimes. Parents can help here also by assisting you as a computer monitor or a guest lecturer.

Accept the reality that some events are just out of your control. Do the best you can each day, but never expect perfection from your students, your administrators, the parents, or yourself. Be satisfied with small positive steps toward success and you and your students will thrive even in the most chaotic community.

Finally, take a well-deserved vacation when possible. Another important antidote for teacher burnout is to become involved in self-absorbing hobbies, something entirely different from what you teach. Leave school at school.

Too often, weekends as well as nights are filled with teacher-related activities. People who are not teachers often observe that teachers just can't let go. When teachers socialize, what do they frequently talk about? Teaching! The axiom "Teaching is not a job, it is a way of life" is a living statement. If someone ever asks you to "get a life," you can say that you have one, thank you, and it is teaching.

chapter 1

REFLECTIVE ACTION IN TEACHING

How do we prepare our students to thrive in the high-tech world of the 21st century? We learned how to conduct research in libraries, using encyclopedias and other "hands-on" materials. Now we must teach our students how to do research on the ever-changing, ever-expanding Internet. We learned to make political and economic decisions mainly by reading the newspaper and watching television newscasts to inform our votes. Our students will gain most of their information online, and they will have to be able to sort opinion from fact among the hundreds of points of view they will see from around the world.

We learned how to read, write, and do arithmetic from books and workbooks, but now we will use CDs and computer programs to assist our students in learning the basics. We will enrich their curriculum with an amazing array of high-tech ideas such as those found on www.schoolnotes.com, a site where teachers can share curriculum ideas and teaching strategies with one another. Merrill Education, an imprint of Prentice-Hall and Pearson Education, which publishes this book, offers teachers a website that brings together a variety of resources. In fact, this book has its own web page, www.prenhall.com/eby. You can use this page as a doorway to Merrill's general methods resources site.

Of one thing we can be certain: Nothing is going to stay the same very long.

In January 2000, a recent college graduate went to a job interview at an Internet firm in Boston. Ravi Chatpar was taken aback when, instead of being interviewed about his education and experience, he was asked to "build something with Legos." He was given 5 minutes to build whatever he wanted and then he and the interviewers would talk about it. Other job seekers are being asked to solve mathematical brainteasers and riddles to demonstrate their capacity to think under pressures. Some candidates are asked to participate in group games that test their ability to collaborate with others.

Is our K–12 curriculum going to keep pace with and prepare our students to thrive on the changes in our social and economic environment? The answer depends largely on you. As new teachers, you will be offered similar opportunities to demonstrate your problem-solving skills, your ability to collaborate with others, and your capacity to think outside the box and design new learning experiences that will generate enthusiastic responses from your students.

One thing has not changed. Despite the rapid growth of and dependence on technology, we all still need to feel that someone cares for us. All students who enter every classroom every year yearn for a teacher who will like them; a teacher who will inspire them to do their best; a teacher who will listen and perceive their needs and longings. There is no high-tech shortcut for this fundamental truth.

Noddings (1992) , recognized that "the desire to be cared for is almost certainly a universal human characteristic. Not everyone wants to be cuddled or fussed over. But everyone wants to be received, to elicit a response that is congruent with an underlying need or desire" (p. 17). Caring is a way of being in relation, not a set of specific behaviors.

The best, most creative, caring, and reflective teachers realize that—like parenting— good teaching takes time and understanding. Good teaching resembles good parenting in that both require long periods of time and continuity to develop. Good parents and teachers create an environment that encourages trusting relationships and work continually to strengthen that foundation of trust (Noddings, 1992).

This book describes classroom strategies and methods that you can use to become a caring and reflective teacher so you will thrive as a teacher. We believe there are two major traits that help teachers develop the kind of caring relationships that encourage students to relate to ideas, to their peers, and to others in their world. The first trait is *withitness*, which refers to a combination of caring and perceptiveness that allows teachers to focus on the needs of their students. The second trait is rooted in withitness. It is the ability to monitor your own behaviors, feelings, and needs and to learn from your mistakes. We call it *reflective action*. One of the most important things you can do to develop withitness and reflective action is to get to know yourself and understand your own needs and desires to be cared for. We will return to this theme repeatedly, because your need to receive respect and affection from your students is something you must recognize and deal with effectively before you can care for others. We'll begin by examining the concept of withitness and then describe reflective action.

Withitness

Kounin (1977) videotaped classrooms in action to discover the differences between well-managed, smoothly functioning classrooms and poorly managed, disorderly classrooms. Although he expected to find that well-managed classrooms were governed by a common set of rules and discipline strategies, he found no such relationship. Instead he found that the most smoothly functioning classrooms were led by teachers whose management styles were characterized by a high degree of alertness and the ability to pay attention to two things at once.

Kounin labeled the characteristic that distinguished good classroom managers from poor ones *withitness*. The good managers he observed knew what was going on in their classrooms at all times. They were aware of who was working and who was not. They were also able to overlap their instruction with monitoring of student behavior. As a result, they were able to alter a presentation at the first sign of student restlessness or boredom. If a minor disruption occurred between students, the teacher perceived it immediately and was likely to move a student or otherwise prevent the disruption from growing.

Withitness is expressed more through teacher perceptiveness and behavior than through words. Eye contact, facial expressions, proximity, gestures, and actions such as stopping an activity demonstrate teacher withitness to students. These teachers are able to continue teaching a lesson while gesturing to a group or standing next to an overactive student who needs to refocus on the lesson. These are examples of the concept of overlapping, in which the teacher is able to deal both with student behavior and the lesson at the same time.

Kounin also studied what he called the *ripple effect*, a preventive discipline strategy that he found to be particularly useful in elementary classrooms. Kounin observed a student in his own college class reading a newspaper during the lecture. When Kounin reprimanded the student, he observed that his remarks caused changes in behavior among the other members of the class as well. "Side glances to others ceased, whispers stopped, eyes went from windows or the instructor to notebooks on the desk" (1977, p. 1). In subsequent observations in kindergarten classrooms, Kounin found that when teachers spoke firmly but kindly to a student, asking that student to desist from misbehavior, the other students in the class were also likely to desist from that behavior as well. When teachers spoke with roughness, however, the ripple effect was not so strong. "Children who witnessed a teacher desist another child with anger or punitiveness did not conform more nor misbehave less than those witnessing a teacher desist another without anger or punitiveness" (p. 10).

Reflective Action Builds on Withitness

Withitness is an essential foundation for becoming a reflective teacher. Perceptive teachers constantly observe conditions and gather information to make good judgments about what is happening in a classroom and what can or should be done to address it. Withitness continually raises the quality and level of reflective thinking because it helps teachers observe more accurately and collect more complete information about classroom conditions. Reflective teachers plan for variations in student response, constantly monitor students' reactions to classroom events, and are ready to respond when students show confusion or boredom. Reflective teachers actively monitor students during group activities and independent seat work, looking for signs that students need clarification of the task or the teacher's expectations. They also consider the quality of developing student relationships, and note how students interact with ideas, with their peers, and with others in various settings.

Can withitness and reflective action be learned? We believe so. If you are willing to examine the cause-and-effect relationships in your classroom honestly and search for reasons for students' behaviors, you are likely to develop your withitness in the process. If you are willing to ask other adults to observe your interactions with students and give you feedback on how you respond to various situations, you will be able to make changes and improve the quality of your withitness radar and responses. If you are willing to discuss classroom problems openly and honestly with your students, in a problem-solving manner, you are likely to learn from them what their signals mean.

For example, Judy once visited a second-grade classroom where a teacher planned the morning activities to go from reading to math to science without a break. By the time the teacher asked the students to put away their math books and take out their science books, the grumbling and murmuring and shuffling feet had grown to intolerable proportions. With no trace of withitness, this teacher's voice went higher and higher as she scolded the children and told them to be quiet and listen, keep their hands and feet still, sit up, and pay attention. This happened over and over until lunchtime. A reflective, caring teacher using withitness as a tool would have perceived that the student grumbling signaled a planning problem—one that could be easily solved by allowing the children to move and stretch for a few minutes before starting another lesson.

Principals and supervising teachers often note that withitness and reflective thinking grow with experience. That growth is symbiotic. The more withitness teachers develop, the more reflective they are likely to become. Similarly, the more reflective teachers are about how their own needs may conflict with the needs of their students, the more withitness they display. Few first-year teachers exhibit consistent and accurate withitness. They develop it gradually as they reflect on the effects of their actions and decisions on their students' behavior.

For example, a beginning teacher may gradually become aware that her lessons are too long for the students' attention spans. From that time on, she will be sensitive to whether a particular lesson is moving too slowly or lasting too long.

On another day, the teacher may notice that whenever a certain student is made to establish eye contact, the student ceases to misbehave; the teacher reflects on this and actively begins to use eye contact as a way to connect not only with this student but with others. Then, after further observation and discussion with a colleague, the teacher may realize that in some cultures children learn that making eye contact with adults is a sign of disrespect—so this strategy probably will not work with them.

In response to a serious disruption, the teacher may notice that using a strong, confident voice causes the students to pay attention, whereas using a tentative, meek voice causes their attention to wander. Through reflecting on these experiences, the teacher develops two effective strategies for redirecting student behavior, and begins to learn which is more effective in a given situation. Her active self-reflection is the first step toward developing greater withitness, and her increasing withitness contributes to greater self-reflection.

A MORAL AND ETHICAL BASIS FOR REFLECTIVE ACTION

Reflective action is a time-consuming practice that may involve an emotional risk for the individual willing to engage in it. Personal examination of why you do something and how you can do something better can result in feelings of discomfort. When you engage in reflective thinking about actions you have just taken or are about to take, you may become critical of your own behavior or your motives. Peters (1991) observed that reflective practice involves a personal risk because it requires one to be open to an examination of beliefs, values, and feelings about which there may be a great sensitivity.

When teachers are engaged in reflection about their decisions, actions, and behaviors, they are likely to begin asking themselves questions such as "Why do I have this rule?" "Why do I care so much about what happens in my classroom?" "How did I come to believe so strongly about this element of my teaching?"

When teachers ask themselves this type of searching question, they may find a need to reexamine their beliefs and values. For example, teachers who have been raised and educated in traditional settings where children were "seen and not heard" unless responding to a question by an adult may expect the same behavior from their students. But, imagine that such a teacher observes a classroom where students are allowed to interact, discuss their ideas with other students, and take part in spirited discussions with the teacher. Based on past assumptions, the beginning teacher may feel very uncomfortable in a classroom with this noise level and consider the behavior of the students to be rude. If, however, the teacher is willing and able to ask, "Why am I uncomfortable with this noise level? Is it because I was never allowed to speak up when I was a child? How did I feel about the rules when I was a child? How do I feel about them now? What are the differences in the way these children are learning and the way I learned? What do I want my future students to learn, how to be quiet and orderly or how to be curious and assertive?"

When teachers confront confusing and ambiguous questions like these with honesty, they are becoming "real." Honest self-reflection can lead to new understandings of how your beliefs influence your present choices and actions. Continued reflective thinking can lead you to begin clarifying your philosophy of life and teaching, your ethical standards and moral code.

Do you think it is necessary for you as a teacher to know what you stand for, what you believe and value? Is it important that you be able to state clearly the ethical and moral basis for your decisions? Strike (1990) notes two important reasons for teachers to have a well-articulated philosophy of teaching and code of ethics are that (a) they work with a particularly vulnerable clientele and (b) the teaching profession has no clear set of ethical principles or standards. Strike believes that, in the matter of discipline and grading, the most important ethical concepts are honesty, respect for diversity, fairness, and due process. He also believes that teachers must be willing to consider the ethical implications of equity in how they distribute their time and attention to students, avoiding playing favorites. Are these part of your personal code of ethics?

It is likely that you believe your students ought to have the attributes of honesty, respect for diversity, and fairness. If so, it is important that you demonstrate these behaviors for them, for it is well known that teachers are important models of moral and ethical behavior for the students they teach. As Ryan (1986) noted:

> Research has now confirmed what humankind long ago recognized intuitively: People with power and prestige are imitated by those around them. And, although some teachers may not think of themselves as people with power and prestige, the children they teach certainly see them as such. Children watch their teachers to find out how grown-ups act. Therefore, teachers need to be constantly aware of the powerful influence that their actions in the classroom have on students. (p. 231)

Your students are your clients. They are quite vulnerable to the influence of their teachers' beliefs and ethics. Teachers are important role models for behavior and character. In classrooms that we observe, the teacher's character and moral code sets the standards and the tone or climate for the classroom. If the teacher is fair, students are influenced to treat others fairly. If the teacher is impulsive and selfish, students are likely to behave the same way. When teachers demonstrate a willingness to listen openly and honestly to others' points of view, students begin to respect the opinions of others as well. When teachers are closed and rigid in their approach to teaching and learning, students mold their behavior into a search for right answers and rote learning.

Gilligan (1982) asserts that the concepts of caring and responsibility are essential elements of moral development. Teachers may express these qualities by showing respect for students' feelings and taking responsibility for meeting students' needs without shifting the blame for their low performance on other factors. Noddings (1992) expresses the need for ethical caring in schools because schools are where human beings learn how to interact. She proposes that caring is the basis of the golden rule. Caring as a moral attribute is probably high on the list of most aspiring teachers. Many people choose the career of teaching because they care deeply about the needs of children in our society. They are also likely to feel responsible for meeting the needs of their students.

Occasionally, you may observe teachers who seem to have lost the ability to care for others because they are overwhelmed with meeting their own needs. They tend to put the blame on others for their students' failure to behave or achieve. But reflective, caring teachers willingly accept that it is their responsibility to design a program that allows their students to succeed. They work every day to balance their own needs with the needs of their students. To achieve this goal, they are willing to learn systematic ways of reflecting on their own practice so that they can enhance their students likelihood to succeed. Other moral attributes that teachers cite as important in their personal lives and in their work with children are honesty, courage, and friendliness.

DEFINITIONS OF REFLECTIVE THINKING AND ACTION

In *How We Think: A Restatement of the Relation of Reflective Thinking to the Educative Process*, John Dewey (1933) defined *reflective thinking* as the "active, persistent and careful consideration of any belief or supposed form of knowledge in light of the grounds that support it" (p. 9). An analysis of this carefully worded statement creates a powerful verbal image of the reflective thinker and correlates with the concept presented here of a person consciously choosing to use reflective action in teaching.

The first descriptive adjective, *active*, indicates one who voluntarily and willingly takes responsibility for considering personal actions. Reflective action includes an energetic search for information and solutions to problems that arise in the classroom. Dewey's use of the word *persistent* implies a commitment to thinking through difficult issues in depth, continuing to consider matters even though it may be uncomfortable or tiring to do so. Although some teachers may begin to seek knowledge and information, they may be satisfied with easy answers and simple solutions. In contrast, the reflective teacher is rarely satisfied with quick answers. Instead, he continually and persistently seeks to fine-tune and improve ways to teach students and manage classroom events.

The careful thinker is one who has concern for both self and others. Teachers who use reflective action want to improve their classroom performance and bring the greatest benefit to the lives of their students. They believe that teaching is relational—meaning that the quality of interactions in the classroom sets the tone for learning. Using reflective action, such teachers set out to create positive, nurturing classroom environments that promote high self-esteem and concern not only between teacher and students, but also among students and their peers. Less caring teachers are likely to consider their own needs and feelings to be of greater importance than those of their students. Because they do not reason with care, they may make unreasonable demands on their students or fail to sense and address important student needs.

Dewey's phrase, "belief or supposed form of knowledge," implies that little is known for sure in the teaching profession. The teacher who uses reflective action recognizes the value of informed practice, but maintains a healthy skepticism about various educational procedures and theories. While a less reflective teacher might be persuaded that there is only one right way to teach, the reflective teacher knows that individual students may need different conditions for learning and a variety of incentives to be successful. A less reflective teacher might adopt each new educational fad without questioning its value; the reflective teacher greets these new ideas with an open but questioning mind, considering whether it is valuable and how it can be adapted to fit the needs of the class.

The final phrase in Dewey's definition, "in light of the grounds that support it," directly relates to the reflective thinker's practice of using evidence and criteria in making judgments. While less reflective teachers may jump to conclusions quickly based on initial observations or prior cases, the reflective teacher gathers as much information as possible about a problem, weighs the value of the evidence against suitable criteria and then draws a tentative conclusion. After a conclusion is made, the less reflective teacher may stick to it rigidly, but the reflective teacher will reconsider that conclusion whenever new evidence or information becomes available.

Although persistent and careful thinking is important to the reflective teacher, such thinking does not automatically lead to change and improvement. Dewey also acknowledged the importance of translating thought into action, and specified that attitudes of open-mindedness, responsibility, and wholeheartedness are needed for teachers to translate their thoughts into reflective actions.

Schon (1987) concurs with Dewey's emphasis on action as an essential aspect of the reflective process. He defines the reflective practitioner as one who engages in "reflection-in-action." This kind of thinking includes observing and critiquing our own actions and then changing our behaviors based on what we see. Reflection-in-action gives rise to on-the-spot experimentation. We define a problem, consider how we have addressed it in the past, and think up and try out new actions to test our tentative understandings of them. This process helps us determine whether our moves change things for the better. An on-the-spot experiment may work, or it may produce surprises that call for further reflection and experiment.

Schon (1987) also notes that reflectivity in teaching leads to "professional artistry," a special type of competence displayed by some teachers when they find themselves in situations full of surprise, ambiguity, or conflict. Just as physicians respond to each patient's unique array of symptoms by questioning the patient and then inventing, testing, and creating a new diagnosis, Schon believes that reflective teachers also respond to the unexpected by asking questions such as, "What are my students experiencing? What can I do to improve this situation? How does my students' performance relate to the way I am teaching this material?"

Often, during the process of reflection, individuals find that a new, surprising event contradicts something they thought they already knew. When this happens, reflective individuals are able to cope with paradoxes and dilemmas by re-examining what they already know, restructuring their strategies, or reframing the problem. They often invent on-the-spot experiments to put their new understandings to the test or to answer the puzzling questions that have arisen from the event.

Reflective action is made up of many elements and is related to an individual's willingness to be curious and assertive to increase self-awareness, self-knowledge, and new understandings of the world in which we live and work. It is not something that occurs easily for most of us and it takes time to develop. Writing of this idea, Brubacher, Case and Reagan (1994) cite the children's story of the Velveteen Rabbit to suggest that becoming a reflective practitioner has much in common with the process of becoming "real." As the Skin Horse explained to the Rabbit, becoming "real" takes time, and happens after a toy has been loved so much that it loses its hair and becomes shabby. In the same way, becoming a truly reflective teacher involves time, experience and, inevitably, a bit of wear around the edges!

A Graphic Model of Reflective Action in Teaching

Consider that as writers, it is our responsibility to connect with you in the same way teachers must connect with their students. We reflect on our memories of ourselves as beginning teachers and think about what we wanted to learn and needed to know to be successful. In this third edition of the book, we have used feedback from readers of previous editions, as well as our own continuing research, to fine-tune the material we want to present.

We know that sometimes students learn better by seeing a picture or a graphic model of a complicated idea. The model of reflective action we present in this edition has changed from the first and second editions because we are continually reflecting on how to make it more understandable and usable. Still, we recognize that any model is over-simplified and relies on the readers to fill in details and examples with their own imagination. With feedback from you, we will continue to refine our thinking in future editions. This is exactly how your own teaching can improve over the years if you are willing to seek critical feedback, reflect, and grow as a result of your experiences.

When you think of your school years, no doubt several of your past teachers come to mind. Maybe you had a favorite teacher who reached out to you in a way that made you feel valued and important. Perhaps one of the reasons you are reading this book is that your interactions with a caring teacher helped instill in you the desire to influence others in the same way you were influenced. On the other hand, you may have had a negative experience with a teacher and determined to enter the teaching profession to help ensure that more caring individuals become the teachers of the future. You have probably heard the term, the *art of teaching*. One aspect of the art of teaching is that each of us enters the teaching profession carrying a unique set of experiences with people and with institutions. From these experiences, each teacher develops a unique perspective—or set of expectations—through which we view the world and from which we determine what we think life in a classroom should be like.

In the field of education, our perspectives or expectations work a little bit like the visual artist's perspective. For example, imagine that three artists have been asked to paint the same landscape. Figure 1.1 shows the artist on the left painting the scene as she views it. Notice how she has chosen to depict the boat in relation to the sunset and the lake.

In contrast, note how the middle artist's view differs. He focuses on a close-up of the pine tree, with the boat farther in the distance. If you compared the two paintings, you might not realize from the first that there were pine trees in the original scene. Finally, look at the third artist's canvas. How does her view compare with the first two? There is no lake at all in her painting.

Over time, artists develop particular perspectives that become associated with their style of art. In the same way, your unique teaching and learning perspective will lead you to notice some things and overlook others—during your teacher preparation courses, and throughout your teaching career. There is nothing wrong with having a perspective or set of expectations about teaching—in fact, you can't help having one. However, it is important to remember that one's personal perspective is not the only view or interpretation of events. In fact, there are at least as many different perspectives for an event as there are participants in it!

Figure 1.1   Different perspectives create a point of view.

Why does the existence of different perspectives matter in becoming an effective, reflective teacher? Let's explore what happens to a teacher who fails to recognize how to take advantage of different frames, compared with one who does.

Teacher Enters with Expectations.   A teacher preparing a lesson works from a personal perspective or set of expectations about what makes a good lesson, how students should act, and what effective teachers do. When it is time to actually teach the lesson, this set of expectations functions almost like a picture in the head of what is about to occur.

Figure 1.2   Teacher has a view of how lesson will proceed.

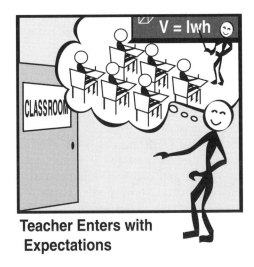

Unforeseen Problem Occurs.   Unfortunately, students don't always share the teacher's perspective for a lesson. This can occur for several reasons. Perhaps the students' experiences with school differ greatly from those of the teacher, or perhaps a physical need (e.g., hunger, fatigue) prevents a student from paying full attention to the teacher's input. For any number of reasons, an unforeseen problem or challenge can (and often does!) arise during even the best-prepared lessons.

Unaware Teachers Continue.   Like an artist who chooses to paint a close-up of a figure, some teachers focus only on those students or events that are doing what they expect or want to see. These teachers lack withitness. They fail to notice disruptive students' behaviors or needs. For example, the teacher pictured here focuses only on the student who is paying attention to the lecture. Perhaps you have been in a classroom where the teacher does not address unexpected, and often undesirable, behaviors. Sometimes the teacher seems unaware that there is even a need to change the pace or interact with a particular student. How long will students continue to learn in such a setting?

Figure 1.3   Students' responses do not match what the teacher expected.

Unforeseen Problem Occurs

Figure 1.4   Some teachers focus only on students who fulfill expectations.

Unaware Teachers Continue

Reflective Teachers Use Withitness.   In contrast, the most effective, caring teachers monitor the ever-changing climate of the classroom by paying attention to students' non-verbal and verbal responses. We use the term *withitness* to describe the combination of caring and perceptiveness that such teachers possess. When events deviate from expectations, a withit teacher responds by changing pace in a lesson, moving about the room, and interacting with students in an effort to redirect and refocus attention and learning.

Teacher Puts Problem into Perspective.   Successful teachers do not stop thinking about a problem when the bell rings. Effective teachers have learned the value of reflecting on negative classroom events and considering how those events might have been prevented. You will often find reflective teachers reviewing an event, seeking to explain for themselves what caused the problem to occur. For example, as the teacher in this drawing reviews the math lesson, the teacher may blame it all on a particular student who is known as a "troublemaker." This easy solution can be easily supported

Figure 1.5   Teacher notices behavior of all students and responds quickly to unexpected events.

Reflective Teachers Use Withitness

Figure 1.6   Teacher reviews the event and creates a tentative explanation for it.

Teacher Puts Problem into Perspective

by recalling several instances where the student exhibited disruptive behaviors in the past. As with most easy solutions, this one may only cover up the real issues. Reflective teachers will not be satisfied with such a hasty conclusion.

Teacher Widens the Perspective.   A caring and reflective teacher understands that a particular point of view can limit perceptiveness and withitness. This teacher examines the first conclusion about the "troublemaker" in class, and recalls that this student seems to exhibit the disruptive behavior about five minutes before the lunch bell. Thinking back to the students' schedules, the teacher suddenly realizes that the misbehaving student (and several others) help in the cafeteria on Tuesdays and Thursdays. Perhaps the math lesson deteriorated as students grew anxious about arriving on time for their special lunchroom jobs. Recognizing that a different perspective exists for the classroom event, this teacher then rules out the troublemaker idea, and looks further into the event, wondering if there was anything about the way the lesson was presented that also contributed to student restlessness.

From this example, you can see how vitally important it is to spend time on self-reflection. By rushing out the door to another appointment, or turning your attention away from the problems you face to do paperwork, you may miss valuable opportunities to develop your capacities for withitness and reflective action. We cannot emphasize enough the importance of this first step. Without reflection, there is unlikely to be any growth of withitness. Without reflection, there is little motivation to take action.

Teacher Does Research and Invites Feedback.   In our example, the teacher's honest self-reflection leads to the first important action step, inviting the feedback of respected colleagues or looking for other resources to help explain the unexpected classroom event. In this case, the concerned teacher shares the math experience with a colleague, who has a different perspective to offer. "Did you have something besides the chalkboard for students to look at?" the colleague asks. "Perhaps they needed something more concrete to focus on. I would use some blocks to demonstrate the mathematical operation more concretely."

Figure 1.7   Teacher reexamines tentative explanation and considers alternatives.

Teacher Widens the Perspective

Figure 1.8   Teacher turns to colleagues and other sources for feedback on the problem.

Figure 1.9   Teacher gathers new information to create a new perspective for the problem.

Teacher Redefines the Problem.   Rather than simply adopt someone else's interpretations, the reflective teacher gathers information and uses it to help reexamine earlier thinking. In this case, the reflective teacher's willingness to redefine the problem results in a completely new perspective, and the teacher realizes that the students may need to work with THEIR OWN blocks to understand the concept. "Empty hands!" thinks the teacher. "They lost focus and misbehaved because they had NOTHING TO DO WITH THEIR HANDS!"

Teacher Creates New Action Plan.   Once the reflective teacher widens the perspective and redefines the problem in terms of students' needs, the next step is to devise an action plan to meet their needs. The teacher imagines the students working with manipulatives at their own desks. This leads to more action steps of locating appropriate materials and setting them up in the classroom in time for the next math lesson.

Teacher Predicts Possible Outcomes.   However, reflective teachers don't just devise an action plan and rush back to the classroom to carry it out. Rather, they continue with their self-reflection long enough to consider the potential outcomes of their new plan, considering possible pitfalls or problems that may arise as they put their new plan into action. As

Figure 1.10   Teacher makes a plan that sets up new expectations.

this teacher reflects on the desirable effects of using manipulatives in her math lesson, there is also a need to address the possible contingency that students could easily misuse the materials, causing noise and disruption. By imagining the plan in action and visualizing potential problems, the teacher is able to take steps to prevent the problems. In this case, the teacher considers how to talk with the students about the appropriate use of the blocks. The reflective teacher is likely to imagine passing out the blocks and rehearses ahead of time the procedures and rules to be used. "When Juanita hands you your blocks, you are to leave them alone until I tell you what to do next." Thinking ahead is one of the most important aspects of reflective action that helps teachers gain confidence in their own effectiveness. Each successful cycle of reflective action results in enhanced withitness, heightened enthusiasm, greater expectations for success, and greater maturity as a teacher.

Figure 1.11   Teacher predicts possible outcomes that could occur.

Professional Standards for Teachers

The reflective action model we have presented here is our way of articulating a set of thought processes and action steps that encourage self-understanding and professional growth. As a beginning teacher, you may want to be able to demonstrate your professional growth and your unique teaching style, talents and abilities to others. You may need to do this to earn your teaching credentials, or after that, to compete successfully for a teaching position. The National Board for Professional Teaching Standards (1999) sets forth five propositions of accomplished teaching as fundamental requirements for professional teachers to be able to demonstrate. The board believes that "excellence in teaching is the sum of human qualities like judgment and improvisation, expert knowledge and skill, and unflagging professional commitment." The five propositions follow:

1. Teachers are committed to students and their learning.
2. Teachers know the subjects they teach and how to teach those subjects to students.
3. Teachers are responsible for managing and monitoring student learning.
4. Teachers think systematically about their practice and learn from experience.
5. Teachers are members of learning communities.

We hope that you see the links between these five core propositions of excellence in teaching and the processes we've described as reflective action steps. To clarify these links, we believe that teachers who are committed to their students are those who use withitness to perceive their students' needs and are further willing to reflect alone and collegially to meet those needs. Teachers who are determined to know the subjects they teach and how best to teach them are willing to use reflective action steps to do research and examine and reexamine their frames of problems that arise in their classrooms. Teachers who want to grow in their management capabilities are willing to ask colleagues for feedback on management problems and issues and consider contingencies before they arise to prevent management problems from occurring.

The fourth core proposition is that teachers think systematically about their practice and learn from experience. What does it mean to "think systematically?" We've tried to offer one version of systematic thinking in this chapter. Our reflective action model is just that—a system of thinking and acting to improve your practice and learn from your experience. Our model is purposefully collegial as we concur with the fifth core proposition that teachers are members of learning communities.

USE THE WORLD WIDE WEB AS YOU CREATE YOUR PROFESSIONAL PORTFOLIO

Today, one of the most important learning communities for the busy professional is the World Wide Web, with countless resources on every educational issue and topic.

If you want to be able to demonstrate your professional accomplishments as well as your ability to think systematically and learn from experience, there is no better vehicle than the creation of a professional portfolio. Martin-Kniep (1999) describes portfolios as:

> . . . collections of purposeful and specialized work, capturing a process that can never be fully appreciated unless one can be inside and outside someone else's mind.
>
> Portfolios are history in the making. They are fluid, even though they can freeze a moment and make it look as if it has a clear beginning and end. They are museums of our work and thinking—displaying our successes, experiments and dreams. (p. 1)

Professional portfolios have been endorsed by the National Board for Professional Teaching Standards, but are rarely used. At the end of each chapter in this book, we have provided activities that we believe will assist you in creating your own professional portfolio. For example, in this chapter, we make suggestions to help you clarify and articulate your unique philosophy of teaching and learning. We suggest that you use our model of reflective action in teaching as the basis for demonstrating your systematic thinking as well.

By accessing the Merrill Education General Methods Resources Site (http://www. prenhall.com/methods-cluster), you will discover an introduction page that can give you access to chat rooms, message boards and links to other sites. By researching these educational materials, you may discover new ideas to add to your statement of philosophy, or you may find that certain issues cause you to challenge your existing philosophy, thereby widening your perspective and causing you to reflect more deeply on what it is that you believe.

As you create your professional portfolio, you may want to refer to Merrill's web page and other educational resource sites to discover new methods, or to do further research on an educational topic that interests you. Each portfolio section is divided into reflective action steps. Doing research and asking for feedback is always an important reflective action choice. You may do this with colleagues in your school, or you may want to invite feedback from a broader range of colleagues on the World Wide Web using the chat room and message board features found within each topic of the Merrill site.

Because the underlying idea of reflective action is that actions change as a result of our reflection, we do not expect that you will write one philosophy of teaching today and keep it for many years. Rather, we believe that you will write one draft of your philosophy today and revise it many, many times during the course of your career. When you think your philosophy has changed, it is important to return to that page in your portfolio and revise it accordingly.

⊃ Reflective Actions for Your Professional Portfolio
My Philosophy of Teaching

Use Withitness

Visit a classroom and use all your senses to observe and describe how the teacher uses space and other resources. How are the students' desks arranged? Where is the teacher's desk? Does the room feel crowded or spacious? Are there activity spaces? If so, for what purpose are they used? Observe and describe the use of light, color, and decorations. What do you hear when you walk into this classroom? How does the room smell? Are there any tastes associated with your visit?

Put Your Philosophy into Perspective

Take photos or draw a sketch of this classroom and include them in your portfolio, along with your written reflections. As soon as possible after your classroom observation, draw a sketch of how you would arrange this classroom to make it fit your preferences.

Widen Your Perspective

Would you like to be a student in the classroom you visited? Why or why not? Would you like to be a student in the classroom you sketched for yourself? Why or why not?

Do Research and Invite Feedback to Learn More

Ask yourself, "How does the classroom environment demonstrate one's philosophy of teaching?" Discuss your question with colleagues. Read articles or books about the effects of various physical arrangements on students' sense of well-being and motivation. Brainstorm with a colleague to create a list of moral and ethical attributes that are highly valued by humankind (e.g., honesty, courage, fairness).

Redefine Your Personal Philosophy

Select four to six of the qualities you brainstormed that you value most. Describe how your classroom environment will represent these values.

Create an Action Plan that Reflects Your Philosophy

Write a paragraph or two about why each value you identified is important to you and how you will attempt to model and teach those concepts to your students. Consider this paper a first draft of your philosophy. For additional pages, remember that teaching is a very creative career. The talents that teachers use include art, music, interior design, drama, photography, and cartooning. What are some creative talents that you will use to create a unique and welcoming classroom environment for your students? Include sketches of the bulletin boards, centers, or class projects that you will design to enhance your classroom environment.

Predict the Possible Outcomes of Your Plan

After you write the first draft of your philosophy, consider again what are the likely effects of your philosophy on your students' experience. What elements of your philosophy will your students welcome and respond to in a positive way? What elements of your philosophy might be a "hard sell"? How will you convince students of the importance of these elements? Add a paragraph that describes your understanding that philosophies change with experience and that you intend for your philosophy to be a dynamic one, based on your future experiences and the needs of your students. Also, write a statement about how you will plan for contingencies and learn from your mistakes. Revise and refine your philosophy as the year goes by. The final draft goes in your portfolio.

References

Brubacher, J., Case, C., & Reagan, T. (1994) *Becoming a reflective educator: How to build a culture of inquiry in the schools*. Thousand Oaks, CA: Corwin Press.

Dewey, J. (1933). *How we think* (rev. ed.). Lexington, MA: D.C. Heath.

Gilligan, C. (1982). *In a different voice*. Cambridge, MA: Harvard University Press.

Kounin, J. (1977). *Discipline and group management in classrooms.* New York: Holt, Rinehart and Winston.

Martin-Kniep, G. (1999) *Capturing the wisdom of practice: Professional portfolios for educators.* Alexandria, VA: Association of Supervision and Curriculum Development.

National Board for Professional Teaching Standards. (1999). *What teachers should know and be able to do.* On-line: Washington, DC: NCATE Webmaster. Access at www.nbpts/standards/intro.html

Noddings, N. (1992). *The challenge to care in schools*. New York: Teachers College Press.

Peters, J. (1991). Strategies for reflective practice. *Professional and Continuing Education, 51,* 83–102, San Francisco: Jossey Bass.

Ryan, K. (1986). The new moral education. *Phi Delta Kappan, 67,* 228–233.

Schon, D. (1987). *Educating the reflective practitioner*. San Francisco: Jossey-Bass.

Strike, K. (1990). The legal and moral responsibility of teachers. In J. Goodlad, R. Soder, & K. Sirotnik, (Eds.), *The moral dimensions of teaching* (pp. 188–223). San Francisco: Jossey-Bass.

chapter 2

PLANNING A HEALTHY, SAFE ENVIRONMENT FOR LEARNING

When you walk into a classroom, you can sense a particular climate or environment within a few moments. A multitude of sensory images enters your consciousness—sights, sounds, and smells, for the most part. The way the room is arranged, its messiness or neatness, wall decorations, the movements and noises made by the students, and the smell of chalk dust or an animal cage all combine to create a unique flavor or climate in the classroom. The behavior, body language, and facial expressions of the teacher and students give you the most important clues about what life is like in this classroom. You may sense healthy elements such as excitement, energy, joy, cooperation, and pride, or you may sense debilitating elements such as fear, aimlessness, frustration, and tension. These are all components of the classroom environment, which is largely established by the teacher during the first days and weeks of the school year.

This chapter describes in some detail what reflective teachers think about and how they make decisions to promote a healthy classroom climate that encourages student achievement and satisfaction. It also describes how reflective teachers think about the psychosocial environment of their classrooms and how they carefully structure classroom expectations and incentives to promote enduring patterns of achievement and interest in school.

A Good Beginning for the School Year

Studies show that it is the teacher who establishes the particular climate of each classroom. Given identical classrooms in the same school, identical materials and resources, and the same clientele, each teacher creates a unique learning environment based on a unique set of expectations, beliefs, attitudes, knowledge, effort, and repertoire of teaching strategies and skills. You have experienced the power of the teacher for many years as a student. It is likely that you still enter every classroom on the first day of a new course hoping that the teacher will be interesting, fair, knowledgeable, and caring.

Many people think that inner-city schools serving less affluent students are deadly and sterile, while suburban schools serving middle-class students are vital and stimulating. In reality, though, a great variety of classroom environments exist within each school. Talented, caring, and reflective teachers in inner-city schools can and do make learning a joyful experience, and their classrooms shine with goodwill, understanding, wit, and creativity. There are, however, just as many careless, nonreflective teachers in rural areas and in the suburbs as there are in the inner cities. In any environment, teachers who give little thought to their job or to their students create a classroom environment characterized by anxiety, disorder, anger, and despair.

Unfortunately, great social and economic disparities exist in the world. Children, who have not created these differences, are their victims. School historically has been the great equalizer, the means to rising out of poverty, the chance to make the most of one's potential. Reflective, caring, and creative teachers know they can make a significant difference in students' lives, and they work especially hard at creating a positive, healthy classroom environment to counteract the effects of poverty, discrimination, and neglect.

ORGANIZING THE PHYSICAL ENVIRONMENT

The classroom appearance makes a statement about the extent to which the teacher cares for the environment in which the class lives and works. It may be untidy or neat, colorful or drab; filled with objects, plants, animals, and children's art or left undecorated and unkempt. No two classrooms are alike; each has its unique environment. However, some classrooms (and their occupants) bloom with health, vitality, and strength, while others appear sickly, listless, and debilitated.

Studies of teacher planning show that during the days immediately preceding the school year, teachers are primarily concerned with setting up the physical environment of the classroom. Reflective teachers want to come to school several days before their contracts call for them to be there. They hang posters, decorate bulletin boards, and carefully consider ways to arrange the students' desks, tables, bookcases, and other furniture to fit their curriculum plans and the needs of their students. You know from the many years you have spent in classrooms as students that a bright, colorful, cheerful, and stimulating classroom leads you to expect that school will be interesting and that the teacher celebrates life and learning. You also know that drab, undecorated spaces lead to expectations of dullness and boredom.

How to arrange the desks is a complex issue. Often the room contains many more desks than it was designed to hold comfortably. The number of students in a classroom may vary from 15 to 35, and the precise number of students is not known until the last minute, making planning difficult. Generally, though, teachers know approximately how many students they will have, and they set about arranging the desks in a way that uses space economically and strategically. Their plans are governed by an image of themselves and their students in teaching and learning experiences.

While arranging the classroom, reflective teachers envision its "activity flow"—what it will be like when the classroom is filled with students. This imaging process helps reflective teachers decide how to arrange the furniture in the room. As with other important decisions, each option has both advantages and disadvantages. Desks can be arranged in rows, circles, semicircles, and small groups. Each arrangement influences how students work and how they perceive their environment. Rows of desks provide an advantage in keeping order but leave little space for activities (Figure 2.1). A large circle of desks can be used if the teacher envisions that teaching and learning experiences will take place in the center of the circle, but it will be difficult for all students to see the chalkboard (Figure 2.2).

Doyle (1986) reports that students placed in open (nonrow) arrangements spend more time working together, initiating their own tasks, and working without teacher attention compared with students in traditional rooms. Teachers who value cooperative group learning experiences over teacher-centered learning experiences often use clusters of four to six desks (Figure 2.3).

Jones (1987) recommends organizing the classroom into shallow concentric circles, no more than three rows deep (Figure 2.4). In this setting, the teacher can maintain eye contact with all students and is able to move quickly to the side of any student who needs assistance or a reminder to pay attention. The increased physical proximity allows the teacher to circulate more easily to provide individual help.

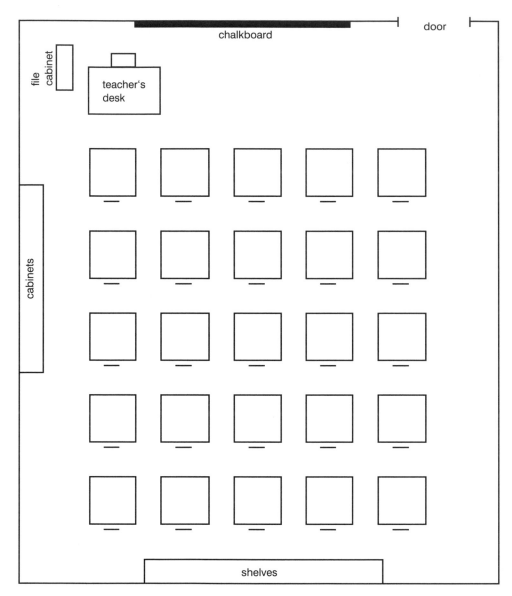

Figure 2.1   Classroom arrangement: rows of desks.

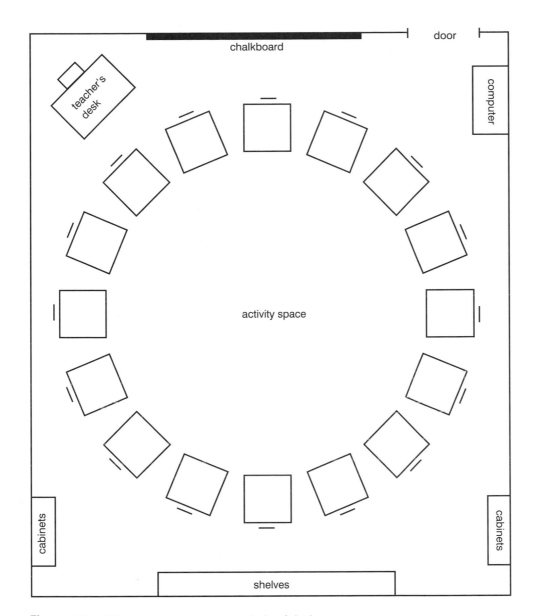

Figure 2.2   Classroom arrangement: circle of desks.

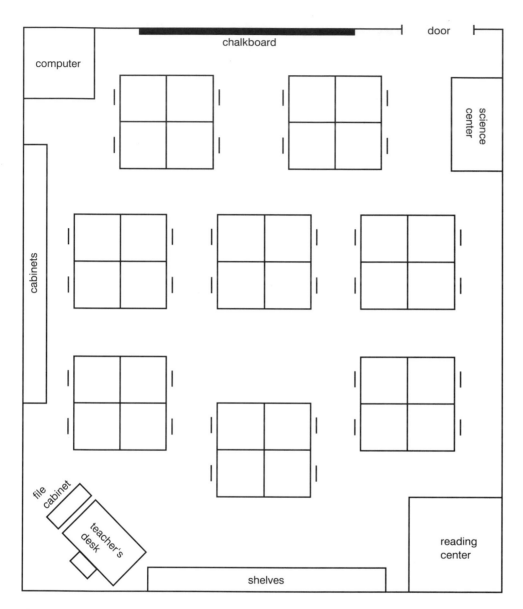

Figure 2.3 Classroom arrangement: clusters of desks.

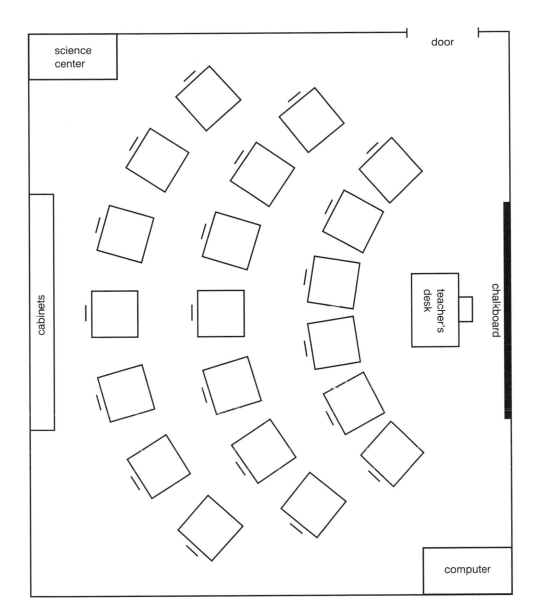

Figure 2.4 Classroom arrangement: concentric circles.

Activity and work spaces can be arranged by using bookcases and room dividers or simply by arranging tables and chairs in the corners of the room. Some teachers bring in comfortable furniture and rugs to design a space just for quiet reading. Computer or listening stations must also be designated. Room arrangement and the use of space are highly individualized decisions. Teachers make these decisions to fit their personal image of what a classroom should be, by considering what they value most highly and how the room arrangement fits these values as well as the curriculum and grade level of the class.

Reflective teachers also consider the effects of the physical arrangement of the room on developing a healthy classroom environment. Rows of desks connote order and efficiency but do little to build a sense of community. Clusters of desks promote cooperation and communication among groups of students. Large circle or concentric circle arrangements encourage communication and sharing among the entire class. Many reflective teachers change their room arrangements depending on the goals of a particular learning experience and thus create a variety of classroom environments to fit a variety of purposes.

The First Day of School

The physical environment and schedule of the classroom may lead students to expect certain things about the way teaching and learning will occur during the school year. These expectations are reinforced strongly during the first few minutes of the first day of school. For example, consider the students' experience on their first day of school in the following elementary and high school classroom scenarios (Figures 2.5 and 2.6).

You can probably recognize the teachers in these opening day scenarios and can give them names and faces from your own experiences. You have been exposed to a variety of teaching styles, methods, attitudes, and philosophies as consumers of education. Now you will soon become teachers yourselves. What style will you have? How will your students perceive you? What values and principles will you model? How will your students feel when they walk into your classroom on the first day of school?

Teaching Styles

Each teacher in these scenarios has a unique *teaching style*, a result of personality, philosophy, values, physical and emotional health, past experiences, and current knowledge about the effects of a teacher's behavior on the classroom environment. There are three broad descriptors of teaching styles, (a) *authoritarian*, (b) *permissive*, and (c) *democratic*.

Authoritarian teachers tend to plan furniture arrangements to maintain order in the classroom and plan schedules that seldom vary. Authoritarian teachers believe it is their sole responsibility to make all class rules and establish consequences for misbehavior. Such teachers tend to rely on teacher-centered lectures, discussions, and assignments. It is the student's role to obey the rules and do all assigned work satisfactorily.

In the opening-day scenarios, Miss Adams represented a moderately authoritarian teacher, while Mrs. Destry and Mr. Green are so authoritarian that they could almost

The scene is an elementary school. It is the first day of the new school year. In one corridor, several classroom doors are open. We see and hear four teachers greet the students in their classes.

Room 101

Miss Adams is standing at the doorway. As children walk in, she says, in a calm, even-toned voice, to each of them, "You'll find your name on a desk," as she gestures toward six clusters of desks. "Sit in that desk and wait quietly." The children obey and the room is quiet within. When all the children have entered, Miss Adams goes into her classroom and quietly shuts the door behind her. The beginning bell rings at precisely that moment.

Room 102

Mr. Baron is nowhere to be seen. Children enter the classroom looking for him, but when they don't see him, they begin to talk and walk around the room. The desks are arranged haphazardly in ragged rows. Two boys try to sit in the same desk, and a scuffle breaks out. The beginning bell rings. Suddenly Mr. Baron comes running down the hall, enters the room yelling, "All right, you guys, sit down and be quiet. What do you think this place is? A zoo?"

Room 103

Mr. Catlin is standing at the door wearing a big smile. As each child enters, he gives the child a sticker with his or her name on it. "Put this sticker on a desk that you like and sit in it," he says. The children enter and quickly claim desks, which are arranged in four concentric arcs facing the front of the room. They talk with each other in the classroom. When the bell rings, Mr. Catlin enters, leaving the door ajar for latecomers.

Room 104

Mrs. Destry is sitting at her desk when the children enter. Without standing up, she tells the children to line up along the side of the room. They comply. When the bell rings, she tells a student to shut the door.

If we were able to enter the classrooms with the students, this is what we might see, hear, and experience after the beginning bell ceased.

Room 101

Miss Adams stands in front of the class. She has excellent posture and a level gaze. As she waits quietly for the children to find their seats, she looks at each child eye to eye. They settle down quickly. When the classroom is perfectly quiet, she begins to talk.

"I see that you have all found your desks. Good. Now we can begin. I like the way you have quieted down. That tells me that you know how to behave in school. Let's review some of the important rules of our classroom."

Pointing to a chart entitled "Class Rules," she reads each aloud and tells the children its significance. "Rule 1: Students will pay attention when the teacher is speaking. This is important because we are here to learn and there can be no learning if you do not hear what the teacher is saying. Rule 2: Students will use quiet voices when talking in the classroom. This rule is important because a quiet, orderly classroom is conducive to learning. Rule 3: No fighting, arguing, or name calling is allowed."

The children listen attentively to all items. They do not ask questions or comment on the rules. After the rules are read, Miss Adams assigns helpers for class jobs. The newly appointed monitors pass out the reading books, and the children begin to read the first story in their books. Miss Adams walks quietly from desk to desk to see that each child is reading.

(continued)

Figure 2.5   First day of elementary school scenario.

Room 102

Mr. Baron rushes in and slams some books and papers on the desk. Some of them land on the floor nearby. Stooping to pick them up, he says, "Sit down, sit down, or I'll find cages for you instead of desks." The children sit down, but the noise level remains high.

"Enough! Do you want to begin the school year by going to the principal's office? Don't you care about school? Don't you want to learn something?" Gradually, the noise diminishes, but children's voices continue to interrupt from time to time with remarks to their teacher or to fellow classmates.

Mr. Baron calls roll from an attendance book. He does not even look up when a child says "Here" but stares intently at the book. He has several children pass out books at one time, resulting in more confusion about whether children received all the necessary books. Finally, he tells them to begin reading the first story in their reading books. Some do so, others do not. Mr. Baron begins looking through his file cabinet, ignoring the noise.

Room 103

Mr. Catlin walks throughout the room as he talks to the class. From time to time, he stops near a child and puts his hand on the child's shoulder, especially a child who appears restless or insecure. This action seems to help the child settle down and pay attention.

"Welcome back to school! This year should be a good one for all of us. I've got some great new ideas for our math and social studies programs, and we'll be using paperback novels to supplement our reading series. But first, let's establish the rules for our classroom. Why are we here?"

A student raises her hand. Mr. Catlin reads the name tag sticker on her desk and calls on her by name. "To learn," she says timidly.

"Exactly!" Mr. Catlin agrees. "And, what rules can help us to learn the most we've ever learned in a single year?"

Several children begin to call out responses at the same time.

"Wait a moment, class. Can we learn anything like this?"

A chorus of "No's" is heard.

"Then what rule do we need to solve this problem?"

A child raises his hand, is called on, and says, "We need to raise our hands before we talk."

"What a fine rule," Mr. Catlin says with a broad smile. "How many agree?" The hands of most children go up. Mr. Catlin spots one child whose hand is not raised. He walks over to that child, kneels next to the child's desk and says, "Do you agree that this rule will help you learn this year?" "Yes," says the child and his hand goes up.

After the class has established and agreed on several other class rules, Mr. Catlin talks about the reading program. He offers the children a choice among five paperback novels, distributes them, and tells the children to begin reading. As they read, he circulates around the room, stopping from time to time to ask questions or make comments about the stories to individual children.

Room 104

Mrs. Destry regards the children in their line with an unfriendly gaze. When a child moves or talks, she gives that child a withering stare. From a class list, she begins to read the students' names in alphabetical order, indicating which seat they are to take. The students sit down meekly. No one says a word or makes a sound.

"Now, class, you will find your books in your desks. Take out your reading books and turn to the first page." Going down the rows, each child reads a paragraph aloud while the other children sit silently and listlessly, following along in their books.

Figure 2.5

The scene is a high school. It is the first day of the new school year. In one corridor, several classroom doors are open. We see and hear two teachers greet their classes.

Room 205

Mr. Evans is waiting at the front door, welcoming his students. The students enter the classroom and can be heard saying, "Hello, Mr. E." Mr. Evans says hello and that he's glad to have each student in class. He tells them to locate their seats by looking at the overhead in the front of the room. He has a seating chart shown on the overhead. Students begin to sit down and talk about their summer experiences.

After the bell rings, Mr. Evans walks to the center of the room and waits for quiet. The students look up and begin to prepare themselves for Mr. Evans's beginning remarks. One bulletin board in the front of the room is completed in the school colors and includes a picture of the school mascot, a pennant, and words from the fight song. The other bulletin board is filled with mathematical symbols and sayings by famous mathematicians. Along the top of the chalkboard is a set of very colorful geometric designs.

A set of rules is posted conspicuously on one of the walls of the room:

Rule 1: Respect each other.
Rule 2: Participate in class.
Rule 3: Help one another.
Rule 4: Everyone tries 100%.

Mr. Evans begins by saying, "Welcome to the best high school in the city. I hope each student has found his or her seat using the chart on the overhead. I believe that it is important that you know how to use such items as charts and graphs. I like to take every opportunity to use mathematics in my classroom. In addition, I would like to review the rules of this classroom. If you have any questions related to the rules, we should discuss them immediately. If you have suggestions for any additional rules, we may want to include them in the initial set of rules I've listed."

Room 206

Mr. Green leaves the teacher's lounge about 30 seconds before class starts. When he arrives at his classroom, the bell rings. Some students are still outside talking with friends. Mr. Green yells at the students to "get inside or I'll begin writing detention slips on the first day." The students begin to take seats or lean against the side shelves.

As you look around the classroom, there is nothing on any of the bulletin boards. Student books are stacked on the side shelves. They are obviously ready to be distributed to the class.

Mr. Green tells the students to "shut up" so that he can call the roll and tell students where their seats are going to be. He stands behind a podium and begins to call names and assign seats. As students go to their seats, they continue talking among themselves. Frequently, Mr. Green calls for silence, but the noise level does not diminish very much.

After the students are seated, Mr. Green complains that this is a bad beginning to the school year and warns the students again that he is not afraid to send them to detention if they don't know how to behave. He has used this tactic in the past, and he will use it with this class if necessary.

With no discussion of goals, rules, or expectations, Mr. Green appoints some of the boys to pass out the textbooks and writes, "Read Chapter 1" on the chalkboard. Some students begin to read, while others continue to talk with each other. Mr. Green gets out his detention slips and begins to write names on them.

Figure 2.6   First day of high school scenario.

be called autocratic. Teachers who exhibit these leadership styles seem to have as their primary goal a quiet, orderly classroom climate. There is little positive social interaction in the class. Individuals compete for grades and the teacher's attention. Some students attempt to please the teacher by any means possible, while others revolt and undermine the teacher's efforts to control students' behavior. A positive sense of community is rare in a classroom led by an autocratic teacher; the only sense of community that may develop among the students is a shared sense of resentment or even rebellion.

At the other extreme are teaching styles that have been called *permissive* or *laissez-faire*. Teachers who employ a permissive style, such as Mr. Baron in Figure 2.5, appear tentative and powerless. They make few rules and are inconsistent in establishing or delivering the consequences for misbehavior. They accept excuses and seem unable to assert authority over academic work or student behavior. Confusion is the chief characteristic of the classroom climate created by such a permissive teacher. Students don't know what is expected or how they can succeed. Limits are fuzzy, leading to a constant testing by students of how much they can get away with. Little sense of community can develop within a permissive classroom because students often learn to play one against the other to get their way.

A third type of leadership is the *democratic* style. Democratic teachers, represented in Figures 2.5 and 2.6 by Mr. Catlin and Mr. Evans, are neither permissive nor autocratic. They are firm and reasonably consistent about their expectations for academic achievement and student behavior. They discuss the need for rules with their students and involve them in establishing the specific rules and consequences for the class. From time to time, they may initiate a reevaluation of certain rules to update them and make them more usable and meaningful. Democratic teachers assert their power to make decisions but are willing to listen to their students' reactions, needs, and desires. The result is that the sense of power and ownership is distributed among students and the teacher in the same way that it is distributed in a healthy community.

Perhaps you may be considering the important question, "Is it possible to control and decide on my teaching style, or is it simply a function of my personality?" The more information you can gather about how teachers create healthy climates for learning, the more power you have to gain self-understanding and control over this and other important matters pertaining to teaching and learning. Evertson (1989) has demonstrated that when teachers learn to examine their own practices and behaviors, they can learn to use the more productive and positive classroom practices and discontinue less effective methods.

To identify the most effective classroom management strategies, Emmer, Evertson, and Anderson (1980) conducted a study about how teachers begin the school year and establish their expectations with students. They were especially interested to learn how teachers who are effective classroom managers begin the school year. They hoped to discover some basic principles of effective classroom management that could be taught to beginning teachers. They selected 27 third-grade classrooms in eight elementary schools for their study. Observers were present in each of these classrooms during the first few weeks of school. Using criteria for effective management developed by the team of observers, the 27 teachers were classified into two categories: more effective and less effective classroom managers.

Both groups of teachers had rules and procedures planned for their classes. What distinguished the more effective managers from the others was that they spent most of the first day and much time during the next three weeks helping the students adjust to classroom expectations and understand the rules and procedures established for the class. Like Miss Adams and Mr. Catlin, the teachers began describing their carefully planned rules and procedures as soon as most students had arrived at the classroom. In some cases, but not always, students were asked to suggest rules for the class. The rules and procedures were explained clearly, with examples and reasons.

More effective managers did not rely simply on a discussion of the rules. They spent a considerable amount of time during the first week of school explaining and reminding students of the rules. One of the most effective ways to communicate your expectations to your class is to lead them through a rehearsal on how to follow the procedures. Teachers take time to rehearse procedures, such as how to line up for lunch or what to take out of their desks for math class. Many teachers teach students to respond to specific signals, such as a bell or a hand signal to call for attention. Emmer et al. (1980) observed, "In summary, the more effective managers clearly established themselves as the classroom leaders. They worked on rules and procedures until the students learned them. Teaching content was important for these teachers, but they stressed, initially, socialization into the classroom system. By the end of the first three weeks, these classes were ready for the rest of the year" (p. 225).

The reflective teacher, guided by moral principles, also recognizes that it is not simply a matter of establishing leadership that is important; the style of leadership counts as well. Miss Adams, Mr. Catlin, and Mr. Evans quickly established that they were the classroom leaders, but Mr. Catlin's style of leadership best exhibited the underlying moral principles of caring, consideration, and honesty as he interacted with his students. The result is that students in such an environment return the caring, consideration, and honesty to the teacher and exhibit it in their interactions with one another.

In contrast, less effective managers (exemplified by Mr. Baron and Mr. Green) did not have well-thought-out procedures. Although teachers like Mr. Baron always have rules, the rules are often vague and the teachers tend to tell the class the rules and procedures quickly without spending time discussing and rehearsing what they really mean. Others, like Mrs. Destry, try to move quickly to academic matters. They seem to expect the students to be able to comprehend and retain the rules from a single, brief statement. They do not teach the class routines and procedures. As a result, they are often found to waste many hours of class time during the year as they remind the students again and again to behave.

The way the two groups of teachers monitor the behavior of their students is also critical in establishing a clear set of expectations for students. The Emmer study disclosed that less effective teacher-managers did not actively monitor students' behavior. Instead, they busied themselves with clerical tasks or worked with a single student on a task while ignoring the rest of the class. The consequence of vague and untaught rules and poor monitoring was that the children were frequently left without enough information or a good enough example to guide their behavior.

From this study, you can conclude that if you expect your students to obey the rules of your classroom, you must give them clear directions, allow them to rehearse the procedures until they get it right, and actively observe while your students work, showing them that you expect them to pay attention to the task and do their work.

Preventive Discipline Strategies

Maintaining a positive learning environment is one of the most important daily functions of a teacher. In many ways a teacher is an orchestra conductor where students are playing a variety of instruments at different levels of mastery and varying frequencies and tonal ranges. At times, the teacher must stop and ask, "Are we all playing the same musical arrangement?"

The classroom management task of a teacher, like that of a conductor, is to inspire students to want to work together in harmony, learn to listen and pay attention to the leader and grow to care for and respect the contributions of each of their fellow classmates.

If the conductor allows a few members of the group to get away with disruptive behavior that is off key or out of sync with the goals of the entire group, the consonance of the class can be quickly destroyed. Teachers, even more than musical leaders, have a moral obligation to provide the best educational opportunities for all students, and this includes providing an environment that is conducive to learning. All too often the average student is lost because of distractions caused by a few. A teacher who spends an inordinate amount of time disciplining the same students over and over is forfeiting the education of others. Maintaining appropriate discipline procedures shows that you care, not only about your students, but for your subject matter as well.

Don't buy the lie that good teachers don't have discipline problems. Every teacher has students who present new behavioral challenges every year. Students come from a variety of family and emotional backgrounds that are usually beyond our control. In part, because of the prevalence of action movies, computers, and video games, some students (and even a few parents) demand an "infotainment" approach to learning. They have become so used to split-second actions and reactions that anything outside this genre is perceived as boring. Although technological learning can enhance achievement, we must also help our students to understand that much of education is a challenging learning experience which at times includes persistence and labor.

Jim Hicks has discovered over his long tenure as a high school science teacher that discipline problems are minimal when class members see their teacher as a good person who is knowledgeable about the subject matter and tries hard each day to produce meaningful and appropriate learning activities. Displaying enthusiasm about the lesson promotes a stimulating environment that inspires students to behave similarly. The adage that students will look at your heart before they look at your mind is true.

Jim also finds that one important way to build mutual respect in his class is to show his interest in his students' lives and extracurricular activities. He tries to attend school plays, sports events, debates, or other activities in which his students are participating. He believes that this communicates to his students that he has a genuine interest in them and a desire to know them as real people. Teachers may be one of only a few adults that students have contact with each day. In fact, teachers may spend more hours each day with young people than their parents do. Students need positive attention from the adults they respect and they will respond by giving their positive attention in return.

Jim also believes it is essential to communicate your own feelings to your students. For example, if you are is ill and having a difficult time teaching, tell this to the class at the beginning of the period and remind them that you might not be yourself today. If you are under unusual stress for a variety of reasons, disclose this information. It is not unusual for a teacher to say, "You know, it won't take very much to set me off today."

At the same time, you must respect the emotional life of your students. Young children and adolescents are sensitive about peer group pressures and evaluations. A teacher who castigates or ridicules a disruptive student unfairly in front of the class may not only alienate this student for the rest of the year, but also may lose respect from the rest of the class, especially if the class perceives the infraction less harshly than you do. Instead of a public rebuke, Jim Hicks suggests that you take the student aside for a private discussion. Communicate that you want the behavior to stop but that you are not interested in embarrassing the student in front of the class. Be calm, positive, but firm, and explain the behavior needed to be corrected and why it is important that you correct it. Describe the consequences that will ensue if the student continues with the disruptive behavior and then be prepared to follow through with the consequence. Do not say something that is unreasonable or that you know might never happen. For example, if you were to say, "You're out of here!" or "You are history!" you might lose the students' respect if the student is returned to class by a school administrator who sees the situation differently than you do.

Teachers may feel especially concerned about what to do when a student's behavior seems potentially dangerous. Threatening behaviors or other deleterious actions on the part of students require your immediate attention and action. It is important for a teacher to gain control immediately in the face of potentially harmful situations. At the time you are hired by a school district, you should ask about district policies and procedures regarding behavior that might put students and teachers in danger. New policies of zero tolerance of drug use and against bringing potentially dangerous weapons to school are in place in many districts.

Maintaining appropriate discipline in your class depends on an excellent support system from, and good communication among, you and other faculty members and administrators in your school and district. If students suspect that no matter how outrageous their behavior in class, they will be able to get off the hook somewhere else, then your efforts as an effective orchestra leader have been compromised.

For this reason, it is important to know school policies regarding unacceptable behavior. When a behavior is extremely serious, or the behavior has occurred frequently, it is a good idea to take the time to describe the entire incident in writing, including the student's behavior and the resulting interruption for the rest of the class. A carefully laid paper trail can be used to support your recommendations and gain the respect of your school administrators regarding your decisions about student behavior problems. It will also serve to communicate effectively with the student's parents, so that they understand and accept your concerns about their child's behavior in school.

Remember, your demeanor will say more to the class than any set of words. Young adults watch what you do, and do not necessarily listen to what you say. Showing your students that you care about their education will eventually have a very positive effect on class atmosphere. Perhaps Kahlil Gibran said it best in a letter to Mary Haskell:

> People are always longing for someone to realize their best selves, to believe in them, and demand their best. When we can do this for people we should not be just an ear to them.

TEACHERS' BODY LANGUAGE

Teachers are the ears, eyes, and conscience of their classrooms. When teachers listen well, see perceptively, and think carefully about the needs of their students, they are more likely to be able to control students' impulsive behaviors and help them be their best selves. Many experienced teachers will share their secret methods for managing student behavior. One researcher who studied classroom management found that a great deal depends on the teacher's body language. Effective teachers are able to communicate many important things with eye contact, physical proximity, bodily carriage, gestures, and facial expressions (Jones, 1987). Teachers do not have to be 6 feet, 5 inches tall and weigh 230 pounds to be considered strong and powerful by their students. It is fascinating to observe teachers who are small in stature control classrooms with a glance by standing next to a student who is disturbing the classroom.

Consider the eye contact of the teachers in the first day of school scenario. Miss Adams had a level gaze and met the students' eyes as she looked at each of them at their first meeting. She communicated that she was aware and in control in a positive, nonthreatening manner. Mr. Evans made immediate eye contact with each student in a positive way and demonstrated enthusiasm for the school where he teaches and the students themselves. Mrs. Destry gave the students withering stares that probably caused them to feel anxious and fearful about the year ahead. Mr. Baron and Mr. Green never met the eyes of their students at all, communicating their lack of preparation and confidence to manage the classroom.

Mr. Catlin used *physical proximity* as well as eye contact to put his students at ease and to communicate that he was in charge. Jones (1987) recommends the concentric circle desk arrangement that Mr. Catlin used because it causes students to focus their attention on the teacher and enables the teacher to provide help efficiently by moving quickly to the side of any student who is having difficulty. By moving close to the restless students and placing a hand on their shoulders, he can help them allay their fears and turn the focus to the classroom activity. Room arrangement can help or hinder a teacher's ability to control children's behavior. To use physical proximity effectively, the teacher must be able to step quickly to the side of the misbehaving student, as Mr. Catlin did.

The strong, straight posture of Miss Adams reinforced the students' perception that she was an authority worthy of their respect. Good posture and confident *bodily carriage* convey strong leadership, while a drooping posture and lethargic movements convey weakness, resignation, or fearfulness (Jones, 1987).

Gestures are also a form of body language that can communicate positive expectations and prevent problems. Teachers can use gestures to mean "stop," "continue," or "quiet, please" without interrupting the verbal instruction. When used with positive eye contact, physical proximity, bodily carriage, or facial expression, gestures can prevent small disruptions from growing into major behavior problems.

Facial expressions vary greatly among teachers. They can show enthusiasm, seriousness, enjoyment, and appreciation, all of which encourage good behavior; or they can reveal boredom, annoyance, and resignation, which may tend to encourage misbehavior (Jones, 1987). Facial expressions that display warmth, joy, and a sense of humor are those that students themselves report to be the most meaningful. Candidates training to be teachers may even want to look in the mirror at their own expressions to discover how students see them when they are happy, angry, feeling good about themselves, or upset.

ESTABLISHING RULES AND CONSEQUENCES

In a healthy democratic community, the citizens understand and accept the laws that govern their behavior. They also understand and accept that if they break the laws, certain consequences will follow. Healthy democratic classrooms also have laws that govern behavior, although they are usually called *rules*. In the most smoothly managed classrooms, students also learn to understand and accept the consequences for breaking a rule from the very first week.

In the opening-day scenarios, each teacher established rules and consequences for the classroom differently. Miss Adams had established a set of rules beforehand. She read them to the class and explained why each was important. Mr. Baron, Mr. Green, and Mrs. Destry did not present a clear set of rules. Their actions indicated that they expected the students to discover the rules of the classroom. These are likely to be quite consistent in Mrs. Destry's classroom; but in the cases of Mr. Baron and Mr. Green, we suspect that the rules may change from day to day. Mr. Catlin had planned an entire process for establishing rules. His process involved the students in helping to establish the class rules based on shared expectations and consequences.

Two different types of consequences are used to guide or shape student behavior. *Natural consequences* are those that follow directly from a student's behavior or action. For example, if a student gets so frustrated while working on an assignment that he rips the paper in half, the natural consequence is that the work will have to be redone from the beginning. If another student wakes up late, the natural consequence is that she misses the bus and has to walk to school, arrives late, and suffers the embarrassment of coming to class tardy. In these cases, there was no adult intervention; the consequence grew directly from the student's behavior.

Logical consequences are those the teacher selects to fit students' actions; they are intended to cause students to change their behavior. For example, a teacher may decide that the logical consequence of not turning in a paper on time is that the student must stay in for recess or miss another activity period to finish the paper. When the paper is turned in, the logical consequence is that the student may go out to recess or take part in the activity period.

The difference between a punishment and a consequence is that a consequence is not arbitrary and is not dispensed with anger or any other strong emotion. To work effectively, logical consequences must be understood fully by the students. The teacher must describe them and explain the connections between the action and the consequence so that students understand the justification for the consequence. They must be applied consistently to all students who exhibit the behavior.

In many classrooms, teachers write a set of rules on a large piece of posterboard that is prominently displayed. Many teachers try to word the rules in positive ways, describing what they expect rather than what they forbid. Many teachers also write specific consequences for each rule on the same poster for all students to see. For example, an elementary teacher may display these rules:

Class Rules	Consequences If Not Followed
We wait in line courteously.	Go to the end of the line.
We listen to the teacher.	Lose 5 minutes of free time.
We turn in work on time.	Finish during free time.
We work and talk quietly.	Take a time-out.
We treat others with respect.	Write a letter of apology.

At the middle or high school level, the posted rules and consequences may resemble these:

Class Rules	Consequence If Not Followed
Work quietly in study hall.	Attend after-school study hall.
Use appropriate language.	Write an essay on swearing.
Maintain school property.	Clean and/or repaint property.
Turn in assignments on time.	Three late assignments equals a grade reduction.

USING POSITIVE CONSEQUENCES AND REWARDS

Jones (1987) focuses on preventing discipline problems by helping students develop self-control. One way to assist students in developing self-control is through the use of positive consequences or incentives for learning and behaving cooperatively. To this end, Jones has examined familiar and widely used teacher practices and has recommended ways to refine these practices to make them more effective and to eliminate negative side effects. For example, he examined the familiar incentive systems of grades, gold stars, and being dismissed first and discovered that these systems appear to benefit only the top achievers; they are not genuine incentives for students who cannot realistically meet the established criteria.

Jones also noted that if teachers offer incentives that are not particularly attractive to many students, they will not positively affect student behavior or achievement. He uses the term *genuine incentives* to distinguish those that students perceive as both valuable and realistic for them to earn from those that students perceive to be of little benefit or impossible to achieve.

Jones uses the phrase *Grandma's Rule* to describe a familiar teaching practice: "First, eat your dinner; then you can have dessert." Applied to the classroom, this rule requires that students first do what the teacher expects; then they can do something that they genuinely want to do. Examples of genuine incentives that many students prize are computer activities, films, or free time in which students can choose and play games in small groups and learning experiences in art, drama, and music.

If students are to continue to perceive these favored activities as genuine incentives, they must be delivered as promised. Some teachers promise the incentive but run out of time and do not deliver on their promises. Another counterproductive practice is continually to threaten to reduce or eliminate the incentive if students do not cooperate. Still others deliver the reward even when the work is not done acceptably. When this occurs, the students learn that they can have dessert even if they do not eat their dinner—that is, they can get the reward without doing their work. This practice can destroy the balance of trust between student and teacher so that when the teacher establishes incentives, the students are skeptical that they will be delivered as promised.

When delivered as promised and as earned, genuine incentives can promote increased achievement among individuals and groups and can cause peer pressure to encourage good behavior. Caring, reflective teachers attempt to understand the real needs and desires of their students and to provide incentives that meet these needs.

Many schools have designed schoolwide systems of behavior management based on Canter's (1992) theory known as *assertive discipline*. According to this theory, teachers have the right to expect good behavior from their students. In these schools, the rules and consequences are the same in every classroom. A set of procedures is established for the first, second, and third infraction of each school rule. For example, the first offense causes the student's name to go on the board and serves as a warning. If students are disciplined for the second time, a check goes by their names, and they must write the rule 25 times. For a third offense, students lose recess or stay after school, and parents are notified of the student's behavior.

In assertive discipline systems, individuals or classrooms often can earn positive rewards for demonstrating their cooperation with the rules. For example, a school may establish a Friday afternoon movie with popcorn for students who have not received any citations for misbehavior during the week.

TWO-WAY COMMUNICATION WITH PARENTS

Discipline problems are less likely when teachers communicate their expectations to students and parents so that everyone is working with the same set of policies. Communication with parents needs to occur early in the school year. Teachers should clearly explain the policies, procedures, and rules that govern the classroom and should establish procedures for parents to ask questions and voice their concerns.

Vernice Mallory teaches fifth grade in a neighborhood of small homes and apartments that houses a diverse population of African Americans, Caucasians and recent immigrants from Asia, Mexico, and Central America. In the Reflective Action Case 2.1, Vernice describes the ways she builds effective two-way communication with the parents. You will notice that as Vernice reflects on the processes she uses in her classroom, the elements described in the Model of Reflective Action do not appear in the order given in Figures 1.2–1.9. As you have no doubt observed, teachers do not reflect on events in any one set order or pattern. Still, it is evident that Vernice exhibits all six of the reflective actions as she discusses how she establishes rapport and trust with her students' parents.

Case 2.1 ⟲ Reflective Action

Vernice Mallory, Fifth-Grade Teacher,
Edison Elementary School, San Diego, Calif.

Use Withitness

At the beginning of this year, I noticed that many of my students were not turning in their homework on a regular basis. I knew I had to attack this problem right away before a pattern was established.

Put the Problem into Perspective

I have been teaching for many, many years and I have found that one thing hasn't changed. To prevent discipline problems, it is absolutely necessary to establish good quality two-way communication with parents early in the school year. This policy holds true for every ethnic group. What has changed is that there seems to be less and less supervision at home because so many parents are working so hard to support their families these days.

Parents are the child's first teachers and I believe that children respond better when they know their parents are behind them. When I hear other teachers criticize parents and say that they won't come to conferences, I believe that it often occurs because teachers erect barriers between themselves and the parents. They don't try to understand how the parents feel. For example, many African American parents come from an old school: God first, preachers second, and teachers come right next to God and the preacher. So it isn't that they don't respect the school or the teacher. Something else comes between them and feeling comfortable visiting their children's classes. Some African American parents may believe that when they send their children to school, the teacher is the boss and has the right to do whatever it takes to make the child learn. But I'd rather work as partners with parents so I build a partnership.

Widen Your Perspective

For me, teaching has been a learning process from day one and will be until the day I retire. I've read many books about teaching and discipline systems in my career and I've attended many workshops to learn new methods, but I know I still have a lot to learn. In this case I think I learned the most from the parents themselves. They were the ones who could best tell me how to meet their needs.

Do Research and Ask for Feedback

Each year, I have to learn what the parents of my students are thinking about. I don't wait for the fall open house. In the second week of school, I send home a notice inviting all the parents to come to my classroom for a kaffeeklatsch or get-together. I don't make the note formal or threatening. It might look something like this:

Hi,

I'm your child's teacher this year and I want to get to know you. Let's all get together and discuss the plans for this year. In Africa, there is a saying that it takes a whole village to educate a child, and this goes for our neighborhood too. So come next Wednesday at 1:00 to meet your child's classmates and their parents. We'll discuss homework policies, attendance, parent involvement, and whatever else piques your interest.

Signed, Vernice

_____ Yes, I can attend

_____ No, I cannot attend. A more convenient time for me is _____ .

When the parents come for my get-togethers, they may be skeptical at first, but when I greet them in a friendly way, they respond with enthusiasm. I always do a survey of my parents at the meeting. I ask the question, "What are your strengths and interests?" Then I try to make a place for them in my classroom, putting their strengths to work. By the way, this get-together includes the students, too. I want my students to see their parents at school and to have positive role models in their homes and neighborhood.

In the middle of the year, I call another meeting. We sit down and discuss anything the parents are concerned about or are not pleased with. We discuss class parties and schedules. I remind them of my expectations. If a new parent has moved to the neighborhood, the meeting gives them a chance to meet the other parents. A feeling of community bonding develops.

At the end of the year, I invite parents to help us make class ribbons and autograph books. The culminating activity of the year is something I developed to celebrate the diversity of our classroom and to bring all of us together again. I have a potluck and the parents make all of the food representing their cultures.

Devise a New Action Plan

Getting back to my problem with homework supervision: At the first parent get-together, with the students sitting there listening, I tell their parents to expect homework every day. I show them how I write the homework assignments on the board and then I tell them that they are expected to sign their names on the students' finished homework every day. In this way, we all understand each other, and I am confident that the parents know what I expect.

After the first meeting, I invite the parents to come be part of the program, based on their strengths and interests. For example, one parent loved math, so she led a math tutorial. Another parent wrote that her main interest was African American culture. She taught all the students to wrap material around their heads into authentic African crowns. Another parent volunteers to do physical education because his strength is physical fitness. One even teaches ballroom dancing. If the parent has to bring in a small child, I let her. I'd rather have her bring her child and do her good work for our classroom than stay at home. My classroom has a variety of dolls and games the young child can use to keep busy while the parent works with the students.

Predict Possible Outcomes

The majority of parents come to the meeting, but for the ones who don't I follow up and ask them to come in at their convenience. I don't limit them to any time of day. I make time for them. I make myself available because I believe that getting my students' parents to work with me is one of the most important parts of my job.

When parents have had bad experiences with other teachers, and they have made up their minds that they don't trust schools or teachers, I have to build trust. I had a parent who was absolutely irate because the child's homework was too hard for him to understand and he couldn't help his child. I tried to convince him that the homework was not for him, it was for his child, but that if he really wanted to learn, he was welcome to come in while we were doing math. A few weeks later, he walked in my classroom and I nodded him to an available seat. He sat very quietly. When the class was over, I went to him and he said, "Math isn't the way it was when I was in school." He started coming in every day for about two months. I asked him if he wanted to sit by his son and he did. He sat by his son and they learned fractions together.

At the end of the year, during the pot luck, every child in my classroom gets a special award, even if he just sharpened a pencil for me. And at the same time, I present awards for positive parenting to the parents. We all feel proud of our village of children that we have worked together to raise.

Discipline Systems That Build Character and Self-Esteem

Lickona (1992) confronts a complex issue that teachers face today in his design of a system called moral discipline. He acknowledges that fewer students come to school with attitudes of respect for adults or schools: "Many are astonishingly bold in their disrespect for teachers and other authority figures" (p. 109). He has observed student teachers and first-year teachers confront the harsh realities of working with students who bring their anger and resentment to school each day.

Lickona believes that the teacher is the central moral authority in the classroom and for many children the teacher functions as the primary moral mentor in their lives.

"Exercising authority, however, doesn't mean being authoritarian. Authority works best when it's infused with respect and love" (1992, p. 111).

To create a moral discipline system for your classroom, Lickona suggests involving your students in establishing the rules in a cooperative, mutually respectful manner. He describes how Kim McConnell, a sixth-grade teacher at Walt Disney Elementary School in San Ramon, California, develops rules with her students on the second day of school.

She arranges her classroom into groups of four students each because she believes it is important for students to have a support group. She asks each group to brainstorm rules that will help them do the following:

1. Get our work done.
2. Feel safe.
3. Be glad we're in school.

When they have written their rules on large pieces of paper, she shows them the list she has created. As a group, the class synthesizes the best elements into one list that serves as the class rules for that year.

Lickona compares the system of moral discipline with the system of assertive discipline and observes that assertive discipline is a fixed system that uses the same consequences for all types of behavior. Moral discipline, in contrast, focuses on the specific needs of each class and uses logical consequences that help students understand what they have done and what they must do to improve their moral conduct.

For example, with a rule such as, "Use respectful language in this classroom," the consequences (designed by the students in cooperation with their teacher) might be:

> *First occasion:* Take a time-out of 5 minutes and state or write the language you used that was disrespectful. Tell why it was disrespectful and to whom.
>
> *Second occasion:* Write a letter of apology to the person or class to whom you were disrespectful.
>
> *Third occasion:* Bring up your own behavior at a class meeting; ask for feedback on how you can stop using this type of language. Write a plan for improving your language and present it to the class.

HUMOR IN THE CLASSROOM

Csikszentmihalyi and McCormack (1986) recognized the importance of enjoyment in the learning process in a study they conducted on the influence of teachers on their students. When they asked students to tell them who or what influenced them to become the kinds of people they are, 58 percent mentioned one or more teachers, with descriptions such as these:

> Mrs. A. was influential because her class was a lot of fun. After all these years, I found out for the first time that I really liked English. It was really fun, and I've kept up my interest even though I'm not doing as well as other kids. (p. 419)

Csikszentmihalyi and McCormack (1986) believe that teacher enthusiasm, a sense of humor, and the ability to make learning enjoyable are vitally important in the classroom because they are connected with trust and meaningfulness. "How can young people believe that the information they are receiving is worth having, when their teachers seem bored, detached, or indifferent?" they ask (p. 419).

Loomans and Kolberg (1993) have written a book called *The Laughing Classroom*, which is filled with motivating strategies for teachers to use in all areas of the curriculum. They identify four styles of humor-oriented teaching. The Joy Master is a teacher who inspires students to become warmhearted and humane toward one another. She might use a strategy such as creative debate in which students are assigned a role and debate an issue. Abe Lincoln may be debating on one side and Charlie Chaplin on the other.

The Fun-Meister uses slapstick and clowning as a motivational technique. When teaching a mathematical operation, the teacher may pretend to make mistakes so that students catch them, thereby giving the students a reason to monitor the teacher's demonstration more carefully. Peals of laughter may fill the room as the students point out the teacher's error. This style of teaching, however, can have its dark side, as fun-meisters sometimes mock others, including their students, causing students to laugh at one another's mistakes.

A third type of humorous teacher is the Life Mocker, and this type is almost entirely negative from the students' viewpoints. Teachers who are cynical and sarcastic may cause a few laughs, but the students may experience this style as coldhearted and dehumanizing.

A fourth style is the Joke Maker. Teachers who have a way with telling stories and jokes are always entertaining for their students. These stories can be very instructive and provide insight as examples of an abstract concept. Occasionally, teachers can use jokes or stories that are experienced as insults or stereotypes that have a negative effect on students.

The Laughing Classroom is an excellent resource for teachers at all grade levels and can assist you in planning humorous activities that are supportive, positive and healing.

Scheduling Time for Active Learning

DAILY AND WEEKLY SCHEDULES

Teachers at all levels believe they cannot fit everything they want to teach into the school day. Charles (1983) cites "dealing with the trivial" as one of teachers' greatest time robbers (p. 243). When teachers simply try to fit everything into the day, they are as likely to include trivial matters as important ones. A reflective teacher weighs the relative importance of each element of the school program and allocates time accordingly. This may mean eliminating certain items entirely and carefully scheduling the minutes of the day to meet students' most important needs.

Schedules differ from grade to grade depending on the relative importance of the subject at that grade level and the way the school is structured and organized. The most frequently used structure in elementary schools is to place students into grade-level *self-contained classrooms* in which one teacher has the responsibility for teaching all the academic subjects. In other cases, students may have a homeroom but their academic subjects are *departmentalized*, meaning that teachers specialize in one academic area and students move from class to class during the day.

For example, the primary grades are usually structured as self-contained classrooms, and primary teachers often schedule reading and language-arts activities for up to one-half of the school day. The intermediate grades may be self-contained or departmentalized; but in either case, math, science, and social studies activities are usually given more time than they are at the primary grades. In junior high school, the schedules are likely to be departmentalized, meaning that each teacher specializes in one subject and teaches it to several classes of students during the day.

No two schedules are alike. Teachers in self-contained classrooms are usually allowed great discretion in how they allocate time. Typically, state requirements mandate how many minutes per week are to be allocated to each of several subjects, but teachers make varied plans within those prescriptions. For example, the state may require a minimum of 150 minutes of math per week. Teacher A may schedule 30 minutes per day; teacher B may schedule 40 minutes for four days; teacher C may schedule 45 minutes on Mondays, Wednesdays, and Fridays with brief review periods on other days.

Elementary class schedules may be rigid or flexible. They may be the same every day or vary greatly. They may be governed by bells or by the teacher's own inner clock. Charles (1983) recommends that, regardless of how it is determined, "the daily classroom schedule should be explained in such a manner that students know what activities are to occur at each part of the day and how they are to work and behave during those activities" (p. 10). When students know the schedule, they can learn to manage their own time more efficiently. A teacher who uses a consistent schedule may create a permanent display of the schedule on a bulletin board; a teacher who varies the schedule from day to day can write the current schedule on the chalkboard each morning.

The conventional wisdom of teachers is that the most difficult subjects should be scheduled early in the day when students are most likely to be attentive. Reading or language arts is frequently the first subject of the day in a self-contained classroom, followed by math. Science, social studies, art, and music compose the afternoons. This may be the preferred schedule, but often school constraints make it difficult to achieve. Physical education, art, and music may be taught by other teachers in separate classrooms. The schedule for these special classes may affect the classroom teacher's schedule. Some classes must be scheduled for special classes in the morning, causing classroom teachers to adjust their plans.

PLANNING TIME

Teachers may be annoyed when special classes interrupt their scheduled lessons, but they appreciate one important side effect: when the class leaves for art, music, or physical education, the classroom teacher has a planning period. Planning time is usually part of the teacher's contract and is designed to provide opportunities for individual or collegial planning. Teachers of self-contained classrooms have complete discretion over their planning time, but departmentalized teachers frequently hold meetings during their planning time to discuss how they will plan and deliver their shared curricula.

Teachers use planning time in various ways, some productive and others less so. Charles (1983) recommends that teachers use this time as efficiently as possible by "prioritizing tasks, giving attention to those that are absolutely necessary, such as planning, scoring papers, preparing for conferences, and preparing instructional materials and activities. Also high on the list should come those tasks that are difficult or boring, leaving for later those that are most enjoyable" (p. 244). Less efficient teachers may use the time for socializing, complaining, smoking, eating, reading magazines, or making personal telephone calls. Later they complain that the school day is too short and that they have too much work to do at home.

Charles (1983) recommends that routine tasks such as watering plants, cleaning the room, feeding animals, and distributing materials should not be done during planning time or by the teacher at all. The teacher who is an efficient time manager delegates as many of these routine tasks as possible to student helpers. This has two effects that contribute to a healthy classroom environment: (a) it reduces the stress teachers feel about time, and (b) it provides a sense of responsibility and meaningful accomplishment for the student helpers.

Most reflective teachers want to create a classroom in which students can meet their basic human needs for belonging and achievement. To accomplish this, they consider every aspect of the environment as it relates to children's needs. They arrange the furniture to meet students' needs for a sense of belonging; they create rules and schedule time to meet students' needs for security; they provide opportunities for students to write about and discuss their other feelings and needs. They do this because they want to create a nurturing sense of community in their classroom as a means of enhancing successful achievement.

⊃ Reflective Actions for Your Professional Portfolio
A Sample of Your Classroom Management System

Use Withitness

Visit a classroom and observe and record how time is used. Is a schedule posted? If so, is it followed rigidly or flexibly? If not, how is the schedule determined? Keep a record of how much time is spent on academic, nonacademic, and classroom management concerns. Also, observe what the rules are in this classroom and how the rules are communicated to students. Do the students seem to understand and accept the rules?

Put Problem into Perspective

Create a schedule that you would use if this were your classroom and you had control over the resource of time.

Widen Your Perspective

How do you want time to be used in your classroom? What are the rules you consider most important to establish for your students? Remember the philosophy of teaching that you wrote in Chapter 1, and look for classroom management strategies that are congruent with your philosophy.

Do Research and Invite Feedback to Learn More

Read articles about the classroom management strategies you are interested in. Visit and talk with a teacher using them. Look up the topic of discipline and classroom management on the world wide web. Try the Prentice-Hall methods cluster web page at www.prenhall.com/methods-cluster or other teacher resource pages such as thegateway.org or schoolnotes.com. These web pages have articles about effective discipline or they will link you to other sites that have a huge variety of tips and strategies teachers have found to be useful.

Redefine the Issue

From all these resources, you can begin to synthesize the methods and strategies that work best for you. Write your current ideas of which discipline and classroom strategies fit with your philosophy of teaching and how you will incorporate these strategies into your classroom.

Create an Action Plan

Create a schedule that incorporates the best of your ideal use of time with the realities of your school environment. Write about the balance you try to achieve with this revised schedule. Write down the rules you believe are most effective. Write the consequences or incentives that fit each rule. Describe how you can explain these rules to your class and how you can incorporate students' suggestions into the class rules. Include these pages in your portfolio.

Predict the Possible Outcomes of Your Plan

Ask some students to look at your schedule and rules. Ask them to tell you how effective they think your plan is. Probe as you question them to find out what they really think. Ask them to be as honest as possible with you and then be prepared to make alterations if you receive some useful feedback.

References

Canter, L. (1992). *Positive Behavior Management for Today's Classroom.* Santa Monica, CA: Canter & Associates.

Charles, C. (1983). *Elementary classroom management.* New York: Longman.

Csikszentmihalyi, M., & McCormack, J. (1986). The influence of teachers. *Phi Delta Kappan, 67*(6), 415–419.

Doyle, W. (1986). Classroom organization and management. In M. Wittrock (Ed.), *Handbook of research on teaching* (3rd ed.) (pp. 392–431). Upper Saddle River, NJ: Merrill/Prentice Hall.

Emmer, E., Evertson, C., & Anderson, L. (1980). Effective classroom management at the beginning of the school year. *Elementary School Journal, 80*(5), 219–231.

Evertson, C. (1989). Improving elementary classroom management: A school-based training program for beginning the year. *Journal of Educational Research, 83*(2), 82–90.

Jones, F. (1987). *Positive classroom discipline.* New York: McGraw-Hill.

Lickona, T. (1992). *Educating for character.* New York: Bantam.

Loomans, D., & Kolberg, K. (1993). *The Laughing Classroom.* Tiburon, CA: H J Kramer.

chapter 3

Celebrating Diversity in Your Classroom

As soon as they succeed in getting a teaching position, most teachers are eager to get into their classrooms to arrange furniture, establish schedules, put up bulletin boards, consider rules and consequences, and plan major units of study. But surprises are inevitable when school starts and the classroom is filled with students from many backgrounds who have a variety of abilities, talents, and needs.

The first day of school can be daunting for a teacher who has spent a lot of time and energy planning the perfect beginning for the school year. Some students may appear to be totally uninterested while others seem to be intent on disrupting the teacher's plans. Most classrooms today are likely to have some students who are struggling to understand and speak English. Many new teachers find themselves sitting at their desks, wondering, "Whatever made me think I could do this?" Even experienced teachers often find themselves comparing their new classes with last year's, thinking, "These students have so many more needs than last year's group!" They may be forgetting that last year's class had made a whole school year's worth of progress when they parted at the end of the year.

Teaching today's diverse student population is most definitely a challenge. Students bring a wealth of different perspectives to the classroom, whether they are from mainstream U.S. homes or homes where multiple languages are spoken. We three authors believe that all students are teachable, and we hope you do too. Teachers who have faith in their students' abilities to learn are the ones who are able to make the most significant and positive differences in their students' lives.

Stephanie Collom, a Fresno, California, resource teacher at Hidalgo Elementary School, where native English speakers are rare, observed that "All the children come to school with faith in me, as their teacher. I have to find ways to support their learning so that that faith is justified. I also have to have faith in their abilities as learners and find a way to make sure that they succeed."

Many teachers begin their careers expecting the students and the curriculum to resemble the students and curriculum they experienced when they were in school. It is sometimes a shock to realize how much has changed in education in a very short time. Today's students come to school from many backgrounds, not only in experiences, but in language exposure and perceptions of what school is about. To add complexity to the issue, it seems that as our student body becomes more diverse, the state-mandated curriculum is becoming more focused on meeting a single set of standards for all.

Teachers in today's schools are expected to teach the traditional skills to a nontraditional group of students. In addition, teachers are expected to diversify their instructional methods in ways that support students' self-esteem, knowledge of technology, and ethnic and language backgrounds. An added challenge in working with diverse populations is the different expectations that parents from different cultures bring to the school.

Celebrating diversity is vastly different from *tolerating* diversity. At the end of the 20th century, the goal seemed to be for teachers in multicultural settings to show acceptance of students' differences. In the current—and, it is hoped, more enlightened—century, teachers have the goal of finding ways to encourage all students to value their own cultural heritage and appreciate the contributions of their classmates from other diverse backgrounds.

One of the major factors that affects learning is the difference in language. To teach effectively, teachers must understand how language is acquired and know how to adjust their assessment, curriculum, and planning to take advantage of the multiple language-centered perspectives contained within almost every classroom.

Language Acquisition and the Classroom Teacher

The research into language acquisition issues has become rich and productive. Linguists and educators working together have discovered effective ways to support students in their acquisition of new languages and content knowledge. It is vital that classroom teachers understand the implication of the language acquisition theory so they can provide the scaffolding necessary for their students to be successful in the classroom (Krashen & Terrell, 1983).

Krashen (1982), in his study of language acquisition, makes a distinction between language *acquisition* and language *learning* that is vital to the support of students in the classroom in their gradual acquisition of fluency in a new language. Krashen's research demonstrated that language acquisition is a natural process. He observed how easily and readily young children acquire their home language without formal teaching, and no drill and practice! Natural language acquisition is a gradual interactive process based on receiving and understanding messages, building a listening (receptive) vocabulary, and slowly attempting verbal production of the language in a highly supportive, nonstressful environment.

He recommends that teachers duplicate these conditions as much as possible in the classroom to foster the acquisition of a second language. According to this theory, teachers will be most successful in teaching English if they plan interactive learning activities and speak or write in words selected to match their students' level of understanding. This concept is termed *understandable language* or *comprehensible input*, and it is to be used with props, gestures, pictures, and other strategies that all contribute to the child's acquisition, and eventually to the production, of the language.

LANGUAGE SCAFFOLDING

Scaffolding is a term used in teaching that involves modeling and demonstrating a new skill. It requires a highly interactive relationship between the teacher and the student while the new learning occurs. Anderson (1989) cites Jerome Bruner's work with mothers and children as the first reference to scaffolding. As a mother reads aloud to a toddler, she may simplify the book to meet the attention span and interests of her child, calling the child's attention to material that is appropriate and eliminating material that is beyond the child's current capacity. She is also likely to allow the child to interact with her as they read and discuss the words and pictures on each page. This flexible and simplified interaction allows the child to connect new ideas to existing schemata at the child's own level.

Teachers can apply scaffolding in the classroom by reducing complex tasks to manageable steps; helping students concentrate on one task at a time; stating explicitly what is expected and interpreting the task for the student; and coaching the student using familiar, supportive words and actions. A teacher coaching a student through a difficult task must provide sufficient scaffolding through the use of hints and cues so that the student can succeed. As students become more skillful, the scaffolding can be reduced and finally eliminated.

Scaffolding is an especially valuable technique for the primary teacher because most young students require supportive interaction and accommodation to their existing vocabularies to learn new skills. But scaffolding is also appropriate for upper-level students when the tasks are complex or the students have difficulty with the language.

For some beginning teachers, scaffolding may not come naturally because they may not have experienced scaffolded learning in their own school experiences. This technique can be learned only by reflecting on the needs of students, gathering the latest information on such techniques from reading and talking to experienced teachers who have used the techniques successfully, and gradually adding such strategies to personal repertoires.

Scaffolding academic language supports students' successful participation in content area instruction. Academic language is language associated with school subjects such as mathematics, science and social studies. It places a higher cognitive demand on the listener or speaker.

Cummins (1986) identified two types of language that students acquire. The first, Basic Interpersonal Communication Skills (BICS)—or social language—is learned more quickly and easily than the second, Cognitive Academic Language Proficiency (CALP)—or academic language. Academic language scaffolding supports the student in CALP, the language necessary for the student to participate successfully in classroom learning opportunities.

For students to participate successfully in academic lessons in the classroom, teachers use a series of scaffolding strategies that include modeling academic language; contextualizing academic language using visuals, gestures, and demonstrations; and supporting the students in the use of academic language through active learning activities.

Susan McCloskey, a kindergarten/first-grade teacher at Greenberg Elementary School in Fresno, California, provides a perfect example of language scaffolding as she teaches her students the concepts of *same* and *different*. She begins her lesson by modeling. She takes two large teddy bears and holds them up for the students to see. "These are the same," she says. She puts one bear down and picks up a stuffed bunny. "These are different," she says. She asks students to come to the front of the class and hold two of the stuffed animals. The other students repeat the words "same" and "different," depending on the animals the child is holding. Ms. McCloskey then has the students draw pictures of their favorite foods. They show their pictures and talk about the fact that some children like the same foods and others like different foods. During recess she photocopies some of the drawings onto a large sheet of paper and when they return to the classroom she arranges the students into pairs, making sure each pair has a relatively strong English speaker. (All of her students are English language learners so she doesn't have the advantage of strong English models, other than herself and classroom volunteers and aides.)

Ms. McCloskey demonstrates while she gives the instructions for the activity. She tells them to cut out the pictures as she models cutting out the pictures. She tells them to paste pictures that are the same on a piece of construction paper. She models choosing two pictures of hamburgers and placing them together on a large sheet of construction paper. She repeats, "These are the same," as she points to the two hamburgers. The students work together, some talking in English, some in Hmong, their native language. Ms. MsCloskey moves around the room supporting the students, asking questions about "same" and "different." To anyone observing this activity, the lesson is obviously a success.

At the end of the lesson, Ms. McCloskey adds the piece that scaffolds the students into new levels of language. As each pair completes the task, they bring the paper to Ms. McCloskey. She points to one group of pictures on the construction paper and asks, "Why did you put these together?"

The first child says, "Same." "Yes," confirms Ms. McCloskey. "They are all the same. This is a hamburger. This is a hamburger. This is a hamburger. This is a hamburger. They are all the same," she says as she points to each hamburger on the page. She then asks, "Why did you put these together?" as she points to the hot dogs. The child responds, "This is hot dog. This is hot dog. This is hot dog. This is hot dog," as he points to each one. "They all same." Ms. McCloskey then asks the other child in the pair the same questions. Because this child has been watching and listening, she responds in phrases just as Ms. McCloskey has modeled. In just a few minutes these two children have moved from one word responses to simple sentence responses with the teacher's language scaffolding. Many teachers would have been pleased that the students had completed the task correctly and would have put a smiley face or star at the top of the page without using the "teachable moment" and providing the vital language scaffolding part of the lesson. Knowing how children acquire language is a necessary part of effective teaching with English language learners.

THE STAGES IN LANGUAGE ACQUISITION

Students who are acquiring a new language go through predictable stages (Krashen & Terrell, 1983). The stages begin with students listening to language. They are taking in, or receiving, language at this stage and it is often called the *silent period*. Teachers should be aware that students are processing the language they are hearing and it is important that the language be contextualized so that it is understandable. After this silent or preproduction period, students move into the early production stage where they can give one- or two-word responses. They then move into speech emergence where they are attempting to speak phrases and short sentences but still making grammatical errors. They then move gradually into intermediate fluency where their sentences lengthen and their errors decline. Finally, over time, they become fluent in English.

Teachers need to be aware of these stages so that they can adapt their questioning strategies and expectations to support students' progress. It is especially important that teachers actively seek ways to keep English language learners involved in the classroom community. Allowing students to sit idly, not engaged or processing the instruction that is going on in a classroom is never acceptable, but teachers must be armed with strategies to use in engaging students.

Leveled questions are used when teachers adapt the way they ask questions so that students can answer or respond to them according to their language acquisition stage. The use of leveled questions enables a teacher to include English language learners in the classroom activities and support their active engagement which, in turn, supports their language acquisition. To level the questions, the teacher must observe the students and note the way in which they interact in English. Once the teacher knows the level at which the students interact in English, the questions the teacher poses to the students can be adjusted to assure the students' success in answering. This may involve the teacher using gestures, visuals, or slowing the speech slightly while asking the questions. The teacher asks the question in a way that encourages the student to answer by pointing to a visual, giving a one word response or a complete sentence or explanation depending on the student's level of language acquisition. The teacher's role in using this strategy involves knowing the student's level of English acquisition and providing enough context in the question so that the student can respond, either verbally or nonverbally, with understanding and confidence.

OPTIMAL LEVELS OF INSTRUCTION

Reflective teachers who want to encourage each student to function at the highest level of achievement monitors the student's level of understanding closely to see what interventions are needed. Lev Vygotsky, a Russian cognitive psychologist, identified the optimal level of instruction for each student as the *zone of proximal development* (ZPD). The ZPD for each student is based on the level at which the student can no longer solve problems alone but must be supported by a teacher or more knowledgeable peer (Dixon-Kraus, 1996). For the teacher to be able to provide instruction for all students at their optimal learning level, or ZPD, the teacher must use reflective actions to gain an understanding of the student's needs. This is especially vital for students who have special needs or who are learning English as their second language.

Five Factors in Meeting the Needs of Diverse Students

Whether a student is learning English as a second (or third) language or just having difficulty absorbing academic content, there are five factors that reflective teachers consider when planning and implementing instruction.

The first factor is *comprehensible input*. The teacher looks at the lesson and asks, "Is the instruction I am giving understandable to my students?" If the students are confused or simply not "getting it," the teacher must consider how to make the instruction more understandable. It is important to give explanations while demonstrating something. The teacher may want to ask, "Am I just talking or am I modeling, using pictures, gestures, and real objects to demonstrate the concepts I am trying to get across? Am I using words that I have defined and demonstrated? Am I relating new concepts to past experiences, giving examples, showing instead of telling?"

Good explanations require a lot of thought. Giving multiple examples supports understanding. Giving non-examples is also very helpful. For example, when teaching about the characteristics of mammals, a teacher might say, "A zebra and an elephant are both examples of mammals; fish and birds are not examples of mammals."

The second factor to consider is *quality of the verbal interactions* with and among your students. Ask yourself, "Am I providing opportunities for the students to interact with one another? Do the students have an opportunity to use hands-on materials? Are they given a chance to see the practical importance of what they are being asked to learn?"

The third factor is the *contextualization* of the language experiences you provide for your students. In other words, are new words and ideas presented within a context so the students can link the vocabulary and concepts to a bigger picture? One of the biggest factors in a student's ability to comprehend language is how well that language is supported by context. The direction, "Take out your science book," when spoken while holding up the science book is easily understood even by a student who knows no English, or a student who can't hear well. Just getting in the habit of supporting instruction with the use of gestures, visuals, and showing while telling is highly supportive of language acquisition and student understanding.

The fourth factor to consider is *selecting strategies* for teaching and grouping that serve to reduce student anxiety rather than aggravate it. Students who are anxious about being called on or to speak aloud in front of their peers often have difficulty processing information or even listening attentively. Krashen (1982) calls this the *affective filter*, an emotional process that prevents the learner from hearing or processing new information. Teachers who want to diminish or eliminate the likelihood of triggering a student's affective filter, must find ways to create a classroom climate that encourages and motivates students while reducing their anxiety.

One important consideration for you to reflect on is the way you ask questions and respond to errors. If students know that making an error is not going to cause them to be ridiculed in front of the class, they are much freer to answer questions and take risks. It's not enough to refrain from embarrassing students, however. There should be a consistent monitoring of the verbal interactions among students as well. A "no-tolerance rule" related to student ridicule proves a healthy classroom climate, conducive to learning. This happens only when the teacher models it, discusses it openly, and tolerates no negative verbal interactions among the students.

The fifth factor to be considered is how to increase the *level of active involvement* of students within the classroom. Opportunities to actively engage in classroom activities designed to practice and gradually master the skills being taught are as vital to language acquisition as they are to other aspects of student learning. Activities that let students work in small groups on projects that use new skills and problem-solving strategies also require the students to engage in verbal interactions and contextualize the language they are using—and generally serve to reduce anxiety.

When all five of these factors are considered in scheduling the school day and planning individual lessons and activities, the classroom becomes a community of learners. The reflective teacher observes the classroom climate and uses withitness to perceive any indications of discord or anxiety that may be standing in the way of learning. Planning time for purposeful student interaction is a vital building block for developing a strong sense of community. Students need time to interact and get to know one another. As they know more about each other, they will begin to value the diversity and uniqueness of the individuals who make up the community.

Two of these important goals can be achieved by using cooperative group activities as a strategy for teaching in your classroom. Language acquisition for English language learners is enhanced by taking part in a cooperative group effort where communication skills are required to complete an assigned task and increased understanding and appreciation of diversity occurs as well.

Slavin (1995) reports that cooperative groups may actually improve race relations within a classroom. Studies suggest that students who participate in multiracial teams choose one another for friends more often than do students in control groups. Researchers attribute this effect to the fact that working together in a group as a part of a team causes students to promote more differentiated, dynamic, and realistic views (and therefore less stereotyped and static views) of other students (including peers with disabilities and students from different ethnic groups) than do competitive and individualistic learning experiences (Johnson & Johnson, 1984).

INTERACTIVE GOAL SETTING

Teachers can support the growth of their students' levels of performance by using interactive goal setting as a natural forum for celebrating growth and setting goals for the future.

Vince Workman a fifth-grade teacher in Fresno, California, sets aside time to discuss his students' accomplishments with them during each of the six grading periods in the school year. He schedules these student conferences throughout the year, recycling back through his class in about the same order so that students can expect to meet with him for goal setting every six weeks. Because Mr. Workman and his students work together to select samples for the student portfolios, he begins the conferences by asking the students to talk about the work they have accomplished since their last student/ teacher conference. Students talk about the work they have chosen to share and then, together, the teacher and student look at the grade-level standards and decide which of the standards have been met or are in the process of being met. They decide together on an appropriate challenge for the next week.

For example, Alberto, a student who is reading at about the third grade level, has set a goal of reading two library books a week. He is keeping a reading journal and a vocabulary notebook to monitor his own understanding of the books he is reading and focus on building his English vocabulary. Mr. Workman encourages him to use the new words he is learning everyday and often calls on Alberto in class to share some of the new words he is practicing. Because vocabulary study is one of Alberto's self-selected goals, he is much more motivated to keep working on his vocabulary journal. Mr. Workman talks to him briefly almost every day about new words he is exploring and celebrates Alberto's growing word knowledge frequently through simple responses such as, "That's a great word for that, Alberto. Explain where you first found that word and some of the ways you have found to use it." Alberto's first vocabulary goal was to learn two new words a day. He has increased his goal each six weeks so that he is now focusing on six new words each day. His vocabulary journal helps both Alberto and Mr. Workman to keep track of the progress he is making.

Building Self-Esteem and Intrinsic Motivation

Maslow (1954) first described human beings' *hierarchy of needs.* He recognized that people have basic physical and emotional needs that must be satisfied before the individual can attend to the higher need for achievement and recognition. If the lower needs are not satisfied, the individual is preoccupied by trying to meet them, and higher-level needs disappear or are pushed into the background. This explains why hungry or tired students cannot learn efficiently. All their capacities are focused on their need for food or sleep. To satisfy the real hunger needs experienced by many students, some schools provide breakfast, snacks, or milk so that students can pay attention to school tasks.

But what happens when the student has plenty of food and adequate shelter and is well rested? Then "at once other (and 'higher') needs emerge," and these become dominant (p. 375). The need for safety and security follow basic physiological needs, and the need for love and belonging follow safety needs. Imagine two classrooms, one led by an autocratic or permissive teacher in which students feel threatened, insecure, and isolated; the other led by a democratic teacher in which students feel safe, secure, cared for, and connected with other members of the class community. In the latter setting, students are more likely to have their needs met and therefore be ready and able to achieve greater success in academic work.

Raths (1972) also identified eight emotional needs that people strive to satisfy. These include the need for love, achievement, belonging, self-respect, freedom from guilt, freedom from fear, economic security, and self understanding. Raths believes that children whose needs are not satisfied exhibit negative, self-defeating behaviors such as aggressiveness, withdrawal, submissiveness, regressiveness, or psychosomatic illness.

Raths recognizes that teachers cannot satisfy the many unmet needs experienced by all the students in their classrooms. However, he does believe that "children cannot check their emotions at the door and we should not expect them to. If unmet needs are getting in the way of a child's growth and development, his learning and his maturing, I insist that it is your obligation *to try* to meet his needs" (1972, p. 141). Raths's book *Meeting the Needs of Children* contains many pages of specific suggestions about what teachers can do to help meet children's emotional needs so that they are free to learn.

THE ENHANCING EFFECTS OF SUCCESS

All individuals want to win or succeed. Virtually all students who walk into a classroom on the first day of school hope that this year will be *the* year, that this grade will be *the* grade, and that this teacher will be *the* teacher who will make it possible for them to succeed. Some enter secure in the knowledge that they've succeeded before, but are still anxious about whether they can duplicate that success in this new situation. Others enter with a history of failure and harbor no more than a dim hope that they can succeed if only they can overcome their bad habits and learn how to succeed.

Winning and success are the most powerful motivations for future effort and achievement that we know of. Glasser (1969) noted:

> As a psychiatrist, I have worked many years with people who are failing. I have
> struggled with them as they try to find a way to a more successful life. From these

struggles I have discovered an important fact: regardless of his background, his culture, his color, or his economic level, *he will not succeed in general until he can in some way first experience success in one important part of his life.* Given the first success to build upon, the negative factors . . . mean little. (p. 5)

It is possible to restate Glasser's message as a significant principle of teaching and learning: When an individual experiences success in one important part of life, that person can succeed in life regardless of background, culture, color, or economic level. Glasser's book *Schools Without Failure* (1969) has caused researchers and practitioners to reflect on the fundamental goals of education and to reexamine what students need from the school environment to succeed.

It is especially important for children who may have been raised in culturally different settings to experience success in their new school environments. Caring, reflective teachers are quick to perceive that children new to the school or the community need to experience success very quickly in order to adjust well to their new surroundings. Assign new students a task that you are sure is well within their capability and then show your acceptance and satisfaction with the work they accomplish.

The same is true for students who may appear indifferent or even resentful of school and teachers. Try to understand that they may have a history of being unfairly treated by other, less caring teachers. Students who have faced failure repeatedly often develop negative attitudes toward schoolwork and frequently mask their need for approval with defensive and disruptive behaviors in an effort to hide their hurt and shame. You can be the teacher who helps them change their behavior by perceiving their need for success and structuring some tasks to fit their unique talents and abilities so that they can experience the true and lasting joy of succeeding and being productive.

Glasser (1993) believes that students need to feel safe, happy, and proud of themselves in a classroom if they are going to become convinced that schoolwork is worth the time and effort. To enlist their support, he recommends that you allow your students to know you as a human being, not just as an authority figure. Isn't it true that the better you know someone and the more you like them, the harder you will work for that person? Glasser asks you to use that same principle when establishing the expectations and procedures for your classroom. He suggests the following:

During the first few months you are with your students, look for natural occasions to tell them:

1. Who you are.
2. What you stand for.
3. What you will ask them to do.
4. What you will not ask them to do.
5. What you will do for them.
6. What you will not do for them. (1993, p. 32)

CLASSROOMS AS COMMUNITIES

How does a class of strangers or competitive individuals develop into a community? As with all the other important classroom effects discussed in this chapter, the teacher has the power to create a positive, healthy, mutually supportive, and productive classroom environment from the first day of school. Through furniture arrangement, schedules, the teacher's body language, words of welcome, rules, consequences, and interaction with the class, the teacher demonstrates a unique leadership or teaching style to the students. A sense of community is also achieved through honest, open communication of needs and feelings among students and their teachers.

Sandra Jackson, an African American woman who taught high school for several years in an urban school, recalls that "to create a community of learners in which the climate is open and conducive to dialogue and conversation, teachers must act in ways that students gain trust in them, and they in their students. This means that teachers must resist the urge to be in control and attempt to manage learning" (Jackson, 1995, p. 142). But Ms. Jackson also recognizes that students need and expect their teachers to demonstrate a sense of authority; otherwise, the students may doubt the value of the course and the teacher's knowledge . Reflective teachers explore this dilemma thoroughly, looking for ways to teach that strike a balance between demonstrating openness and acceptance of students' opinions and establishing a legitimate sense of authority and limits.

CLASSROOM MEETINGS

One method that democratic teachers often use to build mutual caring, consideration, and honest expression of opinions and perceptions is to schedule classroom meetings to discuss problems confronting the class. The classroom meeting was first described by Glasser (1969). Some teachers hold regularly scheduled classroom meetings each week; others schedule them only when necessary. When Judy Eby taught fifth grade, she scheduled hers just before lunch on Wednesdays so that it was in the middle of the week. One of the most important effects of a classroom meeting is the sense of community created when the students and teacher sit down to solve problems together.

For a detailed account of how to initiate and lead a class meeting, refer to Glasser's book *Schools Without Failure*. An abbreviated description is all that can be included in this chapter. The seating arrangement for a class meeting is a single circle of chairs, so that each member of the class can see the teacher and all other members of the class. The teacher establishes rules and consequences for the meeting. These usually consist of a rule about one person speaking at a time and accepting the ideas and opinions of others without criticism or laughter. It is important that as the leader of the meeting the teacher be nonjudgmental. When expressing anger or other feelings, class members are encouraged to use "I" statements.

The meeting may be divided into several parts. For example, the teacher may open with an unfinished statement such as "I sometimes wonder why . . . " or "I am proud of . . . " or "I am concerned about. . . . " Going once around the circle, every member of the class is encouraged to respond to this opening statement. The teacher makes it clear, however, that any individual can simply say, "Pass." Opening the class meeting in this way has the advantage of allowing everyone to speak at least once during the meeting and may bring out important issues that need discussion.

The second part of the meeting can be devoted to students' concerns. The teacher opens this discussion by asking who has a concern. When a problem is expressed, the teacher moderates discussion on that issue alone until it is resolved. Issues are seldom resolved easily in one meeting; but class members can raise a problem, express different ideas and opinions, and then offer solutions. When a reasonable solution is worked out, the teacher's role is to restate the solution and suggest that the class try it for a week and discuss how it worked at the next classroom meeting. Other student concerns can then be expressed.

The third part of the class meeting can address the teacher's concerns. The teacher can bring up a problem by expressing personal feelings or stating expectations for future work. Students' responses can be brought out and discussed and solutions proposed. The sense of community that develops from expressing needs and opinions, hearing other perspectives, and solving problems together is translated into all aspects of life in the classroom. When an argument occurs during recess or when students perceive something as unfair, they know they can discuss it openly and freely in a class meeting. When the teacher needs more cooperation or wants higher-quality work, this issue can be brought up in a class meeting. Mutual understanding, tolerance for opposing views, and a way to resolve conflicts results in a strong sense of ownership and commitment to the academic, social, and emotional goals of the class as a whole.

After several weeks of class, when the members of your class have demonstrated that they have established a sense of trust and respect for you and for one another, the classroom meetings may even be used to discuss racial and ethnic issues. Students may bring up issues relating to their ethnic differences, or the teacher can raise the question of how students perceive prejudice in their own lives. These discussions may have the effect of preventing some conflicts related to ethnicity.

TEACHING STUDENTS HOW TO RESOLVE CONFLICTS

No discussion will prevent all conflicts, however. Every classroom has the potential for conflict because of the difference in personalities and points of view. How the teacher handles such differences can be a critical factor in establishing a safe, healthy classroom climate.

In many schools, especially middle and high schools, conflicts have escalated to violent confrontations. Students bicker, threaten, and harass one another. Conflicts among racial and ethnic groups in schools cause local or even national headlines in the news every week. Truancy is epidemic in some areas. Traditional discipline programs, involving scolding and suspensions, do not appear to improve this situation. What can we do? What will you do when you are confronted with these situations? In some learning communities, teachers are teaching students how to be peacemakers and resolve conflicts for themselves and their peers. Johnson and Johnson (1991) provide a curriculum for such programs in their book *Teaching Students to Be Peacemakers*. Through the use of role plays and other learning opportunities to practice conflict-resolution skills, students learn how to negotiate and mediate when conflicts arise.

Laurie Mednick, a fifth-grade teacher at Kellogg School in Chula Vista, California, teaches fourth-, fifth-, and sixth-grade students the communication skills they need to resolve conflicts peacefully. Basing her work on the belief that conflict is inevitable and can even be healthy if dealt with in an honest and caring manner, Laurie sponsors the Peace Patrol program at her school. She describes this program in Case 3.1.

Case 3.1 ⟳ Reflective Action
Teaching Students to Resolve Conflicts

Laurie Mednick, Fifth-Grade Teacher,
Kellogg Elementary School, Chula Vista, California

Use Withitness

I was very troubled by the apparent lack of concern my students felt for other people. Instead of treating one another with respect, many of my students were involved in behaviors such as fighting, tattling, putting each other down, and interrupting when others were talking.

Put Problem Into Perspective

My original belief was that the students were mirroring the prejudices of the society in which we live.

Widen Your Perspective

Not willing to accept or perpetuate these behaviors, I asked myself, "How can I help these children to understand that people are different and have different ideas and perceptions, but that they are still very important? How can I help them learn to resolve their own conflicts? How can I teach them to make better choices for themselves?"

Do Research and Ask for Feedback

I went to see mentor teachers in my district who were investigating a new Peace Education curriculum and asked them what programs or methods were helpful in building self-esteem. I gained an enormous amount of insight and information from these people as well as an enthusiasm to continue my search.

I did a literature search at a university library on the topic of Peace Education and found that this topic is a major concern to teachers across the country and that a number of programs are designed to address this issue. This search took about two months. I became so interested in the topic that I wrote my master's thesis on the subject.

Redefine the Problem

I decided that this problem was larger than my own classroom. My students would benefit most if the whole school got involved. This decision was a direct reflection of my values, because I believe that each individual is important and must be shown respect and value, even if you don't agree with them. I also believe that there are alternatives to violence and that we need to teach these alternatives to our students.

Create an Action Plan

I began my new effort by teaching my students to be more attentive listeners and how to solve problems among themselves without telling the teacher. We also began to practice sharing our feelings using "I" messages (e.g., "It hurts my feelings when you call me that name. I don't like it.")

Then I began to use role-playing three to four times a week to involve my students in sharing feelings and practicing conflict resolution by listening to each other with respect. The students were receptive to the curriculum. They loved being treated with respect by their peers. The class as a whole became very cohesive and helpful toward one another.

After implementing these strategies in my classroom, I selected 30 other fourth-, fifth-, and sixth-graders from other classes to become part of a Peace Patrol program for the entire school. I taught them the same communication and conflict management skills that I had used in my classroom. I meet with the Peace Patrol twice a month for continued training. Each day they wear their blue jackets out on the playground and help other students resolve their conflicts peacefully.

Now in our school, when a conflict occurs between students, a Conflict Manager takes the students involved to a quiet corner or passageway to discuss the event. The patroller listens to each student and then asks them to suggest solutions. If a solution can be found by the children themselves, the Conflict Manager writes a brief report about the conflict and the solution. Copies of the report are given to the students, their teachers, and the principal.

Predict Possible Outcomes

I was concerned that not all teachers would take seriously the reports written by student peace patrollers, so I brought up this problem at a staff meeting. As a faculty, we have agreed that whenever we receive a Peace Patrol report, we show our respect for these successful conflict management encounters by congratulating the students for resolving their conflicts peacefully. I feel very proud of the role I took in developing this program for my school community.

Effective communication between teacher and student is based on mutual trust that grows from the basic moral principles of caring, consideration, and honesty. Reflective teachers who are guided by these moral principles express them in the classroom by listening empathetically—or, as in the case of the Peace Patrol in Ms. Mednick's class, by teaching students to listen empathetically. Listening is one of the most important ways of gathering subjective information about students' needs to make informed judgments about why students behave the way they do.

Discussions between teacher and student must be guided by consideration for the child's feelings and fragile, developing self-concept. There is also a great need for honest, open exchanges of feelings and information among all members of a classroom. A sense of community and shared purpose grows from a realistic understanding of one another's perceptions and needs.

Using Assessment Devices to Identify Students' Needs

In many ways the teacher's role in diagnosing students' needs is similar to the role of the medical doctor in diagnosing disease. Doctors get information from observing and talking with patients about their medical histories. Similarly, teachers observe and talk with their students to assess their learning histories. But some important information needed for an accurate diagnosis cannot be observed or discussed. Just as doctors may find that laboratory tests provide them with valuable information about the patient, so teachers may find that achievement tests and other assessment procedures can provide them with valuable data about their students.

Many school districts use nationally normed standardized tests to assess the academic achievement their students make from year to year. The typical standardized test consists of reading, spelling, English, mathematics, science, and social studies exams given over a period of several days. The teacher does not write the questions or establish the criteria to fit a particular classroom. Instead, the tests are created by nationally recognized testing companies, and the items are written to approximate what is taught across the nation in each subject area at each grade level.

Statistical calculations of test scores provide information about a student's performance. The score may be translated into a percentile or a grade-equivalent score. These interpretations are done by comparing the student's raw score with the raw scores of the sample population. A *percentile rank* tells you what percentage of the people tested scored below a given score. For example, if Joe receives a percentile rank of 78, this means that 78% of the students at Joe's grade level scored lower than he did.

Grade equivalent scores were created by test publishers especially for use in schools. The results are reported as a function of grade level. For example, if Sally receives a grade-equivalent score of 4.2, this means that her performance is similar to students who are in the second month of fourth grade. If Sally is in the fourth grade, her score tells the teacher that Sally is doing about as well as she is supposed to be doing. If Sally is in the second grade, the score tells the teacher that Sally is capable of functioning like students who are two years above her current grade level. But if Sally is in sixth grade, her score alerts the teacher that Sally is functioning like students who are two years below her current grade level.

When they are used to inform teachers about students academic needs, standardized tests provide numerical scores that can be used to document the growth of students in their abilities to read, work math problems, and answer questions about academic subjects such as science, social studies, English grammar and spelling.

Because standardized tests are written by English speakers and assume that students are fluent in the English language, there is a potential for misunderstanding by students who are learning English as a second language. Standardized tests also require that standardized procedures be used for administering the exams. All students must hear the same instructions, work under the same time limitations, and have access to the same tools and materials during the test (Tanner, 2001).

English language learners often have difficulty demonstrating their true abilities on standardized tests because the teacher is not allowed to vary or interpret the instructions that are a part of the standardization of the test. For students with a limited English vocabulary, the instructions may not be clear and the students may not understand what is expected of them. They may be able to perform the tasks if they understand the directions but are unable to demonstrate their true abilities when the instructions are a mystery to them.

The use of standardized tests varies widely from district to district. In some schools, they are used to diagnose learning difficulties of individuals so that corrective measures can be taken. In other school systems, the test results are published in local newspapers to compare how well students from different schools are doing in the basic skills. This practice is a controversial issue among educators. The tests were not designed to be a measure of excellence among schools, but the public and the press have come to believe that they can be used that way.

INTERPRETING DATA FROM STUDENTS' CUMULATIVE FILES

Standardized test scores are recorded in a permanent file for each student. This record of information, called the *cumulative file* (often referred to as a *cume file*) is kept on each student in a school. Each year, the classroom teacher records in the students' files data such as information about the student's family, standardized test scores, reading levels, samples of written work, grades, and notes on parent–teacher conferences. At the end of a school year, the cume files are stored in the school or district office until the next year when they are distributed to the students' new teachers.

Obviously, these files contain much useful information for teachers to use in preliminary planning. By studying them, the teacher can make judgments about placement in reading, math, or other study groups before meeting the students. Alert teachers may discover information about a student's home environment, such as a recent divorce or remarriage, that can help them in communicating with the student. Some files may reveal little about the students; others may be overflowing with records of conferences and staffings that signal that the student has exhibited a special need or difficulty.

Many teachers resist looking at their students' cume files before meeting the class. Tracy Kidder's (1989) *Among School Children* provides a realistic look at the entire school year of a fifth-grade class in upstate New York. In the opening chapter, which describes the beginning of the school year, the teacher, Chris Zajac, reflects on the value of cume files as she ponders what to do with a student named Clarence, whose negative attitudes toward school have become apparent on the first day of school.

> Chris had received the students' "cumulative" records which were stuffed inside salmon-colored folders known as "cumes." For now she checked only addresses and phone numbers, and resisted looking into histories. It was usually better at first to let her own opinions form. But she couldn't help noticing the thickness of some cumes. "The thicker the cume, the more trouble," she told Miss Hunt. "If it looks like *War and Peace* . . . " Clarence's cume was about as thick as the Boston phone book. And Chris couldn't help having heard what some colleagues had insisted on telling her about Clarence. One teacher whom Chris trusted had described him as probably the most difficult child in all of last year's fourth-grade class. Chris wished she hadn't heard that. (p. 8-9)

While data and observations about students made by former teachers may be a valuable resource for planning, many reflective teachers, like Chris Zajac, are aware of the power of the self-fulfilling prophecy, in which their own expectations may influence the way their students behave or achieve in school. Good and Brophy (1987) define *teachers' expectations* as "inferences that teachers make about the future behavior or academic achievement of their students" and show that the self-fulfilling prophecy occurs when "an originally erroneous expectation leads to behavior that causes the expectation to become true" (p. 116).

When cume files contain data and descriptions of low academic achievement or misbehavior, nonreflective teachers may assume that the students are unteachable or unmanageable. On the first day of school, the teacher may place them at desks set apart from the rest of the class or hand them textbooks from a lower grade. These teacher behaviors tell the students how the teacher expects them to behave and perform in this class. If these expectations are consistent over time, they are likely to affect the students' self-concepts and motivations in such a way that they achieve poorly and behave badly. In contrast, consider the possible effects of warm and encouraging teacher behavior on these students. If the teacher builds rapport with the students, includes them in all classroom activities from the first day and works with them to establish their achievement levels and needs, it is likely that their behavior and achievement will improve during the year.

Reflective teachers who understand the great influence of their expectations on their students prefer to assess the strengths and needs of each student independently in the first few weeks of class. They may read the cume folders at the end of September to see how their assessments fit with those of the students' previous teachers.

A good case can be made for either point of view: using cume folders for preliminary planning or waiting to read them until the students are well known to you. This is an issue that you will need to decide for yourself. Perhaps if you understand the power of teacher expectations, you can find a way to use the information in the files to establish positive expectations and resist the tendency to establish negative ones.

AVOID LABELING STUDENTS

Tests and other recorded information about a student can sometimes cause teachers and parents to think about students in oversimplified terms, or labels. Whether you gain information about your students through formal assessments or informal interactions, it is important to avoid the temptation to categorize or stereotype particular students. You can probably recall a time in your own life when you were burdened with a label you resented. Perhaps you dealt with a nickname you detested, or with an academic designation that failed to capture your real potential. Being able to learn about your students and act in their best interests without labeling requires a great deal of care and reflection. How often a quick perusal of a cume file, a glance at a standardized test score, or a few days of observation in the classroom have led a teacher to label a student as a *slow learner*, *behavior-disordered*, or *underachiever*. These labels can stick for life! When communicated to students and their families (whether indirectly or directly), such labels can have disabling effects all by themselves. Many labels imply that a student is deficient in some way, and contribute to a self-fulfilling prophecy where further erosion of self-concept and self-confidence causes even more severe learning difficulties.

Students with excellent school performance can also suffer from labeling. Some teachers refer to their most capable and willing students as *overachievers*. This pseudo-scientific term is attached to students whose test scores are only moderate, but whose grades and work habits are excellent. The implication is that these students are working beyond their capacity, and this is somehow seen as a negative characteristic by some teachers (and some peers).

Students with high test scores on standardized tests, especially IQ or achievement tests, are frequently labeled as *gifted*. At first glance, this label may appear positive: Certainly many parents seek it for their children. But careful reflection reveals that this label can be as damaging as any other. Rimm (1986) notes that "any label that unrealistically narrows prospects for performance by a student may be damaging" (p. 84). A gifted label tends to narrow the expectations of performance for that student to a constant state of excellence. Any performance less than excellent can be interpreted by the student (and/or the parent) as unacceptable.

The gifted label also has other negative implications. If 2% to 5% of the students in a given school are labeled as gifted, then what are the other 95% to 98% of the students? Not gifted? What is the hidden consequence for a sibling or a good friend of a gifted student? Or what about the students who score a few percentage points below the cut-off score for a particular gifted program? What do we call them, *almost gifted*?

Broader labels also carry damaging consequences. The term *minority* carries a connotation of being somehow less than other groups with respect to power, status, and treatment. Terms such as *economically disadvantaged*, *culturally deprived*, and *under-privileged* may also create stress and anxiety among those to which they are applied.

These may be especially insidious because they fail to acknowledge the value and unique contributions of various individuals or groups.

As you become aware of the various strengths and needs among your students, you can work to address them without relying on labels. Students who are learning English can be joyfully released to work with a special tutor and be warmly welcomed back to the classroom. Children who encounter difficulty working in large group settings can spend part of their day in small groups and build interaction skills in larger groups under carefully designed conditions. Children who learn more quickly can be challenged to extend their thinking through engaging inquiry projects. No matter what their unique need, our students can be welcomed to our classrooms as unique and valued individuals—labeled only as important, cared for, and wanted.

AUTHENTIC ASSESSMENTS FOR A DIVERSE STUDENT BODY

In this text, we use the term *authentic assessment* for evaluation procedures that take into account each student's unique and various needs for clarity and support to demonstrate what they are truly capable of doing. Most authentic assessments are designed by teachers in their own classrooms to match what has just been taught. Authentic assessment tasks are similar or identical to actual tasks that students routinely accomplish in the classroom setting, unlike standardized assessment tasks, which tend to be very unlike everyday classroom activities (Herrell, 2000).

In Chapter 11, we provide a much more expanded discussion of assessment issues and examples of authentic assessment tasks and procedures. We raise the issue in this chapter because assessment procedures have become such a controversial issue as they relate to student diversity.

USING PRETESTS TO DIAGNOSE STUDENTS' NEEDS

Pretests are assessment devices designed to gather useful information to plan what students need to learn and what teachers need to teach. At the beginning of a term or a unit of study, teachers use pretests to determine what skills and knowledge pertaining to the subject students already have mastered. Pretests can take the form of brief short-answer quizzes or teachers may ask students to write a paragraph or two telling what they already know about a topic to be studied. They may also describe any study they have done on the topic in another year or another class, family trips, or other experiences that relate to the topic about to be explored.

The best use of pretests occurs when the teacher and the student discuss the results and share their insights into what the student needs to do next. For example, a pretest may reveal a pattern of correctable mistakes in a mathematics operation. The teacher may be able to reteach the process quickly, and the student will be able to proceed successfully. In another instance, the pretest may reveal that the student has mastered the material already, and the conference may then focus on an enriched or accelerated learning opportunity for that student while the others are learning the material.

PLACEMENT AND GROUPING DECISIONS

Standardized tests are frequently used to qualify students for special programs such as special education programs, classes for the gifted, or bilingual education programs. In most cases these types of placements are no longer made solely on the basis of test results but also include opportunities for the parents and teachers involved in the student's education to provide information and share in the decision.

For many years teachers used pretests and standardized test scores to determine students' placement in reading groups for instructional purposes. In recent years, teachers are using more authentic types of reading assessments such as Marie Clay's (1989) *Observation Survey of Early Literacy Abilities* and reading observations called *running records* to document students' reading abilities, use of strategies, and cueing systems. In kindergarten and first grade classes, the students are grouped in flexible reading groups for guided reading instruction. They read small paperback books for this instruction so that the groups can remain flexible. The small books can be read in one reading group period and then students can be regrouped whenever they show the need. This is helping to eliminate the old, traditional "speedboats, sailboats, and rowboats" reading groups that were set in concrete and served to convince students that they were poor readers because they were always placed in the low (rowboats) reading group and stayed there for their entire elementary school careers. Teachers today are finding that grouping can help students to learn, if the grouping is done with careful reflection. Heterogeneous groups where each student has a special function are being used frequently in classrooms because students get more opportunities to interact, work together to solve problems, and discuss the task to be done.

Teachers may also use data from pretests, observations, and running records to create cooperative groups and partners for peer tutoring. To strengthen student motivation and interaction, many teachers employ the cooperative team concept. Cooperative groups typically consist of three to five students who are assigned a set of tasks to complete by cooperating with and assisting one another. Each student in the group has an assigned function and the group must work together to complete the assignment. Cooperative groups are extremely effective when they are given instruction in working together to achieve their goals. In some classrooms, teachers use pretest data to decide which students to assign to each team. Often teachers use cooperative groups to promote peer coaching and interactive assistance among their students. In this case, a team of four students may consist of one student with strong performance, two with moderate performance, and one with relatively weak performance in the subject area. Similarly, peer tutoring dyads may consist of one skilled and one less-skilled student, or one student with very little English vocabulary and another student who speaks the same home language but can speak English at a higher level. These are simply examples, other types of cooperative group placement decisions, for different purposes, are also possible.

PERFORMANCE SAMPLING

Performance sampling is a form of authentic assessment in which a student is observed accomplishing academic tasks and is evaluated on the way in which the tasks are done. Performance samples are well-named because the teacher observes a sample of the student's performance in a given academic tasks. The following are examples of the types of tasks used in performance sampling:

- working math problems
- responding to a writing prompt by creating a prewriting activity, writing draft paper, and then revising the paper
- researching a topic in science or social studies and creating a poster or overhead transparency to demonstrate the main concepts that were researched.

Performance sampling is particularly appropriate for assessing English language learners because the degree of achievement they can demonstrate is based on their ability to perform the task rather than their fluency in English (Hernandez, 1997).

Portfolio assessment is a term that refers to a system for gathering observations, performance samples, and work samples in a folder or portfolio; regularly analyzing the contents of the portfolio; and summarizing the students' progress as documented by the contents of the portfolio (Herrell, 2000) . Often students are involved in selecting work to be kept in the portfolio. Students are also involved in the review and summarization of the work, setting goals for future work, and the sharing of the contents of the portfolio with parents (Farr & Tone, 1994).

This approach to assessment is particularly appropriate for English language learners and special education students because it allows assessment based on actual sampling of the students' work and the growth they are making with less dependence on scores on standardized tests, which are often difficult for these students to understand (Hernandez, 1997). Portfolio assessment allows students to demonstrate their content knowledge without being so dependent on English fluency or reading ability. The focus in this approach to assessment is celebration of progress rather than focus on weaknesses.

THE SELF-FULFILLING PROPHECY

Children are extremely perceptive beings. They have withitness, too, at least as far as perceiving how to meet their own needs. They understand and react to subtle differences in adult expectations. In classrooms from preschool to graduate school, students focus their withitness on teachers to pick up the cues of whether the teacher likes and respects them. They also pick up cues on just exactly what the teacher expects of them. Then they look around and see how the teacher's expectations differ for each of their classmates as well.

One effect of the students' withitness about teachers' expectations is known as the *self-fulfilling prophecy*. The process appears to work like this: (a) the teacher makes a decision about the behavior and achievement to be expected from a certain student; (b) the teacher treats students differently depending on the expectations for each one; (c) this treatment communicates to the student what the teacher expects and affects the student's self-concept, achievement motivation, and aspirations either positively or negatively; (d) if the treatment is consistent over time, it may permanently shape the child's achievement and behavior.

Many studies of how teachers' behaviors display their expectations have been done and replicated to confirm earlier findings. Good and Brophy (1987) found that some teachers treat low achievers this way:

1. seat them far away from the teacher
2. call on them less often
3. wait less time for them to answer questions
4. criticize them more frequently
5. praise them less frequently
6. provide them with less detailed feedback
7. demand less work and effort from them (p. 55)

Using the self-fulfilling prophecy to your and your students' advantage can occur if you expect the best from all students and truly believe that all students can and will succeed this year. This was demonstrated in the early 1960s when a researcher informed teachers that he had a new assessment instrument that would identify which students were ready to make enormous changes that year. After making this official sounding announcement, the researcher gave the students a simple achievement test, which he did not even score. He selected students at random and reported to their teachers that these were the students who had demonstrated great potential for making academic progress this year and the teachers were encouraged to support them. A year later, the students who were randomly selected and identified as having great potential to learn had made great progress in academic areas.

Teachers who carefully structure their classroom lessons to ensure success are frequently baffled by the tendency of some students to fail to succeed even under optimal conditions. Rimm (1995) observes that there is no single cause for underachievement, nor is there a single cure. Also, no consistent characteristics are associated with underachievement. Some underachievers are bossy and aggressive; others are lonely and withdrawn. Some are slow and perfectionistic; others are hurried and disorganized. A few have adopted a behavior pattern of learned helplessness because of previous experiences in school, overly high expectations at home, or even because of their position in the family as the youngest child. These students perceive that they are certain to fail at whatever they try, so they have learned not to try. They may also have learned to manipulate others to do things for them by acting helpless.

Students from culturally diverse backgrounds or those raised in poverty may underachieve because of low self-esteem or a lack of experiences such as family trips, or little exposure to English reading materials in the home. Marc Elrich, a sixth-grade teacher in Washington, D.C., was frustrated to find that even though he and his colleagues had created a curriculum celebrating diversity and talking about it as a source of strength, he was unable to change his students' own preconceptions about their self-worth. One year 27 members of his class of 29 students were either African American or Hispanic and had been raised in academically disadvantaged neighborhoods. Mr. Elrich observed that even at age 10 or 11, most showed very low self-esteem and had low expectations for their future. He enriched his curriculum with many examples of

African American and Hispanic literature and other contributions to art and music. Still, the stereotype within the students didn't seem to change.

In a discussion with his students exploring the issues of race, Mr. Elrich heard his African American students attribute negative racial stereotypes to themselves. "Blacks are poor and stay poor because they're dumber than whites (and Asians)," they said. "Black people don't like to work hard. White people are smart and have money. Hispanics are poor and don't try hard because, like blacks, they know it doesn't matter."

Teachers like Mr. Elrich are not willing to accept the status quo. They keep trying to create a therapeutic classroom environment that will encourage their culturally diverse students to raise their own hopes and expectations to appropriate levels. He reflected on how to teach them to like themselves. He considered the frequently used strategy of setting aside a month for studying black history but decided that this was not an adequate remedy. "These students aren't naïve," he said. "What are the other eleven months? White history months?"

Marc hasn't solved this problem yet. Neither has our society. But, as teachers, you will have an opportunity to confront this difficult issue and create new educational opportunities to improve your students' view of themselves and encourage the people of our nation to grow together rather than apart. There is good news on this topic, however. In recent years there are growing resources available to teachers in the form of multicultural literature to read and discuss in the classroom. Many of the new publications focus on the things all cultures share in common and celebrate the differences as variety and uniqueness.

Adrienne Herrell (2000), one of the authors of this book, has compiled a book titled *Fifty Strategies for Teaching English Language Learners* which can be a valuable resource for teachers at any grade level who have multilingual students in their class. The strategies include step-by-step instructions and real-life classroom examples that we don't have room to describe in this text. These 50 strategies can be helpful for reflective teachers who want to widen their perspective and create action plans to meet the needs of their diverse student body.

⟳ Reflective Actions for Your Professional Portfolio
AN EXAMPLE OF YOUR STUDENT NEEDS ASSESSMENT PLAN

Use Withitness: Creating a Cultural Bridge

Arrange to interview one student. Select a student whose culture is different from yours. Talk with the student about what is important and valued in his or her family. Share your own memories of growing up with that student. Look for common experiences and discuss your differences. Ask questions to learn about how this student prefers to learn. Sample questions are provided here, but you may want to make up your own as well.

Do you learn easily by reading about something?

Do you learn well by listening to a teacher explain something?

Do you need for the teacher to write examples on the board?

Do you learn best by having somebody show you something or by working alone?

Do you need a quiet room or can you work when others are talking or when the TV is on?

Does it bother you when there is movement around you?

Put the Issue into Perspective

From your interview, write an initial assessment of what conditions this student needs to learn and feel safe and comfortable in your classroom.

Widen Your Perspective

Ask yourself what else you need to know to make a thorough assessment of this student's needs. Ask yourself whether your preferred way of learning may serve as a blinder in assessing students who are different from you. How do you learn how to meet the special needs of students with physical handicaps, learning difficulties, and cultural or language differences? What strategies can you use to meet their needs and provide them with opportunities to experience pride and success?

Assess your own strengths and talents according to Gardner's seven intelligences:

1. verbal
2. mathematical reasoning
3. music
4. visual arts
5. physical/kinesthetic
6. interpersonal
7. intrapersonal

Which are your greatest strengths; your weakest areas? Do you wish to strengthen your talents or your weaknesses in your own life? Do you believe it is more important to strengthen your students' talents or develop the areas in which they are weak?

Do Research and Invite Feedback

What can you find on the World Wide web that relates to this issue? Try a chat with other teachers on the Merrill Methods Cluster page or on Schoolnotes.com.

    If possible, try to meet the student's family and learn what the parents' hopes and expectations are for their child. Write in your journal what you have to teach this child and what the child can teach you.

Redefine the Issue

Write another draft of your plan to create classroom conditions that you believe to be important for this student to learn effectively. Include in your plan ideas for encouraging students with differences to feel safe and comfortable in your classroom.

Create an Action Plan

Design a learning experience that will allow your students to choose from a variety of learning activities that take into account several ways of knowing or types of intelligence. Write a description of your plan that shows how students can use each type of intelligence to accomplish something of value.

Predict and Plan For Possible Outcomes

Imagine yourself teaching the multiple intelligence learning experience you designed. Try to imagine the positive and negative effects on your students. What are they likely to gain from it? What could be the troublesome areas? Will they expand their strengths or weaknesses? What else can you do to improve your plan?

References

Clay, M. (1989). *Observation survey of early literacy abilities.* Portsmouth, NH: Heineman.

Cummins, J. (1986). Empowering minority students: A framework for interaction. *Harvard Review*, 56, 18–36.

Farr, R., & Tone, B. (1994). Portfolio performance assessments. Fort Worth, TX: Harcourt Brace.

Glasser, W. (1969). *Schools without failure.* New York: Harper & Row.

Glasser, W. (1986). *Control theory in the classroom.* New York: Harper & Row.

Glasser, W. (1993). The quality school teacher. New York: Harper & Row.

Good, T., & Brophy, J. (1987). *Looking in classrooms* (4th ed.). New York: Harper & Row.

Hernandez, H. (1997). Teaching in multilingual classrooms. Upper Saddle River, NJ: Merrill/Prentice Hall.

Herrell, A. (2000). *50 strategies for English language learners.* Upper Saddle River, NJ: Merrill/Prentice Hall.

Jackson, S. (1995). Negotiating self-defined standpoints. In S. Jackson & J. Solis (Eds.), *Beyond comfort zones in multiculturalism* (pp. 47–69). Westport, CT: Bergin & Garvey.

Johnson, D., & Johnson, R. (1984). *Circles of learning: Cooperation in the classroom.* Alexandria, VA: Association for Supervision and Curriculum Development.

Johnson, D., & Johnson, R. (1991). *Teaching students to be peacemakers.* Edina, MN: Interaction.

Kidder, T. (1989). *Among schoolchildren.* Boston: Houghton Mifflin

Krashen, S. (1982). *Principles and practices of language acquisition.* Oxford: Pergamon Press.

Krashen, S., & Terrell, T. (1983). *The natural approach: Language acquisition in the classroom.* Oxford: Pergamon Press.

Maslow, A. (1954). *Motivation and personality.* New York: Harper & Row.

Raths, L. (1972). *Meeting the needs of children.* Upper Saddle River, NJ: Merrill/Prentice Hall.

Rimm, S. (1995). *Why bright children get poor grades.* New York: Crown.

Slavin, R. (1995) *Cooperative learning* (2nd ed.). Boston: Allyn & Bacon.

Tanner, D. E. (2001). *Assessing academic achievement.* Needham Heights, MA: Allyn & Bacon.

chapter *4*

HOW TEACHERS PLAN
SCHOOL PROGRAMS

O ne of classroom teachers' most important responsibilities is to plan the *curriculum*, the course of events and learning experiences for their students. To illustrate the complexity of the planning process, here is a brief account of some of the issues that Lori Shoults faced during her first three months at Seth Paine Elementary School in Lake Zurich, Illinois.

When I first walked into my empty classroom in August, I was greeted by a big box of textbooks. I had been hired by this school district because of my interest in and enthusiasm for the whole language approach to teaching reading and writing. So I had the freedom to create my own curriculum rather than rely on the texts. With that freedom came a lot of hard work.

It was hard to plan before knowing my students, especially the first year, when I didn't even know what second graders were like. I wanted the curriculum in my classroom to be fully integrated. I wanted science and social studies to be a part of reading and writing. I examined all the textbooks in great detail. I made lists of skills that were taught in the English, phonics, and spelling books. I looked for topics from the science, social studies, and reading basals. I divided the year into two- or three-week integrated units on topics such as plants, weather, light, magnets, dinosaurs, animals, and safety.

Within these units, I taught my reading and English skills every morning in a new poem that was related to the unit's theme. I distributed a poem to the students, and they glued it into their folders. We read the poem once just to enjoy its ideas and sounds. Then each day, I asked the students to look for examples of phonics rules, word structures, types of sentences, and punctuation. I focused on two or three new skills each day.

Because I used the whole language approach, the students chose their own reading materials from the books in our room or in the library. To encourage them to read, I decided to use a reading incentive program, which gave credit or rewards for the number of books each student read. But when I further considered this idea, I found that it had a lot of drawbacks. Children who read short, easy books would appear to get more credit than those who read long, challenging books. I talked to other teachers to find out what they had tried. One teacher told me about a system of having students keep track of the number of minutes they read rather than the number of books. When I considered this approach, I concluded that it was more productive than focusing on the number of books read because my goal was for the students to read longer stories and books rather than just counting books. It also seemed more fair because students at different achievement levels read books of different lengths. This system gave equivalent credit to each student for time spent reading at every reading level.

The social studies textbook focused on the concepts of community and geography. I decided to have an overall theme of community, which I implemented by establishing a simulated community in the classroom. We had a teacher, a sheriff, a mayor, a meteorologist, a banker, and a gardener. Students signed up for the jobs they wanted and rotated every week. The learning stations in the class were community sites such as a post office (letter-writing center), a greenhouse (science center), a newspaper stand (writing center), a telephone company (listening center), a library (reading center), a toy store (learning games), and a computer lab.

My organizational problems grew more difficult each day. At the beginning of the year, I tried to do it all at once. In addition to my regular reading, writing, and math programs, I set up five rotating math enrichment stations, the community stations, a geography program, and literature circles in which students discussed books they were reading on their own. I wasn't able to get to all of these things as I had planned. I kept running out of time during the day. The students were confused. They were always asking me when we were going to do different things.

So I sat down and planned for one special activity each day. On Tuesdays we would do community stations, on Wednesdays we had our literature circles, and on Fridays we had math enrichment stations. I thought it would be better to have a consistent schedule. The students wanted to know what to expect, and I felt better knowing when to plan for each activity.

For mathematics, I examined the basal text and believed that I could cover the skills in more interesting ways. I wanted to teach with more hands-on activities and use fewer math pages. I decided to use the Everyday Mathematics program (Bell, 1990) for teaching concepts and use the textbook for practice and review. I also gave the tests from the math book. After using this approach for several months, I found that the students were able to do the textbook tests successfully. More important to me, they were enthusiastic about math. Even my lowest-achieving students felt confident participating in math activities.

After three months of teaching, I believed that I was beginning to think like a teacher. At the beginning of the year, my schema for teaching and learning was rudimentary, leading me to make most decisions by trial and error. But later I felt I had expanded my knowledge and experience base to the point that when I reflected on a decision, I had a much better understanding of the consequences of my actions.

As Ms. Shoults' account shows, teachers face a multitude of complex issues and judgments in their classrooms. As a teacher, Ms. Shoults has a great deal of freedom to decide what to teach and when to teach it, but behind the scenes, her decisions are influenced by many forces, both past and present. For one thing, history and tradition exert powerful influences over what is taught in schools. The three Rs have served as the basis for planning in U.S. schools for more than a century, and there are active and vocal groups of citizens who believe that the primary goal of K–12 schools should be to instill these basic skills in their students.

Some groups believe that schools are the custodians of the culture and that the primary goal of education should be to develop good citizenship and understanding of the great ideas and literature produced by Western civilization. Others believe strongly that the primary goal of a modern education is to teach students how to use reasoning, problem-solving, and communication skills as a means of learning how to learn so that they are able to gather the information they will need in their lives.

Still others believe that the new wave of computer technology available to future generations makes older forms of learning obsolete. They call for an emphasis on the use of technology in K–12 schools to prepare students for a future that will be vastly different from the present. There is also a growing trend toward creating school programs that are multidisciplinary and multicultural by design, with a new emphasis on investigation, inquiry, research, experimentation, and conflict resolution.

Ms. Shoults discovered how difficult it is to plan so many school programs all at once. Like many beginning teachers, she wanted to incorporate the best ideas from all of the influential groups she had read about in her teacher education program. At times the responsibility seemed so overwhelming that she might have wished that there were just one standard curriculum for all teachers to follow.

How School Curricula Are Planned
NATIONAL STANDARDS IN THE PLANNING STAGE

Many nations have uniform standards for school curricula. Individual teachers plan their daily programs to coincide precisely with national expectations. In some countries, if you were able to visit several schools in various cities at the same time of the school year, you would find the students using the same textbooks and working on the same chapters as students in other cities and rural areas of that country. Periodically, all children attending the schools take national examinations as a means of testing whether they have learned the requisite material and, at the same time, whether schools are accomplishing their mission of teaching the national curriculum.

Other countries, including the United States, have no such tradition of a uniform mandated curriculum. Historically, the regulation and supervision of K–12 curriculum has resided with the states; and although many states have established curriculum guidelines and examinations, there has also been a strong public sense that the best curriculum is the one planned at the local level based on local interests, values, resources, and the needs of a particular group of students in each school district.

Recently, however, some school districts have been criticized by the media or by citizen watchdog groups because their students have performed badly on a variety of tests and measurements of academic progress. As a result of the public's perception that some school districts prepare students for the world much better than other school districts do, a debate is growing over the value of establishing national standards for student performance. Concurrently, there are movements to establish national standards for the preparation of teachers and for teaching effectiveness.

In 1994, Congress formalized efforts to address school reform in its Goals 2000: Educate America Act. It was intended to improve learning and teaching by providing a national framework for education reform. Goals 2000 includes eight goals that have had a great effect on local, state, and national directions. The act was revised in 1996 and will likely be amended in the future. Despite its changing nature, you will want to be familiar with the eight goals, which include provisions for the following:

1. school readiness
2. school completion
3. student achievement and citizenship
4. teacher education and professional development
5. mathematics and science

6. adult literacy and lifelong learning
7. safe, disciplined, and alcohol- and drug-free schools
8. parental participation

As you can see, each goal in the list is vital in creating a society of lifelong learners. You may even want to organize your own professional goals according to these eight areas, adding others you believe are also important.

In response to the public's desire to be able to measure and compare the progress of students across the nation, Congress mandated the Department of Education to provide a set of assessment tools to measure K–12 students' subject-matter knowledge in five areas. They produced a document known as the National Assessment of Educational Progress (NAEP), which is commonly referred to as the nation's report card. NAEP provides benchmarks for each subject area. A *benchmark* is a statement describing what students should be able to do or demonstrate at various grade levels.

Another source of updated information about national and state standards in education is a website managed by the Putnam Valley Central Schools in Putnam Valley, New York. Access this site at **http://putwest.boces.org/Standards.html.** When you log on, you will have the choice of reviewing the latest national standards or see the most recent curriculum frameworks for each state.

As is often the case in a vigorous, multicultural democracy such as the United States, there is little agreement about the form that educational standards should take or how they should be used. Subject-area specialists, for example, argue that their disciplines are so different from each other that standardizing performance expectations across the disciplines would be impossible (Viadero, 1993).

Many other philosophical debates concern the purpose of national standards in education. Before establishing one set of universally accepted standards, educators will need to agree on issues such as whether the national standards and benchmarks ought to describe basic or minimal competency in each subject area or whether they ought to describe how experts perform. A national debate remains over the value of emphasizing content or process knowledge in most subject areas, and this causes the authors of standards and benchmarks to disagree about whether to assess content knowledge or performance standards.

STATE CURRICULUM GUIDELINES AND STANDARDS

In the United States, each state has a department of education that has traditionally taken responsibility for establishing guidelines for curriculum development. Recently, these state departments of education have become much more interested in measuring achievement as well.

Currently, there are many attempts to create statewide standards for learning and achievement. Brooks & Brooks (1999) observe that most standards-based reform efforts are illogical because they ignore the differences in the way students learn and the diversity of experience that students have from their multicultural backgrounds. State standards depend on constructing or buying standardized assessments that equate test results with student learning. These systems tend to reward schools whose students score well on the assessments and sanction schools whose students don't. Brooks and Brooks decry the "un-deviating, one-size-fits-all approach to teaching and assessment in states that have crowned accountability king. Requiring all students to take the same courses and pass the same tests may hold political capital for legislators and state-level educational policymakers, but it contravenes what years of painstaking research tells us about student learning" (p. 20).

Brooks and Brooks (1999) advocate the constructivist philosophy of learning that is based on the concept that learners control their own learning. They caution curriculum and testing designers to recognize that controlling what students learn is virtually impossible. Educators may structure tests and curriculums to ensure that all students learn the same concepts at the same time, but the fact is that each student still constructs his or her own unique meaning through his or her own unique cognitive processes.

Constructivists such as Brooks and Brooks (1999) believe that only by analyzing students' understandings and ways of learning and then customizing our teaching approaches to each student's cognitive processes can we hope to increase student achievement. This constructivist approach to learning and assessment of learning is closely aligned with the concept of reflective action in teaching we put forth in this book. Reflective action in teaching calls for teachers to use their withitness to perceive student needs, which vary widely depending on background experiences, multiple intelligences, and physical development of the brain and nervous system. We concur with Brooks and Brooks when they say that we can set standards for our own professional practice, but not for student achievement.

Another role of state departments of education is to publish curriculum guidelines for all the subject areas in public K-12 education. Many states revise their curriculum guidelines by inviting representative teachers and administrators from all areas of the state to form a committee responsible for considering ways to incorporate both state and subject matter standards into meaningful curriculum outlines. The resulting documents are then published and distributed to all of the school districts they serve.

Curriculum frameworks at the state level change frequently based on the latest research in education. They are also heavily influenced by political pressures and interest groups within the state. As a beginning teacher, you will be expected to become familiar with the latest curriculum frameworks for your state and implement them in your classroom.

EVALUATION AND USE OF TEXTBOOKS

School textbooks have an enormous effect on the curriculum. Elementary school textbooks are undergoing major revisions to meet the demand for updated, student-centered, active learning rather than the older emphasis on receptive, rote learning. Many of these changes are controversial, reflecting the often divisive issues that are hot topics among adults in our society.

One of the greatest controversies regarding textbooks today is the rewriting of social studies textbooks to include multiple perspectives on history. Critics of traditional textbooks suggest that they are written solely from the perspective of the white European male. They believe students should learn history from multiple perspectives. Traditionalists believe that eliminating or ignoring content in the traditional textbooks will misrepresent history and that the subject will become diluted in an effort to please every ethnic group. Reflective teachers attempt to clarify their own values and their own curriculum orientations and beliefs as they make decisions about the curriculum they teach.

When first-year teachers move into their classrooms, the textbooks are already there, in formidable rows or piled in cumbersome stacks. Novice teachers have been told about the importance of individualizing education and meeting the needs of all students in their professional preparation programs. When reality sets in, they realize that many of the materials they need to plan a highly creative program that meets the students' individual needs are not in the classroom. A less reflective teacher will, without thinking, distribute the textbooks and begin teaching on page 1, perhaps emulating former teachers, with the intent of plowing through the entire book by the end of the year.

Reflective teachers, however, are more inquisitive and more independent in their use of textbooks. They ask questions of other teachers: "How long have you been using these textbooks? How were they chosen? Which parts match the school or district curriculum guides? Which parts are most interesting to the students? What other resources are available? Where do you go to get your ideas to supplement the textbook? In your first year of teaching, how did you meet the individual needs of your students when you had only textbooks available to you?"

Less reflective teachers tend to assume without question that the "approved" or "correct" curriculum is the one found in textbooks because it is written by "experts." They attempt to deliver the curriculum as written, without questioning its effects or adapting it to the students' needs.

More reflective teachers consider decisions about curriculum planning to be within their jurisdiction, their domain of decision making. They consult with others, but they take responsibility for deciding which parts of a textbook to use to meet the needs of their own particular class and to match the goals and learning outcomes their state and local curriculum committees establish.

The Constructivist Philosophy of Teaching and Learning

Teachers who have a constructivist basis for their philosophy of teaching and learning are seldom satisfied to use textbooks alone. Constructivists know that students must have a motivation to search for meaning and create their own understanding of the world of ideas. "When students want to know more about an idea, a topic, or an entire discipline, they put more cognitive energy into classroom investigations and discussions and study more on their own" (Brooks & Brooks, 1999, p. 22). They have identified five central tenets of constructivism as a teaching philosophy:

1. Constructivist teachers seek and value students' points of view. This concept is similar to the reflective action process we call withitness,

in which teachers attempt to perceive students' needs and respond to them appropriately.

2. Constructivist teachers challenge students to see different points of view and thereby construct new knowledge. Learning occurs when teachers ask students what they think they know about a subject and why they think they know it.

3. Constructivist teachers recognize that curricula must have meaning for students. When students see the relevance of curricula, their interest in learning grows.

4. Constructivist teachers create lessons that tackle big ideas, not small bits of information. By seeing the whole first, students are able to determine how the parts fit together.

5. Constructivist teachers assess student learning in daily classroom activities, not through the use of separate testing or evaluation events. Students demonstrate their knowledge every day in natural ways. Paper and pencil assessments administered under strict security perpetuates false and counterproductive results and creates myths about the nature of intelligence, creativity, knowledge and accountability.

State and local curriculums address what students learn. Constructivism, as an approach to education, addresses how students learn. The constructivist teacher, in mediating students' learning, blends the what with the how. As a 3rd grader in another classroom we visited wrote to his teacher, "You are like the North Star for the class. You don't tell us where to go, but you help us find our way." Constructivist classrooms demand far more from teachers and students than lockstep obeisance to prepackaged lessons. (Brooks & Brooks, 1999, pp. 21, 23)

TYLER'S BASIC PRINCIPLES OF CURRICULUM PLANNING

Tyler (1949) observed that in planning educational goals, teachers should first consider the needs of the learners, then the needs of society or what he called "contemporary life," and finally the suggestions or recommendations of subject-matter specialists. Since 1949, there has been consistent support for Tyler's elegant (simple, but not simplistic) curriculum planning method. He proposed four fundamental questions that should be considered in planning any curriculum:

1. What educational purposes should the school seek to attain?
2. What educational experiences can be provided that are likely to attain these purposes?
3. How can these educational experiences be effectively organized?
4. How can we determine whether these purposes are being attained? (1949, p. 1)

Reflective educators are likely to use Tyler's basic principles in planning, organizing, and evaluating their programs because they are remarkably similar to the process of reflective thinking. Essentially, he suggests that teachers begin curriculum planning by perceiving the needs of students, gathering information, making a judgment about an educational purpose, selecting and organizing the strategies to be used, and then evaluating the effectiveness of their curriculum plan by perceiving its effects on their students. These are similar processes to those outlined in the model of reflective action presented in Chapter 1.

Although reflective teachers are not likely to memorize Tyler's four questions word-for-word, they are likely to carry with them the fundamental notion of each:

1. What shall we teach?
2. How shall we teach it?
3. How can we organize it?
4. How can we evaluate it?

Reflective teachers ask themselves these questions each year because they have probably noticed subtle or dramatic changes in their communities, subject-matter materials, students, or themselves from year to year that cause them to reexamine their curricula. On reexamination, they may confirm that they want to continue to teach the same curriculum in the same way or that they want to modify some aspects of the curriculum. As teachers grow in experience and skills, most greet each new year as an opportunity to improve on what they accomplished the previous year. Rather than continue to teach the same subjects in the same ways year after year, reflective teachers often experiment with new ways of teaching and organizing the curriculum.

An obvious contrast between more reflective and less reflective teachers is that after teaching for 20 years, a reflective teacher has accumulated 20 years of experience, while a less reflective teacher is likely to have repeated one year of experience 20 times. Reflective teachers want to have an active role in the decision-making processes in their schools, and curricular decisions are the ones that count the most. They also display a strong sense of responsibility for making good curriculum choices and decisions, ones that will ultimately result in valuable growth and learning for their students.

BLOOM'S TAXONOMY OF EDUCATIONAL OBJECTIVES

Benjamin Bloom, a student of Ralph Tyler's, extended Tyler's basic principles in a most useful way. Bloom and his colleagues attempted to respond to the first of Tyler's questions as completely as possible (Bloom, Engelhart, Furst, Hill, & Krathwohl, 1956). In meetings with other teachers, they brainstormed and listed all the possible purposes of education, all the possible educational objectives that they could think of or had observed during many years of classroom experience. Then they attempted to organize and classify all of these possible objectives into what is now known as the *Taxonomy of Educational Objectives.* Their intent was to provide teachers with a ready source of possible objectives so that they could select ones that fit the needs of their own students and circumstances. They also intended to help teachers clarify for themselves how to achieve their educational goals. A third purpose for the taxonomy was to help teachers communicate more precisely with one another.

The taxonomy first subdivides educational purposes into three domains of learning: cognitive, affective, and psychomotor. The *cognitive domain* deals with "the recall or recognition of knowledge and the development of intellectual abilities and skills"; the *affective domain* deals with "interests, attitudes, and values"; and the *psychomotor domain* concerns the development of manipulative and motor skills (Bloom et al., 1956, p. 7).

CLARIFYING EDUCATIONAL GOALS AND OUTCOMES

All three domains are considered to be important in the curriculum because together they support the growth and development of the whole student. Educators used to begin writing curriculum documents by carefully wording their educational goals. An *educational goal* is a general, long-term statement of an important aim or purpose of an educational program. For example, most schools have a goal of teaching students how to read and write, another to ensure that they understand the cultural heritage of the United States, and another to help them develop attitudes and habits of good citizenship.

To translate goals into operational plans, however, most educators today prefer to specify what *outcomes* are expected as a consequence of being in school and taking part in the planned curriculum. Eisner (1985) alerts educators to be aware that goals express intentions but that other factors may occur that alter the intentions in the educational process. According to Eisner (1985), "outcomes are essentially what one ends up with, intended or not, after some form of engagement" (p. 120).

Outcomes are statements that describe what students will demonstrate as a culmination of their learning. Spady (1994) proposes that outcomes must specify "high quality, culminating demonstrations of significant learning in context" (p. 18). A high-quality demonstration means one that is thorough and complete, showing the important new learning the student has gained or demonstrating the mastery of a new skill or process. Outcomes are designed to be assessed at or near the end of a learning period.

Written outcome statements are used to translate goals into actions. They describe what students will be able do as a result of their educational program. If educators can envision what they want students to be able to do or know after a series of learning experiences, they can plan with that outcome in mind. Learning outcomes generally describe actions, processes, and products that the student will accomplish in a given period.

Cognitive outcomes are expressed in terms of students' mastery of content or subject-matter knowledge. For example, kindergartners are expected to master the alphabet, third graders are expected to master multiplication facts, and sixth graders are expected to show mastery of the history of ancient civilizations.

Educators also write many psychomotor outcomes, including strategies, processes, and skills that involve both the mind and the body in the psychomotor domain. For example, elementary students are expected to learn how to decode symbols to read, write, calculate, solve problems, observe, experiment, research, interpret, make maps, and create works of art, music, and other crafts.

Most teachers view affective outcome statements as being related to the development of character. Typically, schools highlight the affective outcomes emphasizing good citizenship, self-esteem, respect for individual and racial differences, and an appreciation of art, music, and other aspects of our cultural heritage.

Individual teachers may write outcome statements for their own classes, but when they work collectively to clarify a set of schoolwide outcome statements, the effect on students is likely to be much more powerful and result in greater growth and change. This enhanced growth is a result of the consistency of experiences that students have in every classroom and with every adult in the school. Many school districts have statements of philosophy (often called *mission statements*) and outcome statements written in policy documents, but they may or may not be articulated and applied in the schools themselves. For effective change to take place, the school faculty must consider its educational purposes each year, articulate them together, and communicate them to the students through words and deeds.

In a classroom, each teacher has the right and the responsibility to articulate a set of educational outcomes for their own students. Working alone or with teammates at the same grade level or subject area, the classroom teacher may want to articulate two to four yearly outcome statements in each of the three domains. Tyler (1949) encourages teachers to select a small number of highly important goals because "time is required to change the behavior patterns of human beings. An educational program is not effective if so much is attempted that little is accomplished" (p. 33).

WRITING USEFUL AND APPROPRIATE OUTCOME STATEMENTS

The wording of outcome statements must be general but not vague. This is a subtle but important distinction. Some school documents contain goals such as "to develop the full potential of each individual." What does this mean to you? Can you interpret it in a meaningful way in your classroom? Can you translate it into programs? Probably not. This goal statement is so vague that it cannot be put into operation, and it would be very difficult to determine whether it is being attained.

An outcome statement should be general, in keeping with its long-term effects. It should also describe, clearly and precisely, how you want your students to change and what you want them to be able to do at the end of the term of study.

Here are some examples of useful *cognitive* outcome statements:

> Kindergarten students will be able to recognize and name all the counting numbers from 1 to 20.
>
> Fifth-grade students will demonstrate that they understand how technology has changed the world by creating a time line, graph, chart, or set of models to show the effects of technology on human experience.

Here are some examples of *psychomotor* (sometimes referred to as *skill* or *process*) outcome statements:

> Third-grade students will be able to measure and compare a variety of common objects using metric units of measurement of length, weight, and volume.
>
> Sixth-grade students will be able to compose and edit written works using a word-processing program on a computer.

Here are some examples of *affective* outcome statements:

> Second-grade students will demonstrate that they enjoy reading by selecting books and other reading materials and spending time reading in class and at home.

> Students at all grade levels will demonstrate that they tolerate, accept, and prize cultural, ethnic, and other individual differences in human beings by working cooperatively and productively with students of various ethnic groups.

In many school programs, outcome statements are intended to be accomplished during the course of a school year. Yearly outcome statements can be written for one subject or across several disciplines. Outcome statements can also be written for a shorter period, such as a term or a month. They are used as guides for planning curriculum and learning experiences for that length of time. At the end of a given time, the teacher assesses whether students have successfully demonstrated the outcome. If not, the teacher may need to repeat or restate the outcome statement to ensure that it can be met.

Some outcome statements may need to be modified because they are too vague. In the following example, compare the first vague statement with the improved second statement:

> *Original outcome statement:*   Students will be able to demonstrate that they understand the U.S. Constitution.

> *Improved outcome statement:*   Students will be able to describe the key concepts in the articles of the U.S. Constitution and give examples of how they are applied in American life today.

Other outcome statements may need to be modified because they are too difficult for the students. Compare these:

> *Original outcome statement:*   Fourth-grade students will demonstrate that they know the key concepts of the Bill of Rights by creating a time line showing how each has evolved during the past 200 years.

> *Improved outcome statement:*   Fourth-grade students will be able to create an illustrated mural showing pictorial representations of each of the articles in the Bill of Rights.

Some outcome statements may need to be improved by adding learning opportunities that will stimulate student interest and motivation to learn the material. Consider the following:

> *Original outcome statement:*   Students will be able to recite the Bill of Rights.

> *Improved outcome statement:*   Students will work in cooperative groups to plan and perform skits comparing how life in the United States would differ with and without the Constitutional amendments known as the Bill of Rights.

Outcome statements are useful guides for educational planning but must be adapted to fit the needs of a particular teacher and class. For this reason, curriculum planning is an evolving process. A curriculum is never a finished product; it is constantly being changed and improved from day to day and year to year.

Examples of Long-Term Curriculum Planning

LANGUAGE ARTS PLANNING FOR THE PRIMARY GRADES

Until recently, the elementary curriculum contained separate subjects called *reading, English, spelling,* and *creative writing.* It was believed that if students learned how to read, spell, and use grammar and punctuation correctly, they would be literate and able to communicate effectively. The language arts curriculum of the 21st century places roughly equal emphasis on cognitive, affective, and psychomotor outcomes. Teachers now tend to believe that the best environment for learning is one that enhances a child's love of reading, writing, speaking, listening, and being creative. But they also know that students must master the basic skills of phonics, sentence construction, and word usage to be proficient readers and writers.

In an integrated language arts curriculum, students listen to or read literary works, write in journals, participate in editing groups, and speak for a variety of purposes. They also have skills lessons to master the proper grammar, punctuation, spelling, and other conventions of the English language.

As a first-grade teacher in Carpentersville, Illinois, Ginny Bailey and her colleagues planned this integrated curriculum together. She explains:

> We began our plan by deciding that we would use thematic units to accomplish the state outcomes. We quickly discovered that language arts cannot be separated from science, social studies, and mathematics when you use a unit approach, so we incorporated those areas into our planning. All of us had attended numerous classes and workshops on using thematic units and had read every book we could find on the subject of using an integrated language arts curriculum in the classroom. But now it was time to sit down and make our plan for the coming school year. We began by going through the science, mathematics, and social studies curriculum guides to familiarize ourselves with what had to be covered in those areas at our grade level. We then studied the Language Arts Outcome Statements. We chose to teach one or two thematic units a month depending on the length of the units.

A brief overview of Ms. Bailey's yearlong plan for an integrated language arts curriculum is presented in Box 4.1.

Box 4.1 Year-Long Integrated Curriculum Plan for First Grade

by Ginny Bailey, Judy Yount, and Sandra Krakow, Woodland School, Carpentersville, Illinois, Barrington Community Unified School District

These three teachers like to use a multidisciplinary approach for curriculum planning. They use themes that may be related to social studies, literature, or science, but all of them incorporate and emphasize language arts activities. In each unit, students read, write, speak, and otherwise investigate the topic. The themes change from year to year, but this is a typical example.

Author Study: Norman Bridwell (Clifford Books)

The purpose of this unit is to make the children feel comfortable in school. Young children relate to these familiar books. For the first week of school, we read the Clifford books and do many art and music activities related to the stories. The students discover that they can learn to read through singing and express themselves through art.

Changes

This unit emphasizes the patterns of cause and effect in life and encourages students to notice that things in the world change and evolve over time. Subtopics include

1. Butterflies and moths
2. Frogs
3. Colors
4. Apples
5. Seasons
6. Self

Zoo Animals

The purpose of this unit is to learn the characteristics of animals and to classify them as mammals, amphibians, reptiles, or birds. It is primarily a mathematics and science theme, but we integrate literature and writing activities in it and culminate the unit with a trip to the zoo.

1. Mammals
2. Amphibians
3. Reptiles
4. Birds

Human Bodies

In this unit, we help students understand their physical and emotional selves. Subtopics include

1. Inside the human body
2. Nutrition
3. Five senses
4. Feelings

Families

In this unit, we emphasize the importance of families and how each family is alike and different. Subtopics include

1. Family members
2. Different types of families
3. Families from different cultures
4. Family homes

Astronomy

The purpose of this unit is to understand that we are part of the universe and how the laws of science govern our lives. Subtopics include

1. Day and night
2. The sun and the nine planets
3. The force of gravity

The Earth

In this springtime unit, we examine earth science concepts and how they relate to our everyday lives. We emphasize the new beginnings that occur in the spring in each of the following subtopics:

1. Rocks and minerals
2. Farm animals
3. Insects
4. Plants

continued

Community Helpers

The purpose of this unit is to acquaint students with the variety of jobs that people in the community do and how interconnected our lives are. Subtopics include

1. Police
2. Fire protectors
3. Postal workers
4. Nurses and doctors

Transportation

The purpose of this unit is to study geography and learn where things are in the world by studying how we travel from place to place. Subtopics include

1. Trains
2. Airplanes
3. Automobiles
4. Ships and boats

AN EXAMPLE OF A MIDDLE-SCHOOL PLAN FOR MATHEMATICS

We will use the subject of mathematics to provide an example of how curriculum plans are designed at the middle-school level. The teaching of mathematics has changed at every grade level. No longer a time for drill and practice, mathematics is often one of the most highly interactive parts of the elementary school curriculum. Manipulatives that primary children use to demonstrate their understanding of number concepts include beans, beads, and number lines. But many teachers also use such motivating materials as pretzels, fish-shaped crackers, jelly beans, or coated chocolate candies. Recently, a little girl was asked how she knew it was math time and she answered, "That's easy! Math is when we have our snacks."

Kendall & Marzano (1995) provide a summary of recommendations made by the National Council of Teachers of Mathematics (NCTM, 1994) and the Mathematics Assessment Framework of the NAEP. These groups stress the importance of teaching mathematics in the context of real-life situations, and they recommend that school curricula should be designed so that the student:

1. effectively uses a variety of strategies in the problem solving process.
2. understands and applies properties of the concept of number.

3. uses a variety of procedures while performing computation.

4. understands and applies the concept of measurement.

5. understands and applies the concept of geometry.

6. understands and applies concepts of data analysis and distributions.

7. understands and applies concepts of probability and statistics.

8. understands and applies properties of functions and algebra.

9. understands the relationship between mathematics and other disciplines, particularly science and computer technology. (Kendall & Marzano, pp. 88–89)

With this emphasis on problem solving and application of mathematical concepts to real-life situations, the curriculum in many elementary schools has changed dramatically from drill and practice to mathematical explorations and investigations. Teachers who try to incorporate these recommendations into their mathematics curricula find that the best way to do it is through the use of projects and multidisciplinary units. A yearlong plan in mathematics will be divided into several strands or concepts with opportunities for reviewing previously learned material from time to time. It may resemble the Long-Term Plan in Mathematics presented in Box 4.2.

Box 4.2   Long-Term Plan in Mathematics

MIDDLE SCHOOL GENERAL MATHEMATICS COURSE

by Pam Knight, Twin Peaks Middle School, Poway, California

From the California Mathematics Frameworks (1992), the goal of mathematics education is to develop mathematically powerful students who can think and communicate drawing on mathematical ideas and using mathematical tools and techniques.

Teachers are expected to plan their mathematics curricula to include the following strands: number, measurement, geometry, patterns and functions, statistics and probability, logic and language, and algebra and discrete mathematics.

At Twin Peaks Middle School the mathematics department has developed a core curriculum. In addition, Pam Knight has synthesized the state's frameworks, textbooks, and other resources into the following year-long plan.

Measurement (Three Days)

This involves hands-on activities in cooperative groups. Students measure classroom contents using standard English units and metric units. They create charts showing the various units of measurement.

continued

Number (Four Weeks)

Students review the operations of whole numbers, fractions, and decimals and use calculators.

Integers and Integer Operations (Five Weeks)

Using a time line from 500 B.C. to the present, students explore the concept of positive and negative numbers. They then learn how to express these concepts in operational terms and how to apply them in operations.

Equations (Six Weeks)

We begin by examining the order of operations, exponential operations, one- and two-step equations, and integers. Students learn to evaluate expressions, do ratios, and solve equations.

Geometry (Four Weeks)

We begin by learning the vocabulary of geometry and then explore area, perimeter, surface area, and volume and learn to measure and construct angles. We then do Euclidean drawing experiences using compass and straight-edge constructions such as tessellations.

Probability and Statistics (Three Weeks)

We begin with an experiment using colored candies. Students tally the colors and then predict the probability of getting each color. They learn to write probabilities as fractions and ratios. They conduct their own surveys and display their results graphically and then make an oral presentation to communicate their findings.

Scale Drawing (End-of-the-Year Activity)

Each student brings in a postcard. They divide up their postcards into square inches. They then transfer their postcard drawings to 12 inch by 18 inch paper using colored pens.

LONG-TERM PLANNING IN SCIENCE

In the high school curriculum, we will use science as an example of how teachers plan long-term goals. Science consists of a survey of the basic ideas in the academic disciplines of Earth and space, life sciences, physical sciences, environmental studies, and the relationship between science and technology. When most of you were in elementary school, you may have learned about science as a collection of facts, laws, principles, and theories that have been found to be important in each of the science disciplines. When this content-oriented approach is used as the basis for curriculum planning in science, students are expected to read, comprehend, discuss, and take tests to demonstrate their mastery of the subject matter. This academic orientation toward science assumes that content is what students must learn to be able to understand science in later schooling.

Project 2061 (an educational study group of the American Association for the Advancement of Science) and the National Committee on Science Education Standards and Assessment (1994) are among several national study groups recommending that we change that approach very significantly. The new recommendations stress the need for students to have realistic, hands-on opportunities to experience the methods and processes scientists use to imagine possibilities, speculate on causes, hypothesize effects, gather and weigh evidence, and reach conclusions.

Reflective teachers who believe in teaching science processes use fewer textbooks and more laboratory experiences. Rather than teach *about* science, they believe that students must learn how to *do* science to understand it. They are likely to create a science curriculum that consists of a series of laboratory and experimental situations in which students observe, hypothesize, experiment, and evaluate their results in each topic of science. They may test rocks or create a model of plate tectonics for earth science. They may observe the moon or simulate an eclipse for astronomy or collect and classify plants and engage in microscopic examinations of pond water for biology. They may build and test simple machines for physics.

Reflective teachers recognize that the process approach provides students with many more opportunities for developing their critical and creative thinking about science than the textbook-centered, content-oriented approach does. Jim Hicks and Chris Chiaverina, two high-school science teachers in Illinois, have created a curriculum that involves their students in active explorations designed to stimulate their curiosity, make them aware of the wonders that surround them, and equip them with skills to help them function effectively in the world. As you can see in their Yearlong Plan in Science, presented in Box 4.3, they build toward a culminating activity in which students do physics at a Great America theme park. In Chapter 5, you will find one of their units described in greater detail, and one of their lesson plans is included in Chapter 6.

The yearlong plan in science may be planned in a variety of sequences. Teachers may decide to offer an Earth and space science unit for the first six weeks, followed by units on life science, then science and technology, and ending with physical sciences. This order may easily be changed; many elementary teachers choose to coordinate their science units with other academic subjects. For example, at the same time as a unit on measurement is presented in mathematics, the science unit may emphasize measurement tools and strategies. When the social studies curriculum focuses on themes of exploration of new worlds, the science unit may be coordinated to emphasize scientific frontiers in technology.

Box 4.3 Year-Long Plan in Science

by Jim Hicks, Barrington High School, Barrington, Illinois
and Chris Chiaverina, New Trier High School, Winnetka, Illinois

Planning as a team, Jim and Chris have incorporated these basic guidelines into their plan for their physics course.

Measurement Techniques (Four Weeks)

Focusing on the question "What is time?" this unit is designed to enrich students' concepts of time. Students learn how to measure short time intervals using stroboscopic photography and a cathode ray oscilloscope (CRO) and how to measure long time intervals using time-lapse photography and motion pictures. Students create motion picture machines called *xeroscopes*. Measurement of length is also covered. To investigate probability, estimation, and errors in measurement, students throw paper snowballs into a hidden trash can to estimate how large the trash can opening is. The probability nature of the second law of thermodynamics is also investigated.

Wave Phenomena in Light and Sound (10 Weeks)

In this unit we deal with reflection of light, refraction of light, and properties of waves associated with light and acoustics. The unit culminates in a field trip to the University of Wisconsin at Whitewater, where students learn the theory of holograms and then make and develop their own.

Forces, Vectors, and Equilibrium (Seven Weeks)

In this unit, students learn that forces come in pairs: action and reaction. We examine the forces of nature—gravitational, electromagnetic, nuclear, and the weak force.

In our exploration of vectors, students learn how to add forces. We examine the directions of forces and how they relate to each other. We construct graphs to demonstrate the effects of various forces and vectors.

Our study of equilibrium demonstrates how to combine forces to make a net force of zero. We examine Newton's first law of motion (an object at rest tends to remain at rest).

Acceleration (Two Weeks)

Using Newton's second law of motion (force equals mass times acceleration), we explore acceleration with ordinary objects. Students design and build a hovercraft and also spend a day measuring the mass of a car by applying a net force and measuring the resulting acceleration.

Kinematics (Five Weeks)

Kinematics is the study of motion. Our students investigate the properties of motion and its relationship to time, velocity, and acceleration through racetrack games. We also study projectile motion and circular motion, which extends the study of motion to two dimensions.

Work and Energy (Three Weeks)

We discuss all the types of energy that can be observed and learn to classify them into kinetic and potential energy.

Momentum (Two Weeks)

We explore practical applications of the concept of momentum by focusing on automobile safety, especially the use of seatbelts and air bags. We explore forces in collisions. This unit culminates in a field trip to an amusement park to explore energy conservation and circular motion. We have created a guidebook for physics experiences in an amusement park.

Electricity (Two Weeks)

We explore electrostatic forces between stationary charges and charges in motion or current electricity and emphasize their uses in the home and the workplace.

LONG-TERM PLANNING IN SOCIAL STUDIES

As in science, development of the social studies curriculum can follow a content-oriented approach or a process-oriented approach. Educators committed to an academic or content-oriented view of social studies believe that students need to know and understand the important facts, persons, events, and sequences in the history of our country and the world. Also important to the academic orientation toward social studies are the important concepts that distinguish various cultures and the basic facts about world geography. Recent critics of U.S. schools have decried the lack of knowledge of history and geography among young people. Televised tests and magazine quizzes have demonstrated that many young people lack knowledge about geography. Content-oriented curriculum planners seek to improve this condition by providing history and geography courses that emphasize knowledge and comprehension objectives to teach facts and concepts.

Process-oriented curriculum planners believe that instead of memorizing facts, names, places, and dates, learners should experience the processes of acquiring information on their own. The National Center for History in the Schools (1994) provided benchmarks for teaching students how to do think historically, by learning to do their own research in social studies and learning how to use tools such as maps, globes, atlases, charts, graphs, and other resources to enable them to find information when the occasion demands it. The credo of this orientation toward curriculum development can be summed up in the adage, "Give a man a fish and he will be hungry the next day; teach him to fish and he'll never go hungry again."

Decision making is also a key focus in the process-oriented approach to teaching social studies. Harlan Cleveland defined social studies as "the study of how citizens in a society make personal and public decisions on issues that affect their destiny" (Bragaw & Hartoonian, 1988, p. 9). To accomplish this, Bragaw and Hartoonian suggest that the curriculum planner must make sure that students do the following:

1. Develop an information base in the social sciences.
2. Think using the logic and patterns of history and the social sciences.
3. Communicate with others about social science data.
4. Make enlightened personal and policy decisions and participate in civic activities.

David Ramert is a social studies teacher at Francis Parker Upper School in San Diego, California. When asked what he would like new teachers to know about long-term planning, he reminisced about his first years of teaching.

> When I began to plan my U.S. history course, I read several textbooks written for my course and I knew that I couldn't teach all the material in one year, nor did I want to. I reasoned that it can't all be of equal value. Some parts are definitely more equal than others, but how was I to decide which parts to emphasize? I began to look for events and ideas that would be most likely to stimulate high-school students' interests and imagination and involve them in discussion. At the time I had a personal interest in political cartoons that have been published in newspapers for several centuries. I believed that these could be used effectively

to spark student interest in controversial issues, which, in my view, is what history is about. U.S. history can be viewed as one controversy after another from Columbus to Clinton.

I also wanted to seek out primary sources rather than rely on textbooks alone. You can yap for hours about Christopher Columbus and students will yawn and doodle. But show them the letter he wrote home to Spain describing the natives of this new land, their facial features, clothes, crops, and what they valued, and students sit up and start asking questions. They are surprised to learn, for example, that Columbus' men learned that the natives would trade gold for bits of pottery or scraps of leather. Because of his own values, Columbus forbid his crew to continue in this exchange because it wasn't fair. He had a moral problem with that. This experience offers students an interesting contrast to the present-day image of Columbus as a destroyer of an ancient culture.

Basically, what I want to accomplish by teaching U.S. history is for my students to scuttle all the simplistic, black-and-white notions of history that they read in the newspaper and see on television. When they leave my class I want them to have learned how complex human beings are and how complex every historical event has been and continues to be. Controversy is the middle name of my course. No one is spared, not even the teacher.

My responsibility as a teacher of U.S. history is to present a survey of the entire span of our nation's history, but my responsibility to myself is to give an emphasis to the stories that best illustrate the controversial nature of historical events. There have always been so many different interest groups seeking attention and power. So, to plan my year, I selected the most interesting and controversial topics in the textbook and organized them chronologically. I begin with Colonial America, emphasizing the demographics, peoples' life spans, diseases, and the rise of public schools. Then I move on to the American Revolution, the Declaration of Independence, the Constitution and the new nation, the Jeffersonian Era, Nationalism and Western expansion, Jacksonian America, and issues leading to the Civil War, beginning with the struggle over slavery. I always spend too much time on the Civil War.

From there I go to Reconstruction, Industrialization, Immigration, and Urbanization in the late 19th century. I choose to do the Spanish American War and the controversial issue known as "U.S. Imperialism." I deal with the rise of the populists and progressives which takes us through World War I. Then I move on to the 1920s as the era of wonderful nonsense, the Jazz age. Then, in contrast, we learn about the economic collapse of 1929, the Great Depression and the New Deal of the Roosevelt Era. World War II is a complex subject because I have to deal with both the European and the Pacific War. I don't have time to teach it battle by battle, so I focus on political and economic events leading up to the war, the treaties and commitments made by the United States after the war. Lots of controversy there!

That takes us to the Cold War. I give this era a lot of time, looking at both foreign and domestic issues. I remember this era. I lived it as a child. Now most of my students don't know what a Communist is and why our country was so fearful of them. As we reach the 1960s, we discuss the rise of civil rights and civil liberties for all groups, women, Indians, Blacks, Chicanos. I always spend significant time on that era. The College Board exams places a lot of emphasis on this era, on questions relating to the social history of our country. That illustrates one of the major changes in the teaching of history. When I went to school, the teachers used to focus on diplomatic and political history and so did the textbooks. Now, the focus has turned to social history, emphasizing changes in the way people live, interact and view one another. Teaching a year of U.S. history is a constant struggle to get at the truth. Controversy is a tool I use to undo the myths created in students' minds by popular culture's simplistic notions.

You can read a unit plan from Mr. Ramert's U.S. history course in Chapter 5 and a lesson plan in Chapter 6.

REDESIGNING THE CURRICULUM TO REFLECT MULTICULTURAL VALUES

One of the enduring controversies in curriculum planning is how to design curriculum that accurately reflects and honors the variety of cultural values represented by students in our schools. As David Ramert provokes his students to think by posing controversial questions, he is also trying to encourage them to see the world from points of view different from their own.

James Banks, director of the Center for Multicultural Education at the University of Washington, has similar goals when he advises teachers to redesign their curricula to promote "cultural excellence." Banks (1992) believes that the redesigned curriculum should describe the needs and contributions of all Americans, all their struggles, hopes, and dreams. It should not be an add-on to the existing curriculum, but should become an integral part of every subject we teach. Ask students to reflect, discuss, and write about questions such as, "Who am I?" "Where have I been?" "What do I hope for?" Banks believes that when students can answer these questions they will be better equipped to function in their own world, as well as in the larger community that may be populated by people who answer the same questions differently.

To develop a multicultural curriculum for your classroom, no matter what subject you teach, plan learning experiences that reflect the concerns of the diverse cultural groups that make up the class, the school, and the community. Encourage your students to share their different perspectives and opinions and show that you value the different ways that they solve problems and view the world around them.

Reissman (1994) recommends that as you assign learning tasks, consider how each assignment can be used to strengthen intergroup understandings, respect for each other's cultures, and the development of skills that will later be needed in community, national, and global citizenship. Her book titled *The Evolving Multicultural Classroom* may be a valuable resource for you in your curriculum planning.

REDESIGNING THE CURRICULUM USING MULTIDISCIPLINARY THEMES

Students:

> develop knowledge by interacting mentally and to some extent physically with people and objects around them. This interaction requires active involvement.

Knowledge that is poured into a passive mind is quickly forgotten. (Sleeter & Grant, 1994, p. 218)

One side benefit of the multidisciplinary curriculum is that it has led teachers to share what they are doing and work together to plan learning experiences. Teachers who come to school, close the doors of their classrooms, and teach in isolation are becoming a thing of the past. For example, in curriculum planning, many districts team beginning teachers with experienced teachers to develop and share curriculum materials.

This new trend has created an environment in which teachers do not structure their curricula into separate blocks of time. As Beane (1991) points out, when confronted with a problem, individuals do not say, "Now which part of this is science and which part of this is language arts?" Instead, people address problems with a multidisciplinary approach and use whatever resources and content they need to resolve them.

In his analysis of subject-matter teaching, Brophy (1992) emphasizes the importance of teaching fewer topics in more depth. This allows students to have a greater understanding of the topics and lets teachers emphasize higher-order applications. Brophy indicates that state curriculum guides and textbooks should be modified to accomplish this task, and in many cases they are being revised to include a greater emphasis on integrated curricula such as whole language programs.

In middle school, much energy is being focused on restructuring the curriculum. In many cases, middle school faculty are reflecting on whether to continue with the concept of the middle school as a mini high school, where students take subject-specific courses, or whether to consider alternative structures that combine subject matter into integrated curricula. Beane (1991) proposes a vision of the curriculum centered on themes rather than abstract or artificial subject areas. He suggests that middle-school curricula could be focused on themes such as "living in the future," "wellness," or "cultural diversity."

When this integrated thematic approach is used in a middle school, the faculty plans together to design curricula that include literature, writing, mathematics, history, science, and health instruction within the selected theme. The result is often a highly motivating set of learning experiences designed specifically for the special needs of young adolescent students. Faculty members also report increased satisfaction with their own careers when they are involved in actively restructuring the curriculum to meet the needs of their students and celebrate their own special interests and talents.

At the middle-school and high-school levels, where teachers are usually responsible for teaching only one major subject area at a time, it may be more difficult to design a multidisciplinary curriculum than it is in elementary schools. It requires that several teachers agree to try this approach and collaborate to plan common goals and themes so that students can experience an integrated, multidisciplinary curriculum even though they still go to math, social studies, and English classes during different class periods.

If a team of secondary teachers decides to plan a multidisciplinary curriculum, it might, for example, choose a common theme such as "change." Individual science, mathematics, language arts, and English teachers then design learning experiences that allow students to identify how things change and to relate these changes to their own experiences. The mathematics teacher might choose to do the unit on renaming fractions during this period to illustrate how number concepts need to be changed to carry out mathematical operations. The social studies teacher may focus on the changes in a community over a period of time. The English teacher will look for a novel or a series of other readings that fit the theme of change and carry out discussions of how change affects the characters' lives and beliefs.

To extend this example of the multidisciplinary curriculum to include a multicultural approach as well, the same teachers can highlight various cultural aspects within the theme. The mathematics teacher can describe the contributions made by various cultures to change the way in which mathematics is done. The social studies teacher can ask students to explore the way changes in the community have affected various cultures and encourage students to express how these changes are experienced today by their own families. The English teacher can select a variety of readings on the theme of change, each one expressing the point of view of a different cultural or ethnic group.

We can also find examples of high schools that are using the integrated curriculum. One is the Humanitas Program in the Los Angeles Unified School District. This program integrates English, social studies, and art; some teams also include philosophy, mathematics, science, studio art, or dance. The Humanitas Programs are built around themes such as "women, race, and social protest"; "the Protestant ethic"; and "the spirit of capitalism." Students take core classes in these thematic programs that may include literature, writing, artistic expression, and discussion of social issues. They attend regular subject-matter classes for mathematics, science, and physical education. Teachers who work with the Humanitas Program are responsible for planning the program together; and as a result, they report that they believe a spirit of renewal and empowerment was missing when they worked alone.

PLANNING CURRICULUM FOR A MULTICULTURAL, BILINGUAL CLASSROOM

Ruth Reyes teaches sixth grade at Washington School in downtown San Diego, California. This school follows a special policy of developing biliteracy among all its students. All classes are taught in both Spanish and English. In her class, Ms. Reyes teaches one day in Spanish and the next day in English. Her curriculum is designed to allow students to move from one language to another very flexibly. When she designs a unit of study, she selects resources in both English and Spanish. The students use both or select the ones that fit their own level of language development.

Ms. Reyes uses a yearlong theme that she calls Environment/Survival. This theme grows out of her own special interest in biology. It also ties in with the social studies curriculum and grows out of her belief that sixth-grade students need to be aware of the concept of environment and the relationship between human beings and their environment. She wants her students to leave her class with a commitment to saving our natural environment. She also wants them to begin to develop survival skills and strategies to improve their own environment.

Ms. Reyes describes how she translates this important goal into daily learning experiences that cover the state- and district-mandated curricula for math, science, social studies, and language arts. Ms. Reyes describes the process this way:

I looked through the course of study provided by the school district and the curriculum guides from the state and the school district. Then I opened up all the teacher's manuals for the textbooks we use in sixth grade. As I looked for a way to organize all this material into meaningful chunks, it was clear to me that I should use the social studies curriculum as the basis for planning. At sixth grade, we focus on the study of world history and geography. That's a perfect fit with my interest in the environment and its relationship to mankind. I can teach the historic material and at the same time bring in contemporary issues and show how they relate to each other.

But before I plunge into the yearlong thematic curriculum, I spend the first week of school assessing students' interests and needs. My goals are to get to know my students and learn their strengths and interests. For that week, I use a short literature book that really interests me. This year, I used Kurusa's (1981) *The Street Is Free* and the Spanish edition, *La Calle Es Libre*. This book about the rainforests fits my theme and allows me to introduce the major ideas we'll be studying all year long. The students do a lot of reading, writing, discussion, and group assignments so that I can observe them as they work together. I spend most of my time during that week observing and taking notes on students as they are working in various groupings. I try to identify what each student enjoys, what is easy, and what is a challenge for each of them. As I walk around with my clipboard, and I take notes on computer labels (one label per student), which I can then transfer to their portfolios without rewriting, I look for as many positives as possible and also jot down what appears to be challenging for each student. Everyone in my class is learning a new language so I have to be alert when I hear them speak in the unfamiliar language, so that I can encourage them and plan activities that will allow them to be successful.

During the second week of school, we begin our study of the first social studies/literature unit for the year. The topics that are covered in the social studies curriculum include: Early Man, the Beginning of Civilization, Ancient Hebrews and Greeks, India, China, and Rome. For language arts, I locate several literature books that are related in some way to each of these topics. We spend about three weeks on each novel. For example, with the study of Early Man, I use a book about a girl who lived during the Ice Age who has to help her family survive by moving to a winter cave. See, it fits my theme in every way. For math and science, we study the time lines and the ages of prehistoric Earth. We also write word problems for math involving the characters in the novel.

I am not rigid in my organization of the whole year, but we spend about three weeks per book. For some historical eras, we read two or three books. I try to get each book in Spanish and in English. When this isn't possible, then I get similar books on the topic so that my students can choose to read in English for one book, Spanish for another.

We begin a new unit by brainstorming what we already know about rainforests. We make a chart of what we know and put it up in the classroom. Then we make another chart of what we want to learn about rainforests. Based on what we want to know, I create five categories and divide the class into five groups. Each group focuses on researching one of the categories, such as animals or trees. Each group researches their topic for about three days and then they begin to organize their material into a book. They use the computer to write, edit, and illustrate their books. When they are completed, they teach what they have learned to the rest of their classmates. The books they write become part of the school library's collection for the rest of the year.

When I think of what my students experience during the entire year, I want them to see that every subject is related to each other. When they see the connections between subject matter, I feel that I have been successful. Some children come to school believing that to do math, they have to use a math book. I want them to learn that we do math every day of our lives. I also want them to see the relationships between different authors and their style. We concentrate a lot on comparing and analyzing in my room. Whenever we read a new book, we are constantly looking for ways that this book compares to other books we've read or to the social studies book or to some idea in math or science. When I hear my students making these analyses, I believe my methods of teaching are validated.

TIME LINES THAT FIT YOUR GOALS AND OUTCOME STATEMENTS

Time is the scarcest resource in school. Reflective teachers who organize time wisely are more successful in delivering the curriculum they have planned than are teachers who fail to consider it. Teachers who simply start each subject on page 1 of every textbook and hope to finish the text by June are frequently surprised by the lack of time. In some cases, they finish a text early in the year, but more often the school year ends and students never get to the subjects at the back of the textbook. In mathematics, some classes never get to geometry year after year. In social studies, history after the Civil War is often crammed into a few short lessons at the end of the year.

Will you be satisfied if this happens in your classroom? If not, you can prevent it by planning the time you will give to each element or subtopic of each subject area you are going to teach. This may seem like an overwhelming task at first, but it can be less threatening if you understand that you are not required to plan every outcome and objective for every subject before the year begins. You need to give the entire curriculum an overview and determine the number of days or weeks you will allot to each element.

Begin by examining the textbooks in your classroom, looking at the way in which they are organized. Most books are divided into units, each covering a single topic or collection of related topics within the academic subject. Mathematics books are likely to contain units such as "place value," "operations," "measuring," and "geometry." History books are divided into units on "exploration," "settling the New Frontier," "creating government," and others. English books contain units such as "listening," "writing," and "speaking."

Curriculum units are excellent planning devices because they show students how facts, skills, concepts, and application of ideas are all related. The alternative to planning with units is planning a single, continuous, yearlong sequence of experiences or planning unconnected and unrelated daily experiences. Units will be used as the basis for planning throughout the rest of this book.

Decide if the units in your school's textbooks are valuable and important as well as whether you agree with the way they are organized and the quality of learning experiences they contain. Consider whether using the textbook will result in achieving the outcomes in your school curriculum guide. Will it result in achieving the goals and outcomes you have for your class? If the textbook learning experiences match your outcomes, you can plan the year to coincide with the sequence of units in the book. If the textbook does not coincide with your planned outcomes or if you disagree with the quality or the organizational pattern of the book, you have several options. You can plan to use the book but present the units in a different order. You can delete units, or you can use some units in the book as they are written but supplement with other materials for additional units not covered or inadequately covered in the book. The most adventuresome and creative teachers may even decide to use the textbook only as a resource and plan original teaching units for the subject.

In any case, you should carefully consider the amount of time you want to allot to each unit you plan to teach. Create a time line, chart, or calendar for each subject and use it as you judge how much time to spend on each subtopic. For time-line planning, you can divide the school year into weeks, months, or quarters. For a subject such as mathematics, you may think about the year as a total of 36 weeks and allot varying numbers of weeks to each math topic you want to cover during the year. For a subject such as language arts, you might think of the school year as eight months long and create eight units that involve students in listening, speaking, writing, and reading activities.

You may divide the year into four quarters for subjects such as science or social studies with four major units planned for the year. These examples are only suggestions. Each subject can be subdivided into any time segment, or you may combine subjects into interdisciplinary units that involve students in mathematics, science, and language arts activities under one combined topic for a time.

Making reasonable and professional judgments about time-line planning depends on having information about your students' prior knowledge and their history of success or failure before the year begins. The pace of your curriculum depends to some degree on the skills and knowledge your students have acquired before you meet them. But your own expectation for their success is also important. You want to avoid the trap many teachers fall into of reviewing basic skills all year because a majority of your students have been unsuccessful in the past. If you expect them to succeed in your curriculum and be ready to move on to new challenges, then you should provide them with new challenges. They are likely to respond to your positive expectations.

The time lines you create at the beginning of the year need not be rigid and unchanging. They are guidelines based on the best knowledge you have at the time. As the year progresses, you will undoubtedly have reasons to change your original time line. Students' needs, interests, and success will cause you to alter the pace of the original plan. Current events in the country, your classroom, or your local community may cause you to add a new unit to your plan. Interaction with other faculty members may bring you fresh insights about how you want to organize the way you allocate time in your classroom.

COLLABORATIVE LONG-TERM PLANNING

Long-term planning, either individually or collectively, is an important job for teachers. If you are teaching in a self-contained classroom, you have the freedom to write your own outcomes as long as they relate to the district and state guidelines. If you are working in a team-teaching school, you will need to articulate your vision of student outcomes to your teammates and adjust yours to include their ideas as well as your own. In either case, the outcome statements you create will improve with experience. As you see the effects of your original outcome statements, you will reflect on them and find ways to improve them with each succeeding year.

When you begin teaching, you may be assigned to a curriculum task force or planning committee. In discussions with your colleagues, you are likely to gain new insights and information, but you may also experience frustration with points of view that differ from your own. When this occurs, remember the five different curriculum orientations of teachers. That may help you see things from a different perspective. Be prepared to speak assertively about your own ideas and beliefs. You may be the one to suggest innovative ways of dividing the curriculum into units. Although your ideas may meet skepticism or resistance from some teachers, it is quite appropriate for you to articulate them because schools rely on fresh ideas from faculty members with the most recent college or university training to enhance the curriculum and create positive innovations and change.

⮌ Reflective Actions for Your Professional Portfolio
A SAMPLE OF YOUR LONG-TERM PLANNING

Use Withitness

Observe a classroom in action for a few hours and try to infer what the goals are from what you see taking place. Write what you perceive to be the major affective, cognitive, and psychomotor goals in effect.

Put Curriculum Planning Into Perspective

You have a personal philosophy of education. From this philosophy, what are some of the major affective, cognitive and psychomotor goals that you have for your students generally? Write these goals.

Widen Your Perspective

Now consider a particular group of students that you are observing or working with at the present time. Based on your perception of these students' needs, what are your highest-priority educational goals? Write at least one cognitive, affective, and psychomotor outcome statement that matches both your philosophy of education and the particular needs of these students

Do Research or Invite Feedback on Your Goals

Visit a school and ask to see the mission statement and curriculum goals or outcomes for that site. Ask a classroom teacher to describe his or her goals and show you the long-range plans. Talk with the teacher about how the school's mission statement and goals affected the class curriculum. Research goal and outcome planning on the World Wide Web sites **www.prenhall.com, www. schoolnotes.com** and **thegateway.org.** You can join chats online or leave a message on the message board and get responses from teachers around the world. You may also like to try links to professional journals such as *Educational Leadership,* a publication of the Association of Supervision and Curriculum Development at www.ascd.com, where you can read their latest articles on goal setting and curriculum planning.

Redefine Your Goals

Do these visits to educational websites or to real classrooms cause you to rewrite your original outcome statements? As with other aspects of teaching, we must always be open and willing to change.

Devise a New Action Plan

Imagine that you have been hired to teach in the school that you are currently visiting. Create a series of themes that you'd like to use for the grade level you'd most like to teach. Describe how you would integrate the subject areas into each theme.

Predict the Consequences of Your Plan

Using the themes you selected for your grade level, sketch out a brief yearlong plan using months or quarters of the year as units of planning. What would be the major goals or outcomes in language arts, social studies, math, and science for each month or quarter? How do they relate to the theme?

References

Banks, J. (1991–92). Multicultural education: For freedom's sake. *Educational Leadership, 49,* 4.

Beane, J. (1991). Middle school: The natural home of the integrated curriculum. *Educational Leadership, 49*(2), 9–13.

Bell, M. (1990). *Everyday mathematics: First grade teachers' manual.* Evanston, IL: Everyday Learning.

Bloom, B., Engelhart, M., Furst, E., Hill, W., & Krathwohl, D. (1956). *Taxonomy of educational objectives: Cognitive domain.* New York: Longman.

Bragaw, D., & Hartoonian, M. (1988). Social studies: The study of people in society. In R. Brandt (Ed.), *Content of the curriculum* (pp. 9–29). Alexandria, VA: Association for Supervision and Curriculum Development.

Brooks, J., & Brooks, M. G. (1999). In search of understanding: The case for constructivist classrooms. *Educational Leadership, 57*(3), 18–24.

Brophy, J. (1992). Probing the subtleties of subject-matter teaching. *Educational Leadership, 49*(7), 4–8.

Eisner, E. (1985). *Educational imagination.* New York: Macmillan.

Kendall, J., & Marzano, R. (1995). *The systematic identification and articulation of content standards and benchmarks.* Aurora, CO: Mid-Continent Regional Educational Laboratory.

Kurusa. (1981). *The streets are free (Las calles son libras).* Caracas: Ekare-Banco del Libro (Spanish version); New York: Annick Firefly Books (English version).

National Center for History in the Schools. (1994). *National standards for United States history: Exploring paths to the present.* Los Angeles: Author.

National Committee on Science Education Standards and Assessment. (1994). *National science education standards.* Washington, DC: National Academy Press.

National Council of Teachers of Mathematics. (1994). *Curriculum and evaluation standards for school mathematics.* Reston, VA: Author.

Reissman, R. (1994). *The evolving multicultural classroom.* Alexandria, VA: Association for Supervision and Curriculum Development.

Sleeter, C., & Grant, C. (1994). *Making choices for multicultural education.* Upper Saddle River, NJ: Merrill/Prentice Hall.

Spady, W. (1994). Choosing outcomes of significance. *Educational Leadership, 51*(6), 18–22.

Tyler, R. (1949). *Basic principles of curriculum and instruction.* Chicago: University of Chicago Press.

Viadero, D. (1993, June 16). Standards deviation: Benchmark-setting is marked by diversity. *Education Week,* 14–17.

chapter 5

Planning Thematic Units for Authentic Learning

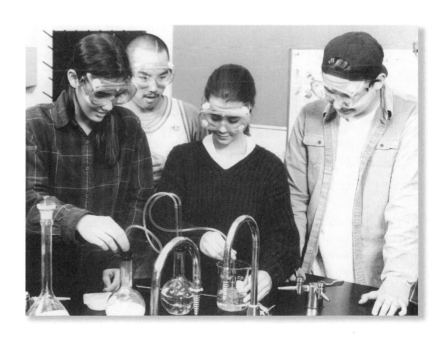

Do you have a vision of yourself teaching a roomful of students who are excitedly investigating, experimenting, discussing, and reporting on what they are learning? Beginning teachers and student teachers often report that what they want to do most is create a learning environment that motivates their students to want to come to school and learn as much as they can about important matters.

Current national standards and state curriculum guides are also the products of the vision of experienced teachers, working in collaboration to provide beginning teachers with guidelines on what to teach and how to teach it. These documents encourage teachers to create programs that develop students' deeper understandings of a few important subjects rather than provide them with superficial surveys of data. At the local school district level, teachers are responsible for translating the curricular visions described at the national or state level into practical classroom learning experiences. The word *vision* is carefully chosen in this discussion because at the local level teachers and principals are asked to develop a common vision and create a mental image of what they want to accomplish with students.

One of the most natural and authentic ways to translate a vision of core curriculum goals into practical classroom experiences is to plan thematic units of study that engage students in actively seeking information on a topic that has meaning in their lives. Many teachers, like Ruth Reyes and Ginny Bailey, described in Chapter 4, use a series of thematic units for their long-term planning. There is something refreshing and inherently motivating for both teachers and students who are using this plan. A unit of study lasts a specified number of days or weeks, during which time everyone is motivated to investigate and find out everything they can about the topic. Then, during an exciting culmination, the students proudly display what they've learned. After a brief period devoted to assessment, the unit ends, and a new one begins. When this rhythm is established in a classroom, complaints of boredom or repetition are rare from students or the teacher. The pace is quick, the goals are clear, and the expectations are high when everyone is involved in a thematic unit on an interesting, challenging topic.

How Teachers Plan Thematic Units

No other model of curriculum development involves teachers in a more active and professional capacity than do the planning, teaching, and evaluation of thematic curriculum units. They appeal greatly to reflective teachers who want to be part of the decision-making process and use their own creative ideas and methods. However, planning thematic curriculum units also adds greatly to the responsibility of classroom teachers. To create a successful unit, teachers must be willing to gather information and create an excellent knowledge base about the topics they've chosen so that the learning experiences will be based on accurate information. They must also be willing to work with their colleagues to make sure that their curriculum units do not repeat or skip important material in the elementary curriculum. They must take care to articulate their units with what was covered in earlier grades and what their students will learn in subsequent years.

Even when teachers decide that they want to create their own thematic curriculum units to translate curricular visions into actual classroom experiences, many are not certain how to begin to create a unit or what can or should be covered in each one. In this chapter, we examine how teachers decide what units to teach and how they organize the learning experiences in a curriculum unit to ensure that students learn the knowledge, skills, and processes that are intended when a unit is planned.

DECIDING ON UNIT TOPICS

A single teacher can work alone or with colleagues to translate state and local curriculum outcomes into units of study. Working alone, a single teacher analyzes state and local outcome statements to be implemented at that grade level in math, science, social studies, language arts, and fine arts. The teacher also examines the curriculum materials supplied by the school district, looking for themes or topics. The teacher may choose to look for topics within a subject, such as a math unit on fractions, a science unit on magnets and electricity, or a social studies unit on the electoral process. Other units may be interdisciplinary—that is, designed to include information and material from several subjects at one time. For example, a theme of "change" may include learning experiences in science, math, social studies, and literature.

Although many teachers choose to work alone, other teachers at the same grade level frequently work together to create units of study. When this occurs, their combined knowledge and ideas are likely to result in a much more comprehensive set of units and a greater variety of learning experiences. Whether a teacher works alone or with a team, the first step is to decide on a series of curriculum units that correspond to the major educational goals in a subject or several subjects for that grade level.

Unit topics may be suggested or recommended by the district curriculum guide and the textbooks purchased for the subject area. Teachers can decide to use the suggested topics in either the order presented or a different order. Teachers may choose to delete or add units to those recommended to fulfill the needs of their students.

Teachers may decide not to use units for every subject throughout the year. Instead, they may choose to teach a subject as an unconnected series of lessons. They may use units occasionally to highlight a particular topic in the curriculum. Sometimes teachers are able to plan units that combine more than one subject area, such as language arts and social studies or math and science. No two teachers will use the same units in the same order. Teachers have much discretion in planning units that fit their own strengths and the students' needs.

When a series of units is planned for a subject, each unit within the series is then developed in planning sessions that may begin in the summer before school begins or take place in after-school meetings during the year. Often teachers plan the first unit during the summer so that it is ready for the fall. Later units are then planned during the school year. Once a unit has been planned, it can be reused in subsequent years, although reflective teachers usually review their older units and revise and update them before teaching them a second or third time.

CREATING A CURRICULUM UNIT
USING REFLECTIVE ACTIONS

When reflective teachers approach the development of a curriculum unit in a subject area, they first consider their long-term goals for that subject. They may begin with the question, "What are my major social studies goals this year, and what should I include in each unit of study to accomplish these goals?" Or they may begin by considering the core outcomes they are expected to achieve during the year, and plan curriculum units that will encourage their students to learn the content and enhance the skills that make up those outcomes.

In the following example, each small picture represents one part of the reflective action process that we encourage teachers to use as they plan curriculum.

Use Withitness

Teachers who think and plan using the reflective actions described in Chapter 1 are likely to consider the cues they perceive from their students' interests and talents when planning thematic units. As they plan curriculum, they tend to ask themselves, "What do my students need to learn? How do they enjoy working? What learning experiences will motivate my students to become actively engaged in the learning process?"

Put the Unit Theme into Perspective

When they have decided on a topic, teachers who use reflective actions then begin by using their curriculum guides and state mandates for the subject. They sketch out a preliminary draft of a unit and begin to consider some interesting ways to teach it. The first draft may resemble something they've read in a curriculum guide, or perhaps even the type of unit plan they recall from their own school experiences.

Widen Your Perspective

Reflective teachers are also likely to establish some criteria for selecting certain content or methods while omitting others. These decisions are likely to be made on the basis of the teacher's values and moral principles or philosophy of teaching. As reflective teachers consider what to include and what to exclude, they ask themselves, "What knowledge and skills do I believe that my students need most to succeed in school or in life? How can this curriculum assist them in developing what they need most? What attitudes do I want to instill among my students? How can this unit help them to attain those attitudes? What values do I want to model for my students during this curriculum unit? How can I best model those values for them?"

Do Research and Invite Feedback

At many points along the way, reflective teachers are likely to do additional research on the subject or on teaching methods they can include in their new unit. They are also likely to talk with other trusted colleagues about how they have taught the subject. Many teachers share their unit plans with others, but most agree that sharing a unit plan is very much like sharing their recipes for making spaghetti sauce. No two sauces or units are identical. Still, a trusted colleague can point out things for the beginning teacher to consider, share strategies for motivating student interest, and suggest new materials to include in the unit.

On many educational websites there are examples of teacher-made units available to teachers and education students. It would be possible to simply copy one of these and claim the work as your own. Don't. We three authors want to encourage you to get the benefit of going through the process of creating your own unit based on your unique strengths and interests. Using another person's unit plan as a place to begin or as a model for the structural elements is a great idea, but then adapt it and change it to fit your philosophy of teaching, your understanding of the world, and your knowledge of the subject matter. Once you've created your own unit plan, you'll understand one of the great joys of teaching—the pride of designing learning experiences that keep you and your students coming back for more each day, asking, "When can we work on our unit study?"

Redefine the Unit Topic and Goals

What changes have occurred to you as a result of your interaction with colleagues? Do you have a new and original way to approach the topic? Have your basic goals changed?

Write Your Action Plan

Now the fun part begins. Teachers who use reflective action tend to enjoy the process of combining all the content materials and methods they've learned during planning into an original set of learning experiences that fit their own teaching style and the needs of their students. No two thematic units are ever alike. Even when teachers plan together up to this point, they are likely to interpret the materials they have gathered differently and add their own spin to the way they teach the unit.

Throughout the process of planning and teaching the unit, teachers who use reflective action are likely to be asking themselves, "How can I adapt the materials I have available to meet my goals? What new instructional materials shall I create to teach this material effectively? What risks are possible if I try to teach this unit my own way?

Which risks am I willing to take? What gains are possible if I take these risks? Do the possible gains outweigh the risks?

During a thematic unit, teachers create original bulletin boards, group activities, work or activity sheets, processes for promoting student interaction, methods to assess student accomplishments and ways to allow their students to perform or display what they have learned. For many reflective teachers, these opportunities for creativity are one of the most important sources of pride and are often cited as one of the most significant perks of their careers.

Predict Possible Outcomes

All teachers encounter problems in teaching and managing their classrooms. But teachers who use reflective action are able to prevent some of these because they try to imagine the consequences of their plans before putting them into action. For example, if you are planning to introduce some innovative learning materials to motivate students, you may try to consider what types of behavior management problems might develop.

Teachers who use reflective actions in their thinking and planning expect these kinds of difficulties. Spinning out consequences may prevent some problems, but realistically, others are likely to occur, When they do, the teachers repeat all the reflective action steps again. They use withitness in the midst of the problem to observe what is happening and respond appropriately. Afterward, they talk with the students themselves or with their colleagues to reframe the problem and create a new plan.

PUT YOUR PLAN INTO ACTION AND USE WITHITNESS AGAIN

The day you present your new unit plan to your students is usually an exciting day for you and your class. A sense of heightened expectation fills the room as you reveal the plan. Students may have a lot of questions. You will be able to answer some but not all of their questions right away. You will use withitness during the initial presentation to get feedback from your most important critics: your students. They will give you cues as they react to the plan with excitement, confusion, fear, or increased motivation to learn. You can also discuss the first day's presentation with your colleagues and get ideas about how to reframe the plan for yourself or for your students. After the first day, you will be even better equipped to spin out the consequences of certain parts of the plan. If your students react with fear or confusion, you can make changes now, before it's too late. If they react with excitement, you can consider adding even more challenging material to the plan.

Reflective teachers are also able to laugh at their own mistakes and learn from their errors in judgment without an overwhelming fear of the consequences or feelings of guilt. As they plan their thematic units, they are likely to encounter difficulties in locating suitable materials. When this happens, they become adept at scrounging for the materials they need or they substitute and go on.

When they begin to teach their units, some of the lessons they planned are likely to turn out quite differently than they expected, but they simply assess, regroup, and reteach as needed. As the unit nears completion, they may discover that, due to their students' choices and actions, some unplanned effects occurred. These are simply accounted for and evaluated along with the outcomes that were planned.

Throughout the process of planning, organizing, teaching, and evaluating a thematic unit, good communication skills are necessary. Reflective teachers must often convince or persuade their colleagues or administrators to allow them to take the time, spend money, take certain risks, and establish certain priorities necessary to teach their thematic units the way they want. Assertiveness is an important trait in curriculum development, especially considering the very different curriculum orientations that various members of the faculty adopt.

Conflicts may arise with students as well. When reflective teachers introduce a creative new way to learn a difficult subject, some students may react by stating their own preferences. When this occurs, teachers who use reflective actions simply begin the cyclical process anew by perceiving what needs the students have that have not been sufficiently addressed in the plan so far and accommodating those needs in a revised version of the unit plan.

SEQUENCING LEARNING EXPERIENCES IN UNIT PLANS

Your goals are established; your basic plan is in your mind or sketched out in print. Now you must consider how to begin your unit so that it engages students' attention, how to end your unit so that it gives them a realistic and valuable payoff for their hard work, and how to pace the events and the learning experiences from day to day. In other words, you need to establish a sequence of events that will accomplish your learning goals and motivate your students to work hard over a period of time. Practically speaking, the process of sequencing the events in a curriculum unit takes place near the end of organizing your unit, as you can see in the following steps:

1. Define the topics and subject matter to be covered in the unit.
2. Define the cognitive, process, and affective goals or outcomes that tell what students will gain and be able to do as a result.
3. Outline the major concepts that will be covered.
4. Gather resources that can be used in planning and teaching.
5. Brainstorm learning activities and experiences that can be used in the unit.
6. Organize the ideas and activities into a meaningful sequence.
7. Create lesson plans that follow the sequence.
8. Plan evaluation processes to measure student achievement and satisfaction.

Analysis will reveal that these statements correspond to Tyler's (1949) four questions. Items 1, 2, and 3 pertain to Tyler's question "What shall we teach?" Items 4 and 5 relate to the question "How shall we teach it?" Items 6 and 7 respond to the question

"How shall we organize it?" Item 8 answers the question "How will we know if we are successful?"

When seen in print, as they are here, these steps appear to depict an orderly process, but curriculum planning is rarely so linear. Instead, teachers find themselves starting at various points in this process. They skip or go back and forth among the steps as ideas occur to them. For example, a team member may begin a discussion by showing a resource book with a particular learning activity that could be taught as part of the new unit. Discussions may skip from activities to goals to concepts to evaluation to organization. Nothing is wrong with this nonlinear process as long as teachers are responsible enough to reflect on the overall plan to determine if all of Tyler's questions have been addressed fully and adequately. When the plan is complete, it is important to review it and ask, "What are the outcomes I expect from this unit? Are the learning experiences directly related to the outcomes? Is my organization of activities going to make it possible for my students to achieve my outcomes? Are the assessment systems I've established going to measure the extent to which the students have accomplished the outcomes?"

Thematic units vary in types of learning experiences and in organization. Some subjects, such as math, are organized very sequentially; others are not. The type of learning experiences also vary greatly depending on the subject, the resources available, and the creativity or risk taking of the teacher.

Most teachers use the textbook or a district curriculum guide as the basis for planning and as an important resource. *Do not limit yourself, however, to a single textbook as the only source of information in planning or teaching your unit.* A good textbook can be a valuable resource for you as you plan and for your students as they learn about the topic, but a rich and motivating unit plan will contain many other elements.

Supplemental reading materials from libraries or bookstores might include biographies, histories, novels, short stories, plays, poems, newspapers, magazines, how-to books, and myriad other printed materials. Other resources to consider are films, videotapes, audiotapes, and computer programs on topics that relate to your unit. Many interesting student-centered computer programs allow your students to have simulated experiences, solve problems, and make decisions as if they were involved in the event themselves. A good example is the computer game called *Oregon Trail,* distributed by the Minnesota Educational Computer Consortium (MECC), in which the student travels along the Oregon Trail, making decisions about what supplies to buy, when and where to stop along the way, and how to handle emergencies. This program can enrich a unit on westward expansion by providing more problem-solving and critical-thinking experiences than reading and discussion can ever yield.

Many educational games also provide students with simulated experiences. Some are board games that can be purchased in a good toy store or bookstore. Others are more specialized learning games sold by educational publishers or distributors. Your school district probably receives hundreds of catalogs from educational publishers. Locate them and find out about the many manipulative and simulation games available on your topic.

Consider field trips that will provide your students with experiences beyond the four walls of the classroom. Which museums have exhibits related to your topic? A simple walk through a neighborhood to look for evidence of pollution or to view variations in architecture can add depth to your unit. If you cannot travel, consider inviting a guest to speak to your students about the topic. Sometimes parents are excellent resources and are willing to talk about their careers or other interests.

In thinking about how to organize a unit, many reflective teachers prefer to begin with a highly motivating activity such as a field trip, a guest speaker, a simulation game, a hands-on experiment, or a film. They know that when the students' initial experience with a topic is stimulating and involving, interest and curiosity are aroused. The next several lessons in the unit are frequently planned at the knowledge and comprehension levels of Bloom's taxonomy to provide students with basic facts and concepts so that they can build a substantial knowledge base and understanding of the topic. After establishing the knowledge base, teachers can design further learning experiences at the application, analysis, synthesis, and evaluation levels to ensure that the students are able to think critically and creatively about the subject. This model of unit planning is not universal, nor is it the only logical sequence, but it can be adapted to fit many topics and subjects with excellent results.

Examples of Thematic Units

The following sections illustrate the processes that teachers use as they select, order, and create unit plans in several subjects from the elementary curriculum. Because each teacher has a personal curriculum orientation and philosophy, the process of decision making is more complex when teachers plan together than when they plan alone. The following examples demonstrate how teachers create their own curriculum units and what they put down on paper to record their plans for teaching. You will notice many variations in the way in which units are created and what they contain, depending on their purposes and the philosophies and values of the teachers who create them.

CREATING A MULTIDISCIPLINARY PRIMARY UNIT

Some units of study cross the boundaries among subjects or disciplines such as math, science, language arts, and social studies. For example, a unit on ancient Rome may incorporate many communication and language-arts skills in what is primarily a social studies unit.

Curriculum plans that include learning experiences from more than one subject area are called *multidisciplinary* or *interdisciplinary* units. To create such units, teachers frequently choose themes or topics and plan learning experiences that involve students in reading, writing, speaking, science investigations, mathematical problem solving, music, and art. A single teacher can certainly plan and teach a multidisciplinary unit, but we've found that the units planned by two to four teachers are often more exciting because they incorporate each teacher's different perspectives and strengths. For example, at Woodland School in Carpentersville, Illinois, three first-grade teachers often plan their whole language thematic units together. Ginny Bailey, Judy Yount, and Sandra Krakow recently planned an interdisciplinary unit on "change," highlighting the changes of butterflies and moths.

The three teachers know that teachers often have difficulty fitting in all the subjects of their busy curricula. They find that by using a thematic unit, they can teach several subjects simultaneously. To plan a unit, these teachers use a graphic organizer known as a planning web. They sit down with a large piece of paper and write the thematic topic in the middle of the page. They write the various disciplines they want to cover at different positions on the paper and brainstorm learning experiences that fit the topic under the appropriate subject area. An example of one of their planning webs is shown in Figure 5.1.

Through their observations of the students they teach, the three teachers learned that, in the minds of first-grade students, reading and writing are closely related. Their interdisciplinary thematic units allow students to read, write, and investigate interesting topics such as caterpillars, cookies, and planets. In each unit they select appropriate topic-specific children's books of fiction, nonfiction, and poetry. They locate songs on the topics when possible. Skill teaching is embedded in the unit, within the context of the literature, poetry, or music. The science and social studies facts and concepts are easily mastered by students when they are presented in the context of hands-on experiments and are reinforced by illustrated stories, poems, and songs. Math concepts are introduced by counting, measuring, sequencing, and patterning games and activities appropriate to each unit. A written planning web called Unit Theme: Changes is presented in Box 5.1, describing some of the specific learning experiences and how the unit is evaluated.

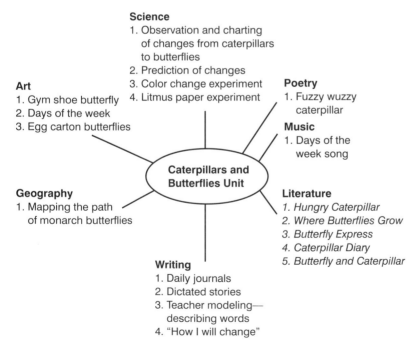

Figure 5.1   Planning web for a thematic unit
Source: Ginny Bailey, Judy Yount, and Sandra Krakow, Woodland School, Carpentersville, Illinois.

Unit Theme: Changes Subtopic: Butterflies and Moths

A FIRST-GRADE UNIT PLAN

by Virginia Bailey, Judy Yount, and Sandra Krakow, Woodland School, Carpentersville, Illinois

Description

This primary learning unit was planned to provide students with a set of varied learning experiences to understand the concept of change, with an emphasis on changes in the life cycle of living things.

Cognitive goal: Students will understand that all living things change over time.

Affective goal: Students will accept change as a natural part of their own lives and environment.

Psychomotor goals: Students will use observation skills to identify changes. They will use writing and speaking skills to report what they have learned through observation.

Nature Walk

Before the nature walk, students are asked to imagine what they might find out about caterpillars and butterflies on their walk. During the walk, they look especially for cocoons. When they return to the classroom, they discuss their findings. They predict whether the cocoons they found will become butterflies or moths. Then they write about what they saw on their nature walk.

Observing Caterpillars

Caterpillars ordered from a science supply dealer arrive in plastic jars. Students observe them climb to the top of the jar preparing to form a chrysalis. In just a few days, they begin to spin their chrysalis. They remain in this form for three or four days and then emerge as butterflies or moths.

As a follow-up activity, students are asked to illustrate the various changes they observe. A strip of 18-inch by 6-inch paper is prepared for each child. Children fold the paper into fourths and draw each stage of a butterfly's development: (1) egg on a leaf, (2) caterpillar, (3) chrysalis or cocoon, and (4) butterfly or moth.

In groups of four, children evaluate their products and check the proper sequence. Each child can then tell the other children a story about his or her butterfly.

Color Changes

In a learning center, students experiment to discover how colors change. Working with diluted red, blue, and yellow food color, the children use an empty cup and an eye dropper to mix colors and experiment on their own to create new colors from the original primary colors.

Children's Literature

The teacher collects a variety of picture books related to change. Some books will be read aloud by the teacher and used as a focus for discussion. Others will be selected by the children to read on their own.

Caterpillar/Butterfly Art Activity

Students create a wiggly caterpillar by cutting 12 cups from an egg carton. They make a small hole in the bottom of each cup, tie a knot at one end of a piece of yarn, and string the 12 cups together. Then they add paper eyes and decorate the caterpillars with crayons or paint.

They create a butterfly by cutting out 3 of the 12 cups from an egg carton for the body. Then they add wings and pipe-cleaner antennae.

Gym Shoe Butterfly

Each child places his or her gym shoes on a large piece of pastel paper (arches facing out) and traces the shoes into a butterfly shape. The child then cuts out the shape and adds antennae. The child can write a poem inside the butterfly shape.

Days of the Week

Students create a caterpillar with seven circles cut from construction paper. They then copy one name of each day of the week on each circle and glue them onto a background paper in the correct order. Afterward, they added a face, legs, and antennae. Students learn a song about the days of the week.

How People Change

Students bring in pictures of themselves as babies and put them on a bulletin board. Current school pictures are also arranged on the bulletin board. Students have to try to match the baby pictures with the current pictures of their classmates. Discussions focus on how people change (observing differences in size, hair, and other physical features) and what people are able to do at different ages. As a follow-up, students write in their journals about how they have changed.

continued

Growth Charts

Charts on the students' current heights and weights are initiated during this unit. Each student measures and weighs a partner. These data are recorded on a wall graph. The charts are updated three times during the year.

Poetry about Change

Poems about caterpillars and butterflies, seasons, and other changes are distributed frequently during the unit. Students read them, memorize and recite them, discuss them, and illustrate them. The poems are also used to teach language structure and vocabulary skills. A poem is projected onto a screen using an overhead projector. Students also have copies of the poem on their desks. We teach skills such as these:

1. Reading from left to right
2. Finding and reading individual words
3. Using the context of the poem to decode words
4. Learning specific phonics skills (such as beginning sounds, endings, rhyming words)

Art/Nutrition

Create a caterpillar out of fruit, vegetables, and peanut butter. Eat it for a snack and discuss its nutritional value.

Unit Evaluation Activity

Provide students with a paper that has the beginning of three paragraphs (shown later in this box). Use a copy on the overhead projector and clarify for students how to begin and what is expected.

Because primary students are unable to write all that they know and have observed, this evaluation can be extended by asking children from an upper elementary grade to interview the primary children and write the younger students' responses for them.

This week, I learned about butterflies and moths. First, I learned _____

_____ .

Next, I learned. _____ .

Finally, I learned. _____ .

DEVELOPING A MATHEMATICS UNIT FOR THE MIDDLE SCHOOL

Mathematics is generally thought of as a subject that does not lend itself to multidisciplinary planning, but recently many teachers have begun experimenting with ways to connect mathematics to other subject areas and life experiences. As Piaget demonstrated, mathematics is a subject that requires early experiences with concrete examples and hands-on experiences allowing students to manipulate materials to understand mathematical relationships. Only in the upper intermediate grades can students be expected to understand these same relationships at an abstract level without the need to "see" them in a concrete way. Many teachers like to plan their mathematics curriculum using thematic units so that students have many opportunities to experience and investigate the mathematical relationships they are learning.

Mathematics is also a subject that requires lateral thinking, reasoning, and problem-solving strategies that cannot be taught in a sequential series of lessons. Current mathematics units encourage students to explore mathematical relationships and select from a variety of strategies to set up and solve problems. Skillful computation is no longer sufficient as an outcome or performance expectation; it is also important that students be able to apply mathematical operations to real-life problems and tasks.

Based on these organizational principles, an effective curriculum unit in math is likely to (a) present new skills and concepts in order of difficulty; (b) initiate new learning with concrete, manipulative experiences so that students can understand the concepts involved; (c) teach students a variety of problem-solving strategies; and (d) provide examples, tasks, and problems that call on students to apply their newly learned skills and strategies in lifelike situations to problems they can relate to and want to solve.

Mathematics is an example of a *spiral curriculum.* This means that certain concepts and skills are taught every year but in an upward spiral of difficulty. Each year begins with a review of skills from previous years, then introduces new skills and concepts. For this reason, the topics of mathematics units are likely to be similar from year to year, but the way in which these topics are addressed and the complexity of the concepts vary greatly. Mathematics education now emphasizes problem solving and investigation as a means of developing mathematical power. Whenever possible, real situations and problems are becoming the basis for the curriculum.

A good example of a mathematics unit that involves students in realistic investigations and problem solving is presented in Box 5.2, Television Viewing Habits. Pam Knight created this unit for her sixth-grade students. She uses it during the first week of school to engage her students' interest in mathematics, help to develop a sense of confidence in their mathematical power, and show them how useful and important mathematics can be in their everyday lives.

AN EXAMPLE OF A SOCIAL STUDIES UNIT IN U.S. HISTORY

Social studies combines several academic disciplines, including geography, history, economics, political science, anthropology, sociology, and psychology. By adding learning experiences in literature and the arts, a teacher can fairly easily create a high-quality

Box 5.2 Television Viewing Habits

A MIDDLE SCHOOL MATHEMATICS UNIT

by Pam Knight, Poway School District, Poway, California

Description

This unit functions both as a personal exploration of how students use their free time and as a mathematics investigation. Students keep a log of all the time they spend watching TV every day for a week. With parental permission, students may also log the TV viewing habits of their parents. After a week of data gathering, students carry out a variety of mathematical calculations and interpret the data they collected.

Cognitive and Skill Outcome Statements

- Students will be able to collect and record data accurately and efficiently.
- Students will be able to calculate percentages of time spent watching television and compare those with percentages of time spent doing other activities.
- Students will be able to create bar and circle graphs based on the data they collected and the percentages they calculated.
- Individually, students will interpret the data they collected about their own television-viewing habits.
- As a class, students will combine their data with that collected by other members of the class to make interpretations and generalizations regarding TV-viewing habits of their age group.
- Individually, students will write articles describing the conclusions and generalizations they reached from this study.
- In small groups, students will make oral presentations on the findings of their group.

Affective Outcome Statement

Students will become aware of the amount of time they and their classmates spend watching television and will make value judgments about whether they want to continue spending their time in this way.

continued

Calendar of Events

I plan this investigation for the first week of school. It gives me insight into the students' incoming work habits and mathematical power.

FIRST WEEK OF SCHOOL

Friday: Introduce unit and distribute data collection materials. Assign students the task of collecting data, beginning Sunday, on the amount of time they watch television. Because video games are played on a TV screen, my students also decided to count the time spent playing video games. I ask students to be as honest as possible and to keep track to the nearest quarter of an hour.

SECOND WEEK OF SCHOOL

Monday–Friday: Data collection continues. Discussions in class focus on data collection problems and techniques.

THIRD WEEK OF SCHOOL

Monday: BAR GRAPHS Individually, students create bar graphs demonstrating the amount of time they watched TV each day of the preceding week.

Tuesday: CALCULATING PERCENTAGES AND CIRCLE GRAPHS Individually, students calculate the amount and percentage of time they spent sleeping, in school, in after-school or weekend activities, and watching television, as well as extra time not spent watching television. They create circle graphs showing these percentages.

Wednesday–Friday: DATA INTERPRETATION Cooperative groups combine class data in order to answer these questions:

1. Which grade level watches more television? Explain how you came to this conclusion.

2. Which day of the week do people watch the most television? Explain how you came to this conclusion.

3. Who watches more television in general: boys or girls? Does any particular age group watch more television? How did you come to your conclusions?

4. By using data about parent viewing habits, have you discovered any relationship between the television-viewing habits of a parent and the habits of a child?

FOURTH WEEK OF SCHOOL

Monday: WRITING ARTICLES   Individuals are assigned to write an article about their conclusions about the television-viewing habits of middle school students. They must answer the questions "Who? What? When? Where? and Why?" in the articles.

Tuesday–Wednesday: ORAL PRESENTATION PLANNING   Cooperative groups plan presentations on the findings of their groups. They create visual displays to show the data they collected.

Thursday: ORAL PRESENTATIONS   Cooperative groups present their findings to the rest of the class.

Friday: UNIT EVALUATION   Students evaluate their accomplishments in this unit. Individuals participate in a teacher-student conference to discuss the points each student earned in the unit. Cooperative groups discuss the processes they used in their group planning sessions, the visual displays they made, and the effectiveness of their oral presentations.

multidisciplinary thematic unit. If your goal is also to infuse the unit with multicultural learning experiences, then social studies is a very appropriate subject. Typically, the social studies curriculum is designed as an ever-widening circle of ideas, in keeping with the developmental stages of students. In the early grades, the curriculum centers on the home and the community; the middle grades focus on the states and the United States; concepts related to nations and the world are dealt with in the later grades. At each level, teachers can find many interesting ways to address the issues and contributions of various cultures.

Primary teachers often create units on the community, including maps of the school neighborhood, history of the community, roles of community helpers, economic activities related to stores in the community, and other similar experiences. To make this unit a valid multicultural experience, primary teachers invite family members of the students to participate by sharing their cultural heritage with the rest of the class.

Upper elementary teachers frequently create units on the life experiences and cultural beliefs of the first citizens of North America, the Native Americans. They also bring in the wide variety of contributions made by the people who immigrated from Asia, Europe, Africa, and Central and South America. Upper-grade teachers may offer units comparing nations of the world in terms of culture, geography, politics, economics, and history.

U.S. history is a topic that is taught in elementary, middle and high schools. It is an example of the spiral curriculum, where students are introduced to a topic in elementary school, revisit it at middle school, and then learn more about it in high school. As a teacher planning curriculum for a subject such as U.S. history, the trick is finding a way to engage the learners' interest in a subject they think they already know. David Ramert uses controversy to generate interest.

In Chapter 4, Mr. Ramert described an overview of how he plans for a year of U.S. history. One of his favorite units of study is the Jacksonian Era, spanning 1828 through 1840 (Box 5.3). This period includes many of the controversies related to the changing status of the American Indian in the United States. Because he relishes teaching the controversial issues that he finds throughout history, he enjoys challenging students to examine how President Jackson created policies that dealt with who gets to create Indian policy, and the changing status of American Indians in the burgeoning United States. Mr. Ramert challenges his students to think about the questions that Jackson and other U.S. politicians at the time posed, such as "Are Indians citizens? Are they people? Do they get to vote? Do they have any of the rights provided by the Constitution?" Some of these questions were answered during Jackson's presidency, for better or worse.

Mr. Ramert allocates only five to seven days of class time to this important era in our history. His Jacksonian Era Unit Plan presented here illustrates one of the most perplexing dilemmas faced by high-school history teachers. One academic year is about 180 days, and each of the exciting and valuable eras of our history must be brutally condensed to fit within this time limit. In this unit of study, there is no time for a hands-on project, but David does view it as a separate and unique unit of study because it deals with so many overriding issues that are still meaningful to our culture today.

Using a form of authentic performance-based assessment, David informs his students of the essay questions on the first day of the unit. On the final day, they write their essay responses to these questions. There are no surprises. At the beginning of the year, the students tend to ask, "Are these really going to be the questions on the test?" He does this to relieve anxiety and worry about what they are expected to learn. He tells them what he expects them to learn on the first day and gives them an opportunity to demonstrate it on the final day. He may vary the essay questions to fit the academic levels of different classes. Advanced-placement classes will be offered more complex questions.

To determine grades in his course, David assigns a point value to each unit of study and combines these points to assign a letter grade at each reporting period. Every assignment has a point value based on its importance as an assignment. A quiz might be worth 10 points, while a test may be worth 50 points. Each student's numerical score is entered in the grade book as a ratio made up of the student's score above the possible score, for example $9/10$ or $45/50$. These ratios can then be converted to percentages—90%—which are then translated into letter grades. Examples of this type of grading system are found in Chapter 11 in the section called Computation of Grades.

TWO SCIENCE TEACHERS COLLABORATE TO CREATE A HIGH SCHOOL SCIENCE UNIT

Chris Chiaverina and Jim Hicks are high school science teachers who believe that the world is a richer and more interesting place when people are aware of the principles of physics that operate around us. They plan their physics units to replace students' misconceptions

Box 5.3 Model Unit Planning

JACKSONIAN DEMOCRACY

by David Ramert, U.S. History Teacher, Francis Parker Upper School, San Diego, California

Description

We deal with the questions, "Was Jackson a curse or a blessing? Was he good for this country or bad? The Jacksonians viewed themselves as guardians of the constitution, of individual rights and promoters of equality. Is that view of themselves accurate? It illustrates some of the enduring contraditions of our country since its inception. It was the era of the common man, and the rise of the common man, but that term applied only to white male property owners. It was known as an era of Jacksonian Democracy, even though it didn't apply to women, Blacks or Indians.

Outcomes

I start with questions, such as those in the description above. My outcomes grow from these questions. Students will write answers to these questions at the end of the unit to show what they have learned and to demonstrate that they are able to view the Jacksonian era and others in U.S. History in all its controveries.

> *Question 1:*   Was Jackson a curse or a blessing in our country?

> *Question 2:*   Was he defender of the constitution in the area of individual liberty and human rights and equality? Was that view of themselves valid?

Time Line

DAY ONE

I pose my two basic questions (see above) as dramatically as I can and back them up by writing them on the black board. As I write, I tell the students that these are the essay questions that they will have to deal with at the end of the unit. The questions remain there in writing for all of us to see so that we all stay focussed. I also provide a handout that lists the questions, the subject matter outline and the list of readings.

For the remainder of the class period, I introduce Andrew Jackson. Who was he? Where did he come from? Why did he cough and spit puss and blood every day?

DAY TWO

What was the vocabulary of the Jackson era? What was Jacksonian democracy? Who was the common man at that time? What was the frontier aristrocracy? How was it similar to the Marxian struggle between the classes?

continued

Day Three

What was Andrew Jackson's Indian policy? What were the contradictions of that policy? What was the role of the Supreme Court in deciding the status of Indians? What was the "trail of tears?" What did it mean for the future of the Indian? How did this era determine the present day status of the Indian in the U.S.? Why can Indians now have gambling casinos on their reservations? Isn't it interesting that the Indians have turned the tables on the white man? Now, they get the white man drunk and take their money at their gambling casinos.

Day Four

What were the major political issues of the Jackson Era? Why did he kill the bank of the United States? How much of his presidency was vindictive because of his electoral loss in 1824? What was universal manhood suffrage? Who was actually eligible to vote at the end of his term? How did his economic policies help to create the panic of 1837? What were the petticoat wars? How much of his presidency was purely personal? Why did his view of women and the rights of women cause his vice president to resign?

Day Five

What was the issue known as states rights? What was the struggle that divided the federal government and the states? What court cases illustrated these state rights? Is nullification of federal law a valid concept? Is it possible or legal for a state to secede?

Day Six

What is the legacy of Andrew Jackson? We review our questions for essays by brainstorming answers to the controversial questions. (See David's Lesson Plan in Chapter 6)

Day Seven (Evaluation) Students write essays.

I pose both the basic questions and they choose one to write. Essays are worth 50 points toward a final grade in the course and are evaluated on the following criteria:

   There must be a thesis statement that takes a stand on the controversial question posed. (10 pts)

   It had better be interesting and keep me awake. (10 pts)

   Quote from primary sources or the text to support your statements. (10 pts)

   Use the vocabulary of the era of study correctly and appropriately. (10 pts)

   You must argue your controversial issue using evidence and examples from the era and the people and events we studied. (10 pts) about science as a dull and abstruse body of knowledge with a new view that science consists of exciting opportunities to satisfy their curiosity about how things work.

Working as colleagues, the two teachers have created a number of science units that begin with concrete explorations that encourage students to explore and investigate science phenomena. When they begin to create a new unit, they think about spectacular opening demonstrations to pique the students' interest in the topic. They report that they work very hard to plan and teach science units that are full of active exploration, real-life applications, and opportunities for students to experience the wonders of science. The say the payoffs for them and their students are worth the effort. When a student looks at Mr. Hicks with a light in her eyes and says, "Hey, that's neat!" he knows that all the work that went into the lesson was well spent. Their unit on Wave Phenomena is presented in Box 5.4.

The curriculum of any subject or of a combination of subjects may be subdivided into thematic units of study that are often highly motivating to students and a source of pride for the teachers who create them. Teacher-crafted curriculum units are often very creative and original products. For teachers who choose to create them rather than rely on textbook lessons and content, units are a way of individualizing the curriculum to capitalize on the interests and talents of the teacher and the students.

MODEL UNIT PLANNING

Box 5.4 Wave Phenomena
A HIGH SCHOOL PHYSICS UNIT

by Chris Chiaverina, New Trier High School, Winnetka, Illinois
and Jim Hicks, Barrington High School, Barrington, Illinois

Description

In this unit about wave phenomena, we study both sound and light waves. As with all our units, we begin with dramatic and puzzling demonstrations by the teacher to generate students' interest in the topic. Students then explore waves in a qualitative laboratory experience in order to observe them in action. This enables students to construct their own meaning and understanding of the properties of waves. During class discussions, we probe students' preconceived ideas about the phenomena and help them unlearn their preconceptions in order to construct more accurate understandings. Only after students have experienced the phenomena in action do we introduce mathematical relationships. At this point, students do a quantitative laboratory experiment in which they learn to express their new understandings in a formula or mathematical expression.

continued

Outcome Statements

COGNITIVE OUTCOMES

- Students will investigate wave phenomena and identify key features of light and sound waves.
- Students will distinguish between energy transfer by waves and particles.

SKILL AND PROCESS OUTCOMES

- Through kinesthetic learning experiences, students will derive the relationship among wave speed, wave length, and frequency.
- Students will investigate constructive and destructive interference of waves and apply the principle of superposition.
- Students will demonstrate how sound is produced and transmitted.

AFFECTIVE OUTCOME

Students unlearn their preconceived notions of physical phenomena and replace them with scientifically accurate observations and understandings.

Time Line and Calendar of Events

SLINKIES AND HUMAN SLINKIES

Students create and observe waves in the hallways using Slinkies. They explore their views, preconceptions, and observations of wave phenomena and examine different types of waves. Mathematical relationships are derived from students' observations. Students learn to communicate what they have observed about the speed of waves, what happens when waves meet and interfere with each other, and other basic properties of waves using mathematical expressions.

SOUND WAVES

We explore what happens when sound waves meet and interfere with each other. We discuss acoustics and how sound is produced and perceived. We look at the sources of sound, including musical instruments, and how sound is recorded and reproduced. We make Edison record players so that students can experience the reproduction of sound.

LIGHT AND ITS PROPERTIES

Using mirrors and lenses, students look at how light interacts with matter. As a culminating activity, we go to the University of Wisconsin, where the students attend college classes and create their own holograms. They keep a journal of their observations on this trip.

SOUND AND LIGHT SHOW

In the school auditorium, we use loudspeakers connected to a signal generator. Students line up in the regions in the auditorium that have no sound because of wave interference. We also explore how the walls act as acoustical mirrors. Using primary colors, we produce all the other colors of the spectrum by mixing light.

Evaluation Plan

Students complete both quantitative and qualitative laboratory explorations, worksheets, and paper and pencil tests. They take notes and write reports on holograms and the sound and light show. They create acoustical and optical devices.

> *Tests and quizzes:*   50 percent
>
> *Laboratory experiments:*   25 percent
>
> *Homework:*   20 percent
>
> *Special projects:*   5 percent

Resources

Edmund scientific catalogue. 101 E. Gloucester Pike, Barrington, NJ 08007; (609) 547-3488.

Exploratorium science snackbook. San Francisco: Exploratorium Museum Store; (800) 359-9899.

Edge, R. (1981). *String and sticky tape experiments.* College Park, MD: American Association of Physics Teachers.

Freier, G., & Anderson, F. (1981). *A demonstration handbook for physics.* College Park, MD: American Association of Physics Teachers.

Hewitt, P. (1987). *Conceptual physics.* Palo Alto: Scott, Foresman.

Liem, T. (1981a) *Invitations to scientific inquiry.* El Cajon, CA: Science Inquiry Enterprises.

Liem, T. (1981b). *A potpourri of physics teaching ideas.* College Park, MD: American Association of Physics Teachers.

The physics teacher. American Association of Physics Teachers (AAPT), 5112 Berwyn Rd., College Park, MD 20740.

The science teacher. National Science Teachers Association (NSTA), 1742 Connecticut Ave., NW, Washington, DC 20009.

⤶ Reflective Actions for Your Professional Portfolio
A SAMPLE THEMATIC UNIT PLAN

Use Withitness

Visit a class and talk with the teacher about unit plans. Ask to see samples of unit plans used in the class. Then ask to observe the students at work on their unit study.

Put the Unit Plan into Perspective

Brainstorm and make a list of possible unit topics that interest you. We always advise that you create your first unit plan around a strength or long-standing interest of yours. You will then be highly motivated to seek information on the topic and will have much to share with your students when you teach it.

Widen Your Perspective

How do your interests coincide with the elementary curriculum at the district near you? By reflecting on your interests and looking for a good match with the curriculum, you may be able to decide what grade levels you will enjoy teaching.

Do Research and Invite Feedback

Ask to see the school district's curriculum guides and the state guidelines for curriculum planning for the subject matter of your unit. If you are considering a multidisciplinary unit, it is necessary to examine the curriculum guides for all subjects that will be included.

Visit a school library or media center. Research thematic unit planning on the World Wide Web sites **www.prenhall.com, www. schoolnotes.com, and thegateway.org**. Locate resources that you could use in the thematic units you are considering. Interview the librarian to ask for suggestions for other resources on that topic. Include these materials in your unit resource list.

Show your initial plan to the classroom teacher or to other trusted colleagues. Brainstorm and share ideas for the unit topic together. Ask your colleague to predict possible roadblocks or other sources of difficulty standing in the way of implementing your unit plan successfully. Ask for advice about the types of materials you need to gather or create. Ask for suggestions about teaching and assessment strategies that are appropriate for your unit.

Redefine Your Unit Plan

Select one unit theme and brainstorm ideas for the cognitive, affective, and psychomotor outcomes that are possible for your students. Select another interesting theme and do the same thing. Now compare the outcomes possible with each theme and decide which one best fits the needs of the students and also fit the principles that guide your teaching philosophy. Sketch out an initial plan for the theme you choose.

Write Your Unit Plan

Write the final version of your Unit to include in your professional portfolio. Give your thematic unit an interesting, motivating title. Make a folder for the paper copy of your unit plan so that you can file it for safe-keeping. Keep another copy on your computer.

Predict the Possible Outcomes

Using your cognitive, affective, and psychomotor outcomes as a place to begin, allow yourself to envision your students accomplishing these outcomes. Sketch out a planning web as you brainstorm learning experiences that will allow your students to achieve these outcomes. What are the likely consequences of each step of your plan? Which outcomes will be easy to achieve and which will be difficult? Use a calendar to plan the sequence of learning events for your unit. Create a time line of events for your students and a complementary one for yourself so that your teaching plans coincide with the events in the unit.

Now begin to plan a way to assess the outcomes for your unit. What types of products or tests will you use to evaluate the degree to which your students achieve success on each of the outcomes you have for the unit? Show your assessment plan to a colleague and get feedback on making this important part of your unit a meaningful and accurate representation of what students have learned.

Reference

Tyler, R. (1949). *Basic principles of curriculum and instruction.* Chicago: University of Chicago Press.

chapter 6

LESSON PLANNING AND SEQUENCING

When you think of *lesson plans,* what comes to mind? Perhaps you think of a piece of paper containing detailed directions that describe how to teach something to a class of students. Or perhaps you envision a weekly plan book with brief notations to remind experienced teachers what they plan to accomplish each period in the school day.

Beginning teachers often want to find examples of excellent lesson plans so that they can see how other, more experienced, teachers have organized their teaching. How do they write meaningful learning objectives? How do they ever think of every detailed instruction? How do they write out a way to assess what students have gained from the lesson? It can seem like a mystery to many new teachers.

As with other modern mysteries, the Internet provides new clues and models that can inform and enliven your teaching. Prentice-Hall, the publisher of this book has provided a web page for readers at **www.prenhall.com/methods-cluster**, where you can gain access to a variety of curriculum materials. Almost any search engine on the World Wide Web has a category called *education,* and a subcategory called *K-12 education.* Yahoo, Excite, Logos, and others will lead you to web pages filled with real-life examples of lesson plans in every subject and at every grade level.

For example, Ask Eric Virtual library can be accessed at **http://ericir.syr.edu/Virtual/.** This web page contains a library of lesson plans created by teachers and submitted to ERIC, the Educational Resources International Clearinghouse. The Gateway to Educational Materials is another source of ready-to-use lesson plans at **http://www.thegateway. org/.** Once you've located these web pages, you can bookmark them and refer to them frequently. When you have mastered the art of writing your own lesson plans, you can submit one of your best to these types of organizations for others to see.

This chapter is designed to further demystify the process of writing your first lesson plans. We will describe ways to use the reflective action processes to envision and then describe on paper the goals and objectives you want to achieve, the materials you will need to gather, the step-by-step procedures you will use to teach your lesson, and the assessment devices you will employ to measure what your students have achieved.

Writing Objectives to Fit Goals and Outcome Statements

As you recall from Chapter 5, *goals* are the broad, long-term descriptions of how you want your students to grow and develop; *outcome statements* refer to what you want students to know, understand, and be able to do during a given time. As you try to visualize your students accomplishing these goals and outcomes, it is useful to envision a sequence of events that will lead to successful accomplishment of the goal. Teachers often find it useful to write down these steps as a series of objectives that work together to accomplish the goal or outcome. Reflective teachers rarely plan a lesson in isolation. Rather, they consider each lesson in relation to what students already know as well as what they hope students will be able to do later. This big-picture thinking characterizes reflective teachers, who realize that larger goals guide the selection of smaller daily tasks.

EDUCATIONAL OBJECTIVES

Educational objectives are short-term, specific descriptions of what teachers are expected to teach and/or what students are expected to learn. As described in the *Taxonomy of Educational Objectives* (Bloom, Engelhart, Furst, Hill, & Krathwohl, 1956), educational objectives are intended to be used as an organizational framework for selecting and sequencing learning experiences. Embedded in any large goal (such as teaching children to read) are hundreds of possible specific objectives. One teacher may have an objective of teaching students how to decode an unfamiliar word using phonics and another objective of teaching students how to decode an unfamiliar word using context clues. Another teacher may select and emphasize the objectives of decoding unfamiliar words by using syllabification or linguistic patterns to meet the same overall goal.

Objectives are also used to describe the *sequence of learning events* a teacher thinks will help students achieve a given outcome. Objectives also allow teachers to assess and chart group or individual progress. Teachers can ascertain students' needs more accurately if they have established a guideline of normal progress with which to compare each student's achievement.

Teachers who prefer to be specific about their lesson planning choose to write *behavioral objectives*. These include (a) the conditions under which the learning will take place, (b) the action or behavior that will provide evidence of the learning, and (c) the criteria for success (how well a task must be completed or how often the behavior will occur). For example, a behavioral objective could be written as follows:

After practice-writing the spelling words five times each, the student will write the words when dictated by the teacher, spelling 18 of the 20 words correctly.

This statement includes a description of the *conditions for learning* (after practice-writing the spelling words five times each), *the behavior* (write the words when dictated by the teacher), and the *criterion for success* (spelling 18 of 20 words correctly).

Behavioral objectives can have a positive effect on teaching effectiveness; teachers who use them become better organized and more efficient in teaching and in measuring the growth of students' basic skills. When following a planned sequence of behavioral objectives, the teacher knows what to do and how to judge student success. This system of planning also allows the teacher to better explain to students exactly what is expected of them and how to succeed.

As with any educational practice, however, there are positive and negative aspects to planning this way. Critics of behavioral objectives believe that when curriculum planning is reduced to rigid behavioral prescriptions, much of what is important to teaching and learning can be overlooked or lost. Thus, reflective teachers use behavioral objectives in their lesson planning for those learning events and activities which warrant them and rely on other less rigid objectives when appropriate.

As an alternative form for learning that cannot be predicted and calibrated, Eisner (1985) suggests the *problem-solving objective*:

> In a problem-solving objective, students are given a problem to solve—say, to find out how deterrents to smoking might be made more effective, how to design a paper structure that will hold two bricks 16 inches above a table, or how the variety and quality of the food served in the cafeteria could be increased within the existing budget. In each of these examples, the problem is posed and the criteria necessary to resolve the problem are clear. But the forms of its solution are virtually infinite. (pp. 117–118)

Eisner points out that behavioral objectives have "both the form and the content defined in advance. There is, after all, only one way to spell *aardvark*" (p. 119). The teacher using behavioral objectives is successful if all the children display the identical behavior at the end of the instructional period. "This is not the case with problem-solving objectives. The solutions individual students or groups of students reach may be just as much a surprise for the teacher as they are for the students who created them" (p. 119).

As an example, a problem-solving objective might be written:

When given a battery, a light bulb, and a piece of copper wire, the student will figure out how to make the bulb light.

This objective describes the conditions and the problem that is to be solved, but does not specify the actual behaviors the student is to use. The criterion for success is straightforward but is not quantifiable, and in fact, some of the most important results of this experience are only implied. The teacher's primary aim is to cause the student to experiment, hypothesize, and test methods of solving the problem. This cannot be quantified and reported as a percentage. Problem-solving objectives, then, are appropriate when teachers are planning learning events that allow and encourage students to think, make decisions, and create solutions. For that reason they are frequently employed when teachers plan lessons that are designed to develop critical, creative thinking. They are especially valuable when teachers are planning learning events at the higher levels of Bloom's Taxonomy (1956).

BLOOM'S TAXONOMY

Many teachers use Bloom's *Taxonomy of Educational Objectives* (1956) as the basis for organizing instructional objectives into coherent, connected learning experiences. The term *Bloom's taxonomy* (as commonly used by teachers) refers to the six levels of the cognitive domain described here. Any curriculum project such as a yearlong plan, a unit, or a lesson plan can be enriched by the conscious planning of learning events at all six levels of the taxonomy:

Higher-level objectives
Level 6:   evaluation

Level 5:   synthesis

Level 4:   analysis

Level 3:   application

Lower-level objectives
Level 2:   comprehension

Level 1:   knowledge

Knowledge-level objectives can be planned to ensure that students have a knowledge base of facts, concepts, and other important data on any topic or subject. *Comprehension-level* objectives cause students to clarify and articulate the main idea of what they are learning. Behavioral objectives are useful and appropriate at the knowledge and comprehension levels.

At the *application level,* problem-solving objectives or expressive outcomes can be written that ask students to apply what they've learned to other cases or to their own lives, thereby causing them to transfer what they've learned in the classroom to other arenas. *Analysis-level* objectives and outcomes call on students to look for motives, assumptions, and relationships such as cause and effect, differences and similarities, hypotheses, and conclusions. When analysis outcomes are planned, the students are likely to be engaged in critical thinking about the subject matter. Because the *synthesis level* implies an original response, expressive outcomes are appropriate. They offer students opportunities to use creative thinking as they combine elements in new ways, plan original experiments, and create original solutions to problems. At the *evaluation level,* students engage again in critical thinking as they make judgments using internal or external criteria and evidence. For these levels, problem-solving objectives or expressive outcomes are likely to be the most appropriate planning devices.

For example, in planning a series of learning events on metric measurement, the teacher may formulate the following objectives and outcome statements:

Knowledge-level behavioral objective: When given a meter stick, students will point to the length of a meter, a decimeter, and a centimeter with no errors.

Comprehension-level behavioral objective: When asked to state a purpose or use for each of the following units of measure, the student will write a short response for meter, centimeter, liter, milliliter, gram, and kilogram, with no more than one error.

Application-level problem-solving objective: Using a unit of measure of their choice, students will measure the length and width of the classroom and compute the area.

Analysis-level problem-solving objective: Students will create a chart showing five logical uses or purposes for each measuring unit in the metric family.

Synthesis-level expressive outcome: A group of four students will hide a "treasure" on the playground and create a set of instructions using metric measures that will enable another group to locate the treasure.

Evaluation-level expressive outcome: Students will debate their preference for metric or nonmetric measurement as a standard form of measurement.

When we review the six objectives and outcomes for metric measurement, we see clearly that the first two differ from the others in that they specify exactly what students will do or write to get a correct answer. In addition, the criteria for success are not ambiguous. These two qualities are useful to ensure successful teaching and learning at the knowledge and comprehension levels. After successfully completing these first two objectives, students will have developed a knowledge base for metric measurement that they will need to do the higher-level activities. In the problem-solving objectives, students are given greater discretion in determining the methods they use and the form of their final product. In the expressive outcome statements, discretionary power is necessary if students are to be empowered to think critically and creatively to solve problems for themselves.

Although the taxonomy was originally envisioned as a hierarchy, and although it was believed that students should be introduced to a topic beginning with Level 1 and working up through Level 6, most educators have found that the objectives and learning experiences can be successfully taught in any order. For example, a teacher may introduce the topic of nutrition and health by asking students to discuss their opinions or attitudes about smoking (an evaluation-level objective). The teacher may then provide the students with knowledge-level data about the contents of tobacco smoke and work back up to the evaluation level. When students are asked their opinions again, at the end of the lesson, their judgments are likely to be stronger and better informed.

As in the example about smoking and health, it is often desirable to begin with objectives that call on students to do, think, find, question, or create something and thereby instill in them a desire to know more about the topic. Knowledge- and comprehension-level objectives can then be designed to provide the students with the facts, data, and main ideas they need to know to further apply, analyze, synthesize, and evaluate the ideas that interest them. Figure 6.1 shows a planning device offering teachers ideas for learning events that correspond to each level of the taxonomy.

Learning objectives can be planned at all levels of Bloom's Taxonomy. Behavioral objectives are best suited for knowledge and comprehension levels; problem solving and expressive objectives are best suited for application, analysis, synthesis, and evaluation levels.

Examples of Objectives	Appropriate Action Verbs
Knowledge Level	**Knowledge Level**
Can recognize and recall specific terms, facts, and symbols	Find, locate, identify, list, recite, memorize, recognize, name, repeat, point to, match, pick, choose, state, select, record, spell, say, show, circle, underline.
Comprehension Level	**Comprehension Level**
Can understand the main idea of material heard, viewed, or read. Is able to interpret or summarize the ideas in their own words.	Explain, define, translate, relate, demonstrate, calculate, discuss, express in own words, write, review, report, paraphrase, summarize.
Application Level	**Application Level**
Is able to apply an abstract idea in a concrete situation, to solve a problem or relate it to prior experiences.	Change, adapt, employ, use, make, construct, demonstrate, compute, calculate, illustrate, modify, prepare, put into action, solve, do.
Analysis Level	**Analysis Level**
Can break down a concept or idea into its constituent parts. Is able to identify relationships among elements, cause and effect, similarities and differences.	Classify, distinguish, categorize, deduce, dissect, examine, compare, contrast, divide, catalog, inventory, question, outline, chart, survey.
Synthesis Level	**Synthesis Level**
Is able to put together elements in new and original ways. Creates patterns or structures that were not there before.	Combine, create, develop, design, construct, build, arrange, assemble, collect, concoct, connect, devise, hypothesize, invent, imagine, plan, generate, revise, organize, produce.
Evaluation Level	**Evaluation Level**
Makes informed judgments about the value of ideas or materials. Uses standards and criteria to support opinions and views.	Appraise, critique, consider, decide, judge, editorialize, give opinion, grade, rank, prioritize, value.

Figure 6.1 Curriculum planning using Bloom's Taxonomy

Note: From *Taxonomy of Educational Objectives: The Classification of Educational Goals: Handbook I: Cognitive Domain*, by B. S. Bloom et al., 1956, New York: Longman. Copyright 1956 by Longman. Reprinted by permission.

Planning Lessons for Active Learning

Teachers can use their reflective actions to ensure a high-quality learning experience for their students. They begin by using withitness when they write the first draft of their lesson plan. Reflective teachers try to picture in their minds what a lesson will look like in real life. They try to anticipate what their students need, what they can do easily, and where they will need the most guidance and positive feedback.

Reflective teachers recognize that students are more motivated to learn when they understand why this learning is important. For this reason, they explain the reason for each lesson. When describing your objectives, use words and examples that are easily understood by the students at your grade level. For example, during a science lesson, a reflective teacher might say:

We are doing this experiment today to help you see for yourselves how solids can literally disappear in a liquid. The procedures we are going to use are the same type of procedures that real scientists use when they want to discover something new about the laws of science.

After this initial explanation, students are likely to be eager to begin. They want to get on with the experiment and see for themselves what happens. They enjoy acting as scientists do during the process.

To make learning tasks even more inviting, reflective teachers know it is important to model the physical behaviors or mental processes needed to do the work. Kindergarten teachers model how to write a capital letter A. Elementary teachers demonstrate how to divide a pizza into equal fractions. Middle school teachers show students how to place their hands on the keyboard of the computer. High school teachers do a sample algebra problem on the chalkboard. After modeling, reflective teachers stay just as active a role on the sidelines, encouraging and guiding students as they begin the active process of finding out how things work.

Another role that the most effective teachers take while teaching a new skill is to model internal behaviors (such as problem solving) by thinking aloud while they model the first example for their students. By telling the students verbally what they are thinking when they work on a problem, teachers provide real-life examples of how learning occurs. Thinking aloud is particularly helpful when asking students to comprehend an unfamiliar skill or a difficult concept.

Bayles-Martin (Eby & Bayles-Martin, 2000) suggests that beginning teachers approach the lesson planning experience by thinking of these three steps:

I do (what I will do myself to model a desired action for my students)

We do (how I will set up a learning activity so my students can attempt the action with my help)

You do (what the students will do to practice the action on their own)

During each of the three modeling periods, reflective teachers carefully observe and interact with their students—learning what students already know and where they need extra help. This observation and assessment is critical to the success of any lesson, as well as to the planning and sequencing of future lessons. It also helps to think again about this three-step process when things happen during a lesson that surprise you or upset your plans.

Planning Assessments that Fit Your Objectives

How does a teacher measure success? Chapters 11 covers in detail the topic of assessing students' needs and accomplishments, with a focus on creating authentic assessment systems that describe students' progress over time. In designing lesson plans, however, it is useful to consider some options for assessing students' accomplishments on a single lesson.

Traditionally, the methods used to assess individual achievement are written or oral quizzes, tests, and essays. When elementary teachers want to determine whether the class as a whole has understood what was taught in a lesson, they frequently use oral responses to questions that usually begin with, "Who can tell me . . . ?" These are useful and efficient ways to assess student achievement at the knowledge and comprehension levels of Bloom's taxonomy, but reflective teachers are seldom satisfied with these measures alone. They seek out other methods that are less frequently used but more appropriate in evaluating learning at the higher levels.

Knowledge-level objectives are tested by determining if the student can remember or recognize accurate statements or facts. Multiple-choice and matching tests are the most frequently used measuring devices.

Comprehension-level objectives are often tested by asking students to define terms in their own words. (Only knowledge would be tested if the students were asked to write a definition from memory.) Another frequently used testing device is a question requiring a short-answer response, either oral or written, showing that the student understands the main idea. Essays that ask students to summarize or interpret are also appropriate. Multiple-choice tests are also used as a test of comprehension, but the questions call on the students to do more than recall a fact from memory; they ask students to read a selection and choose the best response from among several choices.

At the *application level,* students are usually asked to apply what was learned in a classroom to a new situation. For that reason, application-level objectives are usually assessed by presenting an unfamiliar problem that requires the student to transfer what has been learned to the unfamiliar situation. Essays in which the students describe what they would do to solve an unfamiliar problem can be used. In classrooms where students are encouraged to use manipulative materials and experiment with methods to solve problems, teachers assess the processes used by the student and the end product such as a hand-drawn or computer-generated design of a new device, a written plan for solving a problem, or a model of a new product. These products may or may not be graded, depending on the teacher's need to quantify or qualify students' success.

Analysis-level objectives may also require that the teacher present unfamiliar material and ask the student to analyze it according to some specified criteria. In these situations, students may be asked to analyze various elements, relationships, or organizational principles, such as the way in which elements are categorized, differences and similarities, cause and effect, logical conclusions, or relevant and irrelevant data.

Again, essays may be used to assess analytical behavior, but the essays must do more than tell the main idea (comprehension) and describe how the student would apply previously learned knowledge. Analytical essays must clarify relationships, compare and contrast, show cause and effect, and provide evidence for conclusions. Other student products that are appropriate for assessing analysis are time lines; charts that compare, contrast, or categorize data; and a variety of graphs that show relationships.

The types of student products that demonstrate *synthesis* are infinitely variable. Written work such as creative essays, stories, poems, plays, books, and articles are certainly appropriate for assessing language-arts objectives. Performances are just as useful, including original speeches, drama, poems, and musical compositions. Student-created products may include original plans, blueprints, artwork, computer programs, and models of proposed inventions. Student work may be collected in portfolios to demonstrate growth and achievement in a subject area.

Evaluating the relative success of synthesis products is difficult. No objective criteria may exist for judging the value or worth of a student's original product. When student products are entered in a contest or submitted for publication, outside judges with expertise in the subject area provide feedback and may even make judgments that the classroom teacher cannot make. Many elementary teachers simply record whether a finished product was turned in by the student rather than attempt to evaluate or grade it.

Evaluation-level objectives call on students to make a judgment. To test a student's ability to make a judgment, the teacher must provide all of the needed data, perhaps in the form of charts or graphs, and ask the student to draw certain conclusions from these data.

Another form of evaluation is to ask students to state their opinions on a work of art or to judge the validity of a political theory, offering evidence to support their opinions. The types of products that students create at this level are critical essays, discussions, speeches, letters to the editor, debates, drama, videotapes, and other forms that allow them to express their points of view.

Like synthesis outcomes, evaluation outcomes and objectives are difficult to grade. A teacher who offers students an opportunity to express their own views usually places high value on independent thinking and freedom of expression. Therefore, the teacher cannot grade a student response as right or wrong. But the teacher can assess whether the student has used accurate, sufficient, and appropriate criteria in defending a personal opinion. Student work that has cited inaccurate, insufficient, or inappropriate evidence should probably be returned to the student with suggestions for revision.

In summary, evaluation of student accomplishment should be directly linked to the lesson's objectives. To assess basic knowledge and skills, behavioral objectives are useful because they state exactly what the student will be able to do and specify the criteria for success. For higher-level objectives, problem-solving objectives may be less precise but still should describe the type of student behavior or product expected and give some general criteria for success.

When teachers plan by writing clear behavioral, problem-solving, and expressive objectives for their lessons, they are, in effect, clarifying their expectations regarding what students will gain from the lesson and their criteria for success. The evaluation section of a lesson plan is then usually a restatement of the criteria expressed in the objectives. You will see an example of this in the sample lesson plans in this chapter.

Predicting Possible Outcomes of Your Lesson Plans

Imagine that you have written your first lesson plan and decide to show it to some experienced teachers and ask them what they think about it. Congratulations! You are using this very important reflective action of inviting feedback. Now, you hope that the veteran teachers will read your plan and look up with huge smiles to tell you that you have done a great job.

What is more likely is that one of the teachers will begin the discussion with, "What if . . . ?" Another will say, "Have you thought about . . . ?" One might even laugh and tell a story about the 'perfect lesson plan' that turned into a disaster in the classroom. When Judy Eby was a student teacher at the University of Illinois in Urbana, Illinois, she planned just such a perfect lesson. Within a unit on animal behavior, she planned a series of lessons in which students were allowed to conduct experiments on live animals. Following her written lesson plan, she asked students to bring in small animal cages to house the animals. The students brought in leftover gerbil cages, bird cages and other small containers. On the first day of the new unit, Judy went to the university and got one white mouse per student and put the mice into the students' cages. But, the mice were smaller and more agile than expected. They quickly squeezed out of the cages and began running around the classroom. Chaos ensued. She asked the students to help catch the mice and put them all into a glass-wall aquarium. No teaching or learning took place that day.

Judy and her master teacher spent the afternoon rethinking the lesson plan without separate cages. They decided to identify individual mice by using different colors and patterns of ink dots so that students could tell their mice apart. Having done this, they went home for the night. But when they returned the next morning, the mice had disrupted the plan again. Baby mice had been born during the night and some of the adult mice were dead or wounded by attacks from their own species. The third revision of this lesson plan called for meal worms instead of mice to be used as the experimental animals.

Most veteran teachers have experienced this type of scenario more than once. Even the best plans can go wrong! Indeed, part of the nervousness many teachers feel before teaching a lesson comes from this very realization. It is hard to prepare for the unexpected!

Even when the basic lesson plan runs smoothly, it is almost a given that some students will require different experiences or explanations to understand the new concept or skill being taught. Some teachers can think on their feet and address student confusion on the spot, but this can be a challenge for a new teacher. We suggest that you consistently plan a second way of introducing or extending any given concept just in case you need it. We think you'll often be glad you did. Relational teachers are aware that students learn differently and that some may need a second strategy to achieve the lesson objective.

As we observe new teachers presenting lessons, one thing we've noticed is that discipline and management problems rarely occur when the lesson content is focused slightly above students' current knowledge base. This is probably because students feel challenged, but not overwhelmed by the experience, so they are engaged in learning and feel happy to cooperate. In contrast, problems seem to arise when a teacher prepares a lesson that covers content the students already know. They act restless and may become disruptive when they believe the teacher is babying them or talking down to them. What should you do when you arrive in a setting, materials in hand, and find out the students have already mastered the content you've planned to teach? Should you press bravely on, working your way through the lesson because it is what you worked so hard to prepare? To do so is to ignore the relational aspect of teaching. We have often seen this, and believe that the biggest reason for this choice is a simple one—the teacher has nothing else prepared.

Often teachers plan their lessons with a set of objectives for the students in their class whose knowledge and skills are at grade level. The phrase *at grade level* means the average or typical level of understanding or skill that most children are able to achieve at that age and in that grade. As teachers gain experience teaching at a grade level, they are able to describe what the typical learner at that grade level can accomplish. Because most children in the class will have skills and knowledge near the average, it makes sense for teachers to plan lessons with difficulty levels conforming to that average.

Reflective teachers realize that in any classroom, there is likely to be a wide range of student achievement and experience. There are bound to be students who have already learned and mastered the concepts being taught. Many kindergarden students come to school knowing the alphabet and how to count to 100. Some high school students could teach the teacher a thing or two about their favorite subjects. Planning for ways to extend the knowledge of these students is just as important to the success of your lesson as is planning for ways to help students who don't understand the concept right away. When you enter a classroom with a plan for extending a lesson's concepts and content, you'll feel more confident and you'll enhance the learning experiences of more of your students.

There are also likely to be students who appear to be completely bewildered during a lesson. Others give no readable cues as to whether they understand the lesson concepts. Some students may sit quietly but refuse to try the learning task you've assigned. Relational teachers accept that there are many reasons students may fail to respond in the ways we hope and plan for. For example, a student may be hungry, tired, or preoccupied with a concern (outside or inside of school) that is more compelling than this lesson. Students may doubt their ability to succeed at the task and avoid it in an attempt to save face, or believe the task is far too easy and therefore not worth the effort to complete.

If you consider reasons a student may not respond appropriately to your lesson, you can begin to write variations in your lesson plan to accommodate these students. For example, if you realize that some students may feel threatened by a particular task such as reading aloud to the entire class from their book report, you can plan an alternate task, such as allowing students to work in pairs and discuss their book reports with a peer. By having a back-up plan, you will know what to do when a student stares blankly instead of working. By visualizing and trying to predict the possible outcomes of your lesson plan, you can avoid these uncomfortable situations, maintain the flow of the lesson and involve all your students more productively.

Writing a Well-Organized Lesson Plan

When teachers plan for day-to-day learning experiences, they are creating lesson plans. Usually a lesson plan is created for a single subject or topic for one day, although some experiential, hands-on lessons may be continued for several days. Teachers in self-contained classrooms must devise several lesson plans each day—one for each subject they teach—unless they choose to use multidisciplinary units. Teachers in the upper grades who work in departmentalized settings where students travel from class to class for various subjects must still create different lesson plans for each grade or group of students they teach. High school teachers may teach several different courses during a year, with a different group of students enrolled in each course. They write distinctly different lesson plans for freshmen than they do for seniors. They must also frequently accommodate different levels of achievement within each grade level, from remedial to advanced placement courses.

In the university or college courses designed to prepare teachers, the lesson plan is an important teaching/learning device. The professor and experienced classroom teachers can provide the aspiring teacher with models of good lesson plans. Students can look on the Internet or purchase books that contain well-written lesson plans. But it is only by actively creating their own plans, that they are able to demonstrate the extent to which they understand and can apply the theories and principles they have learned about reflective thinking and planning.

For that reason, many university and college programs require students to create a number of precise and detailed lesson plans. Sometimes students observe that the classroom teachers they know do not write such extensive plans for every lesson. Instead, these teachers write their lesson plans in large weekly planning books, and a single lesson plan may consist of cryptic notations such as Math: p. 108; or Social Studies: Review Ch. 7; or Science: Continue nutrition. Although experienced teachers may record their lesson plans with such brief notes, novice teachers need to write lessons in great detail to know which resources to gather for a lesson. Writing detailed lesson plans also enables novice teachers to communicate their plans to the professor or mentor teacher, who can provide feedback on the plan before the lesson is taught.

Well-written lesson plans have additional value: They can be shared. A teacher's shorthand notes that serve as a personal reminder can rarely be interpreted by an outsider. If a substitute teacher is called to replace a classroom teacher for a day or longer, the substitute needs to see the daily plans in language he or she can understand and use. Teams of teachers often write lesson plans together or for one another. In this case, they need to have a common understanding of the lesson objectives, procedures, evaluation, and resources.

The form may vary, but most lesson plans share a number of common elements. Three essential features of a complete, well-organized lesson plan are the (a) objectives, (b) procedures, and (c) evaluation. These correspond to the four questions of curriculum planning formulated by Tyler (1949). Lesson objectives specify the "educational purposes" of the lesson. The procedures section describes both "what educational experiences can be provided" and the way they can be "effectively organized." The evaluation section describes the way the teacher has planned in advance to determine "whether these purposes are being attained" (Tyler, 1949, p. 1).

The description, another feature in a lesson plan, is used to identify it and give the reader a quick overview of its purpose or description. Also, a lesson plan often contains information about the resources teachers need as background preparation for teaching the lesson as well as any materials necessary for execution of the lesson.

A suggestion for teachers in this age of computers is to create a basic outline of a lesson plan on a word processor and save it on a disk. Then, whenever you wish to write a lesson plan, you can put the outline on the screen and fill in the spaces. You may also want to take some time to look at various lesson plans posted on the Internet. Many sites are available through commercial publishers, as well as through groups of teachers at local and state levels.

THE REFLECTIVE ACTION LESSON PLAN MODEL

Including all the ideas discussed in this chapter in one lesson plan can sound daunting, but it will become second nature to you with experience. To help you remember the important aspects of a lesson, we offer you a model of a lesson plan based on the concept of reflective action in teaching in Figure 6.2. Take some time to review it now, and see if you can explain why each part has been included. This outline can be copied on your computer disk for use in college and the rest of your teaching career.

After you have put in the title, subject, grade level, and lesson duration, you can describe what you want students to gain from this lesson. We suggest using one to three objectives for each lesson to help you maintain focus and avoid overwhelming students with too many ideas at once. Once you have established your basic objectives for the lesson, think about the students in your class who have special needs. Write notes to yourself to describe how you will scaffold the lesson for students who don't understand or who are learning to speak English. Write notes about enriching the lesson for students who have mastered the concept you are teaching and need a more challenging curriculum. By listing the materials you need ahead of time, you avoid getting part way through the lesson and missing something you need.

The procedures that teachers use for teaching a lesson vary, but we suggest that you think of the your procedures using the I, WE, YOU strategy. Each step of the procedures in our model may help you think through what you will do to prepare for and teach the lesson. The pre-assessment step refers to the process of finding out what your students already know before teaching a new lesson. Reflective teachers use this strategy to avoid behavior problems from bored students as well as from those who do not have a clue what you are talking about. This strategy also helps you to build the background for the day's lesson. For example, to pre-assess students' knowledge of metric measurement, you might want to show a meter stick to your students and ask if they know what it is and what it is used for.

After you have written a draft of your lesson plan, imagine yourself teaching it and consider the outcomes that may result. Think through what you will do if students don't understand or appear to be bored. What can you predict about the reaction of students in your classroom who are learning English? What will they need from you and their classmates to be successful in this lesson? You can see that the outcome prediction is a vital aspect of withitness and reflective action in teaching.

Title of Lesson:

Subject Area:

Grade Level: **Lesson Duration:**

Description: (What will students experience during this lesson?)

Materials and Resources: (What do you need to teach this lesson? What do students need in order to participate?)

Objectives: (What will students be able to do at the conclusion of this lesson?)

　　1.

　　2.

　　3.

Varying Objectives for Individual Needs
How will I vary these objectives for students who
　　a) Don't understand?

　　b) Have already mastered the concept?

　　c) Are presently learning English?

Figure 6.2　Reflective action lesson plan model

(continued)

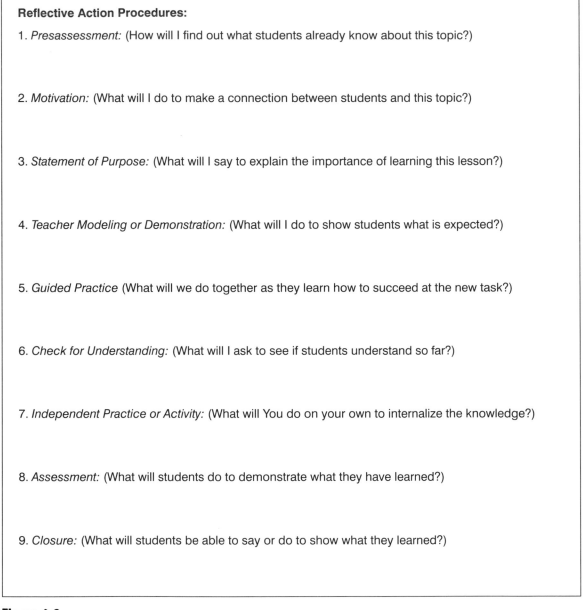

Reflective Action Procedures:

1. *Presassessment:* (How will I find out what students already know about this topic?)

2. *Motivation:* (What will I do to make a connection between students and this topic?)

3. *Statement of Purpose:* (What will I say to explain the importance of learning this lesson?)

4. *Teacher Modeling or Demonstration:* (What will I do to show students what is expected?)

5. *Guided Practice* (What will we do together as they learn how to succeed at the new task?)

6. *Check for Understanding:* (What will I ask to see if students understand so far?)

7. *Independent Practice or Activity:* (What will You do on your own to internalize the knowledge?)

8. *Assessment:* (What will students do to demonstrate what they have learned?)

9. *Closure:* (What will students be able to say or do to show what they learned?)

Figure 6.2

Sequencing Objectives in School Subjects

SEQUENCING OBJECTIVES IN MATHEMATICS

Some subjects are sequential in nature. Mathematics is the best example in the elementary curriculum because its concepts and operations can be readily ordered from simple to complex. Teachers easily can organize the teaching of computational skills in the basic operations of addition, subtraction, multiplication, and division. For example, Outcome Statement 1 describes a possible sequence for teaching an essential understanding about the concept of numbers:

> *Mathematics Outcome Statement 1:* Primary students will be able to show how addition and subtraction are related to one another.

To accomplish this outcome, primary teachers will introduce the students to the concept of numbers and give them concrete, manipulative experiences in adding and subtracting one-digit numbers. Students may act out stories in which children are added and subtracted from a group. They may make up stories about animals or objects that are taken away and then brought back to demonstrate subtraction and addition.

Math textbooks offer a sequence of learning activities and practice of math facts, but reflective teachers find that the math textbook must be used flexibly and supplemented with other learning experiences. Before planning math lessons for a particular group of students, the teacher must pretest their entry level knowledge and skills. Pretests will reveal that some children have already mastered some of the skills in the sequence and do not need to spend valuable time redoing what they already know. They need enriched math activities to allow them to progress. Other children may not have the conceptual understanding of number relationships to succeed on the first step. For them, preliminary concrete experiences with manipulative materials are essential for success.

SAMPLE MATH OBJECTIVES TO FIT OUTCOME STATEMENT 1

Students will be able to

1. Use blocks to show addition of two single-digit integers.
2. Use blocks to show subtraction of two single-digit integers.
3. Use pennies and dimes to show place value of 1s and 10s.
4. Subtract pennies without regrouping.
5. Add pennies and exchange 10 pennies for a dime.
6. Subtract pennies by making change for a dime to show regrouping.
7. Tell how subtraction is related to addition using coins as an example.

These sample objectives are representative of the basic knowledge- and comprehension-level skills needed to accomplish the outcome statement. They can be written in the behavioral objective form, specifying what percentage of correct answers must be attained to demonstrate mastery.

These objectives emphasize basic computational skills that all students need to learn. However, in keeping with the National Council of Teachers of Mathematics' recommendations to emphasize problem solving over computation, reflective teachers are likely to plan lessons that allow students to explore the relationships between addition and subtraction. They are also likely to include many additional math outcomes and objectives at the higher levels of Bloom's taxonomy (1956) to teach students how to apply the math facts and computation skills they are learning to actual problem-solving situations. However, this example does illustrate the importance of matching objectives to outcome statements in a logical sequence. Each of the objectives builds on the one before it. As students master each objective, they are continually progressing toward mastering the outcome statement.

SEQUENCING OBJECTIVES IN LANGUAGE ARTS

Not all subjects in the elementary curriculum are as sequential as mathematics. Language arts consists of knowledge, skills, and abilities that develop children's understanding and use of language. Reading, writing, speaking, and listening are all part of the language-arts curriculum, and each one can and should have its own outcome statement(s). Outcome Statement 2 suggests one illustration of how the language arts curriculum is designed:

> *Language-Arts Outcome Statement 2:*   Students will be able to write standard English with correct spelling, accurate grammar, and well-organized meaning and form.

Again, this outcome statement will take years to accomplish, but teachers at every grade level are responsible for providing learning experiences that build toward the ultimate goal. The objectives to reach this goal may be similar each year for several years but written in increasing levels of difficulty. This is known as a *spiral curriculum.*

SAMPLE LANGUAGE-ARTS OBJECTIVES TO FIT OUTCOME STATEMENT 2

By the end of grade 2, students will be able to

1. Write a sentence containing a subject and a verb
2. Use a capital letter at the beginning of a sentence
3. Use a period or question mark at the end of a sentence
4. Review and edit sentences for complete meaning

By the end of grade 4, students will be able to

1. Write a paragraph that focuses on one central idea.
2. Spell common words correctly in writing samples.

3. Use capitalization and sentence-end punctuation correctly.
4. Review and edit a paragraph to improve the organization of ideas.

By the end of grade 6, students will be able to

1. Write several paragraphs that explain one concept or theme.
2. Use a dictionary to spell all words in a paper correctly.
3. Use correct punctuation, including end marks, comma, apostrophe, quotation marks, and colon.
4. Review and edit papers to correct spelling, punctuation, grammar, and organization of ideas.

By the end of grade 8, students will be able to

1. Write papers with introductory paragraph, logical reasons, data to support the main idea, and a closing statement.
2. Use a dictionary to spell all words in a paper correctly; use a thesaurus to add to vocabulary of the paper.
3. Eliminate fragments and run-on sentences.
4. Review and edit papers to correct spelling, punctuation, grammar, organization of ideas, and appropriateness for the purpose.

By the end of grade 12, students will be able to

1. Write compositions using descriptive language that clarifies and enhances the ideas expressed in the paper.
2. Write compositions that have no significant errors in the proper use of punctuation, grammar, and spelling.
3. Write compositions that synthesize and cite a variety of resources used for information gathering.
4. Write compositions that exhibit a clear personal style and voice.

When teachers have curriculum guidelines such as these, they must still translate the outcome statements and objectives into actual learning experiences that are appropriate and motivating for their students. To pretest how well your students can use written language when they enter your classroom, plan a writing experience in the first week. Analyzing these writing samples will allow you to plan suitably challenging activities for your students. In this example, the second-grade teacher must decide what topics to have students write about and when to limit students to copying teacher-made examples or allow them to begin to write their own sentences. The fourth-grade teacher knows that students will not learn all of these skills in just one writing lesson. It is necessary to provide many interesting classroom experiences so that students will have ideas to express in their writing. The sixth-grade teacher has to plan a series of research and writing experiences so that students will have ample opportunities to synthesize all of the skills required at that grade level.

Curriculum planning of subjects such as language arts is a complex undertaking because it contains so many varied outcomes and objectives. The previous example illustrates only a single outcome for teaching students how to write. Teachers must also plan outcome statements and objectives for reading, listening, and speaking.

SEQUENCING OBJECTIVES IN SCIENCE

As discussed in Chapter 4, the science curriculum should inform students of the basic facts and concepts of science topics but should also allow students opportunities to experience how scientists work. These dual goals of the science curriculum are often expressed as *teaching both content and process.* Here is an example of an outcome statement in science that covers both content and process:

> *Science Outcome Statement 3:*   Students will demonstrate how sound is produced and transmitted.

The following learning objectives show a sequence of learning experiences that allow students to discover some important properties of waves:

SAMPLE SCIENCE OBJECTIVES TO FIT OUTCOME STATEMENT 3

By the end of the unit on sound production, students will

1. Investigate sound production using Slinkies.
2. Investigate waves using water in plastic containers.
3. Write observations, analysis, and hypothesis of how waves behave.
4. Investigate waves using films of waves in slow motion and computer simulations of waves to discover whether their hypotheses are accurate.
5. Discuss observations and theories of sound production as a class with an emphasis on students' articulating their own ideas.
6. Identify key features of waves, define wave terminology, and derive the wave equations through a kinesthetic learning experience. (Under the direction of the teacher, students line up in the hall and simulate the motion of a Slinky. Wave terminology is introduced by the teacher during the experience.)

This set of learning experiences, designed by Jim Hicks and his colleague Chris Chiaverina, begins with hands-on investigations allowing students to observe the sound production. They are involved in the process of science during these learning experiences because they are behaving like scientists investigating unknown phenomena. Content (wave properties and terminology) is introduced by the teachers after students are immersed in the process. Because of its emphasis on exploration, discovery, and communication of findings, the sequence of lessons in science is rarely linear but more often circular or even a figure-eight pattern.

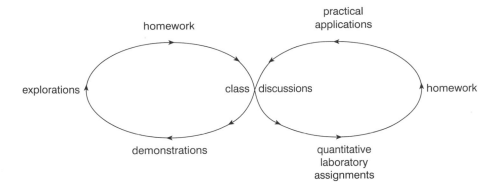

Figure 6.3 Planning sequence for science lessons
Note: Jim Hicks and Chris Chiaverina

Chiaverina and Hicks find that, rather than lecture about scientific phenomena, they first must use a smorgasbord of concrete experiences in which students interact with the scientific materials and literally begin to see the world in a new and more scientifically principled way. The concrete experiences are followed by class discussions that allow time to deal with the students' initial misconceptions about the phenomenon they are exploring. The discussions are very important as students describe their experiences and begin to construct new schemata to fit what they've observed. Hicks and Chiaverina organize a series of lessons to include qualitative demonstrations and explorations followed by homework. The next day, there are discussions to get rid of prior misconceptions and build new scientific schemata. During quantitative laboratory experiences, Chiaverina and Hicks rarely give formulas. Instead, they present open-ended challenges that cause students to translate what they've learned into mathematical language. Following the quantitative labs, they spend time on discussion of practical applications of what they have learned in the unit. Figure 6.3 shows the figure-eight sequence of events that Hicks and Chiaverina have developed for the science courses they teach.

SEQUENCING OBJECTIVES IN SOCIAL STUDIES

Reflective elementary teachers can also see the need for both content and process in their social studies curriculum. They attempt to help their students build a knowledge base in history and geography, but they also give attention and time to teaching students how to acquire information on their own.

Here is an example of an outcome statement in social studies that covers both content and process:

> *Social Studies Outcome Statement 4:*   Students will be able to use a map and a globe to find place names and locations. They will then create a chart listing the countries, major cities, rivers, and mountain ranges in each continent.

SAMPLE SOCIAL STUDIES OBJECTIVES TO MEET OUTCOME STATEMENT 4

At the end of the map and globe unit, students will be able to

1. Identify the seven continents on a world map and a globe.
2. Interpret the country boundaries with a map legend.
3. List the countries in each continent.
4. Interpret the symbol for rivers on the map legend.
5. List the major rivers in each continent.
6. Interpret the symbol for mountain ranges on the map legend.
7. List the mountain ranges in each continent.
8. Create a chart showing the countries, cities, rivers, and mountain ranges in each continent.

In this example, the teacher has planned a set of learning activities that will add to the students' knowledge base about world geography. This set of activities also equips the student with the tools to find and interpret information on maps and globes. This social studies curriculum demonstrates that by employing hands-on learning experiences, students are able to learn both content and processes simultaneously and that they are active rather than passive learners throughout the entire set of activities. An oral or written pretest might consist of having students name or point to certain geographical locations and read and interpret a map legend. The information from the pretest is valuable in planning lessons that use students' existing knowledge and add to it.

SEQUENCING OBJECTIVES IN INTERDISCIPLINARY UNITS

Whenever possible, many teachers enjoy enriching their curriculum units with fine-arts experiences. Primary children are often asked to illustrate math examples by drawing one pumpkin plus two pumpkins or to create 10 different pictures using a rectangle. Songs and rhymes frequently accompany learning about historical events and people. Many such events are dramatized as well. Stories and films are often used to augment many aspects of the curriculum.

In later years, emphasis on the fine arts may decline except in special art and music classes or on special occasions and holidays. This is due, in part, to the crowded curriculum that teachers are required to deliver. Given the prevailing culture of the late 20th century, the fine arts often take a back seat to academic and social subjects. But each teacher must consider the place of fine arts in the curriculum. Reflective teachers are likely to consider the importance of the arts in enhancing the joy of living and to make them an integral part of every learning experience. This has the effect of increasing children's active involvement, creative thinking, and inventiveness.

Here is an example of an outcome statement that includes fine arts with an academic subject:

> *Fine Arts/Social Studies Outcome Statement 5:*   Students will be able to distinguish the important contributions made by various world cultures in sports, art, music, literature, and drama.

SAMPLE OBJECTIVES TO MEET OUTCOME STATEMENT 5

Each learning team of students will be able to

1. Select one country of the world to study.
2. Locate at least three sources of information about that country.
3. Draw a map of the country's geographical boundaries and features.
4. Describe the country's contributions to sports.
5. Play or sing an example of the country's music.
6. Draw examples of the country's art and architecture treasures.
7. Read aloud a story or a poem from that country.
8. Work with other learning teams to create a dramatic event featuring the stories, poems, art, and music of all the countries.

This ambitious set of learning experiences demonstrates how well the fine arts can be incorporated into an academic subject. Cognitively, children who take part in this series of experiences will learn a knowledge base of facts, ideas, and concepts about the world. They will also gain understanding and use of such processes as communication and problem-solving skills. Affectively, they will learn to appreciate and understand differences and similarities among people by sharing the cultural arts of each country.

Sample Lesson Plans

PRIMARY INTERDISCIPLINARY LESSON PLAN

Conchita Encinas teaches in a bilingual first-grade classroom in Chula Vista, California. To encourage her students to interact and use oral language in small groups, she plans many of her lessons using learning centers. For each topic, she designs four activities that students can do independently or in a small group. For example, her spring curriculum includes a unit on plants and growing things. For the lesson on plants and seeds she designs four learning center activities.

She begins the lesson with all the children sitting in a circle, where she provides students with general information in both Spanish and English about plants and seeds. She encourages her students to learn and use new English words related to the topic being studied. Then she introduces the four activities they will be able to explore in the centers. She divides the class into four groups and each group travels from one center to another at 20-minute intervals. At the end of the morning, the students gather in a circle again to share what they have done and learned about seeds and plants. Ms. Encinas reads aloud the stories the children have written at the first center. Her lesson plan for the exploration of seeds and plants is presented in Box 6.1.

SAMPLE LESSON PLAN IN MATHEMATICS

Students like to explore their own world. A large portion of time in the middle school student's world is devoted to watching television. Box 6.2 shows a lesson plan from Pam Knight's unit on television-viewing habits (see Chapter 5). On the surface, this appears

Box 6.1 Primary Bilingual Lesson Plan on Seeds and Plants
A HANDS-ON SCIENCE LESSON DESIGNED FOR LEARNING CENTERS

by Conchita Encinas, First-Grade Bilingual Class, Chula Vista, California

Title of Lesson: Seeds and Plants

Description: Students will explore how seeds grow into plants.

Grade Level: Kindergarten

Lesson Duration: Time for a four center rotation

Materials and Resources: Fruits, vegetables, knife, paper, pencils, posterboard, crayons, rye seeds, paper cups, soil, water.

Objectives of this lesson:

1. Students will observe that seeds are different sizes, shapes, and colors.
2. Students will be able to identify various fruits and vegetables and describe how seeds grow into plants. By doing so, they will increase their English vocabulary and oral speaking and listening skills
3. Students will compare and make graphs to show the variation in number and type of seeds among several different types of plants

Varying Objectives for students who

a) Don't understand?

I will pair them with other students who are likely to understand. The teacher's aide and I will talk with them during the activities.

b) Have already mastered the concept?

They can read or look at books about seeds and plants. They can make graphs on the number of seeds in a plant.

c) Are presently learning English?

I will pair them with other students who are likely to understand. The teacher's aide and I will talk with them during the activities, focussing on vocabulary and oral expression.

Procedures

1. *Preassessment:* Begin in a circle. Review concepts students have already learned about plants. Have students give a thumbs-up signal if they agree, a thumbs-down signal if they disagree with statements such as "Flowers are plants. Plants need water to grow. Plants need milk to grow."

2. *Motivation:* Open up a papaya or cantaloupe and show students the seeds. Tell students that with the seeds for one piece of fruit, it is possible to grow a new piece of fruit for everyone in the room. Discuss how this helps people grow food for everyone in the world.

3. *Statement of Purpose:* Tell students that today they will get to be scientists and investigate how many seeds are in different fruits and vegetables.

4. *Modeling/Demonstration:* Teach children the English words for plants, seeds, garden, grow, and food.

5. *Guided Practice:* Have children repeat these words in the circle and use them while working in the centers.

6. *Check for Understanding:* Ask students to define the vocabulary seeds again. Then, review with the whole group directions for the activities at the four centers. Divide the class into four groups. Assign a rotation schedule so that each group goes to all four centers.

7. *Indpendent Center Activities:*

   Center 1: Students cut out parts of a plant, glue them on a piece of paper, and write a story about it.

   Center 2: Students examine and count a variety of vegetable and fruit seeds, including an apple, cantaloupe, pea pod, and green pepper. They graph the number of seeds in each vegetable.

   Center 3: Students plant rye seeds in a paper cup and discuss what happens to seeds under the ground.

   Center 4: Students identify various vegetables, cut them up, and taste them. They list words about the way each vegetable tastes.

8. *Assessment:* Story boards and stories from Center 1 are read aloud at the closing circle. Graphs from Center 2 are displayed on the bulletin board. Seeds in cups from Center 3 are placed near a window to grow.

9. *Closure:* Students discuss the tastes of different vegetables during the closing circle.

to be a mathematics lesson. However, after analyzing the objectives and activities in it, you will see that it involves the social sciences and language arts as well.

This lesson plan requires more than one class period. One day is needed to prepare for data collection; a week is needed to collect and record the data; and a day or two are required for constructing the bar graphs and describing the findings.

Ms. Knight's lesson demonstrates how students can use mathematics in their lives. They become researchers who collect and organize data. For the data to be relevant, they must be able to analyze them and explain what they found. Finally, the students are expected to make inferences and evaluate an important factor in their lives.

SAMPLE LESSON PLAN IN SOCIAL STUDIES

David Ramert discussed the way he uses controversy in planning his U.S. history course in Chapter 4. In Box 6.3, we can see an example of a lesson that engages students in active discussions on an important, but controversial, topic from the history of the United States. This lesson plan also illustrates the way a reflective teacher designs curriculum so that students know how to succeed, then scaffolds the lessons so that students have many opportunities to get the information they need from readings as well as class discussion. Note David's willingness to adapt the lesson plan to meet the needs of learners who are not fluent in English.

SAMPLE LESSON PLAN IN SCIENCE

The lesson plan for science shown in Box 6.4 is taken from the unit developed by Chris Chiaverina and Jim Hicks described in Chapter 5. Their plan is exciting because they are constantly trying to find ways to make science interesting, practical, and fun. In their words, "if there isn't a common understanding of the application of a concept in science, then it isn't worth teaching." As you read their lesson plan, remember that the philosophy of their approach to science is to use a smorgasbord of examples and demonstrations as well as a hands-on approach by their students. Their lessons clearly meet the expectations of the new science frameworks that require teachers to take an active and exploratory approach to the learning of science.

Conclusions

Lesson plans are scripts that teachers write so that they can present a well-organized set of learning experiences for their students. The objectives of the lesson specify the teacher's expectations for what the students will learn or be able to do as a result of the lesson. When teachers plan objectives that specify the criteria for success, they are clarifying for themselves what the students must be able to do to demonstrate mastery of the skill or understanding of the lesson's concepts.

To plan the procedures of a lesson in advance, many reflective teachers visualize themselves teaching the lesson. They write what they must do to teach the lesson

Box 6.2 Mathematics Lesson Plan

by Pam Knight, Twin Peaks Middle School, Poway, California

Title of lesson: Television-Viewing Habits of Students

Subject area: Mathematics/social sciences

Grade level: Middle school

Description: Students will keep records of the amount of television they watch and present this information using graphs.

Objectives of this lesson:

1. *Application level:*   Students will construct bar graphs using data collected on television-viewing habits.

2. *Analysis level:*   Students will interpret and make inferences based on the analysis of the data gathered by writing a statement that describes the data on the graph.

3. *Evaluation level:*   Students will evaluate their television-viewing habits and the television-viewing habits of the class as a whole.

Varying Objectives for Individual Needs

How will I vary these objectives for students who

   a) Don't understand?
      Provide samples of graphs for students to use as models

   b) Have already mastered the concept?
      Students may design additional research questions about television viewing habits

   c) Are learning English?
      Allow them to work with an English speaking partner on this project. Take time to talk one to one with them about their projects at all stages.

Materials Needed:

Graph paper, rulers, and pencils

continued

Procedures

1. *Motivation:* The lesson begins with a discussion of the observations students have made about their own television-viewing habits. This is an open-ended discussion, and students may talk about types of shows seen (MTV, movies, sports contests, etc.). Ask students: "Do students watch too much television and play too many video games? How much TV do students really watch? Are there methods by which students can gather data on their television-viewing habits?"

2. *Statement of purpose:* We will learn how to gather information and data to make informed decisions about important matters in our lives.

3. *Teacher modeling and demonstration:* Teacher models data collection by surveying students on their favorite TV show. Teacher tallies these data and, with class participation, creates a bar graph of the data at the chalkboard.

4. *Guided practice:* Students duplicate the teacher's tally and bar graph at their desks.

5. *Check for understanding:* Ask questions to determine whether the students know the processes of recording data and constructing a bar graph.

6. *Independent study/activity:* Students gather data on their television-viewing habits for one week.

7. *Check for Understanding:* At the end of the week, students choose ways to display their data using bar graphs. Examples of displaying the data could be the amount of television boys watched compared with the amount girls watched, the amount of television watched on different days of the week, or the types of programs watched. In groups of three, students construct the graph and identify an inference they could make based on their graph. They share their graph and inference and display them on a bulletin board.

8. *Assessment:* Students write in their journals about the activity completed. Students graphs are examined to see if the data have been correctly graphed. The inferences made by students are checked against the constructed bar graphs. The graphs become part of the students' mathematics and social studies portfolios.

9. *Closure:* Students discuss what they have learned about their television-viewing habits. They discuss what the results mean to them. For example, do they think they watch too much television? Do they watch more or less television than they expected? Is the bar graph an effective way to display the data they gathered?

Box 6.3 David Ramert's Lesson Plan

Jacksonian Democracy Unit, Francis Parker Upper School, San Diego, California

Title of Lesson: The Legacy of Andrew Jackson (A review of the unit)

Subject Area: U.S. History

Grade Level: Junior in H.S.

Lesson Duration: 45 minutes

Description: (What will students experience during this lesson?)
Students will be bombarded by comments and statements contributed by everybody in the room about the Jacksonian era. Students will take notes for their essays, hoping they will be able to collect their ideas for the essays they will write the next day.

Materials and Resources: (What do you need to teach this lesson? What do students need in order to participate?) Chalkboard, chalk, ideas, brains engaged, notepaper and pens.

Objectives

(What will students be able to do at the conclusion of this lesson?)

1. Students will use correct vocabulary from the era.

2. Students will contribute ideas (hopefully original) in answer to controversial questions.

3. Students will be able to articulate that Jackson initiated a change in the movement from a republic to a democracy.

Varying Objectives for Individual Needs

How will I vary these objectives for students who

a) Don't understand?
   I walk around during the period to observe students as they write. Those who don't seem to be contributing or writing during class will be invited to an extra tutoring session. As independent school teachers, we are willing to meet with students even on weekends if it is necessary to make certain a student succeeds.

continued

b) Have already mastered the concept?

Occassionally, I have them teach part of a lesson. They prepare a presentation for the class on an area of strength or interest.

c) Are presently learning English?

I tutor them and make arrangements for them to write the essays at home so that they can use their notes, dictionaries, and textbook in their own time. I also allow them to revise and rewrite their essays before they are evaluated.

Reflective Action Procedures:

1. *Presassessment:* (How will I find out what students already know about this topic?) This lesson serves as a preassesment for the essay evaluation for the course.

2. *Motivation:* (What will I do to make a connection between students and this topic?) I ask, "How can this man be the champion of the common man and destroy the lives of thousands of Indians at the same time? Is it possible to be both these things? Do we find these same types of controversy present in every major figure in the history books?"

3. *Statement of Purpose:* (What will I say to explain the importance of learning this lesson?) Today we're going to work together to gather all of the information we need to write our essays separately tomorrow.

4. *Teacher Modeling or Demonstration:* (What will I do to show students what is expected?)

I write two columns on the chalkboard: **Curse or Blessing.** (20 minutes)

I write: (20 minutes)

In what ways did Jacksonians view themselves as Guardians of:

The Constitution Individual Liberty Human Rights Equality

We discuss: **How valid was their view?**

5. *Guided Practice* (What will we do together as they learn how to succeed at the new task?)

I ask the class to brainstorm examples of how Jackson was bad for the country and how he was good for the country. I write their responses in no order of importance.

6. Check for Understanding: (What will I ask to see if students understand so far?)

If a student offers an incorrect response or uses incorrect vocabulary, I probe and question. I may write it so that everyone can see it, but I ask, "Are you sure about this?"

7. *Independent Practice or Activity:* (What will You do on your own to internalize the knowledge?) On the following class day, the students write their own essays on one of the two controversial questions posed in this unit. They must write in ink on lined paper in class for a class period. (see option above for English Language Learners).

8. *Assessment:* (What will students do to demonstrate what they have learned?)

   Essays will be written the next class day. See Unit Plan in Chapter 5 for essay criteria and grading system

9. *Closure:* (What will I say to sum up the unit?)

   Despite all of his enigmas and contradictions, Jackson moved the country one step closer to democracy at a time when democracy was not really popular or "cool," in the rest of the world. Remember, You're going to have to argue both sides of this issue.

successfully and what the students must do to learn the material. Teachers who can visualize the entire process of teaching and learning can write richly detailed lesson plans. When they begin to teach the lesson, they have a supportive script to follow.

As teachers become more proficient and experienced at planning and teaching, their written lesson plans are likely to become less detailed. But for beginning teachers, a thorough, richly detailed plan is an essential element for a successful lesson.

⊃ Reflective Actions for Your Professional Portfolio
THREE SAMPLE LESSON PLANS

Write three sample lesson plans to fit the unit topic you planned in Chapter 5. Include them in your professional portfolio to demonstrate evidence of your curriculum planning abilities.

Withitness: Examine Other Lesson Plans

Ask an experienced teacher to show you his or her lesson plans. Look up lesson plan examples on the World Wide Web. How do these plans differ from the ones in this chapter? Observe a lesson in action and try to perceive the teacher's objectives, procedures, and assessment strategies.

Box 6.4 Sample High School Science Lesson Plan

by Chris Chiaverina and Jim Hicks

Title of the lesson: Sound Production

Subject area: Science

Grade level: High school physics

Lesson Duration?   1-2 class periods

Description: Using a variety of items that vibrate and produce sounds, students investigate sound production.

Objectives

1. *Comprehension:*   Students will become aware of their naïve ideas about sound and be able to describe how sound is produced.
2. *Application:*   Students will make their own source of sound through a device called the hummer.
3. *Knowledge:*   Students will develop their science vocabulary by being able to define and use acoustical terminology appropriately.

Varying Objectives for Individual Needs

How will I vary these objectives for students who

a) Don't understand? Have students review previous laboratory work and movie on waves. Students can explore waves with a pool of water to observe how agitation of a medium generates disturbances.

b) Have already mastered the concept? After building their hummer, students can design a guitar-like apparatus and explain the purpose of changing the tension of a vibrating wire or rubber band.

c) Are learning English? Allow for group work or peer tutoring. Students can explore the wave pool. Students can explore a working model of a hummer.

Materials Needed

Tuning fork, guitar, carpet tubing, music box, 78 RPM record, needle, pencil, "talking strip," Fisher burner, aluminum rod, resin, "sound wagon" toy, rubber bands, file cards, tongue depressors, string

Procedures

1. *Preassessment and connection with previous learning:* Students have done laboratory work, seen demonstrations, and watched a movie on waves. They have also done labs using Slinkies and a ripple tank. After students have observed the demonstration of sounds in the motivation activity, they are asked to relate their observations to the concepts learned in the previous lessons on sound production, including reflection and transmission. They are also asked to relate this to the terminology of wave speed and amplitude.

2. *Motivation:* The teacher demonstrates a variety of common vibrating systems that produce audible sounds. For example, strike a tuning fork and have the students observe if there is a noticeable visible vibration on the fork. Strike the tuning fork and place it in a glass of water and observe what happens. The water will be stirred. The teacher plucks a guitar string and the students listen to the sound.

3. *Statement of purpose:* Students will learn how sound is produced by vibrations.

4. *Modeling/Demonstration:* The teacher then demonstrates some unusual sources of sound. An old record is played with a straight pin. A carpet tube is placed over a Fisher burner, which makes a sound like a fog horn. A talking plastic strip is pulled across a fingernail and delivers a message. An aluminum rod is stroked with rosin and produces a high-pitched tone.

5. *Guided practice:* Students are assigned problems on the sources and transmission of sound. These problems relate to the earlier examples as well as the hummer.5.

6. *Check for Understanding:* Teacher interacts with students while they work on assigned problems.

7. *Independent Activity:* Students produce their own hummer. (a) A rubber band is stretched around a tongue depressor and acts as a vibrating object. (b) A file card is stapled to the tongue depressor and used to amplify the vibrations. (c) A string is attached to an end of the device. (d) The hummer is spun around in a circle by the string, and a sound is produced.

8 *Assessment Plan:* Students create hummers and describe in their own words how the hummer produces sound, using correct acoustical terminology.

9. *Closure:* Students decipher this phrase: "Sound equals vibrations." They demonstrate their hummers.

Put Lesson into Perspective: Choose a topic

Choose a subject or topic for your three demonstration lesson plans. Write an initial description of what you want to accomplish by the end of these three lessons.

Widen Your Perspective

Picture yourself teaching these three lessons. Consider the contingencies you may encounter. What will you do if students don't understand the lessons? What will you do if they already know this material?

Do Research and Invite Feedback

Talk with experienced teachers about what they encountered when they taught the subject or topic you have chosen. Ask them to share their good and bad experiences. Ask them for ideas to use if students don't understand the subject the first time. Ask for ideas to extend your lessons to meet the needs of students who easily master the subject.

Redefine the Lesson: Sequence Your Objectives

Now write three lesson objectives for each of three lessons on your topic. You will have nine objectives in all, each one building on the basis of the previous ones.

Create an Action Plan: Write Three Lesson Plans

Write three sample lesson plans to fit the unit plan you have created. You may wish to use very different types of lessons to demonstrate your flexibility and creativity.

Predict Possible Outcomes of Your Lesson

Show your lesson plans to a knowledgeable teacher and get feedback that will help you to improve them. Make the revisions that you agree with and explain your rationale for elements that you retain. If possible, teach the lessons and then make further revisions. Describe the changes that you made as a result of teaching the lessons.

References

Bloom, B., Engelhart, M., Furst, E., Hill, W., & Krathwohl, D. (1956). *Taxonomy of educational objectives: Cognitive domain.* New York: Longman.

Eby, J., & Bayles-Martin, D. (2000). *Reflective planning, teaching and evaluation for the elementary school.* Upper Saddle River, NJ: Merrill/Prentice-Hall.

Eisner, E. (1985). *Educational imagination* (2nd ed). Upper Saddle River, NJ: Merrill/Prentice Hall.

Tyler, R. (1949). *Basic principles of curriculum and instruction.* Chicago: University of Chicago Press.

chapter 7

AUTHENTIC TEACHING AND LEARNING

Your lessons and unit plans are ready to go. You've taken the time and made the effort to create a safe, encouraging, and stimulating classroom environment. You've clarified your expectations for student behavior and involved your students in the process of creating classroom rules. You've rehearsed the procedures for entering and leaving the classroom, and you know the names of each student and something about their backgrounds and needs. Now you can begin to focus on developing instructional strategies that will promote authentic learning.

The term *authentic learning* is used to distinguish between the achievement of significant, meaningful, and useful knowledge and skills from that which is trivial and unrelated to students' lives. The Wisconsin Center on Organizing and Restructuring of Schools has concentrated on defining standards of authentic instruction. Its studies have led it to conclude that many conventional instructional methods do not allow students to use their minds well and result in learning that has little or no intrinsic meaning or value to them beyond achieving success in school.

These studies recommend establishing standards for teachers to use as guidelines in selecting and learning to use teaching strategies that promote authentic learning. According to their research, the standards for authentic instructional methods should emphasize higher-order thinking, depth of knowledge, connectedness to the world, and substantive conversation and should provide social support for student achievement (Newman & Wehlage, 1993).

As a learner, you may have had teachers who used teaching strategies that stimulated you to use your higher-level thinking and problem-solving skills. You may recall learning experiences that encouraged you to delve deeply into a subject that had real meaning in your life. You may recall class discussions that sparkled with enthusiastic exchanges of ideas and opinions within a social system that encouraged you to challenge yourself to make more and more meaningful accomplishments. If you recall school experiences such as these, you have experienced authentic learning.

Unfortunately, it is likely that you had other teachers who relied on conventional methods that required rote memorization of meaningless material. You may recall learning a lot about little and boring recitations in which students were expected to parrot what they had memorized. You may recall competitive social systems that encouraged only those students who were able to memorize and recite quickly and those who were able to figure out what the teacher wanted to hear. If you recall school experiences such as these, you will need to overcome the natural tendency to repeat learned patterns and challenge yourself to learn to use many new and exciting instructional strategies.

Your personal conception of the teaching-learning process is drawn from your own experiences as a learner, but for reflective teachers it is also drawn from the values and beliefs they hold about what students need to know and how students ought to behave and from perceptions and reflections about the theories and practices of other classroom teachers they observe. To become a reflective teacher, you must make yourself aware of the emerging research and knowledge base about teaching and learning. Gathering information from research is an important attribute of a reflective thinker and teacher.

Schema Theory

The retrieval process is obviously a critical factor in being able to use stored information. Knowledge, concepts, and skills that are learned must be stored in the brain until they are needed. According to the *schema theory*, each subset of knowledge is stored in a *schema*, an outline or organized network of knowledge about a single concept or subject. It is believed that young children develop *schemata* (the plural form of schema) made up of visual or other sensory images. As language increases, verbal imagery replaces the sensory images (Anderson 1989b; Anderson & Pearson, 1984; Bransford, 1983).

For example, an infant stores sensual images in the schemata for mother, bottle, bed, and bath. Later the verbal labels are added. A schema grows, expands, or otherwise changes due to new experiences. If the infant sees and touches a large, round, blue ball, he or she can store sensory images of its size, color, rubbery feel, and softness. At a later encounter, the infant may experience it bounce, and can store these images in the same schema. A year later, when the child learns to say the word *ball*, the label is acted on in working memory and stored in long-term memory within the schema for ball.

Students come to school with varied schema. Some students who have had many experiences at home, in parks, at zoos, in museums, and in other circumstances may enter kindergarten with complex schemata for hundreds of topics and experiences. Other students, whose experiences have been severely limited by poverty or other circumstances, are likely to have very different schemata, and some of these may not match the prevailing culture's values or verbal labels. Similarly, if students come from highly verbal homes where parents talk with them frequently, their schemata are likely to contain accurate verbal labels for stored sensory experiences and phenomena. But students who are raised in less verbal homes will have fewer verbal components to their schemata. This theory complements Piaget's observations of stages of development and helps us understand how a child's vocabulary develops.

Schemata also vary according to their organizational patterns. As children mature, each schema expands to include many more facts, ideas, and examples. In cases of healthy development, the schemata are frequently clarified and reorganized. Learning new information or observing unfamiliar examples often causes a schema to be renamed or otherwise altered. For example, very young children have a schema labeled *doggy* that includes all four-legged, furry creatures. As they see new examples of animals and hear the appropriate labels for each type, the original schema of doggy is reorganized to become simply a subset of the schema *animal*. New patterns and relationships among schemata are forming every day of a child's life when the environment is full of unfamiliar concepts and experiences.

Schema theory helps explain why some students are able to retrieve knowledge better than others. Students who have many accurately labeled schemata are more likely to have the background knowledge needed to learn an unfamiliar concept. Students whose schemata are richly detailed and well organized into patterns and hierarchies are much more likely to be able to retrieve useful information on request than are students whose schemata are vague and sparse.

Reflective teachers who believe that it is in their power to help their students improve their cognitive processing recognize that one of the best ways to do this is to stimulate students to actively create more well-developed, accurately labeled, and better-organized schemata.

At the elementary grade levels, teachers recognize that one of their most important responsibilities is to aid students in schema development with accurate verbal labels. At the earliest grades (especially kindergarten), teachers emphasize spoken labels, teaching students to recognize and be able to name objects and concepts such as numbers, letters of the alphabet, and colors. At the primary grades, teachers emphasize the recognition and decoding of written labels as an integral part of the reading program. When students exhibit difficulties in learning to read, the reflective teacher is likely to plan learning experiences that assist the student in developing schemata that are prerequisites for reading.

Students who have been raised in environments characterized by few experiences with books are likely to have an underdeveloped schema for reading and books. Reflective teachers who consider the needs of the whole individual are likely to provide their students with many opportunities to hear stories read aloud, to choose from a tempting array of books, and to write their own stories as a means of developing a rich and positive schema for the concept of reading.

ADVANCE ORGANIZERS

When teachers want to assist students in retrieving information from their schemata, they provide verbal cues that help the students access the appropriate information efficiently. Teachers can also provide cues to assist students in accurately and efficiently processing and storing what they read, see, or hear. Ausubel (1960) proposed that learners can comprehend new material better when, before the lesson, the teacher provides a clear statement about the purpose of the lesson and the type of information that learners should look or listen for. This introductory statement is known as an *advance organizer*.

When we relate this theory to information processing theory, it is apparent that the advance organizer provides the learner with an important cue as to which schema will incorporate this new knowledge. The learner can be more efficient in processing the information in working memory and transferring it to the appropriate schema in long-term memory than if no advance information was presented.

For example, consider what is likely to happen when a third-grade teacher introduces a lesson on long division with no advance organizer. Some students will simply reject the new knowledge as incomprehensible. But say the teacher tells students to listen for how division is similar to subtraction and how it is the opposite of multiplication. The teacher is providing students with the cues they need to retrieve their subtraction and multiplication schema in advance of the new learning. In the second case, students are more likely to route the new facts into working memory, where they can be processed using the subtraction and multiplication schemata as a framework.

In follow-up studies of Ausubel's (1960) hypothesis, many educational researchers designed experiments that showed the same effects. Therefore, this knowledge has been added to our growing common knowledge base about teaching and learning. In fact, this particular study demonstrates the way in which the knowledge base grows. The original hypothesis and study conducted by Ausubel led others to apply the principle to different types of students and environments. As the hypothesis was confirmed in subsequent studies, the knowledge was gradually accepted as a reliable principle of effective teaching. You probably experience the beneficial effects of advance organizers when your teachers tell you in advance what to listen for in a lecture or what to study for an exam. Now you can learn how to use this principle in your teaching career for the benefit of your students.

Presentation Skills that Increase Clarity and Motivation

Teaching is more than telling. You have been on the receiving end of teachers' lectures, discussions, and other forms of lessons for many years. You know from experience that the way that teachers teach or present material has an effect on student interest and motivation, which are both integral aspects of the classroom climate. You may have been unable to understand the beginning of a lesson taught by a teacher who failed to get the full attention of a class before speaking. You have probably experienced sinking feelings when a teacher droned on in a monotonous voice during a lecture. You may have experienced frustration when a teacher explained a concept once and hurried on, ignoring questions or comments from the class. Reflective teachers are not likely to be satisfied with a dull, repetitive, or unresponsive presentation style. Most of them are anxious to improve their presentation skills to stimulate interest and motivate student achievement.

GETTING STUDENTS' ATTENTION

The introduction to a lesson is very important, whether it is the first lesson of the day or a transition from one lesson to another. As Kounin (1977) found in his study of well-functioning classrooms, transitions and lesson beginnings start with a clear, straightforward message or cue signaling that the teacher is ready to begin teaching and stating exactly what students should do to prepare themselves for the lesson. To accomplish this when you teach, you need to tell your students to get ready for a certain lesson and to give you their full attention. Some teachers use a visual cue for this purpose, such as a finger on the lips or a raised arm. Others may strike a chime or turn off the lights to cue the students that it is time to listen.

It is unlikely that students will become quiet instantly. It will probably take a few moments to get the attention of every student in the class. While you are waiting, stand up straight and make direct eye contact with those who are slow to respond. Watch quietly as the students get their desks, pencils, books, and other needed materials ready for the lesson. The waiting may seem uncomfortable at first. You will be tempted to begin before they are ready because you will think that time is being wasted. Don't give in to this feeling. Wait until every voice is quiet, every chair stops scraping, every desk top stops banging, and every pencil stops tapping. Wait for a moment of pure, undisturbed silence. Then quietly begin your lesson. You will have the attention of every student.

Some teachers use a bit of drama to begin a lesson. They may pose a question or describe a condition that will interest their students. Richard Klein, a teacher at the Ericson School on Chicago's West Side, begins teaching a unit on aviation by asking students what they know about the Wright brothers. The students' replies are seldom very enthusiastic, so he unexpectedly asks them, "Then what do you know about the Wrong brothers?" They show a bit more interest but are still unable to provide many informed responses. So Mr. Klein turns off the lights and turns on a videotape of the Three Stooges in a skit called "The Wrong Brothers." Afterward, partly in appreciation of Mr. Klein's humor, the students show a greater willingness to learn about the real historical events.

Often teachers begin with a statement of purpose, describing how this particular lesson will help their students to make an important gain in skills or knowledge. Still others begin by doing a demonstration or distributing some interesting manipulative materials. Hunter (1982) calls this technique providing an *anticipatory set* both to gain attention and to motivate students to be interested in the lesson. She encourages teachers to use a variety of anticipatory sets appropriate to the lesson content and objective.

In contrast, less reflective teachers begin almost every lesson with: "Open your books to page _____. David, read the first paragraph aloud." This example employs no presentation skills. This nonmethod relies on the material itself to whet the students' interest in the topic. Although some materials may be stimulating and appealing, most are not. The message the teacher gives to the students is, "I don't care much about anything; let's just get through this." The students' motivation to learn drops to the same level as this message and can best be expressed as "Why bother?"

Teachers often display a greater degree of excitement and interest for material they themselves enjoyed learning, and they pass that excitement about learning on to the students. A teacher who reads aloud with enthusiasm conveys the message that reading is fun. A teacher who plunges into a science investigation with delight causes students to look forward to science.

After you gain your students' attention and inspire them to want to know more, you move on to the lesson itself. Presentation skills that you can learn to use systematically in your lessons include the following:

enthusiasm

clarity

smooth transitions

timing

variation

interaction

active learning

closure

Enthusiasm

Animation is the outward sign of a teacher's interest in the students and the subject. Enthusiasm is the inner experience. "There are at least two major aspects of enthusiasm. The first is conveying sincere interest in the subject. The other aspect is vigor and dynamics," and both are related to getting and maintaining student attention (Good & Brophy, 1987, p. 479). Outwardly, the teacher displays enthusiasm by using a bright, lively voice; open, expansive gestures; and facial expressions that show interest and pleasure. Salespeople who use animated, enthusiastic behavior could sell beach umbrellas in the Yukon in January. Why shouldn't teachers employ these techniques as well? You can "sell" long division better with an enthusiastic voice. You can convince your students that recycling is important with a look of commitment on your own face. You can encourage students' participation in a discussion with welcoming gestures and a warm smile.

Is animation something you can control? Absolutely. You can practice presenting information on a topic with your colleagues, using an animated voice and gestures. They can give you feedback, which you can use to improve your presentation. Have yourself videotaped as you make a presentation. When you view yourself, you can be your own best teacher. Redo your presentation with new gestures and a different voice. Repeat this procedure several times, if necessary. Gradually, you will notice a change in your presentation style. You will add these techniques to your growing repertoire of effective presentation skills.

Clarity

The clarity of the teacher's presentation of lesson directions and content is a critical factor in student success. Brophy and Good (1986) listed the importance of teacher clarity as a consistent finding in studies of teacher effectiveness. Their review of research on teacher clarity describes negative teacher behaviors that detract from clarity. These include using vagueness terms, mazes, and discontinuity and saying "uh" repeatedly.

As an example of *vagueness terms*, Brophy and Good (1986) present the following, with ambiguous language in italics:

> This mathematics lesson *might* enable you to understand *a little more* about *some of the things* we *usually* call number patterns. *Maybe* before we get to *probably* the main idea of the lesson, you should review *a few* prerequisite concepts. (p. 355)

The vague terms in this example have the effect of making the teacher sound tentative and unsure of the content. As an introduction to a lesson, it is not likely to capture students' attention or interest. Clarity can be improved, in this example, by exchanging the vague terms for specific ones, resulting in a simple, straightforward statement: "This mathematics lesson will enable you to understand the concept of number patterns. Before we get to the main idea of the lesson, we will review three prerequisite concepts."

Clarity also suffers from what Brophy and Good call *mazes:* false starts or halts in the teacher's speech, redundancy, and tangled words. For example:

> This mathematics lesson *will enab*—will get you to understand *number, uh,* number patterns. Before we get to the *main idea of the,* main idea of the lesson, you need to review *four conc*—four prerequisite concepts. (Brophy & Good, 1986, p. 355)

Even when students attempt to pay attention, they may be unable to decipher the meaning of the teachers' words if the presentation is characterized by the false starts in this example. It is obvious that the way to improve this statement is to eliminate the redundant words. This example is a simple one. Clarity is also reduced when the teacher has begun to present a lesson, is interrupted by a student's misbehavior or a knock at the door, then begins the lesson again. Kounin (1977) observed that the most effective teachers are able to *overlap* teaching with other classroom management actions. That is, they are able to continue with the primary task, presenting the lesson to the class, while at the same time opening the classroom door or stopping misbehavior with a glance or a touch on the shoulder. When teachers can overlap their presentations, the clarity of their lessons is greatly enhanced.

The third teacher behavior that detracts from clarity is *discontinuity,* "in which the teacher interrupts the flow of the lesson by interjecting irrelevant content" (Brophy & Good, 1986, p. 355). This is why lesson planning is so important. Without a plan, teachers may simply begin a lesson by reading from a textbook. As they or the students are reading, the teacher (or a student) may be reminded of something they find interesting. They may discuss the related topic for quite some time before returning to the original lesson. This side discussion may or may not be interesting or important, but it is likely to detract from the clarity of the original lesson.

The fourth detractor from teacher clarity noted by Brophy and Good (1986) is repeatedly saying "uh." It is also likely that other repetitive speech patterns are just as annoying, such as "you know." For the beginning teacher, it is likely that some of these teacher behaviors will occur simply as a result of nervousness or unfamiliarity with the content being taught. It would be interesting to study the hypothesis that these four detracting behaviors decrease as a result of teaching experience. In other words, as a teacher gains experience, the four detracting behaviors subside and clarity increases. Two teacher behaviors found to enhance clarity were an "emphasis on key aspects of the content to be learned and clear signaling of transitions between parts of lessons" (Brophy & Good, 1986, p. 355).

Smooth Transitions

Just as lesson introductions are important to gain students' attention, smooth transitions are essential to maintaining that attention and making the classroom a productive working environment. Transitions occur within a lesson as the teacher guides students from one activity to another. They also occur between lessons as students put away what they were working on in one lesson and get ready for a different subject.

Good and Brophy note that knowing when to terminate a lesson is an important element of teacher withitness.

> When the group is having difficulty maintaining attention, it is better to end the lesson early than to doggedly continue. This is especially important for younger students, whose attention span for even the best lesson is limited. When lessons go on after the point where they should have been terminated, more of the teacher's time is spent compelling attention and less of the students' time is spent thinking about the material. (Good & Brophy, 1987, p. 245)

In addition to moving students to another classroom, transitions between activities and lessons may require that students move from place to place in the room, such as having one group come to the reading circle while another group returns to their seats. Usually students are required to exchange one set of books and materials for another. These movements and exchanges have high potential for noise in the form of banging desk tops, scraping chairs, dropped equipment, and students' voices as they move from lesson to lesson.

Jerky, chaotic transitions are often caused by incomplete directions or vague expectations about student behavior from the teacher. "Take out your math books" is incomplete in that the teacher does not first specify that the students should put away other materials they have been working with. The result may be that the students begin to work on desks cluttered with unnecessary materials.

Often, inexperienced teachers begin to give directions for a transition, and the students start to get up and move around while the teacher is speaking. When this happens, teachers may attempt to talk louder so that they can be heard over the din. A way to prevent this from occurring is to inform students clearly that they are to wait until all directions have been given before they begin to move.

Smooth transitions are characterized by clear directions from the teacher about what is to be put away and what is to be taken out, who is to move and where they are to go. Clear statements of behavioral expectations are also important. The same techniques for getting attention that were described previously apply to the beginning of each new lesson. After a noisy transition between lessons, it is essential for the teacher to have the students' complete attention before beginning the new lesson. The teacher should wait until all students move into their new positions and get their materials ready before trying to introduce the lesson.

The teacher can use a signal to indicate that the new lesson is about to begin. A raised hand, lights turned off and on, or a simple verbal statement such as "I am ready to begin" will signal to the students that they should be ready for the next lesson. After giving the signal, the teacher should wait until the students have all complied and are silent before beginning the new lesson.

In considering strategies that result in smooth transitions, teachers do well to reflect on the students' needs for physical activity. In a junior high or high school, students can move between periods. At the elementary school or in a block period of time in the middle school, it is unrealistic to expect students to be able to sit still through one lesson after another. Some teachers take 5 to 10 minutes to lead students in singing or movement games between two working periods. Other teachers allow students to have a few moments of free time in which they may talk to friends, go to the washroom, or get a drink of water. Some transitions are good opportunities for teachers to read aloud from a story book or challenge students to solve a brain teaser or puzzling mathematics problem. Reflective teachers find that when they allow students a respite and a change of pace during a brief transition period, the work periods are more productive and motivation to learn is enhanced.

Timing

Actors, speakers, and comedians give considerable attention to improving the timing of their presentations. Good use of timing engages the attention of an audience, emphasizes major points, and sometimes creates a laugh. Teachers also work in front of an audience, and class presentations can be improved by considering timing and pacing as a means of getting attention and keeping it. Pausing for a moment of complete silence before you begin teaching is a good example of a way to incorporate timing into your presentation.

In most instances, students respond best to teachers who use a brisk pace of delivering information and instructions. Kounin's (1977) research on the most effective classroom managers demonstrated that students are best able to focus on the subject when the lesson has continuity and momentum. Interruptions result in confusion. When teachers forget to bring a prop, pause to consult a teacher's manual, or backtrack to present material that should have been presented earlier, inattention and disruptive behavior are likely to occur (Kounin, 1977). Jones (1987) found that students' attention improved when teachers gave them efficient help, allocating 20 seconds or less to each request for individual help or reteaching. When this time was lengthened, the result was restlessness and dependency on the part of students.

However, there are times when a pause in instruction can improve your presentation. Researchers have found that it is important to present new information in small steps, with a pause after the initial explanation to check for understanding. Students may not respond immediately during this pause because they need a moment to put their thoughts into words. Wait for them to do so. Encourage questions and comments. Ask for examples or illustrations of the fact or concept being discussed. This pause allows your students to reflect on the new material and allows you to test their understanding.

Variation

Lesson variation is an essential presentation skill for teachers who want to develop a healthy, vital classroom climate. In analyzing classroom videotapes, Kounin (1977) noticed that satiation results in boredom and inattentiveness. If presentations are monotonous, students will find a way to introduce their own variation by daydreaming, sleeping, fiddling with objects, doodling, or poking their neighbors.

Variation is important in any lesson of 30 minutes or longer. Divide your lesson into several segments. Use lecture for only part of the time. For example, include segments of discussion, independent practice, small-group interaction, and application activities. If you cannot break a single lesson into segments, plan to use a variety of strategies during the course of a day. Use quiet, independent work for one subject, group interaction for another, lecture for a third, and hands-on activities for a fourth. In this way, your students will always be expectant and eager for each new lesson. They will feel fresh and highly motivated to learn because of the variety of your presentations. If teachers attempt to address different learning styles in each lesson, they can't help but provide variation in the classroom. All lessons should be checked for activities that address the different learning modalities. This is discussed in more detail later in this chapter.

Interaction

Students thrive on interaction with the teacher and with their classmates. Rather than employing a traditional teacher-to-student, student-to-teacher communication pattern, open up your classroom to a variety of interactive experiences. Pushing the desks into a large circle encourages open-ended discussion from all students. Arranging the desks in small groups encourages highly interactive problem solving. Moving the desks aside leaves a lot of space in the middle of the room for activities. Pairing the desks provides opportunities for peer teaching or partnerships of other kinds. Your presentations can include all these types of activities, and you will find that it is motivating not only to your students but to you as well. You will feel a sense of expectant excitement as you say, "All right, students, let's rearrange the desks."

The need for interaction derives from the powerful motivational need for belonging described by Maslow (1954) and Glasser (1986). When these needs are frustrated or denied, disruptive behavior is likely to occur as a means of satisfying them. When teachers consciously plan interactive learning experiences, they allow students to satisfy their important drive for belonging and thereby prevent unnecessary discipline problems.

Active, Authentic Learning Experiences

Teachers who value authentic learning present material in ways that engage their students in active rather than passive learning by including many verbal, visual, or hands-on activities. Consider a lecture on a topic such as the closed circuit in electricity. Ho hum. Add a visual aid—a poster or an overhead projection. Students sit up in their seats to see better. Now add a demonstration. Turn off the lights. Hold up a battery, some copper wire, and a light bulb. Your students watch expectantly with a new sense of interest.

Turn on the lights again. These techniques are adequate for teaching the students a concept, but none is as valuable as a hands-on experience for in-depth learning and understanding. Picture this scene instead:

After lunch the students come into their classroom to find a battery, a flashlight bulb, and a piece of copper wire on each desk. After getting their attention, the teacher simply says, "Working independently, try to get your bulb to light up." Lights go on all over the room—in children's eyes and in their minds as they struggle with this problem. The motivation to succeed is intense and intrinsic, not tied to any exterior reward. Each individual has a sense of power and a need to know.

The key to authentic learning is in allowing your students to encounter and master situations that resemble real life. Simulated experiences are often just as valuable as real life for elementary school students and are much safer and more manageable for the beginning teacher. While your students may never invent a marketable product, you can simulate this type of exploration by inventing products that are needed in your classroom. You can simulate the debate and communication skills necessary to solve international crises by creating a mini-United Nations in your room, in which each student studies one country in depth and engages in substantive conversations about the varied needs and strengths of each country.

Closure

In the active learning experience example, the teacher can aid the students in comprehending what they've learned by having them share what they did that worked and didn't work. Concepts can be developed by articulating and generalizing what they learned about electricity. Such a teacher-led discussion is an essential part of active, hands-on learning. It provides a sense of closure.

Every lesson or presentation can benefit from some thoughtful consideration to its ending. It is important to allow time for closure. You may use this time to ask questions that check for understanding so that you will know what to plan for the lesson that follows. You may allow the students to close the lesson with their own conclusions and new insights. A few moments spent summarizing what was learned is valuable in any form. If insight is to occur, it will probably occur in this period. At the close of one lesson, you can also indicate what will follow in the next lesson so that your students know what to expect and how to prepare for it.

Systematic Classroom Instruction
DIRECT INSTRUCTION OF NEW KNOWLEDGE AND SKILLS

The curriculum contains a high proportion of basic knowledge and skills that learners must master thoroughly to succeed in the upper grades. Basic language concepts such as letter recognition, phonics, decoding words, writing letters and words, and the conventions of sentence and paragraph construction must be mastered. Basic mathematical concepts such as number recognition, quantity, order, measurement, and the operations used in computation must be learned.

Many models of direct instruction are appropriate for teaching this type of material. They are known as the five-step or seven-step lesson because they have been described in a chronological sequence of steps that results in getting students' attention; reviewing what has been learned up to the current lesson; systematically teaching, modeling, and practicing the new material; then demonstrating individual and independent mastery of what was taught.

The direct instruction model includes the following steps:

1. Create an anticipatory set to interest your students in the lesson by asking a thought-provoking question, providing an interesting visual aid, or using a puzzling and intriguing opening statement about the topic.

2. Connect this lesson with what has come before by providing a short review of previous, prerequisite learning or otherwise describing relationships between the current lesson and other subjects being studied by the class.

3. A short statement of the purpose of learning this new information is likely to convince your students that this lesson has a meaning to their lives beyond just achieving well in school. Tell them what they are going to learn and why it is important.

4. Present new, unfamiliar, and complex material in small steps, modeling each step by doing an example yourself. Give clear and detailed instructions and explanations as you model each process.

5. Provide a high level of active practice for all students. After you model a step, allow every student to practice the example on his or her own or with a learning partner.

6. Monitor students as they practice each new step. Walk around and look at their work as they do their sample problems. Ask a large number of questions to check for student understanding. Try to obtain responses from many students so that you know the concept is being clearly understood by the class. Provide systematic feedback and corrections as you see the needs arise.

7. At the end of each practice session, provide an opportunity for independent student work that synthesizes the many steps students have practiced during the lesson. This may be assigned as seatwork or homework. It is important to check this work and return it to students quickly with assistance for those who have not demonstrated independent mastery of the new material.

When these seven strategies are reviewed quickly, many readers may respond with reactions such as "But isn't that what all teachers do? What is new about these methods?" It is true that many teachers have used these strategies throughout the history of education. Unfortunately, many other teachers have not. We have all observed classroom teachers who take a much less active role than these systematic procedures call for. They assign work, collect it and have students exchange papers and correct it.

On close examination, these seven steps describe methods that would be used by a teacher who takes an active role in helping students process the new information being taught. They are also highly compatible with the concept of authentic learning because students are encouraged to think about what they are learning, construct the new knowledge in a meaningful context, and respond to substantive discussion in a supportive environment for learning. Although direct instruction is frequently associated in peoples' minds with whole-class instruction, you can readily see that these systematic steps can be used during small-group instruction as well.

In selecting appropriate teaching methods and strategies, reflective teachers are likely to look for and discover relationships among various theories of learning and methods of teaching. One such relationship exists between this direct instruction model of systematic teaching and the process of thinking and learning known as *information processing*.

The first step—*begin a lesson with a short review of previous, prerequisite learning*—is a signal to the learner to call up an existing schema that will be expanded and altered in the new lesson. Beginning a lesson with a short statement of goals provides the student with an advance organizer that allows more efficient processing. In practice, these first two steps are often presented together and can be interchangeable with no ill effects.

Current information processing theories suggest that there are limits to the amount of new information that a learner can process effectively at one time (Gagne, 1985). When too much information is presented at one time, the working memory becomes overloaded, causing the learner to become confused, to omit data, or to process new data incorrectly. This overload can be eliminated when teachers *present new material in small steps, with student practice after each step*. This allows learners to concentrate their somewhat limited attention on processing manageable pieces of information or skills.

Teachers who *model new skills and give clear and detailed instructions and explanations* are likely to provide students with the support they need while they are processing new information in their working memories.

Providing students with a *high level of active practice* after each step, and again at the conclusion of a series of steps, is important because the practice enhances the likelihood that the new information will be transferred from working memory to long-term memory, where it can be stored for future use. Each time a new skill is practiced, its position in long-term memory is strengthened.

As teachers *guide students during initial practice and ask a large number of questions, check for student understanding, and obtain responses from all students,* they are also encouraging their students to process the information accurately. Learning occurs when schemata stored in long-term memory are expanded, enriched, and reorganized. Effective teacher questions and checks for understanding cause students to think about new ideas from a variety of perspectives and to update their existing schemata accordingly.

Providing systematic feedback and corrections and monitoring students during seatwork also increases the likelihood that students will process the important points and practice the new skills in the most efficient manner.

VARYING OBJECTIVES FOR STUDENTS WITH SPECIAL NEEDS

As teachers walk around their classrooms and monitor the work of each student, they notice the great differences in the way students work. In every class and for almost every assignment, there are likely to be students who have great difficulty achieving the objective of the lesson. They are not likely to succeed unless the teacher modifies the initial lesson plan to provide them with individual or small-group lessons to reteach the skills they lack. For some children to achieve successful growth of skills and understanding, the teacher must be willing to alter the pace of the lessons, the difficulty of the material, and the criteria for success.

For students who learn more slowly, one modification that is needed is to reduce the volume of material in a lesson. If the grade-level lesson calls for the students to complete 20 problems in one class period, the teacher may reduce this requirement to 10 or

15 problems for a student who works slowly. If 20 were expected of this child, there would be little chance for success, resulting in frustration for both teacher and student. When the pace is lowered, the student has an opportunity to succeed and is likely to show the increase in motivation that accompanies success.

A child may have missed or not learned some important basic skills in previous grades for a variety of reasons. Illness, family problems, emotional difficulties, inferior teaching, or frequent moves may have prevented a child from learning the skills that most students his or her age have attained. In the children's novel *Roosevelt Grady* (Shotwell, 1963), a child from a migrant family moves so often that he never learns what "putting into" means.

> This was his question: When you put something into something else and it doesn't come out even, what do you do with what's left over?
>
> What happened yesterday was exactly what had happened at the school where he'd first heard about putting into. The teacher came to where it seemed she must explain it the very next day. And then what? That time it was the beans that ran out. This time it was celery. And same as yesterday, Roosevelt never got back to school to hear what the teacher had to say. (pp. 19–20)

For students like Roosevelt Grady, who through no fault of their own have not attained the basic skills necessary for a grade-level task, the modification needed is to teach the prerequisite skills before introducing the new material. When these prerequisite skills have been successfully mastered, the student may proceed at the pace of the rest of the class.

Some children in your classroom may have been identified as having *learning disabilities*. This label may mean that a child has one or more of a variety of learning disorders, some physical and others social or emotional in origin. When a student has been labeled learning disabled, a teacher who specializes in working with such students will be called on to create an individualized educational plan (known as an IEP) for that student. The classroom teacher will receive some guidance from the IEP on how to modify lessons for that student.

In some schools, many students come from backgrounds where the primary language of the home is not English. This has implications for instruction and lesson planning. Although these students may be able to understand the content of the lessons, they may not be able to understand the teacher's delivery of the content because of their language differences.

These students are frequently served by English as a second language (ESL) or sheltered English programs. When this is the case, the ESL teacher can assist teachers in assigning appropriate materials and helping students acquire language skills that will help them to succeed. For students learning the language, it is necessary to offer learning experiences that provide context clues using props, visuals, graphs, and real objects. Teachers may need to encourage their classmates to speak more slowly and enunciate more clearly.

Children with hearing impairments need lessons that are modified to provide directions and instruction using visual aids. Similarly, sight-impaired children may require extra auditory learning aids. Less obviously, some children in your classroom may have strong auditory, visual, or kinesthetic learning style preferences. To meet the needs of these children, teachers must modify their lessons to accommodate all three types of learning styles. This is usually accomplished by providing instructions and examples using visual aids to learn such as the chalkboard, books, and written handouts. For auditory learners, the teacher may allow students to use tape recorders to record the instructions and examples given in class. Kinesthetic learners require manipulative materials and hands-on experience to make sense of unfamiliar material. When a teacher provides visual, auditory, and kinesthetic learning aids and experiences, students may modify their own lessons by taking in the needed information in the form that fits their own learning style preferences.

For students who work unusually rapidly and accurately on grade-level material, the task is to provide appropriately challenging learning experiences so that these students are able to continue to make gains even though they have mastered the grade-level requirements. Two standard methods serve the needs of highly able learners: *acceleration* and *enrichment.* Although both strategies are valuable modifications, acceleration is appropriate for sequential subjects such as math, and enrichment is appropriate for other subject areas. An *inappropriate* modification is to give the child more work at the same level. For example, if 20 math problems are required of the students working at grade level, an inappropriate modification is to require the highly able learner to do 40. This practice is common but does not serve the student's real need to be challenged to gain new skills and understanding.

Some acceleration strategies that teachers can choose from include ability grouping, curriculum compacting, and mastery learning. *Ability grouping* requires the teacher to modify the curriculum to correspond to three different groups in the classroom. High, middle, and low groups are created, with variations in material and expectations for success. Reflective teachers must consider the possible negative consequences of lowered self-esteem and the possible positive benefits of academic fit and organizational efficiency when deciding whether or how to use ability grouping in the classroom.

In some schools, ability grouping may be organized across several grade levels. Subjects such as math and language arts may be scheduled at the same time of day, allowing students who work above or below grade level to leave their own classrooms and travel to other classrooms where the instruction is geared to their learning level.

Curriculum compacting can occur in a single classroom. This strategy requires the teacher to pretest students in various subject areas. Those children who demonstrate mastery at the time of the pretest are allowed to skip the subsequent lessons altogether. This strategy compacts the grade-level curriculum for them. Teachers then provide materials at a higher level of difficulty for these students, who typically work on their own through the more difficult material with little assistance from the teacher, who is busy instructing the students at grade level.

Mastery learning is a highly individualized teaching strategy designed to allow students to work at their own pace on material at their own difficulty level. Pretests are used to place students at the appropriate difficulty level. As each new skill is learned, a posttest demonstrates mastery. This technique is described in more detail in Chapter 10.

Enrichment strategies vary according to the imagination of the teacher who creates them. The teacher provides students who demonstrate mastery of a basic skill with a challenging application of that skill. Objectives and learning experiences at the higher levels of Bloom's taxonomy are often used as the basis for enrichment activities. A child who easily masters grade-level material is frequently allowed to investigate or research the topic in greater depth. For outcomes of enriched activities, students typically create an original product, perform an original skit, or teach the class something that they have learned from research.

Modification of lessons is a continual challenge to teachers. It is not easy to decide whether a student needs a modified lesson. Reflective teachers struggle with this decision because they know that when they lower their expectations for a student, one of the effects may be lower self-esteem, creating the conditions for a self-fulfilling prophecy that the student cannot achieve at grade level. But they also know that when adult expectations are too high, students experience little or no success, leading to a similar downward spiral. For beginning teachers, it is wise to consult with other teachers in the school, especially teachers who specialize in working with learning-disabled, gifted, or handicapped youngsters. Talk over your concerns with these specialists and make informed decisions about lesson modifications.

TEACHER MODELING AND DEMONSTRATION

When teachers present new information to students, they must carefully consider the method they will use to introduce it. For students, it is rarely sufficient for teachers simply to talk about a new idea or skill. A much more powerful method of instruction is to model or demonstrate it first and then give students an opportunity to practice the new learning themselves.

A simple example of this technique occurs at the primary grades when teachers say, "First, I will say the word; then you will say it with me." In the middle grades, the teacher may first demonstrate the procedures used in measuring with a metric ruler and then ask students to repeat them. In the upper grades, teachers may write an outline of a paragraph and then ask students to outline the next one.

Teacher demonstration and modeling is an effective instructional technique for almost every area of the curriculum. It is useful in teaching music: "Clap the same rhythm that I do." It is vital in teaching mathematics: "Watch as I do the first problem on the chalkboard." It can be easily applied to the teaching of creative writing: "I'll read you the poem that I wrote about this topic, and then you will write your own."

When teachers circulate throughout the classroom to monitor students as they practice or create their own work, it is efficient to use modeling and demonstration on a one-to-one basis to assist students in getting started or in correcting mistakes.

STRUCTURING TASKS FOR SUCCESS

Researchers have found that the degree of success that students have on school tasks correlates highly with achievement in the subject area. This supports the widely known maxim that "success breeds success." Both formal research and informal discussions with students reveal that when students experience success on a given task, they are motivated to continue working at it or to tackle another one. The number and type of successful learning experiences that students have affect their self-knowledge, leading them to have expectations regarding probable success or failure in future tasks (Anderson, 1989b, p. 93).

To structure tasks for success, a teacher must create a good fit among his or her expectations, student ability, and the difficulty of the task. Rimm (1986), who has specialized in assisting underachieving students reach their potential, describes it this way:

> Children must learn early that there is a relationship between their effort and the outcome. If their schoolwork is too hard, their efforts do not lead to successful outcomes but only to failures. If their work is too easy, they learn that it takes very little to succeed. Either is inappropriate and provides a pattern which fosters underachievement. (p. 92)

When teachers select and present academic tasks to their students, they need to reflect continually on how well the task fits the students' present needs and capacities.

Glasser (1969) has been committed to improving schools throughout his career. As a psychiatrist, he strongly believes that a person cannot be successful in life "until he can in some way first experience success in one important part of his life" (p. 5). Glasser recognizes that children have only two places in which to experience success: home and school. If they are lucky enough to experience success in both settings, they are likely to be successful in their adult lives. If they achieve success at home, they succeed despite a lackluster school experience. But many students come from homes and neighborhoods where failure is pervasive. For these students especially, it is critical that they experience success in school. Glasser's book, *Schools Without Failure*, offers many realistic and practical methods for teachers to develop a classroom environment that breeds success.

MULTIPLE INTELLIGENCES

For students to experience success in school, it is necessary for teachers to understand that each individual perceives the world differently and that there is not just one way to learn or one way to teach. Prior to the emergence of this theory, most people were convinced that there was just one type of intelligence and that all human beings had an intelligence quotient (IQ) that ranged from zero to about 200, with most individuals in the average range near 100, plus or minus 16 points.

Gardner's (1993) emerging theory of multiple intelligences disputes that old belief system. He proposed the alternate theory that human beings have more than one type of intelligence. He originally described seven different intelligences:

verbal/linguistic (word smart)

logical-mathematical (logic and math smart)

visual/spatial (art smart)

musical (music smart)

bodily-kinesthetic (body and movement smart)

interpersonal (people smart)

intrapersonal (self-awareness smart)

Later, he added another intelligence known as the naturalist, describing people who are very smart about nature and natural phenomena. Other researchers have suggested that there are additional intelligences as well. In their teaching and curriculum planning, Eby and Smutny (1990) proposed that there is an intelligence related to mechanical and technical inventiveness. They created curriculum projects that encouraged students to be inventive and expand their technical and mechanical skills.

Teachers who wish to acknowledge and support the varied intelligences of their students try to provide learning experiences that allow students to use their special strengths in learning a subject or skill. For example, when teachers present new material to a class, they are likely to describe it in words and ask for verbal feedback for linguistically talented students. They attempt to provide problem-solving activities related to the subject for logical-mathematically oriented students. They give spatially talented students visual cues and allow them to react to the new material with drawings or diagrams. They may encourage musically talented students to commit the new material to memory via a song or allow them to create a musical response to what they have learned. They set aside time and space for bodily-kinesthetically gifted students to learn with their bodies by modeling, acting out, or pantomiming the material they are learning. For students with a special facility for interpersonal communication, teachers plan stimulating classroom discussions, and for students who are especially good at intrapersonal examination, they provide opportunities for written or oral responses related to how the new material relates to their own sense of self.

Kagan & Kagan (1998) provide a teacher's guide to using the multiple intelligences (MI) in their classrooms, titled *Multiple Intelligences: The Complete MI Book.* This resource suggests three MI visions: matching, stretching, and celebrating. The first vision describes methods teachers can use to match instructional strategies with their students' varied intelligences. The second vision encourages teachers to stretch each student's capacities in their nondominant as well as their dominant intelligence. The third vision suggests ways of celebrating and respecting one another's differences and unique patterns of learning.

Reflective, caring teachers are likely to believe that students must be active learners rather than passive recipients of knowledge. With this philosophy, reflective teachers attempt to plan varied and interesting lessons, which their students view as authentic, meaningful learning experiences.

In this chapter, we have discussed some general presentation skills that can engage the learner's interest in the lesson being taught. We have also focused on the strategies that teachers use to instruct a large group of students in the basic skills of a subject. Because the techniques of direct instruction are used frequently in classrooms, it is important for the beginning teacher to become proficient in planning and teaching lessons of this type.

Although some teachers may rely on direct instruction of the entire class as their major or only teaching strategy, reflective teachers are likely to want to be able to choose from a variety of strategies. The next three chapters offer the beginning teacher a glimpse at a range of teaching methods. From these, you may begin to build a repertoire of teaching strategies to expand your own teaching skills and increase your students' motivation for learning.

⊃ Reflective Actions for Your Professional Portfolio
Presentation Skills

Withitness: Observe Your Own Teaching

To perceive your own teaching performance, it is important to see yourself in action. Teach a lesson that is videotaped. As you observe the videotape of your own teaching, observe your presentation skills and rate your enthusiasm, clarity, smooth transitions, timing, variation, interaction, active learning, and closure. If possible, teach the lesson again, making improvements according to your perceptions.

Put Issue into Perspective: Identify Your Strengths and Weaknesses

As you observe your videotape, allow yourself to see your own strengths and weaknesses. What does your body language say? How does your voice sound? Do you make false starts in your phrasing, such as "Here is an example . . . I mean . . . Look at this. . . . " Do you have eye contact with your students? What facial expressions and gestures are strong and attractive? Which do you want to work on?

Widen Your Perspective

Decide which are your strongest presentation skills at this point in time. Make a new videotape demonstrating these strengths to include in your professional portfolio.

Do Research and Invite Feedback

Choose one of the presentation skills described in this chapter that you want to improve in your own teaching. For example, you may choose *enthusiasm* if you think your presentation style is low-key. For the next four occasions that you have to work with students, focus on the skill and attempt to improve it. Ask the classroom teacher for feedback and work to refine and master this skill to your own satisfaction.

Redefine Your Best Presentation Skills

Videotape a lesson again to see if the presentation skill you worked on has improved. If it has improved, redo your videotape for the portfolio to take advantage of this growth. Plan to review and retape your presentation video frequently as your presentation skills develop and become even stronger. As with every part of your portfolio, improvements and new accomplishments need to be updated every year.

Devise an Action Plan for Your Portfolio

Create a section of your portfolio on teaching strategies and presentation skills. Write a one page description of the videotape so that people looking at your portfolio will know what is on the videotape.

Predict the Outcomes of Your Presentation Skills

Think honestly again about the strengths and weaknesses you observed in your videotaped presentation. What are the consequences that may occur when you are teaching a whole class? What is the next presentation skill you want to improve?

References

Anderson, L. (1989a). Classroom instruction. In M. Reynolds (Ed.), *Knowledge base for the beginning teacher* (pp. 101–115). Upper Saddle River, NJ: Merrill/Prentice Hall.

Anderson, L. (1989b). Learners and learning. In M. Reynolds (Ed.), *Knowledge base for the beginning teacher* (pp. 85–89). Upper Saddle River, NJ: Merrill/Prentice Hall.

Anderson, J., & Pearson, P. (1984). A schema theoretic view of basic processes in reading. In P. Pearson (Ed.), *Handbook of reading research* (pp. 255–291). New York: Longman.

Ausubel, D. P. (1960). The use of advance organizers in the learning and retention of meaningful verbal material. *Journal of Educational Psychology, 51,* 267–272.

Bransford, J. (1983). Schema activation—schema acquisition. In R. Anderson, J. Osborn, & R. Tierney (Eds.), *Learning to read in American schools* (pp. 23–37). Hillsdale, NJ: Erlbaum.

Brophy, J., & Good, T. (1986). Teacher behavior and student achievement. In M. Wittrock (Ed.), *Handbook of research on teaching* (3rd ed., pp. 328–375). Upper Saddle River, NJ: Merrill/Prentice Hall.

Eby, J., & Smutny, J. (1990). A thoughtful overview of gifted education. White Plains, NY: Longman.

Gagne, E. (1985). *The cognitive psychology of school learning.* Boston: Little, Brown.

Gardner, H. (1983). *Frames of mind.* New York: Basic Books.

Glasser, W. (1969). *Schools without failure.* New York: Harper & Row.

Glasser, W. (1986). *Control theory in the classroom.* New York: Harper & Row.

Good, T., & Brophy, J. (1987). *Looking in classrooms* (4th ed.). New York: Harper & Row.

Hunter, M. (1982). *Mastery teaching.* El Segundo, CA: TIP.

Jones, F. (1987). *Positive classroom discipline.* New York: McGraw-Hill.

Kagan, S., & Kagan, M. (1998). Multiple intelligences: The complete MI book. San Clemente, CA: Kagan Cooperative Learning.

Kounin, J. (1977). *Discipline and group management in classrooms.* New York: Kreiger.

Maslow, A. (1954). *Motivation and personality.* New York: Harper & Row.

Newman, F., & Wehlage, G. (1993). Five standards of authentic instruction. *Educational Leadership, 50*(7), 8–12.

Rimm, S. (1986). *Underachievement syndrome: Causes and cures.* Watertown, WI: Apple.

Shotwell, L. (1963). *Roosevelt Grady.* New York: Grosset & Dunlap.

chapter 8

ENGAGING STUDENTS IN CLASSROOM DISCUSSIONS

W hen students become actively and enthusiastically interested in thinking about and discussing an idea, they are experiencing *cognitive engagement,* a powerful new concept for teachers to embrace when they select teaching strategies for their classrooms.

Cognitive engagement results in the opposite of the sterile, passive classroom environment in which students attend listlessly to the lessons and carry out their seat work and homework with little real effort or interest. When students are fully engaged in reading, listening, discussing, or creating, the classroom climate is likely to be as lively and stimulating as a thundershower. When teachers structure classroom discussions to engage their students fully in substantive, meaningful, and highly interactive exchanges of information and ideas, authentic learning is likely to occur, even without the use of hands-on manipulatives.

Can you recall a classroom learning experience so powerful that you have almost total recall of it many years later? When you recall the event, do you feel as if you are reliving it because the memory is still so vividly etched in your mind? Do you think of this event as life changing? Perhaps it altered the way you think about an issue or caused you to change your career goal or provoked you into making a lifestyle change. Bloom (1981) calls these relatively rare classroom events *peak experiences.*

For many students, peak learning experiences occur during especially stimulating classroom discussions in which all members of the classroom community are expressing ideas, opinions, and points of view. Students experience these discussions as authentic, substantive, and valuable. Teachers also have a sense of exhilaration and pride when they are able to create the environment and structure needed for such powerful exchanges. In this chapter, we will examine some of the strategies you can use to stimulate and guide substantive and satisfying classroom discussions.

Asking Questions that Stimulate Higher-Level Thinking

Imagine you are observing a classroom discussion after the students have read a biography of Dr. Martin Luther King Jr. The teacher asks the following questions:

> When and where was Dr. King born?
>
> Who were the other members of his family?
>
> How did King's father and mother earn a living?
>
> What career did Dr. King choose?
>
> What does the term *ghetto* mean?
>
> What does *prejudice* mean?
>
> What did Dr. King accomplish that earned him the Nobel Peace Prize?

As you watch and listen to this discussion, you might reflect on the way you would lead it and the questions you would like to ask the students. Perhaps you think the teacher could use very different types of questions to stimulate higher-level thinking and engage the students in a discussion that connects what they've read to their own lives.

Many reflective teachers use Bloom's taxonomy (Bloom, Engelhart, Furst, Hill, & Krathwohl, 1956) to think of discussion questions that promote the use of higher-level thinking processes. Discussion questions can be readily planned at every level of the taxonomy, just as other learning experiences are planned. The term *higher-level* refers to the top four levels of the hierarchy:

Higher-Level Thinking Processes
> evaluation
>
> synthesis
>
> analysis
>
> application

Lower-Level Thinking Processes
> comprehension
>
> knowledge

In the earlier list of questions, the teacher has asked only lower-level (knowledge and comprehension) questions. But you can plan your discussions to highlight the thinking processes of application, analysis, synthesis, and evaluation. Although this system can be used at any grade level and with any topic, the following examples are taken from the discussion of Dr. King's biography.

KNOWLEDGE LEVEL

At this level, the learners are asked to recall specific bits of information, such as terminology, facts, and details:

> When and where was King born?
>
> Who were the other members of his family?
>
> What were the jobs King's father did to earn a living?
>
> What jobs did his mother do?
>
> What career did Dr. King choose?

COMPREHENSION LEVEL

At this level, the learners are asked to summarize and describe the main ideas of the subject matter in their own words:

> What does the term *ghetto* mean?
>
> What does *prejudice* mean?
>
> How did the church affect King's life?
>
> What did Dr. King accomplish that earned him the Nobel Peace Prize?

While the teacher in the previous example stopped here, a reflective teacher is likely to use those questions only as a beginning to establish the basic facts and ideas so that the class can begin to engage in a spirited discussion of how Dr. King's life and accomplishments have affected their own lives.

APPLICATION LEVEL

At this level, the learners are asked to apply what they have learned to their own lives or to other situations:

> Are there ghettos in this community? What are they and who is affected by them?
>
> Give an example of prejudice that has affected you.
>
> If Dr. King were alive today, what do you think he would be most concerned about? What do you think he would do about it?

ANALYSIS LEVEL

At this level, the learners are asked to describe patterns, cause-and-effect relationships, comparisons, and contrasts:

> How did Rosa Parks's decision to sit in the front of the bus change King's life? How did her decision change history?
>
> In what ways was Dr. King a minister, a politician, and a teacher?
>
> If Dr. King had never been born, how would your life be different today?

SYNTHESIS LEVEL

At this level, the learners are asked to contribute a new and original idea on the topic:

> Complete this phrase: I have a dream that one day. . . .
>
> If there were suddenly a strong new prejudice against people that look just like you, what would you do about it?
>
> How can we, as a class, put some of Dr. King's dreams into action?

EVALUATION LEVEL

At this level, the learners are asked to express their own opinions or make judgments about some aspect of the topic:

> What do you believe was Dr. King's greatest contribution?
>
> Which promotes greater social change: nonviolence or violence? Give a rationale or example to defend your answer.
>
> What social problem do you most want to change in your life?

Some teachers find that Bloom's taxonomy is a useful and comprehensive guide for planning classroom discussion questions as well as other classroom activities. Others find that the taxonomy is more complex than they desire and that it is difficult to discriminate among some of the levels, such as comprehension and analysis or application and synthesis. Other systems of classifying thinking processes are available. Doyle (1986) proposes that teachers plan classroom tasks in four categories that are readily applicable to classroom discussions: (a) memory tasks, (b) procedural or routine tasks, (c) comprehension tasks, and (d) opinion tasks.

Classroom questions and discussion starters can be created to fit these four task levels, as follows:

MEMORY QUESTIONS

Learners are asked to reproduce information they have read or heard before:

> When and where was Dr. King born?
>
> Who were the other members of his family?

PROCEDURAL OR ROUTINE QUESTIONS

Learners are asked to supply simple answers with only one correct response:

> What jobs did King's father and mother do to earn a living?
>
> What career did Dr. King choose?

COMPREHENSION QUESTIONS

Learners are asked to consider known data and apply them to a new and unfamiliar context:

> What does the term *ghetto* mean?
>
> What does *prejudice* mean?
>
> How did the church affect King's life?
>
> What did Dr. King accomplish that earned him the Nobel Peace Prize?
>
> How did Rosa Parks's decision to sit in the front of the bus change King's life? How did her decision change history?
>
> In what ways was Dr. King a minister, a politician, a teacher?

OPINION QUESTIONS

Learners are asked to express their own point of view on an issue, with no correct answer expected:

> Are there ghettos in this community? What are they and who is affected by them?
>
> Give an example of prejudice that has affected you.

If Dr. King were alive today, what do you think he would be most concerned about? What do you think he would do about it?

Complete this phrase: I have a dream that one day. . . .

If there were suddenly a strong new prejudice against people who look just like you, what would you do about it?

What do you believe was Dr. King's greatest contribution?

What can we, as a class, do to carry out some of Dr. King's dream?

Which promotes more social change: nonviolence or violence? Give a rationale or example to defend your answer.

What social problem do you most want to change in your life?

You will notice that the questions in Doyle's four categories are the same as the ones listed in the taxonomy's six levels. Questions at the comprehension and analysis levels are both contained in Doyle's comprehension category, and questions at the application, synthesis, and evaluation levels are contained in the opinion category. Both of these systems offer teachers a comprehensive framework for planning a range of thought-provoking questions. You may choose to write out the questions you ask ahead of time, or you may just remind yourself as you participate in a discussion that you need to include questions from the higher-level thinking categories.

Strategies for Authentic Discussions

In some classrooms, what pass for discussions are really dull and repetitive question-and-answer periods. Some teachers may simply read aloud a list of questions from the teachers' manual of the textbook and call on students to recite the answers. As you probably recall from your own school experiences, when this type of "discussion" occurs, many students disengage entirely. They read ahead, doodle, or do homework surreptitiously. They seldom listen to their classmates' responses; and when it is their turn to recite, they frequently cannot find their place in the list of questions.

Reflective teachers value the process of considering alternatives and debating opinions and ideas. That is how they approach the world themselves, and they are likely to want to stimulate the same types of behavior among their students.

Authentic learning experiences depend heavily on the promotion of high-quality and actively engaged thinking. Teachers who are committed to creating authentic learning for their students do so by planning discussions that stimulate *higher-level thinking processes, problem-solving skills, critical thinking,* and *creative thinking* and acknowledge the *multiple intelligences* of their students.

These terms and concepts can be confusing and overwhelming for the beginning teacher, who may think it is necessary to establish separate programs for each of them. That is not the case, however. It is possible to discover common attributes among them and plan classroom discussions and other experiences that promote high-level thinking, problem-solving skills, and critical and creative thinking in all seven of the multiple intelligences at the same time. One question may pose a problem; another may call for a creative response; a third may be analytical; and a fourth may ask students to evaluate a situation and make a critical judgment. The best (which is to say, the most highly engaging) classroom discussions do all of these in a spontaneous, nonregimented way.

The following sections describe various thinking processes along with alternatives for planning classroom discussions to promote these processes. As you read these sections, reflect on the similarities and differences; look for patterns and sequences; and consider how you would use, modify, and adapt these systems in your classroom.

Although these processes can be applied to both academic and nonacademic areas of the curriculum, we will illustrate how classroom discussions are created and managed, using the topic of racial discrimination as a common theme. In this example, the operational goal is to promote understanding of how racial discrimination affects the lives of human beings and to generate a sense of respect for individuals who are different from oneself.

PROBLEM-SOLVING DISCUSSIONS

Much has been written about the need for developing students' problem-solving and decision-making abilities. This can be done by presenting students with a complex problem and providing adequate scaffolding support for them to learn how to solve problems. Although some solutions require paper and pencil or a hands-on experimental approach, classroom discussion can solve other problems.

To create productive problem-solving discussions, the teacher must understand the processes involved in problem-solving and then structure the questions to guide students through that process. A problem is said to exist when "one has a goal and has not yet identified a means for reaching that goal. The problem may be wanting to answer a question, to prove a theorem, to be accepted or to get a job" (Gagne, 1985, p. 138).

According to cognitive psychologists, the framework for solving a problem consists of identifying a goal, a starting place, and all possible solution paths from the starting place to the goal. Some individuals are efficient and productive problem solvers; others are not. An excellent classroom goal for the beginning teacher is to help students become more efficient and more productive problem solvers.

Nonproductive problem solvers are likely to have difficulty identifying or defining the problem. They may simply feel that a puzzling situation exists, but they may not be aware of the real nature of the problem. Students who are poor problem solvers need experience in facing puzzling situations and defining problems. They also need experience in identifying and selecting worthwhile goals.

When a problem has been defined and a goal established, it is still possible to be either efficient or inefficient in reaching the goal. Efficiency in problem solving can be increased when students learn how to identify the alternative strategies to reach a chosen goal and recognize which ones are likely to provide the best and quickest routes to success. This can be done by helping students visualize the probable effects of each alternative and applying criteria to help them choose the most valuable means of solving the problem they have defined.

As in the teaching of higher-level thinking processes, several useful systems are available to teachers who want to teach students to become better problem solvers. Osborne (1963) proposed the technique known as *brainstorming,* which includes four basic steps:

1. Defining the problem
2. Generating, without criticism or evaluation, as many solutions as possible
3. Deciding on criteria for judging the solutions generated
4. Using these criteria to select the best possible solution

Brainstorming is an excellent way to generate classroom discussion about a puzzling issue. Rather than formulating a series of questions, the teacher supplies a dilemma or a puzzle, teaches the students the steps involved in brainstorming, and then leads them through the process itself.

In discussing the life of Martin Luther King Jr., and helping students to understand the effects of racial discrimination, the teacher might use a portion of the classroom discussion to brainstorm answers to one of the most perplexing questions. For example, the teacher might use brainstorming to expand discussion of the following question:

> If Dr. King were alive today, what do you think he would be most concerned about? What do you think he would do about it?

The techniques of brainstorming call for the teacher to pose the question or problem in such a way that it engages students' interest and motivates them to take it seriously. Because students may not be proficient at discussion of this sort, it is frequently necessary for the teacher to give additional cues and suggestions as a scaffold. In this instance, the teacher might need to pose the original question and then follow it up with prompts such as these:

> What do you think he would be concerned about in our community?
>
> What has been in the news lately that might alarm him?
>
> Who are the people in the world who are presently in need?
>
> What about threats to our environment?

Open-ended questions such as these will generate many more responses than if they were not used. After recording all the student responses on the chalkboard, the teacher leads the students through a process of selecting the most important items for further consideration. This may be done by a vote or consensus. When the list has been narrowed to several important issues, the teacher must then lead the students through the process of establishing criteria for judging the items.

Because the question is related to King's values, one possible criterion is to judge whether King showed concern for the issue in his lifetime. Another criterion might be the number of people who are threatened or hurt by the problem. After judging the items by these criteria, the class makes a judgment about which items would most concern King. Then the process of brainstorming begins again, but this time the problem the class is considering is what King would be likely to do to help solve the problem. Generating responses to the first question—"If Dr. King were alive today, what would he be most concerned about?"—will help students understand the many aspects of racial discrimination that exist today. By selecting one of these as the main concern and generating responses to the question "What do you think he would do about it?" the students will reflect on their own responsibilities to other human beings and on ways to increase tolerance and build a sense of community in their neighborhoods.

To moderate a brainstorming discussion, the teacher faithfully records every response generated by the students, no matter how trivial or impossible it sounds. The teacher then leads students through the process of eliminating the least important items and finally works through a process of establishing criteria to use in evaluating the best possible solutions.

Brainstorming alone does not solve problems. It merely trains students to think productively about problems and consider many alternative solutions. In some classrooms, teachers may wish to extend the hypothetical discussion of possible solutions to an actual attempt to solve a problem or at least contribute to a solution.

GROUP INVESTIGATIONS

Occasionally, a crisis or an unusual event will excite students' interest and concern. When the topic is appropriate, and especially if it relates to the curriculum for that grade level, teachers can allow students to participate in an investigation of the puzzling event to learn as much as they can about the subject and, in the process, learn research and communication skills. Often teachers create puzzling situations or present unusual stimuli as a means of causing students to become curious and learn how to inquire and investigate to gather information that leads to accurate assessments and judgments.

Perhaps there is a change in local government or a national election that students want to know more about. Perhaps a change occurs in the way their own school is managed, or a community event that affects their lives unfolds around them. The first hint of student interest may occur in a classroom discussion. To the extent that reflective teachers are sensitive to their students' concerns, they may wish to allow students time to talk about the event.

The first discussion of the event may simply be time to air students' early opinions and express their feelings about the event. If the teacher decides that the event is a worthwhile issue, the class may be encouraged to read about it, ask questions, or interview other members of the community and bring back their findings for more expanded discussions. These, in turn, may lead students to form small investigative groups that attempt to discover as much as they can about the event and even suggest solutions to the problems or issues under discussion.

The teacher's role in this type of investigative discussion is to encourage students to find out more about the subject and to allow them opportunities to express their opinions and share their findings. The discussion may continue for a few days or a few weeks, depending upon the seriousness of the event and its effect on the students' lives. Under the guidance of a caring, reflective teacher, this type of discussion is authentic learning at its very best.

When teachers want to stimulate curiosity and discussion, they may present a social dilemma or demonstrate a strange event. For example, the teacher may drop a number of different fruits and vegetables into a large, clear bowl of water, asking students to predict and observe which will sink and which will float. Students are encouraged to ask the teacher questions and to formulate hypotheses about floating and sinking objects. As the discussion progresses, the large group discussion may be adjourned to allow small groups to make investigations of their own, reaching their own conclusions. After small group investigations are completed, class members reconvene to share their hypotheses, demonstrate their investigations, and present their conclusions.

DISCUSSIONS THAT PROMOTE CRITICAL THINKING

The term *critical thinking* is not a separate and distinct concept that is different from higher-level thinking processes and problem solving. It overlaps both of them. It is presented here in a separate section because, during the past few years, it has become a field of study with its own research base and suggested classroom processes.

This field of study grew out of the philosophical study of logic, which was designed to train people to think about a single hypothesis deductively to arrive at a rationale conclusion. But in the late 1960s, deBono (1967) observed that, although logical thinkers were prepared to deal with a single issue in depth, they were not prepared to deal with unexpected evidence or ideas.

Using the analogy of digging for treasure, deBono (1967) suggested that, in thinking about a hypothesis, a logical thinker might dig a deeper and bigger hole; but if the hole is not in the right place, then no amount of digging will improve the solution. DeBono believed that a critical thinker would be more flexible than a logical thinker; after considering a problem or issue, the critical thinker would be able to select from a toolbox of thinking skills that allows the individual to clarify where to dig, select from alternative digging methods, use a variety of procedures to analyze the contents of the hole, and judge the worth of what is excavated.

Critical thinking, then, is partially defined as a complex set of thinking skills and processes that are believed to lead to fair and useful judgments. Lipman (1988) points out the strong association between the words *criteria* and *critical thinking*. Through the use of problem-solving discussions, students learn the technique of brainstorming and applying criteria to select the best solution.

But critical thinking is a much more multifaceted concept than problem solving. Critical thinking involves more than simply training students to use a set of strategies or procedures. It also involves establishing some affective goals for students to support them in becoming more independent and open-minded. Paul (1988), director of the Center of Critical Thinking at Sonoma State University in Rohnert Park, California, proposes that some of the affective attributes of critical thinking include independence, avoidance of egocentricity and stereotyping, and suspension of judgment until appropriate evidence has been gathered.

Paul recommends that school curricula be designed to teach students cognitive strategies such as observation, focusing on a question, distinguishing facts from opinions, distinguishing relevant from irrelevant information, judging credibility of sources, recognizing contradictions, making inferences, and drawing conclusions. Because almost every specialist in critical thinking proposes a slightly different set of thinking processes and skills that compose critical thinking, reflective teachers need to judge for themselves which of the strategies to stress in their own classrooms.

Raths, Wasserman, Jonas, and Rothstein (1986) describe a set of thinking operations that they believe compose critical thinking and then provide a wealth of practical classroom applications at both the elementary and secondary levels. The operations they emphasize are comparing, summarizing, observing, classifying, interpreting, criticizing, looking for assumptions, imagining, collecting and organizing data, applying facts and principles in new situations, and decision making.

To train students systematically to become better thinkers, Raths et al. (1986) suggest that teachers select one thinking operation at a time and tell the class that they will be focusing on improving this thinking skill. The teacher then proposes a discussion topic, listens attentively to students' responses, and records them if appropriate. In the following sections, some of their specific suggestions are paraphrased.

DISCUSSIONS THAT IMPROVE OBSERVATION SKILLS

Whenever possible in your curriculum, bring in photos or objects related to the subject you are studying. Invite students to read their stories, essays, or poems aloud for other students to listen and respond to. You may even be able to stage an event to elicit student observation skills. For example, as you study the concept of community, ask some students to role-play a disagreement. Then ask them to describe what they observed, using as many details as they can. Call on as many students as possible and encourage each of them to make their own response to the situation. If they seem to be making impetuous or repetitive observations, guide their thinking with questions that ask them to explain or support their observations.

Show your students that they can observe with all five senses, not just sight. As you study nutrition, for example, allow students to taste a variety of foods and describe their taste observations. During a study of sound waves, provide a variety of sounds and ask students to identify what they have heard. The more students use their five senses and discuss what they observe, the more likely they are to develop accurate, detailed schemata for the subject matter they are studying.

DISCUSSIONS THAT ENHANCE COMPARING SKILLS

In classroom discussions, compare two or more objects, stories, characters, or events by asking students first to tell how the two subjects are the same. Take as many responses as possible. Then ask students to tell how the two are different. This type of discussion can occur in any subject area. You may ask them to compare fractions with percentages in math, George Washington and Abraham Lincoln in history, Somalia and the United States in geography, electric- and gasoline-powered engines in science, or the wording and effects of two different classroom rules in a classroom meeting.

DISCUSSIONS THAT GUIDE CLASSIFICATION SKILLS

Introduce a collection of words or, for young children, a set of manipulative materials appropriate to their grade level. For example, you may use a collection of buttons, small toys, macaroni shapes, or shells. When possible, conduct this type of discussion using cooperative groups. Ask each group to examine the collection, look for distinguishing attributes, and create a system for classifying the objects into groups. During follow-up discussions, a spokesperson for each group can describe the attributes they observed and present a rationale for the classification system they used.

Older children can classify the words on their spelling lists, books or stories they have read, foods, games, clothing, famous people, or television programs. The best results occur when the teacher has no preestablished criteria or notion of right or wrong classification systems. As children discuss the characteristics of the shells or television programs they are classifying, they may discover some of the same attributes that adults have already described, or they may discover a completely original rationale on which to base their categories. The object of the discussion is not to get the most "right" answers but to participate in the open-ended process of sharing their observations and making critical judgments they can defend with evidence.

DISCUSSIONS THAT IDENTIFY ASSUMPTIONS

Use advertisements for products your students want to buy as a means of stimulating a discussion to identify assumptions people make. Show a newspaper ad for a product and ask students to describe what they believe the product will be like based on the advertisement alone. Then discuss the actual product and compare the students' prior assumptions with the real item.

Talk about assumptions human beings make about each other. Ask students to examine the meaning of clothing fads in their lives. Whenever a subject arises that illustrates the effects of making decisions based on assumptions, take the time to discuss these events with your class. For example, ask students to discuss what assumptions are being made when they hear someone say, "He's wrong," or "She's the smartest girl in the class."

SOCRATIC DIALOGUES

One form of discussion that reveals individual assumptions to the speaker and the listeners at the same time is the technique known as *Socratic dialogue*, in which the teacher probes to stimulate more in-depth thinking among students. Teachers who use this method believe that individuals have many legitimate differences in opinion and values. They want to encourage their students to listen to each other to learn different points of view.

To conduct a Socratic dialogue, the teacher presents an interesting issue to the class and asks an individual to state an opinion on the case. With each participant, the teacher probes by asking the student to identify the assumptions and values that led to this opinion. Further questions may be posed to the same student to encourage clarification of the consequences of the student's opinion or the relative importance it has in the student's priorities.

This type of exchange between the teacher and one student may take several minutes and from 3 to 10 questions. While the teacher conducts the discussion with one student, the others are expected to listen carefully, comparing what they believe with what is being said by their classmate. Another student with a different opinion is likely to be the next subject of the Socratic dialogue. When the teacher believes that the most important issues have been raised by the dialogues, then a general class discussion can be used to express how opinions may have been changed by listening or participating in the Socratic dialogues.

DISCUSSIONS THAT ENHANCE CREATIVE THINKING

Can individuals learn to be creative? Perhaps the more important question is, Do individuals learn to be uncreative? More than a century ago, William James (1890) stated his belief that education trains students to become "old fogies" in the early grades by training them to adopt habits of convergent, conformist thinking.

Divergent thinking is the opposite of convergent thinking in that it deviates from common understanding and accepted patterns. Guilford (1967) contributed a definition of divergent thinking that is still well accepted and has become the basis for E. Paul Torrance's (1966–1984) well-known tests for creativity. Guilford describes (and Torrance's test measures) four attributes of divergent thinking: *fluency, flexibility, originality,* and *elaboration.* In other words, a divergent thinker is one who generates many ideas (fluency), is able to break with conformist or set ideas (flexibility), suggests ideas that are new in the present context (originality), and contributes details that extend or support the idea beyond a single thought (elaboration).

Classroom discussions can be designed to help students develop these four attributes of creativity. In a technique similar to brainstorming, the teacher can ask students to generate many responses to a single question as a means of helping them to become more fluent in their thinking. For example, given our topic of King's "I have a dream" speech, the teacher may begin the process with the unfinished sentence, "I have a dream that someday. . . ."

Students may be asked to write their own responses for several minutes before the actual discussion begins. This allows each student to work for fluency individually. Then the ideas on paper are shared, and other new ideas are created as a result of the discussion. To promote flexibility, the teacher may ask students to imagine making their dreams come true and suggest ways that they could do this, using flexible and original strategies rather than rigid and ordinary methods. Finally, to extend the students' elaborative thought, the teacher may select one dream and ask the entire class to focus on it and create a more detailed vision and a more in-depth plan to accomplish it.

Einstein and Infeld (1938) add a further dimension to our understanding of creative thinking:

> The formulation of a problem is often more essential than its solution, which may be merely a matter of mathematical or experimental skill. To raise new questions, new possibilities, to regard old problems from a new angle, requires creative imagination and marks real advance in science. (p. 92)

Problem solving, then, is related to creative thinking. It is readily apparent that the methods described for improving problem solving involve critical thinking and that both involve the use of higher-level thinking processes. Whatever we call it, the goal of aiding students in developing better thinking skills is an integral part of any classroom discussion.

Just as we respect Einstein's ability to pose new problems, so should we respect and develop our own and our students' capacity to ask questions and suggest new ways of solving age-old problems. Certainly, the teaching profession needs people with the capability of regarding old educational problems from a new angle. Often it is the newest and youngest members of a faculty who see things from a helpful new perspective and suggest new ways of dealing with difficult school issues.

Another dimension of creativity involves the production of something useful, interesting, or otherwise valued by at least a small segment of society. In synthesis, a creative thinker is one who poses new problems, raises new questions, and then suggests solutions that are characterized by fluency, flexibility, originality, and elaboration. The solutions result in a product unique for that individual in those circumstances.

DISCUSSIONS THAT ENCOURAGE IMAGINATION AND INVENTIVENESS

In the process of discussing almost any type of subject, teachers always have opportunities to ask students to consider, "What if. . . . ?"

> Imagine living on an island with no electricity. What would your life be like? How would it be different than it is now?
>
> What could we do to make our school a better place?
>
> What would you do if you were the main character in the story? How would your actions change the ending of the book?

For many reflective teachers, these questions are as important as those that test student recall of information or understanding of the main idea. While it is seldom necessary to plan a discussion with the sole intent of stimulating children's imagination, it is a worthy goal to include these types of questions in any classroom discussion.

Another technique is to assign a group of students a certain task that requires them to discuss strategies and invent a method to carry it out. For example, give students a single dollar bill and ask them to discover how high a stack of one million dollar bills would be. Give them a few pieces of cloth and some string and ask them to make an effective parachute. Have each group work together to design one map of the school property. These real-life and simulated tasks provide incentives for authentic discussions on substantive and meaningful topics.

PREWRITING DISCUSSIONS

Another method teachers may use is to focus on images, analogies, and metaphors in creative discussions. These are effective discussions before students begin writing, encouraging students to use these word pictures in their writing as well. Gordon and Poze (1975) suggest that analogies allow us to make the strange familiar and the familiar strange. In discussions, teachers can present an unfamiliar idea or object and assist students in describing it using sensory images or comparing it with another, more familiar concept. For example, when presented with a rusty, old lawn-mower engine, students may be led to describe it according to size, shape, imaginary sounds, or uses. They can compare it with other, more familiar objects. The teacher may ask students what the machine reminds them of. This may generate responses such as "The machine is like my old shoes." Then the teacher probes by asking the child to tell why the machine and the old shoes are alike: "Because they are both old and muddy." Another child may see the machine in a different context: "The machine is like a kangaroo because it has a lot of secret compartments." Discussions like this can begin to have a life of their own and can lead to fresh new ways to express one's ideas.

Do schools enhance or undermine the conditions and processes that encourage creativity? Do textbooks, curriculum guides, rules, regulations, and expectations support the development of creative thinking and the process needed to create a unique product? Caring and reflective teachers do. They work very hard to create stimulating classroom discussions that assist students in learning to become creative thinkers rather than 9-year-old fogies.

DISCUSSIONS THAT ADDRESS MULTIPLE INTELLIGENCES

Thomas Armstrong was asked by a Wisconsin school district to create a format for teaching children to tell time, using all seven of the multiple intelligences described by Gardner (1983) in *Frames of Mind*. To create this set of learning experiences, he linked his instructional objective to "words, numbers or logic, pictures, music, the body, social interaction, and/or personal experience" (Armstrong, 1994, p. 26).

Armstrong told a story about a land of No Time and how confusing it was for people who lived there. The king and queen sent a group of explorers in quest of time, which was rumored to exist beyond their horizons. The explorers met a family named the O'Clocks, who had 12 children: one, two, three . . . twelve.

After telling the story, Armstrong engaged the students in verbal experiences of retelling and restating what they had learned. He asked questions that engaged students in logical and mathematical problem solving to figure out the relationships among the O'Clocks. He used visual aids such as clock faces for spatially talented learners and allowed bodily-kinesthetic learners to act out the times while musically oriented youngsters sang special rhyming songs for each hour.

My name's One O'clock

I tell time

Listen while I sing

My timely little chime

BONG! (Armstrong, 1994, p. 26)

Everyone danced to the tune of Bill Haley's "Rock Around the Clock," and students wrote stories illustrated with clock faces showing different times. In a subsequent discussion, they read aloud and shared their pictures and stories.

As Armstrong plans classroom discussions, he asks himself the following questions to guide himself through the planning process (Armstrong, 1994, p. 29):

Linguistic: How can I use the spoken or written word?

Logical-mathematical: How can I bring in numbers, calculations, logic, classifications, or critical thinking?

Spatial: How can I use visual aids, visualization, color, art, metaphor, or visual organizers?

Musical: How can I bring in music or environmental sounds, or set key points in a rhythm or melody?

Bodily-kinesthetic: How can I involve the whole body, or hands-on experiences?

Interpersonal: How can I engage students in peer or cross-age sharing, cooperative learning, or large group simulation?

Intrapersonal: How can I evoke personal feelings or memories or give students choices?

The Role of the Teacher in Leading Discussions

Discussions that promote the use of critical thinking can be exciting for both students and teachers, but beginning teachers may find it difficult to elicit responses from students who are not used to taking part in such activities. Raths et al. (1986) ask:

What if you ask a wonderful question and the pupils don't respond?
     There is nothing quite so demoralizing for a teacher as a lack of response from students.
     "Now boys and girls, how do you think the sound got onto this tape?"
     No response. Interminable silence. Finally the teacher leaps in to break the tension and gives the answer. Everybody, including the teacher, visibly relaxes. Whew! Let's not try that again. (p. 183)

This example of a nondiscussion is more common than is desirable. Students in your classroom may not have had opportunities to think creatively and express their own ideas. If not, they may be reluctant to do so at first. They may believe that you expect one right answer, just as most of their teachers have in the past. Because they do not know the one right answer, they may prefer to remain quiet rather than embarrass themselves by giving a wrong answer. Your response to their silence will tell them a great deal. If you jump in with your own response, they will learn that their own responses were not really wanted after all.

     Scaffolding is a necessary component of teaching critical thinking and discussion strategies to students. Be explicit about what you do expect from them in a discussion. Tell them that there are no wrong answers and that all opinions are valued. If they still hesitate, provide cues and prompts without providing answers. Simplify or rephrase the question so that they are able to answer it. If the question "How do you think the sound got on this tape?" gets no response, rephrase it. "What sounds do you hear on this tape? Can you imagine how those sounds were captured on a piece of plastic like this? Do you think machinery was used? What kinds of machines are able to copy sounds?" These supporting questions provide scaffolds for thinking and talking about unknown and unfamiliar ideas.

Another consideration in leading discussions is to *value* silence rather than fear it. Silence can indicate that students are truly engaged in reflection. By allowing a few moments of silence, a teacher may find that the resulting discussions are much more creative and productive. Students need time to process the question. They need time to bring forward the necessary schema to their working memories and to consider the question in light of what they already know about the topic. Some students need more time than others to see connections between new ideas and already stored information and to generate a response of their own.

Some teachers consciously use *wait time*, requiring a short period of silence after each significant question is asked. Students are taught to listen quietly, then think quietly for several seconds and not raise their hands to respond until the wait time has passed. Rowe (1974) found that when teachers used a wait time of 3–5 seconds, more students were able to generate a response to the question. Without a planned wait time, the same group of fast-thinking students are likely to dominate all discussions. With the wait time, even slower-thinking students will have an opportunity to consider what it is they do believe before hearing the opinions of others.

Lyman (1989) recommends that teachers employ a system called *listen, think, pair, share* to improve both the quantity and the quality of discussion responses. This technique employs a structured wait time at two different points in the discussion. When a question is asked, wait time goes into effect while students jot down ideas and think about their responses. Students are then expected to discuss their ideas in pairs for a minute. Then a general discussion takes place. After each student makes a contribution, other members of the class are expected to employ a second wait time of 3–5 seconds to process what their classmate has said before they raise their hands to respond.

The quantity and quality of students' responses may be improved by introducing the questions early in the class period, followed by reading, a lecture, or another type of presentation and actual discussion of the questions themselves. This strategy follows the principle of using the question as an advance organizer. Giving students the question before presentation of new material alerts them to what to listen or read for and allows sufficient time for them to process the information they receive in terms of the question. When teachers use this technique, they rarely experience a silent response.

Another strategy that promotes highly interactive discussions involves the physical setup in the classroom. To facilitate critical and creative thinking, students must be able to hear and see one another during the discussion. Arranging the chairs in a circle, rectangle, U-shape, or semicircle will ensure that each student feels like a contributing member of a group.

Meyers (1986) notes that a hospitable classroom environment is the most important factor in engaging students' attention and interest and promoting their creative responses during discussion:

> Much of the success in teaching critical thinking rests with the tone that teachers set in their classrooms. Students must be led gently into the active roles of discussing, dialoguing, and problem-solving. They will watch very carefully to see how respectfully teachers field comments and will quickly pick up nonverbal cues that show how open teachers really are to student questions and contributions. (p. 67)

Reflective teachers are critical and creative thinkers themselves. They welcome opportunities to model their own thinking strategies for their students and plan experiences that encourage the development of their students' higher-level thinking processes. They are likely to make even the simplest discussion an exercise in problem solving, reasoning, logic, and creative and independent thinking. They examine the subjects taught in the curriculum in search of ways to allow their students to learn to think and communicate their ideas. They plan discussions involving the creation and testing of hypotheses in science. They promote thinking that avoids stereotypes and egocentricity in social studies. They teach their students to suspend judgment when they lack sufficient evidence in discussions of math problems. They promote flexible, original thinking in discussions of literature. Discussions in every part of the curriculum can be crafted in ways that teach individuals to think reflectively, critically, and creatively.

In the Reflective Action Case 8.1, Mary O'Donnell, a high school history teacher who has been teaching for two years, describes how she works to develop a classroom climate that encourages active discussion and provides a support system for reluctant participants.

Case 8.1 ⤴ Reflective Action
Developing a Classroom Climate to Encourage Discussion

Mary O'Donnell, History Teacher
Crystal Lake South High School, Crystal Lake, Illinois

Use Withitness

In my classroom, I want to make history come alive so that my students will feel like they not only understand history, but that they feel that they are part of history. To capture my students' interest and give them a sense of ownership, I use a variety of teaching strategies, including having students go out into the community to write and create their own local history. However, it isn't always possible to do such projects. So, even when we are stuck in the classroom, I want to make our discussions about historical events and issues dynamic and exciting.

Put Discussion Plans into Perspective

The first week of school, I plan discussions on interesting topics to train my students to use parliamentary rules and to encourage all of them to contribute to discussions. I tell them that we all want to hear what they have to say. I explain that when someone is speaking, they have the right to speak without interruption until they are finished. For the first few weeks of school, I have to remind students to remain quiet while a classmate is speaking. I try to call on quiet students and encourage them to say what they are thinking. I may stop the discussion for a minute and ask students to reflect on what has been said so far. Then I will ask a quiet student, "Which of the opinions that you've heard do you believe has the most historical merit?" That allows the listener to become an active participant.

Widen Your Perspective

The questions I continually ask myself are "How do I make history relevant to my students' lives? How do I encourage lively discussions that involve as many students as possible? What can I do to help insecure students recognize that their view of history is valid and important to our class so that they will feel comfortable speaking up?"

Invite Feedback

Whenever I get an opportunity to observe other teachers, I focus on their discussion strategies. Craig Pfannkuche, my cooperating teacher during student teaching, was an especially valuable resource for me. His classes always had the liveliest (and loudest) discussions of any I've ever observed. At the end of a class periods, his students would often stay to continue the discussion they had started in class. I wanted to develop that same kind of climate in my classroom.

What I discovered from my observations was that the most successful discussions were led by teachers who had created a classroom climate that made their students feel secure. Students in these classrooms seemed to believe that their opinions were valuable not just to the teacher but to their classmates as well. There was a sense of mutual respect that made the majority of students feel comfortable contributing to the discussions. I knew then that in order to encourage lively and active discussion in my classroom, I had to create a safe and supportive emotional climate for my students.

Redefine Your Discussion Plan Goals

To reach my goal of having lively, diverse, and mutually respectful discussions, I considered using cooperative learning. Although I do find cooperative learning useful for small group discussions, I still find it necessary to allow the class as a whole to express the various opinions they hold on each important issue.

Early in my teaching career, I considered using wide-open, unrestrained discussions in the hope that the students would take the class into all the possible realms, but I quickly found that these discussions could become chaotic and uncomfortable to manage.

Create an Action Plan for an Engaging Discussion

To make my discussions work, I have learned that I must be well prepared with a good list of questions that will elicit the types of student responses that I want. I design my questions to confront students with tough issues and encourage them to use critical thinking in response.

For example, in discussing Christopher Columbus, I may begin with such simple questions as "What were the names of the three ships?" Then I ask, "Why are you all able to recite these names so easily? Why is Columbus so important? Wasn't he just a bad navigator who happened to land on an island in the Bahamas? Does he really deserve the credit he receives?"

Predict the Possible Outcomes

To make my discussions exciting but manageable, I realized that I would have to establish some way to make sure that only one person spoke at a time. I set up a modified form of parliamentary procedure, which requires that the class recognize that the person speaking has the right to the floor until he or she is finished talking. In my classroom discussions, I take the role of parliamentarian. Sometimes I call on students to recognize their right to speak, but as the year progresses and the students show an understanding of parliamentary procedures themselves, I have been able to allow students to speak up when they want to comment without raising their hands. When a person begins to speak in my classroom, the rest of the class has learned to recognize that the speaker "has the floor" until he or she is finished, at which time someone else can feel free to speak.

The most dramatic results of our discussions are evident in my students' essays and other writing assignments. In their written work, students remember and sometimes even paraphrase what they've learned from other students. I find myself using their views as well. My students enjoy our discussions so much that they frequently initiate discussions themselves. I get excited when I notice that my students are beginning to ask one another what they think. As the year progresses, the most outgoing students will call on their quieter classmates to ask them their opinions. When this happens, I believe that my principles of mutual respect for diverse opinions and equal access to knowledge are being successfully passed on to my students.

One major reason that I became a history teacher is to encourage students to take an active civic role as adults in their community. Students who recognize that they have the ability to analyze historical and current events and make critical decisions and judgments about these events will be empowered to become voters, community leaders, and political leaders. Another strong belief that I hold is that each individual should respect the values and opinions of every other individual in our society. Based on these beliefs, I have tried to establish an understanding with my students that respect is the basic social rule of my classroom.

➲ Reflective Actions for Your Professional Portfolio
Videotape and Reflection of Your Class Discussion

Use Withitness: Observe Other Discussion Leaders

Observe a classroom and record the amount of time spent on teacher talk and on authentic student discussions. What amount of time do you want to set aside each day for students to express their ideas in discussion?

Put Discussions into Perspective

Write about your own experiences as a participant in discussions. Do you enjoy contributing ideas? What type of support do you need from a teacher or discussion leader to encourage you to take a more active role?

Write about your own experiences in leading discussions. Are you comfortable in the role of leader? Do you tend to ask good questions spontaneously? Do you need to prepare carefully and write questions ahead of time?

Widen Your Perspective

What type of discussion leader do you want to be? What do you need to do to improve your ability to be that kind of facilitator?

Do Research and Invite Feedback

Plan and lead a discussion with a small group of students. Write the student outcomes you hope to achieve. Do you wish to emphasize students' critical thinking, creativity, or concept formation? Ask an experienced colleague or teacher to sit in the discussion. Have someone videotape the discussion.

Redefine Your Discussion Leading Goals

In response to the feedback you received and your own assessment of the videotape of the classroom discussion you planned and led, write a reflective critique, comparing the result to the outcomes you had hoped for.

As you watch the video, transcribe the questions you asked and categorize them according to Bloom's taxonomy. Keep a tally of the students you called on during the discussion. Were you equitable in calling on students of both genders? How did you encourage students who were reluctant to participate? If you were given an opportunity to repeat this discussion, what would you change?

Now, rewrite your statement describing the type of discussion leader you'd like to be. Add the insights you gathered from this experience.

Create an Action Plan for an Engaging Discussion

Select a topic related to your unit plan (see Chapter 5). Create a set of questions and discussion starters related to your unit.

Predict the Possible Outcomes

What could go wrong when you lead a discussion? Think about it from the students' point of view. What will you do if they don't understand the questions you ask? What will you do if some students sit quietly and seem hesitant to participate? What will you do if some students seem restless or bored? Write some special questions that you think will bring these three groups of students into your discussion.

Remember, some of the best feedback you can ask for is from the students themselves. Ask students to tell you what they enjoyed best about the discussion and what they didn't understand. In a one-to-one situation, ask the quiet students to tell you why they didn't feel like participating and what you could do to help them be more comfortable speaking in a group. Ask the bored or restless students what they needed or wanted to make the discussion more interesting or challenging.

Now, with all the valuable feedback you've received, try out your discussion with a small group of students and have it videotaped. If this video shows your strengths as a discussion leader and demonstrates growth in the areas you identified as needing attention, include it in your portfolio. Add a page to your portfolio describing this section of the videotape so that readers will know what to expect when they view it.

References

Armstrong, T. (1994). Multiple intelligences: Seven ways to approach curriculum. *Educational Leadership, 52*(3), 26–28.

Bloom, B. (1981). *All our children learning.* New York: McGraw-Hill.

Bloom, B., Engelhart, M., Furst, E., Hill, W., & Krathwohl, D. (1956). *Taxonomy of educational objectives: Cognitive domain.* New York: Longman.

deBono, E. (1967). *New think.* New York: Basic Books.

Doyle, W. (1986). Classroom organization and management. In M. Wittrock (Ed.), *Handbook of research on teaching* (3rd ed., pp. 392–420). Upper Saddle River, NJ: Merrill/Prentice Hall.

Einstein, A., & Infeld, L. (1938). *The evolution of physics.* New York: Simon & Schuster.

Gagne, E. (1985). *The cognitive psychology of school learning.* Boston: Little, Brown.

Gardner, H. (1983). *Frames of mind.* New York: Basic Books.

Gordon, W., & Poze, T. (1975). *Strange and familiar.* Cambridge: Porpoise.

Guilford, J. (1967). *The nature of human intelligence.* New York: McGraw-Hill.

James, W. (1890). *Principles of psychology.* New York: Holt.

Lipman, M. (1988). Critical thinking—what can it be? *Educational Leadership, 46*(1), 38–43.

Lyman, F. (1989). Rechoreographing the middle-level minuet. *Early Adolescence Magazine, 4*(1), 22–24.

Meyers, C. (1986). *Teaching students to think critically.* San Francisco: Jossey-Bass.

Osborne, P. (1963). *Applied imagination.* New York: Scribner's.

Paul, R. (1988). *31 Principles of critical thinking.* Rohnert Park, CA: Center for Critical Thinking and Moral Critique.

Raths, L., Wasserman, S., Jonas, A., & Rothstein, A. (1986). *Teaching for thinking.* New York: Teachers College Press.

Rowe, M. (1974). Wait time and reward as instructional variables, their influence on language, logic and fate control. Part 1: Wait time. *Journal of Research on Science Teaching, 11*, 81–94.

Torrance, E. (1966–1984). *Torrance tests of creative thinking.* Bensenville, IL: Scholastic Testing Service.

chapter 9

TEACHING STRATEGIES that INCREASE AUTHENTIC LEARNING

School experiences can be enjoyable for both teachers and students. One way to heighten the enjoyment is to use a variety of teaching strategies and activities. When learning experiences are varied, students are more likely to become actively engaged in the learning process. Their intrinsic motivation to learn is also likely to improve if the skill or knowledge they are learning is presented in a novel and unusual format. To promote the enjoyment of teaching and learning, many reflective teachers are continuously searching for new methods and strategies to motivate and engage their students in the learning process. Developing a repertoire of teaching strategies is also necessary because students' needs and learning styles are diverse. For this reason, teachers must be ready to modify lesson plans and present information more than one way.

The purpose of this chapter is to introduce you to a repertoire of teaching strategies, and encourage you to plan engaging lessons and learning experiences for your students. As you consider each strategy, you will quickly recognize that the descriptions in this chapter are not sufficiently detailed for you to become proficient in using the new strategy. This book can provide only an overview of the descriptions, illustrations, and examples you will need to employ these methods successfully. For strategies that you wish to implement in your classroom, you will need to use the reflective action of initiating an active search for more detailed descriptions of these strategies in books and journal articles or in observations of experienced teachers.

As you read about or select a strategy to try out in a laboratory or classroom, you will find that some of them work for you and others do not. You will need to reflect about what works for you and your students and why. As you think about what works for you, it is quite acceptable for you to combine, adapt, modify, and add your own unique strategies to the ones you read about or observe. Through this process of practice and reflection, you will discover, create, and refine your own unique teaching style.

Examples of Teaching Strategies in Action

DISCOVERY LEARNING

In the 1960s and '70s a phenomenon known as the *open classroom* bloomed, mushroomed, and then faded into obscurity. The underlying philosophy of the open classroom was that students would become more active and responsible for their own learning in an environment that allowed them to make choices and encouraged them to take initiative. To this end, the rows of desks in many classrooms were rearranged to provide more space for activity and learning centers. The curriculum of the open classroom was revised to allow students to choose from among many alternatives and schedule their own time to learn what they wanted to learn when they wanted to learn it (Silberman, 1973).

One of the teaching strategies emphasized in the open classroom was called *discovery learning*. The principle of discovery learning is that students learn best by doing rather than by hearing or reading about a concept. Teachers may still find this strategy an excellent addition to their repertoire. It can be used occasionally to provide real, rather than vicarious, experience in a classroom.

In employing discovery learning, the teacher's role is to gather and provide equipment and materials related to a concept that the students are to learn. Sufficient materials should be available so that every student or pair of students has immediate access to them. Materials that are unfamiliar, interesting, and stimulating are especially important to a successful discovery learning experience. After providing the materials, the teacher may ask a question or offer a challenge that causes students to discover the properties of the materials. Then, as the students begin to work with the materials, the teacher monitors and observes as the students discover the properties and relationships inherent in the materials, asking occasional questions or making suggestions that will guide the students in seeing the relationships and understanding the concepts. The period of manipulation and discovery is then followed by a discussion in which students verbalize what they have observed and learned from the experience (Hawkins, 1965).

A simple example at the primary level is the use of discovery learning to teach the concept of colors and their relationships to one another. Rather than telling students that blue and yellow make green or demonstrating that they do while students watch, the strategy of discovery learning is to provide every student with a brush and two small puddles of blue and yellow paint on white paper and allow them to discover it for themselves. In this case, the opening question may simply be, "What happens when you mix blue and yellow together?" When this relationship becomes apparent and students verbalize it, the teacher can then provide additional puddles of red and white paint and challenge students to "create as many different colors as you can." Experiences can be designed to allow students to discover how and why some things float, what makes a light bulb light, how electricity travels in circuits, and the difference between solutions and mixtures.

Math relationships also can be discovered. Beans, buttons, coins, dice, straws, and toothpicks can be sorted according to size, shape, color, and other attributes. Objects can be weighed and measured and compared with one another. The concept of multiplication can be discovered when students make sets of objects in rows and columns. Many resources in the form of math curriculum projects involving discovery learning are presently being developed for schools because discovery is a part of the problem-solving process, currently a hot topic in education.

INQUIRY TRAINING

Closely linked to the discovery method is a strategy known as *inquiry training*. Teachers who believe that their students must learn how to ask questions and carry out other types of investigations to become active learners often plan lessons that stimulate their students' curiosity and then train them to ask productive questions and use critical thinking, observation skills, and variations of the scientific method to gather information, make informed estimates or predictions, and then design investigations to test their hypotheses.

As an example, a classroom teacher wanted to train her students to think like scientists do, using the skills of observation, inquiry, prediction, hypothesis testing, and experimental design to find out what they need to know. She grouped her students into pairs and distributed a clear plastic glass and five raisins to each dyad. She asked them to predict what would happen to the raisins if they were dropped into a glass of water. Most students correctly guessed that the raisins would sink to the bottom of the glass. The teacher then discussed with her students the need to keep an open mind and not jump to easy conclusions based on prior knowledge. She poured a carbonated lemon-lime beverage into the students' glasses and asked them to predict whether the raisins would sink or float. Each pair of students wrote down their prediction. The teacher generated a chart on the board showing the class predictions.

After recording the predictions, the teacher allowed the students to drop the raisins into their glasses. At first it appeared that the students who predicted that the raisins would sink were correct as the raisins fell to the bottom of the glasses, but as the students watched, several raisins began to rise to the top. In the next few minutes, the students observed a puzzling phenomenon. Raisins moved up and down in the glasses, each at their own pace.

At this stage in the lesson, the teacher encouraged the students to ask questions of her and of each other as they all tried to make sense out of what they were observing. The teacher answered their questions with either "yes" or "no," giving her students the responsibility of articulating the questions and gathering the information they needed to make meaning out of the situation. Soon they began to generate new investigations to discover why some raisins moved up and down more quickly and why some settled to the bottom.

To stimulate your own curiosity and encourage you to use the reflective actions of gathering information, being creative, and being persistent in solving problems, we will not disclose the reasons for the raisins' movement. Try the experiment yourself and try to think like a scientist. If you have opportunities to learn like this yourself, you will be better able to provide your students with the encouragement and support they need without rushing to provide them with answers. You will allow them to take the time they need to inquire and experiment so that they can succeed, and fully experience the "aha" moment, just as scientists do when their inquiries lead them to new understandings.

ROLE PLAYING

When problems or issues involving human relationships are part of the curriculum, teachers may choose to use *role playing* to help students explore and understand the whole range of human feelings that surround any issue. This strategy is frequently used to resolve personal problems or dilemmas, but it can also be employed to gain understanding about the feelings and values of groups outside of the classroom.

For example, to help students understand the depth of emotions experienced by immigrants coming to a new and unfamiliar country, the teacher may ask students to role play the interactions among family members who are separated or the dilemmas of the Vietnamese boat people or others who want to emigrate to the United States but are stopped by immigration quotas.

Successful and meaningful role playing has two major phases: the role playing itself and the subsequent discussion and evaluation period. In the first phase, the teacher's responsibility is to give students an overview of both phases of role playing, so that they know what to expect. The teacher then introduces and describes a problem or dilemma, identifies the roles to be taken, assigns the roles, and begins the action by setting the stage and describing the immediate problem the actors must confront. Roles must be assigned carefully. Usually teachers select students who are involved in the problem to play the role. In an academic dilemma, the roles may be assigned to students who most need to expand their experience with and understanding of the issue. Students who are not assigned roles are expected to be careful observers.

To set up the role-playing situation, the teacher can arrange some chairs to suggest the setting of the event to be played out. During the role play itself, the actors are expected to get inside the problem and "live" it spontaneously, responding realistically to one another. The role play may not flow smoothly; actors may experience uncertainty and be at a loss for words just as they would in real life. The first time a role is played, the problem may not be solved at all. The action may simply establish the problem, which in later enactments can be probed and resolved.

To increase the effect of role playing, Leyser (1982) suggests that after playing a scene out once, the actors exchange roles and play out the same scene so that they grow to understand the other characters' points of view. Actors may be allowed to select consultants to discuss and improve the roles they are playing.

In the second phase, the observers discuss the actions and words of the initial role players. The teacher helps the observers review what they have seen and heard, discuss the main events, and predict the consequences of actions taken by the role players. Following the initial discussion, the teacher will probably decide to have new class members replay the role to show an alternative way of handling the problem. The situation can be replayed a number of times if necessary. When a role-played situation generates a useful solution or suggests an effective way of handling a problem, the situation can be adapted and subsequent role plays can focus on communication skills that will enhance or improve the situation even further.

Role playing has many applications in both the cognitive and affective goals of the curriculum. Through role playing, students can experience history by researching the life of a public figure and taking the role in an historical interaction. Each student in the class, for example, can study the life of a U.S. president and be the president for a day. Frequently, teachers ask students to play the role of characters in books that they have read as a means of reporting their own reading and stimulating others in the class to read the book. Students can enact the feelings of slaves and slave traders, the roles of scientists as they are "doing" science, or the interaction between an author and editor as they try to perfect a piece of writing.

Students can learn new behaviors and social skills that may help them win greater peer acceptance and enhance their own self-esteem. Interpersonal conflicts that arise in the classroom can be role played as a means of helping students discover more productive and responsible ways of behaving. For example, when two students argue about taking turns with a toy in the kindergarten class, the teacher can ask the students to role play the situation in an effort to learn new ways of speaking to one another, asserting their own desires, and creating a plan for sharing the scarce resource. In a classroom, the teacher may notice that one student is isolated and treated like a scapegoat by others in the class. The dilemma can be role played with the role of the isolated student assigned to be played by some of the students who have been most critical and aggressive toward the student. Through this active, vicarious experience, students may learn to be more tolerant and accepting of one another.

SIMULATION

Student drivers drive simulated vehicles before they learn to drive a real car on the highway. Airplane simulators provide a realistic but safe way for student pilots to practice flying in which mistakes lead to realistic consequences without threatening lives. *Simulations* usually involve some type of role playing but also include other gamelike features, such as a set of rules, time limits, tokens, or other objects that are gained or lost through the action of the simulation, and a way of recording the results of the players' decisions and actions. Simulations almost always focus on dilemmas in which the players must make choices, take actions, and then experience feedback in the form of consequences of their actions. The purpose of simulations is primarily to allow young people to experience tough, real-life problems and learn from the consequences in the safe, controlled environment of the classroom.

Many valuable academic and social simulations can be used to enrich the classroom experience and cause students to understand the relationship among their choices, actions, and the consequences. The teacher can purchase or create simulation games. A company named Interact publishes catalogs of simulations in all areas of the curriculum that can be purchased for a relatively small price. These kits include teacher's manuals describing the rules, time limits, and procedures to follow, and a set of student materials that may include fact sheets, game pieces, and record-keeping devices. Titles of some of the simulations they publish include "Zoo," "Dinosaur," "King Lexicon," "Shopping Spree," and "Classroom City."

The role of the teacher during a simulation is to explain the conditions, concepts to be covered, and expectations at the outset of the event. A practice session may be planned to further familiarize participants with the rules and procedures that govern the simulation. After assigning roles or creating groups that will interact, the teacher moderates, keeps time, clarifies misconceptions, and provides feedback and consequences in response to the participants' actions. At the conclusion of the simulation, the teacher leads a discussion of what occurred and what was learned by asking students to summarize events and problems and to share their perceptions and insights with one another. At the end of the discussion, the teacher may compare the simulation with its real-life counterpart and ask students to think critically about what they would do in real life as a result of having taken part in the simulation.

An example of a simulation in economics involves the creation of small companies or stores in which students decide on a product, create the product, set up the store, price and sell the product, and keep records on the transactions. The purpose, of course, is to learn about the principles of supply and demand, as well as the practical skills of exchanging money and making change. Along with the primary goals of the simulation, there are secondary learning experiences. Students are also likely to increase their capacity for critical thinking and to learn about their own actions and decisions regarding competition, cooperation, commitment to a goal, and communication.

Students may simulate the writing of the U.S. Constitution by writing a classroom constitution. After studying various countries of the world, sixth-grade students may take part in a mock United Nations simulation in which students are delegates and face daily world problems presented to them by the teacher.

In language arts, students may establish a class newspaper to learn how news is gathered and printed in the real world. They may even establish a number of competitive newspapers to add another dimension of reality to the simulation. Students may simulate the writing, editing, and publishing processes as they write, print, and distribute their own original books.

Simulations may be used to introduce a unit or as the culminating activity of a unit. They may take a few minutes or the entire year. They may be continued from week to week but played for only a specified amount of time during each session. Some may take a full day or longer. Simulations are powerful learning experiences that may change the way students view themselves and the world.

MASTERY LEARNING

Teaching strategies known as *mastery learning* derive from the philosophy that all students can learn if the task fits their aptitude and they have sufficient time to master the new skill or concept. It is based on the concept that even students with low aptitude for a particular subject can still learn that subject, but that it takes them more time to do so. In other words, students have different *learning rates* rather than different ability levels.

Bloom (1974) created a practical system for instruction using mastery learning. Studies conducted under his guidance have shown that 95% of the students in our schools can achieve the educational objectives established for them, but because they learn at different rates, some students take longer to achieve the objectives than others.

Bloom (1984) also demonstrated that one-on-one tutoring can close the gap between fast and slow learners. In a controlled experiment, he demonstrated that "the average tutored student outperformed 98% of the students in the control class" (p. 5). He attributes this finding to the fact that a tutor is able to determine what each student knows in a given subject and is then able to plan an educational program that begins instruction at the student's level and proceeds at the student's own pace.

The basic structure of the mastery learning model, including adaptations known as *individually prescribed instruction* (IPI) and *continuous progress,* lend themselves best to the learning of basic skills in sequentially structured subjects. Very specific behavioral objectives are written for each unit of study. Pretests are used to assess students' prior knowledge, which then determines their placement or starting level. Working individually, as students master each objective in the sequence of learning, they are able to proceed to the next one. Periodically, unit tests covering several objectives are given to check on the mastery and retention of a whole range of knowledge and skills.

The teacher's role in this process is quite different from teaching skills with a whole class approach. The teacher rarely instructs the entire class at one time. Instead, as students work independently, the teacher monitors their progress by walking around the classroom and responding to requests for assistance. This frees the teacher to work with small groups of students rather than devoting all of the time responding to individual needs.

The value of mastery learning is that it allows students to actively learn new material and skills on a continuous basis. Motivation to achieve also presumably increases because students are working at their own pace and have the prerequisite skills necessary for success. Also, because testing is done individually and they have opportunities to repeat what they did not learn, students should suffer less embarrassment when they make mistakes. The effective goal of mastery learning programs is to help students become independent, self-directed learners.

CONTRACTS FOR INDEPENDENT LEARNING

While mastery learning is appropriate for use only in sequential subjects that require a great deal of independent practice, many teachers are searching for methods of promoting independence and self-directed learning in other subjects as well. An alternative to direct, whole class instruction is the use of independent or group academic learning contracts. A learning contract such as the one in Figure 9.1 is usually created by the teacher at the beginning of a unit of study. The contract specifies one list of required activities, such as reading a chapter in the textbook, finding a library resource and writing a summary of the topic, completing a fact sheet, and other necessary prerequisites for developing a knowledge base on the subject.

A second list of activities is offered as choices or alternatives for students to pursue. This list includes opportunities to do additional independent research or create plays, stories, songs, and artwork on the topic. When learning contracts are offered to develop independence, individuals usually select the activities they want to accomplish. A variation on this strategy would be to combine the concepts of cooperative groups and learning contracts and allow each group to sign a joint contract specifying the tasks and products they will complete.

Science investigations, social studies research projects, and creative language arts activities can be described in learning contracts. The primary advantage of this strategy is that it allows individuals at various ability levels to work on an appropriate amount and type of work during the unit of study. High-achieving students can select the maximum number of tasks and products, and lower-achieving students can select fewer tasks. Theoretically, both types of students can actively learn and experience success during the same amount of time.

GROUP ROTATIONS USING LEARNING CENTERS

Learning centers or stations are areas of the classroom where students can go to do independent or group work on a given subject or topic. Learning centers vary enormously in appearance, usage, and length of time for which they are set up. Teachers who use learning centers use them for a variety of purposes and with a variety of expectations.

Some centers may be informal and unstructured in their use. For example, a classroom may have a permanent science center containing a variety of science equipment and materials. Students may go to the center to do science experiments in their free time. The same classroom may have a permanent reading center furnished with a rug, comfortable chairs, and shelves or racks of books where students can go to read quietly.

Other centers are set up for a limited amount of time and have highly structured expectations. For example, to accompany the unit on settling the western United States described in the learning contract, the teacher may have set up an area of the classroom as a research center. It would contain a computer, with the MECC computer program called "Oregon Trail" turned on and ready for students to use. It would also contain posters and maps of the western United States and a variety of reading materials on the topic. When the unit is finished, the center will be redesigned; new learning materials will replace the ones from the finished unit, and the center will become the focus of a new unit of study.

Westward Expansion of the United States
Required Learning Activities

Date   **Approval**

_____   _____   Read Chapter 6 in the social studies textbook.

_____   _____   Write answers to the questions at the end of the unit.

_____   _____   Locate and read a book on the American West or Indians.

_____   _____   Write a 2–4 page summary of the book.

_____   _____   Play the computer game *Oregon Trail* until you successfully reach the state of Oregon alive.

Alternative Learning Activities

_____   _____   Imagine that you are a member of a wagon train heading west. Write a series of letters back "home" describing your journey.

_____   _____   Write a play about a meeting between Indians and settlers. Find a cast for your play and present it to the class assembly.

_____   _____   Draw or paint a large picture of a scene that you imagine took place during the westward expansion.

_____   _____   Create a song or ballad about life in the west. Be prepared to play and sing it for the assembly.

_____   _____   Create a diorama or a model of a Plains Indian village.

_____   _____   Research the lives of the Plains Indians today. Be prepared to give a speech about the conditions in which they live now and how this is related to the westward expansion.

_____   Create an alternative plan for a learning experience on this topic.

I, _____, agree to complete the following required learning activities by the date_____. In addition, I select two to five alternative activities to pursue on my own. I will present my creative work to my classmates at our assembly on _____.

_____
         student signature

_____
         teacher signature

I have reviewed this contract and understand the work my child has agreed to do. I agree to support this effort.

_____
                parent signature

Figure 9.1   Independent learning contract

In primary classrooms, learning centers are often an important adjunct to reading and language arts. Many teachers set up four or five learning centers or stations with different activities each week. Students in small groups travel from one station to another according to a prespecified schedule. For example, Ms. Bailey uses a weekly theme as the basis for her first-grade language arts program. Each week she sets up activities related to that theme in her five stations: art, math, writing, listening, and reading. To accompany her butterfly theme, students will find books on butterflies to read at the reading station, paper and directions for a writing project at the writing center, paint and brushes to create a picture at the art station, a prerecorded tape to listen to at the listening station, and a math game involving butterflies and caterpillars at the math station.

Ms. Bailey uses five centers—one for each day—and that means each group can visit each center once a week. A poster on the wall (Figure 9.2) shows the schedule of groups and centers.

In Ms. Bailey's classroom, students can go to their stations only after completing their daily work assignments. In her system, the stations extend the students' learning experiences on the weekly theme but are also used as an incentive system for students to complete their required work.

Teachers who work with students who have limited English proficiency are finding that rotations from one learning center to another give the students many rich opportunities to use the English language with their peers as well as with adults. In a kindergarten classroom at Hamilton School in Mid-City San Diego, Susan King recently completed her Cultural, Language, and Academic Development (CLAD) teaching credential. In her classroom, she wants to create a learning environment that enables her English Language Learners to take risks with English so that they develop oral fluency in their new language. In Case 9.1, you can read about how she changed her entire system of teaching within a few months when she became aware that her students were becoming less proficient and quieter under the conventional, teacher-centered system she had been using.

Learning Station Schedule					
Group	**Monday**	**Tuesday**	**Wednesday**	**Thursday**	**Friday**
Blue	Art	Math	Writing	Reading	Listening
Green	Math	Writing	Reading	Listening	Art
Red	Writing	Reading	Listening	Art	Math
Yellow	Reading	Listening	Art	Math	Writing
Orange	Listening	Art	Math	Writing	Reading

Figure 9.2   Learning station schedule

Case 9.1 ⟳ Reflective Action
Establishing Learning Centers

Susan King, CLAD Kindergarten, Hamilton School, San Diego, California

Use Withitness

At the beginning of my first year as a kindergarten teacher, I organized my classroom for whole group instruction in reading and language arts. I used conventional methods in which my students all worked at the same task at the same time, with a great deal of direct instruction from me.

Put the Problem into Perspective

Then I began to perceive that the room was too quiet. Students sat quietly, waiting passively for me to tell them what to do. There were very few opportunities for oral language development using this teacher-centered approach to teaching.

Widen Your Perspective

One day after school, I was thinking about my classroom and I decided that I needed to take some risks and reorganize my entire classroom system to stimulate talking, problem solving, and cooperative learning.

Do Research and Invite Feedback

Our district has designated mentor teachers who are willing to share the teaching strategies they employ with beginning teachers. I arranged to visit a mentor teacher who uses a rotation schedule for her kindergarten-first grade classroom and I learned more in that one day than I could imagine. I was able to see the physical arrangement of her classroom and watch her students travel from one learning center to another. I took pictures of the charts and schedules she used to direct traffic in her room. I also took pictures of the students working at the various centers she had established. From this visit, I was able to envision the changes that would need to be made in my classroom.

Since many of my students are English Language Learners, I also decided to sign up for some courses to get my Cultural, Language, Academic Development (CLAD) credential.

Redefine the Issue

The new knowledge I gained from these visits and courses caused me to become aware of the needs of the students in my class. I became aware of how important it was to include parent volunteers or peer tutors who are familiar with the primary or first language (L-1) of my English language learners in my program. In my classroom, these L-1 languages include Spanish and Laotian.

Create an Action Plan

I recruited Spanish- and Laotian-speaking parents and upper grade students to assist me in my classroom. I also decided to use the resources of my own students who are bilingual. I began to design the materials I would need to get started. In January, I plunged into the whole new system. I set up four different learning stations in my classroom: journal writing, a reading basket, a structured activity center, and the guided reading group. Peer tutors supervised the structured activity center to help children with science, math, and social studies. In all the centers I encouraged my students to talk with each other, share ideas, help each other, and solve whatever problems were at hand. I instructed them to ask everyone in their group for help and then ask the peer tutor or group captain before coming to ask me for help. With this management system, I was free to work with the guided reading group without interruptions.

It took about two weeks for the children to be accustomed to the movement from one area to the next. It took even longer for them to become independent learners. At first they would stand still, waiting for me to come give them direct teaching or instruction about every little step. When I saw this response, of stillness and waiting to be spoon fed, I thought to myself, "What a disservice we are doing to children when we train them to be passive learners. I realized that the whole group teaching I had done for the first five months had caused this response. I had trained them to wait for my every word and not to think for themselves."

Predict the Possible Outcomes

In order to be able to give my full attention to the students in the guided reading group, I had to find a way to organize the learning environment so that the other 25 students were busy and would not need to interrupt me. This felt like a real challenge to me because even though I had recruited parent volunteers, they did not come consistently. So, I went to my colleagues who teach upper grades and asked them to send me some helpers who would like to help in the kindergarten. The response was overwhelmingly positive. Just as my students needed peer tutors, the older children need this type of responsibility to enhance their own self-image.

A resource teacher who visited recently looked around to see the children working so independently. As he left, he told me, "I can't believe this is a kindergarten class. The children are so responsible—so in charge of their own learning."

Cooperative Learning Strategies

Cooperative groups are a welcome change of pace for many students. They enjoy the opportunity to interact with their peers for part of the school day. But teachers may be hesitant to try the strategy for fear that the students will play or talk about outside interests rather than work at the task assigned. Cooperative groups can degenerate to chaotic groups if they do not meet certain conditions.

Imagine that a teacher hears some general ideas about cooperative groups at a conference or reads the first few paragraphs of an article on the strategy. Thinking that it seems to be an intriguing idea, the teacher may hurry back to the classroom, divide the class into several small groups, and tell them to study the Civil War together for a test that will be given next Friday. After a few moments of discussing what they have (or have not) read about the Civil War, the groups are likely to dissolve into chaos or, at best, evolve into groups who sit near one another and talk to one another as each person studies the text in isolation.

When the group has a poor understanding of the goals of the task, the results may be unproductive and frustrating. To prevent this, the teacher must clearly state the goals and expectations of each group task and provide a copy of them in writing so the group can refer to them from time to time. This includes assigning specific duties to each group member which, when combined, result in a smoothly functioning interaction.

Cooperative learning is designed to encourage students to help and support their peers in a group rather than compete against them. This purpose assumes that the perceived value of academic achievement increases when students are all working toward the same goal. Cooperative groups emphasize the notion of pride in one's "team" in much the same way that sports teams do.

Another major purpose of cooperative learning is to boost the achievement of students of all ability levels. The assumption is that when high-achieving students work with low-achieving students, they both benefit. Compared with tracking systems that separate the high achievers from the low achievers, cooperative groups are composed of students at all levels so that the low-achieving students can benefit from the modeling and interaction with their more capable peers. It is also believed that high-achieving students can learn to be more tolerant and understanding of individual differences through this type of experience than if they are separated from low achievers.

Still another point is that cooperative teams are believed to be more motivating for the majority of students because they have a greater opportunity to experience the joy of winning and success. In a competitive environment, the same few high-achieving students are likely to win over and over again. But, a classroom divided into cooperative teams, each with its own high- and low-achieving students, more evenly distributes the opportunity to succeed. To this end, the reward systems do not honor individuals, but depend on a group effort. As in a sports team, individual performances are encouraged because they benefit the whole team.

Johnson and Johnson (1984) provide this description of what cooperative learning is *not*:

> Cooperation is *not* having students sit side-by-side at the same table to talk with one another as they do their individual assignments.

Cooperation is *not* having students do a task with instructions that whoever finishes first is to help the slower students.

Cooperation is *not* assigning a report to a group of students wherein one student does all the work and the others put their names on the product, as well. (p. 8)

LEARNING TEAMS ENHANCE ACHIEVEMENT

Slavin (1995) emphasizes the team concept in cooperative learning. For example, the teacher presents information to the entire class in the form of lectures, discussion, and/or readings. As a follow-up, students are formed into four- or five-member heterogeneous teams to learn the new material or practice the new skills.

These learning teams were designed to provide a way to encourage both individual accountability and group efforts. A baseline score is computed for each team by combining the data from individual pretests. Students then work together and assist each other in learning new material. At the conclusion of the study period, individual posttests are given to determine how well each member of the group has learned the material. Students are not allowed to help one another on the tests, only during the practice sessions. The individual test scores are then combined to produce a team score. But the winning team is not necessarily the team with the highest combined score. The results that count are the *improvement scores*, computed by determining the difference between each individual's original baseline pretest score and the final posttest results and adding these individual improvement scores together to create a final group-improvement score.

For example, students may be pretested on 20-word spelling lists. High-scoring students are grouped with lower-scoring students to study and practice together, with the goal of having all students in the group earn improvement points for their team. One group's scores and points might look like this example:

Name	Pretest Score	Posttest Score	Difference = Improvement Points
John	13	15	+2
Mary	17	14	−3
Jorge	12	19	+7
Carla	10	20	+10

The teacher may use the total score of 16 or calculate an average improvement score for this group, which is 16 divided by 4, for an average group improvement score of 4. This group's score can then be compared with other groups in the class and a competition among the study groups may be used to stimulate interest and motivation in working together to improve everyone's scores. If all groups do well and achieve impressive group improvement scores, then all groups can earn awards or extra privileges. Teachers can design award certificates or plan a menu of extra privileges to encourage students to work hard individually and in cooperation with each other.

COOPERATIVE LEARNING OF THE BASIC SKILLS

Cooperative learning can be used to assist students in the mastery of basic skills such as computing the basic addition, subtraction, and multiplication facts. In a traditional classroom, teachers may prepare students for this assessment by providing them with daily worksheets for practicing and memorizing the math facts. In an effort to motivate students to improve their skills, conventional teachers may post charts for all to read that display the names of students who have reached the criteria and those who have not.

Although this type of competitive environment may please and motivate the high achievers, it is not likely to encourage the remainder of the class. To modify the process of learning math facts from a competitive to a cooperative experience, teachers could adapt the student team achievement division model to fit the needs of their classrooms.

Using a learning team approach, the teacher would begin by giving a pretest of 100 math facts to the entire class. By sorting the pretests into high, medium, and low scores, the teacher can divide the class into heterogeneous groups with equivalent ability in math facts. Each group would contain one of the top scorers, one of the lowest scorers, and two in the middle range.

How the teacher sets up the conditions and expectations for this cooperative learning experience is very important. The achievement goal and the behavioral expectations must be clearly explained at the outset. For example, the teacher may state that the groups are expected to practice math facts for a given time each day. Worksheets, flash cards, and other materials will be provided, and the teams are free to choose the means they use to practice. The goal, in this instance, is to raise all scores from pretest levels as much as possible. A posttest will be given on a certain day, and each individual will have an improvement score, which is the difference between the correct responses on the posttest and the correct responses on the pretest. The group improvement score will be computed by adding up the individual improvement scores. This method of scoring encourages the group to give extra energy to raise the scores of the lowest scorers because they have the most to gain. Top scorers, in fact, may not gain many points at all, since their pretests may already be near the total. Added incentives for this group may be devised, such as a certain number of points for a perfect paper.

The incentives that will be awarded for success depend a great deal on the class itself. The teacher may choose to offer one reward for the group whose scores improve the most or reward each group, depending on their gains. For example, a single reward for the most improved group may be tangible, such as a certificate of success or temporary possession of a traveling math trophy. Less tangible incentives are also important to third graders, such as the opportunity to be first in line for a week, go to the library together during a math class, or eat lunch with the teacher. To spread the incentives to all groups, the points that each group earns may be translated into an award such as 1 minute of free time per point or the opportunity to "buy" special opportunities and materials.

Once students become accustomed to helping their classmates in one subject area, they are likely to take considerable interest in assisting and supporting their members in doing well in other subjects as well. Similar groups could operate to improve spelling, vocabulary, the mechanics of writing, or other basic skills. The membership of each group would be different because students are likely to score differently on pretests for various subjects.

COOPERATIVE LEARNING IN SCIENCE

In many classrooms, the conventional approach to teaching science once centered on textbook reading, discussion, an occasional demonstration by the teacher, and written tests of understanding. But more recently, science curricula have been revised to include many more hands-on experiments and investigations. The current philosophy is that students need to learn how to *do* science rather than simply learn about it.

Hands-on science is an area that has a natural fit with cooperative group strategies. By participating in cooperative science investigations, students learn how scientists themselves interact to share observations, hypotheses, and methods. Although many teachers value these current science goals, they may be reluctant to try them because they are unsure of how to manage the high level of activity in the classroom when science experiments are happening. Cooperative groups can provide the support and structure needed to manage successful science investigation in the classroom.

When a topic or unit approach is taken for teaching science, each unit offers opportunities for cooperative learning. For example, jigsaw groups may study the topic of astronomy, with each studying one planet, creating models and charts of information about their planet, and reporting their findings to others.

Investigations into the properties of simple machines, magnets, electricity, and other topics in physics can be designed by establishing a challenge or a complex goal for groups to meet by a given date. Groups may be given a set of identical materials and told to create a product that has certain characteristics and can perform a specific function. For example, given a supply of toothpicks and glue, groups are challenged to construct a bridge that can hold a pound of weight without breaking. Given a raw egg and an assortment of materials, groups work together to create ways to protect their eggs when they are dropped from a high window onto the pavement below.

Science groups can be mixed and matched frequently during the year, offering students an opportunity to work cooperatively with most other members of their class. This strategy is likely to reinforce the principles of social science as well. For example, during the astronomy unit, the emphasis could be on learning how to come together as a group quickly, quietly, and efficiently when getting started on the day's project. During the bridge-building unit, the groups could practice encouraging everyone to participate, taking time to ask for opinions and suggestions from every member of the group before making an important decision. After completing each unit, the groups should participate in evaluating how they worked together and how well they demonstrated the interpersonal skill emphasized during that unit.

LITERARY GROUPS

Using conventional methods of teaching reading, three homogeneous reading groups based on ability may still be used at many grade levels. Each group reads stories, essays, poems, and plays collected in a basal reader geared for their reading ability. The teacher leads discussions of reading materials and assigns seatwork to be done while he or she works with other groups.

Many upper elementary teachers, however, prefer to use literary materials in their own format rather than as collections in basal readers or anthologies. They believe that students' motivation to read will improve if they are encouraged to choose and read whole books, novels, poetry collections, and plays. A variety of paperback books in sets of six to eight books apiece are needed to carry out this type of reading program.

At Our Lady of Mercy School in Chicago, sixth-grade teacher Roxanne Farwick-Owens has developed a system that allows choice, maximizes cooperative efforts, and holds individuals accountable. To maximize student motivation and enjoyment of reading, Ms. Farwick-Owens believes students must be allowed to choose their reading materials. Each month she provides three or four reading selections, in the form of paperback books, to the class. Students are allowed to choose the book they want to read, and groups are formed according to interest rather than ability level. Ms. Farwick-Owens may advise students about their selections and try to steer them toward appropriate selections, but in the end, she believes that they have the right to choose for themselves what they will read, especially because she has provided only books that have inherent value for sixth graders.

During initial group meetings, students decide for themselves how much to read at a time. They assign themselves due dates for each chapter. Periodically, each group meets with Ms. Farwick-Owens to discuss what they are reading, but most discussions are held without her leadership. Usually, she holds the groups responsible for generating their own discussion on the book. To prepare for this discussion, all members are expected to prepare questions as they read. For example, each person in the group may be expected to contribute three "why" questions and two detail questions per session. Ms. Farwick-Owens reviews the questions each day as a means of holding each individual accountable for reading the material and contributing to the group.

Another task is to plan a presentation about the books—using art, music, drama, and other media—to share with the rest of the class at the end of the month. This allows groups to introduce the books they have read to the other members of the class, who are then likely to choose them at a later date. One group made wooden puppets and a puppet stage to portray an event from Mark Twain's Tom Sawyer. After reading Judy Blume's *Superfudge*, a group created a radio commercial for the book complete with sound effects and background music. Familiar television interview shows are sometimes used as a format, as are music videos.

About once per quarter, two teams are formed to compete in a game show-type tournament. Questions about the books are separated into categories such as characters, plot, setting, authors, and miscellaneous. Each person is responsible for writing five questions and answers on index cards to prepare for the tournament. One student acts as emcee, while another keeps track of the points. The team with the most points wins the tournament.

Ms. Farwick-Owens finds that this cooperative group structure increases her students' social skills, especially their ability to work with others and to find effective ways to handle disagreements. But the primary reason for the program is to help her students see that reading can be enjoyable and that instead of being a solitary pursuit, reading can have a social aspect. Ms. Farwick-Owens believes many of her students may become lifelong readers from this one-year experience.

PEACEMAKING GROUPS

Some cooperative groups are formed for the social purpose of teaching students how to resolve conflicts, handle anger, and avoid violence in their lives. Many schools are taking an active role in training their students to incorporate conflict-management skills in their daily lives. Johnson and Johnson (1991) have created a series of learning experiences teachers can use for this purpose. Students are taught to recognize that conflict is inevitable, and that they can choose between entering into destructive or constructive conflicts. They learn how to recognize a constructive conflict through cooperative group experiences and simulations.

For example, a group of students may be told that they have just won an all-expense-paid field trip to the destination of their choice. Now comes the hard part. Where will the group choose to go? Pairs of students are formed to list their choices and create a rationale for them. Through negotiation, the group must resolve the dilemma and make a plan by consensus.

In other group sessions, students learn to identify how they personally react to conflicts and learn how to be assertive rather than aggressive or withdraw from arguments. For example, one session may be devoted to assisting students in dealing with insulting remarks and put-downs. In another they may deal with a simulated situation in which one student refuses to do her part in a cooperative group assignment. Cooperative group activities such as these are designed to encourage students to seek peaceful solutions in their school environment. Teachers who use these methods are also likely to believe they may be useful to their students as adults and may lead to future generations seeking more peaceful solutions in business, politics, or other issues in their families and communities.

CREATING WELL-BALANCED COOPERATIVE GROUPS

Assigning students to cooperative groups can be the most difficult part of the process for teachers. The philosophy of heterogeneous grouping is excellent in theory, but is difficult to achieve in a real-life classroom. A classroom is likely to have one or two superstars whose ability cannot be matched in some subject areas. Similarly, one or two students may have very unusual learning difficulties or behavior problems. For most types of learning situations, the teacher must simply make the best judgment about the combinations that are about equivalent in ability.

It is advisable to put nontask-oriented students into groups with highly task-oriented teammates so that peer pressure will work to keep them on task. This theory, however, does not always work out in the classroom. Angry or highly restless students may refuse to participate or otherwise prevent their team from succeeding. When this happens, the group itself should be encouraged to deal with the problem as a means of learning how to cope with and resolve such occurrences in real life.

In arranging the room during cooperative group activities, each group should have a comfortable space, and members should be able to face one another and have eye contact with every other member of the group. Separating the groups from one another is also necessary so they can each work undisturbed by the conversations and activities taking place in other groups.

Materials intended for cooperative groups may differ from those used in conventional teaching and learning situations. It is suggested that only one set of materials explaining the task and the expectations be distributed. This causes students in the group to work together from the very beginning. In some cases, each member of the group may receive different information from other members. This promotes interdependence as each member has something important to share with the others.

Interdependence can also be encouraged by the assignment of "complementary and interconnected roles" to group members. These roles will vary with the type of learning and task, but might include discussion leader, recorder of ideas, runner for information, researcher, encourager, and observer.

Tasks that result in the creation of products, rather than participation in a test or tournament, are more likely to succeed if the group is limited to the production of one product. If more than one product is allowed, students may simply work independently on their own products. Members of the group should also be asked to sign a statement saying that they participated in the development of the group's product.

To ensure individual accountability, students must know that they will all be held responsible for learning and presenting what they learned. During the final presentations, the teacher may ask any member of the group to answer a question, describe an aspect of the group's final product, or present a rationale for a group decision.

THE EFFECTS OF COOPERATIVE LEARNING

In a school setting, students learn in classes made up of their agemates, for the most part. With conventional teaching methods, relationships among peers in a class are likely to become somewhat competitive because most students are aware of how well they are doing in relation to their classmates. Grading systems reinforce the competitive nature of school, as do standardized tests and entrance exams.

Individual competition can enhance the motivation for high-achieving students who perceive that they have a possibility of winning or being the best. However, the public nature of competitive rewards and incentives leads to embarrassment and anxiety for students who fail to succeed. When the anxiety and embarrassment are intense, students who recognize that they are unlikely to win no matter how hard they work eventually drop out of the competition in one way or another.

Even when the anxiety over competition is less intense and under control by students with average or high-average achievement, they may become preoccupied with grades to the extent that they avoid complex or challenging tasks that will risk their academic standing and grades.

Despite these negative effects of competition, it is difficult to imagine a classroom without some type of competitive spirit or reward system, and despite its obvious flaws, competition does create an energetic response from many students. Slavin's (1995) models of cooperative group structures are designed to maintain the positive value of competition by adapting it in the form of team competition so that each student is equally capable of winning.

Reflective teachers who undertake some form of cooperative learning will need to be aware of all possible effects and observe for both positive and negative interactions among teammates. When using competitive teams, teachers should take steps to ensure that every team has an equal chance to win and that attention is focused more on the learning task than on who wins and loses. When anger or conflict arise within groups, teachers must be ready to mediate and assist students as they learn the interpersonal and communication skills necessary to learn from their team losses.

Slavin (1995) and Sharan (1984) also report that cooperative groups may actually improve race relations within a classroom. When students participate in multiracial teams, studies show that they choose one another for friends more often than do students in control groups. Researchers attribute this effect to the fact that working together in a group as a part of a team causes students to promote more differentiated, dynamic, and realistic views (and therefore less stereotyped and static views) of other students (including handicapped peers and students from different ethnic groups) than do competitive and individualistic learning experiences (Johnson & Johnson, 1984).

Promoting dynamic interactions among you and your students is the likely effect if you choose to learn and master the use of cooperative learning strategies for your future classroom. All of the teaching strategies presented in this chapter have the potential of creating a stimulating, motivating, and highly interactive learning environment. They are all strategies that enhance the relational aspects of teaching. Simulations encourage interaction; role-playing encourages self-awareness and understanding of others' points of view. Discovery learning and learning centers foster independence and intrinsic motivation, while cooperative groups promote interdependence. By using many of these strategies in your classroom, you will be inviting your students to learn for the sake of learning while at the same time you are providing them with opportunities for becoming reflective and relational human beings.

➲ Reflective Actions for Your Professional Portfolio
Your Plan for Using Cooperative Groups

Use Withitness

Visit a classroom and observe whether competition or cooperation is more highly valued. Give examples of classroom events or incentive structures to support your observation.

Put Issue into Perspective

Do you believe in using competition, cooperation, or some of each to motivate your students to learn?

Widen Your Perspective

From your own experience, do you find cooperative groups enjoyable and stimulating or frustrating and discouraging? What type of role do you usually take in a cooperative group? Do you get impatient with others in your group and wish you could work on the assignment by yourself? How could the structure of the groups you participated in have been improved? Based on your own experience as a learner, are you likely to use cooperative groups in your classroom? Why or why not?

Do Research and Invite Feedback

Visit a number of other classrooms that are using cooperative groups. This is one strategy that cannot be learned by reading alone. Observe the methods other teachers use to form the groups and to assign tasks and responsibilities. Look up the topic of cooperative learning on the World Wide Web pages referred to in Chapter 1. Keep a log of the best ideas you see. Talk with the teachers to learn their best strategies for managing cooperative groups.

Redefine the Issue

After your observations, has your point of view changed? Which are you now more likely to emphasize in your class—cooperation or competition?

Devise an Action Plan for Cooperative Groups

Write a brief plan for using cooperative groups in the grade level you hope to teach. Organize your plan according to subject matter or thematic units. Describe three to five types of cooperative groups you will use to accomplish different purposes.

Predict the Outcome of Various Strategies

Describe an example of a recent classroom event that you observed and tell what you would do to enhance a cooperative attitude among the students. What strategies will you employ to encourage more cooperation? How can you create more positive interdependence? Describe how you will create a climate for cooperation in your classroom.

If possible, ask for an opportunity to field test a cooperative group in one of the classrooms you are visiting. Implement it and have someone videotape the students working on the task while you assist them. Describe the field test for your portfolio. How did you form the groups? What was the task? How did you communicate the task to the students? How did you assign roles and responsibilities? How did you interact with groups as they worked on the task? Critique the results with honesty and reflectiveness, describing what you have learned in the process.

References

Bloom, B. (1974). An introduction to mastery learning theory. In J. H. Block (Ed.), *Schools, society and mastery learning* (pp. 12–21). New York: Holt, Rinehart and Winston.

Bloom, B. (1984). The search for methods of group instruction as effective as one-to-one tutoring. *Educational Leadership, 41*(8), 4–17.

Hawkins, D. (1965). Messing about in science. *Science and Children, 2*(5), 5–9.

Johnson, D., & Johnson, R. (1984). *Circles of learning*. Alexandria, VA: Association of Supervision and Curriculum Development.

Johnson, D., & Johnson, R. (1991). *Teaching students to be peacemakers*. Edina, MN: Interaction Book Co.

Leyser, Y. (1982). Role playing in the classroom: A threat or a promise. *Contemporary Education, 53*, 70–74.

Sharan, S. (1984). *Cooperative learning in the classroom: Research in desegregated schools*. Hillsdale, NJ: Erlbaum.

Silberman, C. (Ed.). (1973). *The open classroom reader*. New York: Vintage Books.

Slavin, R. (1995). *Cooperative learning* (2nd ed.). Boston: Allyn & Bacon.

chapter 10

INTEGRATING TECHNOLOGY INTO THE CURRICULUM

The importance of technology in the classroom cannot be overemphasized as we explore the cyber frontiers of the 21st century. However, for many teachers, technology may seem to be a mixed blessing: exciting and motivating, but at the same time, bewildering and frustrating. To demystify the concept, Jim Hicks traveled to many academic fronts to learn about programs that represent some of the most impressive technology-based K–12 programs in schools today. In this chapter, he describes several programs that provide ideas and practical applications for integrating technology into the curriculum of any discipline at almost any grade level.

In this chapter, we describe what we believe is a glimpse into the educational future, a peek at what may become the norm in most school districts in the next decade. For example, we predict that in the next few years, technology will make it possible for students in one school district to enroll in courses taught by other school districts throughout the United States or even the world.

This chapter can introduce you to a repertoire of technology-based teaching strategies, highlighting methods that employ computers and related systems as teaching and learning tools. As you consider each strategy, you will quickly recognize that the descriptions in this chapter are not sufficiently detailed for you to become proficient in using the new strategy. This book can provide only an overview of the descriptions, illustrations, and examples you will need to employ these methods successfully. For strategies that you wish to implement in your classroom, you will need to use the reflective action of initiating an active search for more detailed descriptions of these strategies in books and journal articles or in observations of experienced teachers.

As you read about or select a strategy to try out in a laboratory or classroom, you will find that some of them work for you and others do not. You will need to reflect about what works for you and your students and why. As you think about what works for you, it is quite acceptable for you to combine, adapt, modify, and add your own unique strategies to the ones you read about or observe. Through this process of practice and reflection, you will discover, create, and refine your own unique teaching style.

The Significance of Technology

Heinz Pagel (1982), a physicist and scientific writer, observed:

> When the great history of this (20th) century is written, we shall see that political events—in spite of their immense cost in human lives and money—will not be the most influential event. Instead, the main event will be the first human contact with the invisible quantum world and the subsequent biological and computer revolutions. (p. 98)

Technology is a valuable tool and can play a pivotal role in education, but communicating with a machine will never replace the spontaneous, invigorating class discussion that takes place between students and teacher when they are actively engaged in puzzling out some dilemma or discussing the relative merits of an abstract idea such as liberty. The most effective teaching is still a human experience and great teachers thrive and take advantage of these teacher–student interactions.

But while it is true that excellent teaching can take place with very little assistance from current technology, most teachers are enjoying the new doors and windows that computers have opened for extending students' learning experiences beyond the classroom walls. We view technology as an essential ingredient in a well run classroom, for the following reasons:

1. *Options*: During any class, using a variety of teaching methodologies with students is very important. This is especially true for long elementary class periods or middle- and high-school double-period classes, such as block scheduled classes and advanced placement classes. Integrating the appropriate technology into your classroom will provide more options. You will have more arrows in your educational quiver.

2. *Currency*: The classroom environment should reflect what is happening beyond the classroom. That is, students should experience the same things on the way home that they see during class. If our students are going to be asked to be technologically literate and interact with a technological world, the classroom must be a point of departure for such an experience. The technological world will continue to advance outside of our classroom whether we like it or not.

3. *Efficacy:* To enhance learning, technological devices can enhance teachers' presentations and make subject matter more meaningful in novel and unusual ways. Students can see changes to variables and subsequent ramifications at the click of a mouse. The "what ifs" can be explored in seconds. Students can generate their own patterns and make judgments when large blocks of data are gathered from many sources and displayed on computer screens.

4. *Coping with Change*: In every historical era, there have been skeptics who believe that because technology changes so rapidly, school curriculums are perpetually out of date and will never keep up. Nonetheless, we believe that by using the most up-to-date technological methods available, teachers are helping their students envision the future and prepare themselves for living in a world in which change is occurring more rapidly than ever. Teachers who keep current themselves and use the most up-to-date technological equipment possible in their classrooms are modeling for students that there is immense value in technology. Students who become accustomed to using technology will be motivated to adapt to the times and keep current with future technological advances.

5. *Advancement:* Many universities and colleges require students to take placement exams on campus through their local area network (LAN) system, hand in class assignments via e-mail, and register for courses that are offered only online. Additionally, networks where students can obtain information by posting information on bulletin boards are common at universities and colleges. Reflective teachers want their students to be technologically literate to compete with others for college entrance or job placements.

What a New Teacher Needs to Know About a School District's Technology Policies

When new teachers are hired by a school district, they face many challenges. Because of the new emphasis on technology-based learning, one of the new challenges is the ability to conceptualize the district's data network and available technology. Rick Bremer, computer resource person for Barrington High School, Barrington, Illinois, believes it is essential for new teachers to ask questions about the technology policies and procedures at the district as soon as possible. New teachers need to:

1. Know the type of platform your district uses and the major software associated with it. If you have a computer at home, you'll want to ask if your computer's software is compatible with the district's software. Can the district's LAN read and process documents using the software on your computer? Mr. Bremer suggests that you begin to save all your school-related programs and documents onto the district's server. This is important not only to provide back up copies of a teacher's work but also to minimize the time a computer is down while it's being repaired.

2. Find out if your district provides a computer technician for computer resource centers (i.e., labs) when your class is using them. Mr. Bremer thinks a teacher should concentrate on teaching and not be concerned with technical problems. "If a teacher is constantly faced with computer problems in a computer resource center, not only is valuable teaching time wasted, but sooner or later, teachers are going to avoid this approach to instruction," he says. "Hence, money spent by the district will be wasted."

3. Always back up your data on disks. Computers are machines and suffer from all machine-related maladies.

4. Leave your computer on during the week when school is in session, but turn it off during extended weekends or vacations. Also make sure you shut off the monitor or have the screen saver working to protect the monitor. This will lengthen the life of your computer.

5. Understand your district's policy regarding the use of nondistrict software. For example, during the summer recess some school districts purge all nondistrict software.

6. Know your district's policy regarding Internet usage by students. Follow these guidelines to the letter. Find out what provisions your district has to prevent students from wandering into undesirable web sites.

7. School districts have the right to look at individual e-mail messages. Be professional with all your correspondence.

8. Get to know your district's technology plan. Be active on technology-related committees.

9. Know the chain of command for computer assistance. Downtime can be kept to a minimum if the right person is contacted at the first sign of a problem.

How Technology Can Enhance Your Teaching

It's a frosty morning and 50-plus high school physics students are ready to tackle the real world as they head to Chicago's O'Hare Field with their homemade accelerometers. The accelerometers are made from simple supplies: a plastic protractor with a string attached to the middle of the protractor and a small weight swinging freely below the curve of the protractor. After check-in and a group picture under the Concourse C sign, the students board an aircraft and settle into their seats with accelerometers poised to collect tangible data. Borrowing a phrase from a well-known financial group, Jim Hicks tells his students that, "Physics is everywhere, everywhere you want to be."

To acquire data for the plane's take off, the students become engineers for a day. Appropriate equations play a significant role in determining answers, but the data is not given. Therefore, a procedure has to be adopted by the group to get the data first. During take off, they record the angle of the string along the accelerometer and then plot acceleration versus time on an sheet of graph paper. Later, they do calculations to estimate the area under the graph, and from these calculations, they determine the take-off speed. Knowing the speed permits them to estimate their take-off distance. After the plane lands, they confer with the pilots to compare their predicted speed with the flight instruments and confirm their distance along the runway by counting marked striped lines.

On this occasion, their predicted take-off speed was within 5 mph of the actual speed recorded by the cockpit instruments. The pilots were impressed with their methods and calculations. To confirm the data collected on the simple accelerators, one of the students has a three-dimensional computer accelerometer with appropriate software taped to her seat. Later, she downloads this data into a laptop computer and displays all of the parameters and graphs needed to answer the laboratory questions.

Yes, the technology of today is faster and more accurate, but both old-school and new-school techniques are needed when students are learning new scientific or mathematical concepts. Without old-school techniques, students miss learning about the advantages of making real-life estimations of data. Mistakes can be made when machines are involved, and no one should accept absurd answers. So, for this field trip the computer only confirmed the answers. Later, when the plane lands at Orlando, and students continue their investigations at MGM Studios, the computer is needed to decipher and analyze the sensations perceived by students as they experience the g-forces of high tech adventure park rides.

Jim Hicks believes strongly that it is important for students not to become technologically dependent and therefore ineffectual when machines break down. For example, a teacher received a note from a frantic mother explaining why her son should not lose points because of misspelled words in his project report. The note states: "Please do not grade down my son's report due to misspelled words. Our spellchecker software was not working last night."

Doing calculations on the back of an envelope is cumbersome, but sometimes we should have a "feel" for the expected answer. Blindly accepting answers from human-driven machines can lead to preposterous conclusions. Students must develop the ability to question answers when solutions do not match estimations. For more difficult situations, like flying an airplane, trust must be put into our machines. However, for events related to and immediately beyond the classroom, students need to develop awareness for sniffing out questionable results.

How do we cultivate this awareness or have our students become stewards of technology? For common, everyday applications, students must learn to do it the hard way first. Two things then emerge: First they will know why the answer is correct, and second, they might develop an appreciation for our technologically driven world.

Not every teacher will be as fortunate as Jim Hicks to be able to teach science on an airplane heading to Orlando. Still, it is good for the rest of us to know that these high-flying teaching strategies exist, so that we can aim a little higher ourselves. School districts may respond to government mandates and parental concerns, but it is also true that assertive teachers have significant influence over how the dollars are spent. Teachers who know and understand the benefits of technology-based education can justify their requests for field trips and purchase orders to outfit their classrooms with the most powerful learning tools of their time. This chapter is written, in part, to help you understand how technology can aid your instruction and then help you justify asking for what you need. Technology can markedly improve the efficiency of your classroom management, the variety and motivating power of your instructional strategies and your ability to extend students' actual or virtual experience beyond the classroom walls.

Managing Your Classroom with (and for) Technology

Technology can assist teachers in classroom management, but at the same time, technology creates new classroom management issues. As a means of making teachers' professional lives more manageable, there are excellent software packages on the market that can be adapted or are designed for seating charts, grades, attendance, lesson plans, room inventories, rubrics, test masters, word processing, spread sheets, etc. Keeping a computer file of these important daily functions saves office space and paper as well.

Many teachers have developed classroom management systems that include having students do their homework on computers. They may "turn in" their papers by e-mailing their homework to the teacher's e-mail address. Independent or group projects can be done by students working on their home or school computers.

When there is a computer laboratory in the school, the classroom teacher and the computer specialist may frequently confer about what the students need to accomplish when they come into the laboratory. Occasionally, the computer specialist will initiate and manage a series of experiences for each grade level.

Having computer activities in a centralized laboratory has certain advantages. The teacher in the lab is likely to be more familiar with various programs and can efficiently select and instruct students in their use. Computer programs can be stored in the lab and distributed easily when students need them. On the negative side, when the entire school must be scheduled for time in the lab, each class may get only an hour or two per week to spend working with the computers.

Media center computers are managed by media center personnel. They may designate one or more computers to be used for CD-ROM research stations. Students use these computers whenever they want to search for information on the CD-ROM encyclopedia, atlas, or other database. Other computers in the media center may be available for a variety of uses, including word processing, tutoring programs, and literature-based software packages. When the media center has a collection of software programs available, students may be allowed to check them out and use them on a computer in the room, getting assistance from media center personnel when needed.

Just appearing on the horizon is a new technology that may revolutionize the way we think about teaching and learning. The Smart Spaces Laboratory provides a potential for people to be able to interact with one another in a life-size and real-time setting. Through the Internet, a teacher and students may be separated by thousands of miles, but they will be able to interact as if they were in the same room. For example, a social studies teacher attending a conference in San Francisco could deliver a lecture to her students in New York City. During the session, the teacher in San Francisco will see her class projected onto a wall in a room at the conference center and students will see her projected on a wall in the classroom. The teacher will appear to her students as if she is really there. A teacher can lecture, perform demonstrations, and view her virtual wall to see student responses. The teacher can respond to questions as they are asked, and students' body language and other important feedback cues will be clearly visible in a real-time lifelike setting.

Does one have to be a technological supergeek to deliver these presentations? No. Through implicit computing, small nested computers around your neck and on your clothes will activate all commands through voice recognition. Universities are researching this technology today. Although the Smart Spaces Laboratory does not appear to be available anytime soon, we should be aware of its possibilities and respect its potential.

In most districts today, students have access to computers in their classrooms as well. Even with a low budget and just one computer in the classroom, teachers can accomplish quite a lot. If you have less than $1,000 to spend on technology, Jim Hicks suggests that you spend it on:

desktop computer	$500 (with CD-ROM and computer VCR interface)
VCR	$150
television	$250 (25-inch screen or larger)
scanner	$80

To purchase a used computer for about $500, try the classified section in your local newspaper or an auction on the Internet or search out a corporation that is upgrading its computers and is willing to sell the old ones at nominal fees or donate them to get a tax deduction. Obviously, the desktops will not be state of the art, but they still will be functional for many educational tasks.

A great deal can be accomplished with just one computer, one VCR, and one television if you create a one-computer classroom setup. The key is to funnel the output from the computer through the VCR. With the proper cable connections, whatever appears on the computer monitor will also be displayed on the television screen.

When teachers have more than one computer for use, they may designate them for specific uses. In the primary grades, rotating schedules are often created that allow each child to use a computer to accomplish a specified task for the week. For example, while studying addition, students may rotate through four to six stations that allow them to practice addition. In a primary classroom, one of the stations may be a computer with a program like Number Muncher (MECC), an addition learning activity.

In the upper grades, students usually sign up to use a computer. Cliff Gilkey, for example, has four computers in his classroom. He has collected a variety of software programs over the years. For some projects, he uses a rotation system that allows one cooperative group to use the computers at a time. He tries to keep the computers busy as much as possible during the day, so he rotates students to the computers for one task or another. During free time, students can choose to use the computer to play educational games.

Beyond the bare-bones budget mentioned above, there are other types of technological equipment that can add greatly to your curriculum options. Jim Hicks suggests that, if possible, you might want to add these items to your shopping list:

laser disc	$500.00
digital camera	$150.00
video camera	$400.00
tripod	$50.00
educational laser discs	$350.00

The laser disc, computer, and video camera can be all connected to the VCR. All four formats can be displayed on a television set. The video camera can be an indispensable educational tool for the classroom. By disconnecting the computer lead to the VCR and connecting a lead from the video camera to the same VCR port, a mounted video camera on a tripod can be turned into a first-class documentation camera.

This setup has unlimited uses for any classroom. For the social sciences, the video camera can be placed on high magnification and documents can be enlarged on the television screen. Maps, charts, pictures, and pertinent documents, which would normally be difficult for some students to see, can be displayed on television with the instructor highlighting revealing features. For the arts, paintings, drawings, and other art forms can be displayed and analyzed in color. For the sciences, lab demonstrations can be magnified so that important features can be examined in detail, especially demonstrations that require a safety shield and for students to be at a safe viewing distance. The use of a video camera in all disciplines is almost unlimited.

A video camera can also be used to record lessons for students who are absent. Also, for teacher absences, a video camera can be used to record a lesson and then allow a substitute teacher to show the material at a later time. Important concepts that are difficult to perform in class can be taped and played over several times for student comprehension. Intricate events that unfold over time can be replayed one frame at a time. Videotaping student laboratory work and class presentation discussions, and then showing vignettes can be an incontestable review session at the end of a unit. However, make sure parents agree to the taping of their children.

There is a plethora of laser disc software for any subject. Bar code readers allow teachers to access specific locations, almost instantly, thereby reducing time to rewind or forward material on videotape. A great quantity of educational material can be stored on laser disc allowing for consolidation of much educational support material.

The information recorded by a digital camera can be downloaded into a computer and then either printed or projected on a television screen. These pictures can be displayed in the classroom at a nominal cost. The pictures from a digital camera can also be used to document accomplishments for portfolios—your own professional portfolio as well as your students'.

If your school district has a photocopy network, you can add to your classroom management system by preparing and binding handouts for each unit of study. At the middle- or high-school level, teachers can prepare a packet of handouts needed for each semester. The typical handout may include a calendar of events, unit objectives, homework assignments with due dates, lab experiments, review sheets, supplementary reading materials, and pictures of key transparencies, all bound together, with each page perforated for easy removal. Students are less likely to lose a bound packet of material than individual sheets that might end up in the wrong folder or be lost. Using colored divider sheets between the units of study lets students easily locate material and allows them to see upcoming work at a glance. Classroom packets are extremely helpful for teachers when students are absent and want to be able to keep up with class assignments.

Enhancing Your Instructional Strategies with Technology

WORD PROCESSING PROGRAMS

Word processing programs are among the most versatile software available for classrooms. Early experiences, especially in the primary grades, may be devoted to simple writing assignments with a dual purpose: composing and learning keyboarding. Many programs are available to teach students how to type and use the special function keys on the keyboard. As students learn to identify letters and numbers, they can often begin to type them before they can hold a pencil and write them on paper.

Learning to operate a keyboard also provides new opportunities for older students with special needs related to small motor functioning. Students with visual and motor difficulties that prevent them from writing neatly or cause them to erase and redo their work can now create neat papers. The delete key may save students from embarrassment and frustration, just as it does for you and me.

When students master keyboarding skills, they are free to compose many types of verbal products, including letters, stories, poems, essays, reports, and plays. Studies have shown that students write longer pieces on a word processor than they do by hand. The other major benefit is that the word processor greatly simplifies the editing and revision processes. Students can learn to use spelling checkers, grammar checkers, and thesaurus programs. Their motivation to write is increased in part because of the attraction of working on a computer, but also because the final products that are printed out are neat and relatively error-free. Rather than experiencing writing as drudgery, students are likely to feel pride and success related to the writing process when they are allowed to compose and edit using a word processing program.

Students with limited English proficiency benefit from writing and composing with a word processor. By pairing a proficient English speaker with a less proficient student, the two can work together at the computer to compose and illustrate stories and poems. In the process, they are communicating orally as well as in writing, giving the less proficient English speaker an opportunity to use the new language in a meaningful context.

Using word processing programs or more specialized desktop publishing programs, students can create newspapers, magazines, posters, invitations to events, and other materials that have the appeal of a professionally published product. Many teachers employ these media to help students create gifts for families, such as published books of poetry or calendars illustrated by the class.

EDUCATIONAL SOFTWARE

Computer programs are available for classroom use that can diagnose students' skill levels in math, reading, vocabulary, and other basic skills and prescribe lessons at the appropriate level. Computers make excellent tutors because they are endlessly patient in waiting for a student response and give the appropriate feedback without emotional side effects. Like manipulatives in mathematics, many computer games provide students with realistic or simulated experiences that allow them to experiment, observe relationships, test hypotheses, and use data to reach conclusions supported by evidence.

There are thousands of software packages to choose from. How do you select the best program for your students? We suggest logging on to the Educational Software Institute, at **http://www.edsoft.com.** You will find many resources at this site, and be able to preview and read reviews about software for every age level and every subject area in the K-12 curriculum. Another website called Superkids at **http://www.superkids.com** provides reviews of software programs that rate them in terms of educational value and ease of use.

Some gamelike programs are useful in expanding students' experiences beyond the classroom walls into simulated journeys, laboratories, foreign countries, earlier periods of history, and the future. Many of these programs increase students' decision-making and problem-solving abilities by offering them opportunities to make choices and get immediate feedback on the consequences of their decisions.

SLIDE SHOW PRESENTATIONS

Jim Hicks uses slide shows to outline the day's activities and inform students of the objectives for class each day. These slides can be stored on a computer and retrieved for any purpose. Students also display what they have learned in a class project by creating their own slide shows using a word processing document displayed on a television screen, or make a PowerPoint demonstration complete with digital pictures, graphs, charts, and lesson plans all on a series of screen snapshots. These slides can be stored for review sessions in class or at a computer resource center. A summary can be written for each day's presentation, which is especially helpful for students who have been absent.

Slide shows are particularly helpful for parent night presentations when course content and expectations need to be outlined quickly. Many teachers post these documents on a bulletin board, but with this setup you have a living document that can be easily updated, deleted, expanded, and stored for future use. Documents can be shared effortlessly with team members. In fact, team meetings can be used to establish the format and content of these slides, thereby making sure every one is on the same page, excuse me, the same slide.

Another powerful tool with slide shows is concept mapping, which allows students to see the total picture and connect key ideas. This educational technique can be used to help students write more coherently in language arts classes as well as assist science students in understanding major conceptual schemes and social studies students in seeing the cause-and-effect relationships of historical events.

Glenn Leto, vanguard biology teacher at Barrington High School, has designed and developed unique technology workstations at each laboratory table in his room. Instead of using two 27-inch television monitors in the front of his class, Glenn has placed a 13-inch color TV and a recycled computer at each of his seven lab stations. Some of these computers were essentially castaways from the Barrington School District. Because each of the seven TVs cost between $80 and $90 each, their cost was about equal to his previous two 27-inch TVs. However, by having a television at each workstation, Mr. Leto believes his students have more intimate contact with the educational material on the screen. "In addition to the glare at certain angles from the larger televisions, students in the back of the room were about 25 feet from either television," he says. This meant students were at about twice the distance they would be if they were watching television at home. Mr. Leto said this distance meant some students were disengaged from the class material on the screen, whose fine print was often unreadable at those distances.

Mr. Leto, who enjoys designing and building educational provisions for his room, wired the entire setup for less than $100. "I put the VCR, laser disc player, and computer in the corner of the room, and then strung one wire to feed the VCR and computer to the remote TV sets, and a second set of speaker wires for the stereo system. I use a scan converter to make the computer display compatible with NTSC standards. This signal can then be sent through the VCR into the TV system. Students can easily swivel the smaller televisions to suit desired viewing angles and control the input locally. If one of the televisions becomes inoperative, I have lost only $\frac{1}{7}$ of my telecast potential, whereas with the two television set up, I would have lost 50%." Mr. Leto alerts teachers who try this system, "The resolution of a 13-inch television is low, so be careful when choosing some interactive software."

Using this setup allows students to see support material while they are engaged in laboratory work. Additional topics on laser discs, video highlights of pertinent information, or computer simulations can be transmitted peripherally while students are doing experiments. This multimedia approach allows students to seek additional sources while they work on laboratory investigations, or see visual examples while Mr. Leto lectures.

Extending Classroom Experiences Beyond the Classroom Walls

There are both low- and high-tech ways to grab students' attention and keep it before and after they leave your classroom. Damian Simmons, a physics teacher at Barrington High School, sets up a white board in the hallway near his classroom. He uses it as a bulletin board with colored markers to highlight messages for students. It can be used to give students a heads-up reminder as they walk down the corridor from class to class. "It can be used to explain homework assignments, list class activities for the day—and other pertinent messages where I don't want to waste board space in the room. It also turned out to be great PR for physics. Chemistry students would often read these messages wondering what, for example, the Car Push Lab was all about."

Jim Hicks photocopies colored photos of students in action doing physics and displays them on a Wall of Science that he created along the entire length of the science corridor. He also adds spectacular photos of science concepts along with intriguing questions and is always gratified to see students browsing these photos before class trying to answer the questions.

Dawn Morden, a sixth-grade teacher in Altoona, Pennsylvania, wanted to provide more relevant, authentic learning experiences to motivate her students to want to learn social studies. She noticed that her students seemed uninterested in the social studies text because they saw little relationship between the text and their own lives. Ms. Morden and a colleague, Connie Letscher, teamed up to create an interdisciplinary, technology-based project that they call "Crossroads to the World."

They begin with literature that stimulates students' interest in traveling, then introduce computer programs that simulate travel, such as *Oregon Trail* (MECC), and *Where in the World is Carmen Sandiego?* (Broderbund). They have also subscribed to an online educational telecommunications network, *WorldClassroom*, that allows students in Altoona to communicate with people all over the world. When students make contacts in other parts of the world, they share "first-hand" information about their communities. Turning next to word processing programs, students write letters to their new friends.

Each student selects a travel destination and writes business letters or sends e-mail messages to chambers of commerce, tourist bureaus, and embassies to gather information about that destination. They use a spreadsheet to prepare their budget for the trip. They consult newspapers and other media to learn about current events or natural disasters in their chosen destinations. Before their journeys, they plan a bon voyage party, complete with invitations to friends and family, using *Print Shop* (Broderbund).

During the actual "travel," students gather information using CD-ROM, laser discs, and other more traditional resources. They document their trips by keeping a daily log on audiotape or a word processor.

COMPUTER-ASSISTED RESEARCH PROJECTS

CD-ROM disks are fast replacing the traditional encyclopedia in most school media centers. Students are able to type in a key word to call up an article on almost any subject. For many topics, they also see a picture or even a short video of the subject they are researching.

Cliff Gilkey, a multiage fourth/fifth/sixth-grade teacher at Frank Paul Elementary School in Salinas, California, was searching for a method to engage the interest of his students, many from families of migrant workers, with limited English proficiency. The social studies material he had available neither matched his students' interests nor gave them positive role models. To meet these needs, Mr. Gilkey created the Local Heroes Project, a social studies investigation and oral history of local Hispanic, African American, and Vietnamese leaders (such as political figures, business people, researchers, and teachers).

The students decided that they would produce videotapes and publish booklets about the local heroes that students in other classes could use as well. Students were asked to identify local heroes that they would like to know more about. The heroes they selected included a Mexican American school board member, a Latina news anchor-woman, African American police chief, the Cuban American city manager, and a Miwok Indian leader.

For this project, students worked in teams of three to four. They developed a set of interview questions by reading and analyzing biographies to see what other biographers included. After preparing the interview questions, they set up appointments to meet the local heroes they wanted to interview. One student asked questions as another operated the videocamera. They transcribed the words of their subjects onto word processors so that they could create booklets about each hero.

This year Mr. Gilkey plans to do the project again with even more technology at his command. He has a new Hyper Studio program that will allow the students to create multimedia presentations and a VCR companion they plan to use to create special effects and credits for their video production.

DIGITAL HIGH SCHOOL IN ACTION

High school students may even travel back in time via the Internet. Tom Berger teaches high school English at Rancho Buena Vista High School in Vista, California. This year he has put his courses online. To view them, log on to **http://rbvhs.vusd.k12.ca.us/~tberger/index.htm** and you will enter the world of a high school sophomore or senior enrolled in one of Mr. Berger's classes. Let's say, for example, that you are a sophomore taking Mr. Berger's honors class in European literature. First, go to the web page containing the course outline to see the topics that are covered this year. After the course begins, you will log on to the web page for daily assignments to see what Mr. Berger will be covering in class this week and learn your homework assignment.

Figure 10.1 shows the online assignments for the first part of September:

English 10 Honors
Daily Assignments

Date Assigned	Assignment	Points	Category	Due Date
9/1/00	Read "Arthur Becomes King" in Literature book. Pages 427–437	10	Class Work	9/5/00
9/5/00	Journal: 2 paragraphs: 1) Write what comes to mind when you think of Arthurian Legends; i.e., movies, characters, etc. 2) Describe a hero or qualities of a hero.	20	Home/ Class Work	9/6/00
9/5–9/6/00	In Class today we took an *"Internet Field Trip"* to England and looked at different locations related to the Arthurian Legends. We also took notes on the historical background of the legends.			

Figure 10.1   Tom Berger's online class assignments

The term *Internet Field Trip* is highlighted on the web page. When students click on it, they are linked to another page on the high school website that has questions about the history and politics of England. Then they click on a link to a website about King Arthur where they can find the answers to their questions. Of course, this is just the beginning of the search, and students may branch off in many directions depending on their interest in the topic.

Mr. Berger plans to create an Internet field trip for each unit of study in both the classes he teaches this year. He structures these Internet activities to link with pre-selected sites because he wants them to encounter quality information from sites that have integrity. In previous years, Mr. Berger would take students to a computer lab and they would search for information on the topic he assigned. Search engines would come up with nonrelated sites that would pull students' attention off track.

Tom posts a web page called Class Standards to ensure that all students are aware of what is expected of them. This page includes his grading, makeup work and computer policy. Here is an excerpt from that page.

Grades and Points

Students should put their best effort into all their assignments. Some class and homework will be checked off for credit, while essays, quizzes, and tests will be evaluated for a grade. Student's grades are compiled in the following categories:

40%   Essays, Tests, & Quizzes

20%   Class & Homework

20%   Final Exam/Project

20%   Participation & Materials

Students receive 10 points every day. Students lose points for absences, tardies, leaving the room, and forgetting materials. To make up points (for excused absences only) students must call my voice mail to hear the homework message AND leave me a message. This way the student will be able to keep up with the class and will be accountable for reading assignments.

Mr. Berger's rules for using the computer are also clearly defined on the Class Standards web page:

Computer Rules
No food or drinks in the room.

Do your assignment, don't play.

Do not aimlessly "surf the net."

We will be using the computers for researching the novels and the histories of our subjects, for publishing our writing, and for creating presentations. It is more important to put your effort into your content rather than creating flashy presentations.

The writing portion of your grade will always outweigh the appearance portion. This is an English class, not a computer class.

Mr. Berger has put a lot of effort into creating and maintaining these web pages for his courses. But, he says it is the most satisfying year of his teaching career. Students use computers at least three times per week, but the work they are doing is similar to what they would do in a noncomputerized English class. In the past, he found that students often disliked English because of its emphasis on reading and writing. Most students are not excited at the prospect of studying grammar and vocabulary. By bringing in technology, we provide students with a hands-on leaning experience. Instead of using pen and paper, students can create Power Point presentations or web pages of their essays, chapter summaries, poem explications, research project and oral presentations in class. The Internet provides a means for students to publish their work. They can create interactive essays incorporating graphics and reader-selected materials.

> In my classroom I have 18 computers that are connected to the Internet and a schoolwide network. The school applied for a California Digital High School Grant which enables us to infuse technology into the existing curriculum. Every student has his or her own network I.D. and folder which enables them to access their work from any computer on campus.

Mr. Berger still lectures, students still read and write, but the difference is that they write on a computer and save their essays to Mr. Berger's network folder.

One benefit of Mr. Berger's web page assignment is that it opens communications with parents and increases their accountability. At a recent back-to-school night, parents were overjoyed to learn that they could log on to the English 10 Daily Assignment web page and know exactly what is expected of their students. One parent provided Mr. Berger with additional links to add to the web page on Arthurian Legends.

Examples of K–12 Technology Programs

THE ONALASKA EXPERIENCE

The Onalaska School System in Western Wisconsin has a five-year technology plan supported by both the community and staff. We present it here as an example of a well-planned infrastructure that makes technology available to every member of the school community.

Kevin Capwell, the coordinator of the program, likens the district's technology plan to an inverted pyramid. "At the bottom of the pyramid are the classrooms with appropriate hardware and software. As the pyramid broadens, each classroom is connected to the school, each school is connected to the district's grid, and finally, the district to the world. Connecting this entire superstructure between schools and district headquarters is fiber optic cable."

The school district was the recipient of a fortuitous technological partnership when it contracted with the local cable company to use the newly installed fiber optic cable system between school buildings for its technological grid. Consequently, every computer in each school is not only linked to appropriate support systems within a building, but to every computer and support system throughout the district. Onalaska Library, which is next to the high school, is also connected to the school system's grid. This permits students and staff to reference any book in both the school district and public libraries. Every classroom has a mounted television set with a VCR. Information can be channeled into each television from a central audio visual department. However, teachers have the flexibility of using their VCRs for in-class videos. The computer-to-student ratio throughout the district is between 1:3 and 1:2. In addition, teachers each have their own computers, plus access to laptop computers that can be checked out day or night.

Because the community–school relationship and communication is an important component in the daily operations of the school district, the district maintains an extensive web site. E-mail addresses for every staff member—teachers and cooks—along with department phone numbers are available from a directory on that site. Community members can also access this site for free from computers at the public library.

Onalaska High School has a long-distance learning program that serves students, staff, and community members. The Distance Learning Lab (DLL) was funded with state and federal grant monies. Many high schools in the area along with the University of Wisconsin, LaCrosse, belong to the DLL consortium which is interconnected by fiber optic cable running at DS3 speed.

The DLL lab itself consists of a regular-size classroom with six to eight student computer stations. Each station has a computer and keyboard under a glass counter desk. A microphone sits on top. Two banks of four televisions each are at opposite ends of the room. One set of four televisions, in the front of the room, is for student viewing while the second set of four televisions in the back of the room is for instructor use, if needed.

This DLL lab allows a student at Onalaska to enroll in a course offered by another school within the consortium. For example, if an Onalaska High School student wants to enroll in an agriculture business class not offered by the district, he can take the course long distance from Holmen High School, a member-school in the consortium. Also, students or community members can take courses offered by the University of Wisconsin at LaCrosse, via the DLL if the class is scheduled at an appropriate time for both DLL consortium schools.

The interaction between students and teacher is live and in real time because of three cameras installed in the DLL schools. Camera No. 1 is mounted next to the front bank of four televisions and automatically shows an entire class of Onalaska students to a Holmen High School teacher, who views them from a second set of TVs in the back of the room. Camera No. 2 at the base of the second bank of four TVs at Holmen High School shows the instructor teaching the course. There is also a Camera No. 2 at Onalaska. If a student at Onalaska has a question at any time during the presentation, he or she presses a bar on the microphone and Camera No. 1 zooms in on his or her face during the questioning. Camera No. 2 at Holmen zooms in on the instructor during the explanation phase. A third camera can be used at any time to clearly show documents on the front table at Holmen. Camera No. 3 at Onalaska remains idle when the instruction is conducted at Holmen, and vice versa. While Camera No. 2 and Camera No. 3 are operating at Holmen, these two views can be seen in a picture-within-a-picture format on the TVs provided for student viewing at Onalaska. The Holmen teacher also has a picture-within-a-picture format so the instructor will be able to see both views simultaneously.

A teacher at one school can teach students from four other schools, with each school shown on a separate TV for instructor viewing. The school's name appears at the bottom of each screen. All together, five classes can use the DLL format: four schools using DLL instruction and one class at the instructor's school. All five classes concurrently receive instruction.

Eagle Bluff Elementary is a two-story building arranged in wings or "pods," with a state-of-the-art media room in the center. One of the many activities planned for this room are staged television productions that can be transmitted to locations within the district or community via cable.

Computer stations are located in the corridors. Six computers at each station are arranged on a huge circular table. Each computer along with keyboard and ear phones is arranged every 60 degrees, allowing ample room for two students, if necessary, to operate one computer. Because the computers are arranged in a circle, all connecting cables are funneled to the back of each computer through the center of the table to connecting links in the floor. From a distance, the area looks wire-free.

All classrooms next to shared corridors contain a computer, VCR, and about 20 students. Huge interior windows in each classroom allow teachers to view any location in the shared corridor. Consequently, teachers can instruct students inside classrooms or in the shared corridor, simultaneously. "Since all of the technology is hooked together, a student finishing a project anywhere within the pod can record it directly to VHS tape and take it home with him," Mr. Capwell adds enthusiastically.

Onalaska High School has computer laboratories for business, language arts, mathematics-science, applied arts (CAD), and foreign language. There are two computer labs for business, one with Macintosh computers and another containing Windows-based machines. The two computer labs, which have at least 30 student stations, are arranged like bookends with a classroom and a teacher business office nested between them. Students can easily attend class discussions, and then adjourn to either lab to perform computer tasks. The entire yearbook and school newspaper are composed on these computers.

The mathematics computer lab is adjacent to the mathematics rooms. It is not uncommon for students to attend class discussion, and then during the same class period adjourn to the computer lab to complete tasks with carefully chosen mathematical software, including ones for remediation and graphical analyses.

The language arts lab is used the most throughout the school. Students can access this room as early as 6:30 a.m. and can stay as late as 9 p.m. These late-night episodes usually take place near the end of a grading period. The room is near an entrance to the school and can be easily accessed by students after school hours.

A school–community alliance forms the heart of this computer lab. Para-professionals supervise this lab during the day, community volunteers at night. Each supervisor is well versed in computer technology so students can get help when working on projects.

The computer aided drafting (CAD) lab, consisting of at least 30 computers, is next to the applied arts classrooms so that students may attend class discussions, and then within just a few feet, work on computer-assisted drawings. Many times students from nearby English classrooms can be found working on writing projects in this computer lab. Digital editing also takes place in the CAD lab. This allows students to produce *Topper TV,* a biweekly show dedicated to news and events about Onalaska High School. Then news anchors, camera operators, and digital video editors are all students.

Onalaska is a district that has infused technology into every aspect of its curriculum and community relations. We hope that you will be able to teach in a district that has such a pioneering spirit.

THE BEARDSLEY MIDDLE SCHOOL EXPERIENCE

Another district that has encouraged and supported teachers to infuse technology into the curriculum is Crystal Lake District #47, Crystal Lake, Illinois. Diane Jensen brings a great deal of expertise to her computer technology instructor position at Hannah Beardsley Middle School (grades 6–8) in Crystal Lake. Teaching is a second career for Ms. Jensen, who was a managing editor of 13 community newspapers when she retired at age 40. The lack of excitement in her career prompted her to go back to college and pursue a career in teaching. She has never looked back and immensely enjoys her teaching assignment.

Ms. Jensen's main responsibility is to teach computer technology skills to students in seventh and eighth grades. Because the different skill levels of her students can present a problem, one focus of the sixth grade program is to make sure there is a minimum level of keyboarding competency for all students.

The first topic in her nine-week course for seventh graders is file management, which is important for data storage and retrieval. After that is a PowerPoint assignment called *About Me,* which helps Ms. Jensen learn more about the students while introducing them to this presentation program. Included in this assignment are requests for information about students' families, plus their activities, hobbies, and dreams for the future. Once they are finished, students take the project one step further: They make their presentations to their classmates.

The major project for seventh graders is a report and presentation on an endangered species, which is a collaborative effort with seventh-grade science teachers, Fran Hicks and Ann Min. The science teachers evaluate the content of the project; Ms. Jensen evaluates its technical side. "I like to say I grade the style and pizzazz whereas the science teachers grade the substance," she says.

Before students get started, they are given two rubrics for grading the project: one from their science teacher and one from Ms. Jensen. That way everyone knows what is expected.

Working with seventh- and eighth-grade language arts teachers, she uses *Inspiration*— a webbing and graphic organizing software program—to teach her students how they can use it to create a book report. Using circles, rectangles, clouds, and a host of other graphics and symbols available in *Inspiration,* students craft a concept flow chart using arrows drawn between main and complementary ideas. With the click of a mouse, *Inspiration* transforms this right brain activity into a traditional outline complete with Roman numerals and subcategories.

Ms. Jensen believes computers can enhance the education of all students, especially special education students. Some special education students do very well on computer tasks. Ms. Jensen doesn't let those labels interfere with how she treats her students. "Several years ago one of my best students was in special education for support and I didn't even know it," she says. "Because some students have a hard time getting ideas on paper, which could result from having trouble with their handwriting, the computer somewhat standardizes each writing assignment. When writing second or third drafts, students readily appreciate, like all of us, that we do not have to rewrite what is correct. By copying and pasting, only the mistakes have to be corrected. Also, there is a creative side to using computers, especially in PowerPoint presentations and web page designs. The computer is seen as less frustrating for many students. I always like to think I teach children, not the curriculum."

One teaching technique to improve efficiency and independence Ms. Jensen uses is the cup on top of the computer. When working on computer tasks students are encouraged to be self-directed with Ms. Jensen as the guide on the side. However, if students do have questions, instead of raising their hands or shouting out distress signals, they place a plastic cup on top of the computer and continue to troubleshoot. "I use this approach so students can keep working even though they need my help in one area. I don't know very many people who can keyboard efficiently with one hand up in the air and the other one on the keys," she says. "Sometimes students remedy their own problems in seconds after the cup alert. Also, neighbors seeing the cup can assist, thereby encouraging students to see themselves as drivers rather than passengers."

The eighth-grade curriculum emphasizes telecommunications. The major project involves students creating their own web pages featuring a social studies topic. Geography is the focus for some of the students; a Civil War battle is the focus for others. As with the PowerPoint science project, this is a collaborative effort and students earn a grade for both classes.

The eighth-grade telecommunication curriculum includes a history of the Internet, e-mail usage, the substance of a URL address and its purpose, vocabulary pertinent to telecommunications, search engines, and netiquette. Students often surf chat rooms outside of the classroom so Ms. Jensen makes them aware of the dangers associated with this type of activity. That is one reason that she and the school's police liaison officer, Terri Nowak, co-teach a lesson on Internet safety and computer crimes. "Young people in this age group think they're invincible and nothing will happen to them. We try to break down that myth. They also think there's nothing wrong with loading someone else's program onto their computer. We hope they'll understand that it is tantamount to stealing," Ms. Jensen says.

Beyond the classroom, Ms. Jensen works with middle-school students who apply what they have learned in the classroom to a real-world experience: the school newspaper. Four to five times a year, *The Beardsley Roar* newspaper provides faculty, parents, and students with a first-class student publication—complete with photos, coupons, advertisements, news and features, editorials, sports, and a Dear Hannah column. The tabloid-format newspaper is published on newsprint at a nearby printing plant. Readers pay 25 cents a copy or $1 for a year's subscription. This is an after-school club activity with students responsible for all content, including advertisements.

The activity is entirely self-supporting with no outside funds. The newspaper provides a sense of community for the school, with the latest issue 20 pages long. The Dear Hannah advice column reveals an openness and sensitivity that rivals national publications. One entry:

Dear Hannah,

I'm having trouble with my parents. You see they are going through a divorce and I don't know what to do. I'm so upset about it that I barely talk to them anymore. I know they are starting to worry, but I just can't talk to them because I am so mad. How can I fix my problem?
Divorce

Dear Divorce,

Your voice will come back, but for now use your writing skills. Instead of talking to your parents, write to them about how you feel. You might learn writing is a powerful thing. It is often easier to write out your feelings than to say them.
Hannah

In addition to mentoring the computer skills of her students, Ms. Jensen assists other faculty members at Beardsley as they develop programs and curricula that make use of technology. Fran Hicks, Jim Hicks's wife, is a science teacher at Beardsley. Jim describes his wife as one of those teachers who expects, and usually gets, quality work from her students. A life science teacher at Hannah Beardsley Middle School in Crystal Lake, Illinois, who has been recognized by her district for her creative curriculum designs, she has the enthusiasm of a first-year teacher but the knowledge of a sage veteran. In the following Reflective Action, Ms. Hicks recalls how one of her favorite curriculum units has changed and developed over the years. New technology, and the support of her fellow teachers has permitted her to keep growing as a teacher as she interacts with her colleagues to develop courses of study that engage her students in a creative and active search for knowledge and, at the same time, holds them accountable for basic skills.

Case 10.1 ⊃ Reflective Action

Fran Hicks, Life Science Teacher
Beardsley Middle School, Crystal Lake, Illinois

Use Withitness

We talk a lot about interdisciplinary studies these days. But what does this term really mean? For me, the answer to this question got a little bit clearer when I began to notice how much it bothered me to see students' science reports filled with misspelled words and grammar errors. I believe that the more emphasis there is on interdisciplinary studies in each classroom, the better the education we are offering. Whether students are in science or in English classes, when answering questions they should be able to spell correctly and use complete sentences with proper grammar.

Put Problem into Perspective

Using a computer-TV interface, I decided to display the most frequently misspelled science words for the week. With a click of a mouse, I can compare this week's list with the previous top 10 to give students feedback on their spelling growth. As E.O. Wilson (1998, p. 57) said, "The ideal scientist thinks like a poet and works like a bookkeeper. . . . .He also writes like a journalist." This quote inspires me, as a science teacher, to educate students to learn that all of our disciplines are needed to produce a quality report.

Widen the Perspective

As the culmination to an ecology unit, I wanted to give students a project that would encourage them to use good spelling and grammar in communicating good science. I wanted to evaluate the unit using something other than a paper and pencil format, so I decided to have them design a poster publicizing various endangered species. I also believed that they would be motivated to do their best if they knew that their posters would be hung up around the school. The posters would also have the effect of making other students aware of the plight of the endangered animals and plants.

Do Research and Invite Feedback

I spent a considerable amount of time in the school and community libraries researching the most current material that was available to make sure that the students would have ample resources. I also talked to my colleagues Ann Min, another science teacher, and Diane Jensen, the computer instructor, to get their perspectives on this topic. Ann and Diane suggested that since the school had a new Windows™ computer lab, it might be possible to create PowerPoint™ presentations. I also asked for, and received, assistance on this project from the language arts teachers and Marilyn Harfst, the media director, making this even more of an interdisciplinary unit.

Redefine the Problem

With all of this input, I began to see that making posters was just the beginning of what my students could do to generate interest in saving endangered species. We could turn this project into a school-wide curriculum plan that encourages students to think like scientists and communicate their ideas effectively using the latest technology.

Devise New Action Plan

The new plan that developed from this collegial planning is that each student will take the role of a fundraiser for the World Wildlife Federation. Their goal is to get money for a project that will protect an endangered species of their choice. Each student must create and present an informative and persuasive presentation using PowerPoint™. To do this they must go beyond just researching the background of their endangered animals or plants. They also have to focus on the problems that are threatening the existence of the animal or plant and come up with a plan that will effectively save it from extinction. Then, they must use technology and good English skills to produce a PowerPoint™ presentation.

Predict Possible Outcomes

We wanted our students to understand from the outset what was expected of them and how they could succeed. Each of the teachers in the project created a separate evaluation rubric. Diane's rubric is used to grade the technical skills, the language arts rubric is used to check for spelling errors, and my rubric evaluates the science content. We give these rubrics to students at the beginning of the unit, so that they know up front what we expect of them.

TRACKING THE RETURN OF SPRING ON THE INTERNET

When one enters Ann Min's seventh- and eighth-grade physical and life science room, the place oozes with science. Its easy to understand why she is one of the first middle-school science teachers in Illinois to attain the coveted National Board Certified Teacher designation. Ms. Min challenges her students each day to hypothesize, evaluate, and reach a consensus when finalizing answers. The Internet plays a pivotal role in her seventh-grade life-science curriculum *Cycles*. Beginning on Groundhog Day, she coordinates her curriculum unit called *The Return of Spring* with the Annenburg Foundation's online program titled, *Journey North* at **http://www.learner.org/jnorth/current.html.**

On campus, students are assigned to teams that monitor the return of springlike conditions around Hannah Beardsley Middle School. Teams monitor tulips, Monarch butterflies, earthworms, and robins. "By recording soil temperature as a function of days, number of hours of sunlight each day, arrival dates of certain birds, emergent dates for assigned plants, correlations are noticed between measured variables," says Ms. Min.

The student teams fill out a template of information and then log onto the Internet. The Annenburg Foundation's web page processes the information and shares it with the world. Each group identifies its position by latitude and longitude. After downloading information weekly from the Internet, the seventh graders tape robin stickers onto a huge map of the United States at locations where robins were sighted. Because this map is in the hallway, all students in the school are virtually able to see a wave of springlike happenings starting in the south and traveling north.

To heighten interest in scientific observation skills, the Annenburg Foundation picks 10 mystery schools. Students are asked to locate these mystery schools by observing weekly data from the unknown 10 schools.

There is an international flavor tossed into the mix for the Monarch butterfly group. Each fall, Ms. Min has her students mail paper butterflies to middle-school students in Mexico. "The fall mailing, of course, symbolizes Monarch butterflies heading south for the winter," Ms. Min explains. When the Monarch line hits the city in the spring, the middle-school students in Mexico mail the butterflies back to her students. But Ms. Min adds a twist to this. "Our students have to write in Spanish to the students in Mexico, and the students in Mexico write in English to the students at our school." This is truly an international as well as an interdisciplinary project.

The Advantages of Teacher-to-Teacher Networking

A major premise of the reflective action model presented in this text is that teachers learn a great deal by interacting with respected colleagues. We encourage beginning teachers to ask for feedback when they have questions or problems. One of the best methods teachers use today to interact and exchange ideas is networking. While networking still occurs on the telephone or in meetings, the Internet has created many more exciting opportunities for "meeting" people and interchanging ideas.

Today, teachers and their students can belong to a community of learners willing to share ideas, explain complex issues, or suggest alternative solutions. And while other forms of networking may invoke travel expenses or long-distance telephone charges, most information from Internet networks is free.

Jim Hicks belongs to a physics teacher support group called Physics Northwest in northwestern Illinois. It consists of about 90 active members plus a working e-mail list of more than 125 teachers. The face-to-face monthly meetings are informal and usually take place in the early evening to meet the needs of busy teachers' lives. At each meeting, several members and other colleagues give demonstrations or discuss an educational issue. Between meetings, members contact one another via e-mail and receive valuable information on the group's Internet web page at **http://campus.northpark.edu/physics//org/physicsnw.html**. The networking among members is vigorous and the information gleaned from one another is astonishing. Members who missed a meeting can read the minutes and there is a constant flow of messages from teachers seeking help or information. In our model of reflective action in Chapter 1, we stress the need for teachers to ask for feedback from respected colleagues. Networking groups such as Mr. Hicks's membership in Physics Northwest provides an extensive opportunity for information and feedback for beginning and experienced teachers alike.

New teachers are sure to receive many responses from fellow teachers willing to share their valuable resources and expertise. Perhaps not all the responses will be useful or match the teachers' teaching style. It is the responsibility of the teacher who requests the information to reflect on all the responses and make use of the material that is most appropriate and useable. This is true of all Internet exchanges. There is always more information than we can possibly use and we must be willing to consider each source to determine its value.

We encourage teachers at all levels and subject matter to join network groups to help support and promote excellent teaching techniques. It is only when we work together and pool our resources that the students of this nation will have the best education possible.

⊃ Reflections for Your Professional Portfolio
Your Plan to Use Technology in Your Classroom

Use Withitness

Visit a classroom where technology is used. Keep a log of how the teacher uses technological equipment. Take notes about the way the classroom is set up so that students can gain access to the computer. Observe the students to see how they respond to using technology. Are they active and motivated by this type of learning?

Put Problem into Perspective

Consider what you would do in the classroom you have observed. How would you rearrange furniture and equipment to improve students' access to the equipment? What would you add in the way of technology?

Widen the Perspective

Think about a curriculum unit you are planning for this course. What type of learning experiences do you have planned that feature the use of technology? How will you use the equipment to make your presentations for the unit? How will students use the technology to create their final products?

Do Research and Invite Feedback

Talk to the computer coordinator at the school you are visiting. Find out what plans the school has to fund their technology purchases. Tell the coordinator about your curriculum unit and ask for ideas to incorporate more technology into it. The Prentice-Hall Methods Cluster web page which you can access at

http://www.prenhall.com/eby provides you with additional material on using technology and has links to other sites on using technology in the classroom.

Redefine the Problem

Reflect on the reasons we teach with technology. Is it just to make our lives easier or are there fundamental changes in the way people view the world these days because of the technological changes. We have access to more information than we can possibly use on the Internet. What do you want your students to be able to do with all of this information? How can your curriculum unit help them achieve your goal for them?

Devise New Action Plan

Rewrite your curriculum unit to include more options for technology both in your presentations and in the way your students research and gain information. Add several new technological options for students to make presentations on what they've learned.

Predict Possible Outcomes

Refer to Case 10.1 in this chapter. Note how Fran Hicks and her colleagues provided rubrics for evaluation at the beginning of her unit on endangered species. Create one or more rubrics for your curriculum unit that can be used to evaluate the use of technology as well as the content or subject matter. Imagine yourself giving these rubrics to your students at the beginning of the unit so that they will know what they have to do to succeed.

References

Pagel, H. (1982). *The cosmic code: Quantum physics as the language of nature.* New York: Simon and Schuster.

Wison, E. (1998). *Consilience.* New York: Alfred A. Knopf.

chapter 11

ASSESSING AND REPORTING STUDENT ACCOMPLISHMENTS

What is good work? As a teacher, you may find evaluating students' accomplishments among the most difficult judgments you have to make. You have worked hard to create authentic learning experiences. Now, how can you create an assessment system that allows students to demonstrate what they learned? How can you create an assessment system that allows students a range of possibilities to demonstrate their particular strengths and talents? How can you create an assessment system that is fair and that your students can understand?

Educators committed to providing authentic learning for their students also seek meaningful and useful assessment systems that provide information that allows students to develop their skills and knowledge base.

How Teachers Select and Use Assessment Devices

One piece of the authentic learning puzzle is the linking of grading and reporting criteria with the criteria used in the learning process. When students know what the criteria for success are and see how they relate to the learning experiences in the classroom, the learning environment seems fair to them (Guskey, 1994). Varying evaluation procedures is also seen as beneficial. No one evaluation strategy works well for all subjects, grade levels, or student learning styles. For that reason, students should have a variety of ways to earn their grades.

Imagine you are a teacher planning a unit on astronomy for your classroom. You have gathered some interesting learning materials, including filmstrips on the solar system, National Aeronautics and Space Administration (NASA) material on the space shuttles and telescopes, and many exciting books with vivid illustrations. You've planned a field trip to an observatory and invited an astronomer to visit the classroom. You have worked out a time line for several weeks' worth of individual and group investigations and projects.

But now it is time for you to think about evaluation and to clarify your values regarding complex evaluation issues. How will you know what students have learned at the end of this unit? What do you expect them to learn? What techniques will you use to find out whether they have learned what you expect? What about the possibility that they may learn something different from what you expect or even that some students who become very actively engaged in the study may learn more than you expect? How will you know what they learned? How will you assign students science grades at the end of this unit? How will you communicate to the students' parents what each has gained from it?

The following sections describe a variety of assessment devices. Each one has many uses and applications. Each one provides answers to different questions teachers have about evaluation. To illustrate how they compare and how they complement one another, each will be applied to the astronomy unit described previously.

Reflective teachers will consider each alternative and decide whether and how to use such measures in their own classrooms. Recognizing that this introductory text can provide only minimal information about each assessment method, the reflective teacher will want to search actively for more information about certain methods to fully understand their value and use before incorporating them into a program that affects children's lives.

INFORMAL OBSERVATIONS

Teachers use informal observation intuitively from the first moment the students enter the classroom at the beginning of the term. They watch groups to see how students relate to one another; they watch individuals to spot patterns of behavior that are either unusually disruptive or extremely productive. To manage a classroom effectively, "withit" teachers are alert to the overt and covert actions of their students at all times.

Informal observations also have academic implications. Teachers who observe their students while teaching a lesson are able to evaluate their understanding. Spotting a blank look, nervous pencil tapping, or a grimace of discomfort on a student's face, the teacher can stop the lesson, check for understanding, and reteach the material to meet the needs of the students who didn't understand.

As students read aloud, primary teachers observe and listen for patterns of errors in decoding words. They may also listen to the expression in the student's voice to determine whether the student is comprehending the material or simply saying words aloud. They listen for signs that indicate whether the student is interested in or bored with the material. An additional tool in informal observation is asking the student pertinent questions to check for understanding and determine the student's thought processes. This one-to-one interaction provides data and information not measured in any paper-and-pencil test.

By observing the student read, asking a few questions, and comparing the results with those of other students of the same grade or age, the teacher is able to assess many things, including (a) the extent to which the student is able to use phonics and context clues to decode reading material, (b) the student's approximate reading level in terms of sight vocabulary, and (c) the student's comprehension level. In addition, the reflective teacher uses the informal observation to gather information about the student's affective qualities, including confidence level, interest in the subject or in reading itself, amount of effort the student is willing to give to the task, and expectations the student has about success or failure in the subject.

By observing as students write or by reading what they have written, teachers can gather similar data about children's writing abilities, interests, and expectations. As students work out unfamiliar math problems, teachers are careful to observe who works quickly and who is struggling. Then they can gather the struggling students together for an extra tutoring session.

In the astronomy unit, the teacher may observe as students take part in discussions to determine the extent to which various students understand the concepts. When students are visiting the observatory, the teacher will watch them to learn about their interests in various aspects of the topic. When an astronomer visits the classroom, the teacher will listen to the students' questions to assess the depth of their understanding.

Informal observations are one of the most powerful assessment devices the teacher can use to gather information about children's learning patterns and needs. Teachers may gather data about a student from academic and psychological tests, but in the end, it is the informal observation that most teachers rely on to understand the test data and make a final evaluation about appropriate placement or a grade value for a student's work.

PERFORMANCE TASKS TO SHOW MASTERY OF OBJECTIVES

In contrast to informal evaluations, which provide useful subjective information, behavioral objectives are relatively formal and provide useful objective data about what students have learned. Do not assume that teachers choose one or the other of these two devices. Many reflective teachers know that it is valuable to gather both objective and subjective data. They may choose behavioral objectives as a means of gathering hard data about what students have achieved during classroom learning experiences and compare those data with the subjective information they have gathered during their informal observations.

To plan an assessment system based on students showing mastery of certain specified outcomes or objectives, the teacher must begin before teaching the lesson. By preplanning a unit with specific outcomes or a lesson with concrete behavioral objectives, the teacher specifies each skill that students should be able to demonstrate at the conclusion of the lesson and the criteria for success. Teachers then plan learning experiences that are linked with the outcomes. After each objective has been taught and students have had an opportunity to practice the new skill, a quiz, worksheet, or other assessment product asks students to demonstrate that they have mastered the new skill and can perform it with few errors.

When each lesson is introduced, the teacher describes the prespecified criterion for success to the students. The criterion may be a percentage or a minimum number of correct responses. For example, the following behavioral objective specifies 80% (or 16 of the 20 possible items) as the acceptable demonstration of mastery of this objective:

Spelling Objective: When the teacher reads the list of 20 spelling words aloud, students will write 80% of the words, using correct spelling and legible handwriting.

A criterion-referenced test such as the weekly spelling test common in many classrooms demonstrates whether the students have mastered the new skill. To record student achievement, teachers may write the percentage of correct responses that each student attained in a grade book.

For more complex objectives, teachers design performance tasks that require students to demonstrate what they have learned. Marzano, Pickering, and McTighe (1993) describe a system that allows teachers to design performance tasks that measure growth in communication skills, information processing and other such complex acts. For example, students may present oral reports on a NASA satellite launch and the teacher may evaluate their knowledge and communication skills by using a rubric such as the following (Marzano et al. 1993, p. 85):

Rubric for Communication Skills and Oral Presentations
4. Clearly and effectively communicates the main idea or theme and provides support that contains rich, vivid, and powerful detail.
3. Clearly communicates the main idea or theme and provides suitable support and detail.
2. Communicates important information but without a clear theme or overall structure.
1. Communicates information in isolated pieces in a random fashion.

CRITERION-REFERENCED QUIZZES AND TESTS

Quizzes are frequently used with behavioral objectives to determine whether students are successfully gaining each new skill or bit of knowledge in a unit of study. Quizzes are generally short, consisting of only a few questions or items, and are thought of as formative assessments, providing teachers with a way to know whether the students are learning the material day by day.

Tests, however, may consist of many items and are generally thought of as summative assessments. Tests are often given at the end of a unit and contain a variety of items that measure students' achievement of content and skills that have been taught during a period.

In both cases, the term *criterion-referenced* refers directly to the criterion established for each behavioral objective. Each item on a criterion-referenced test should match an established criterion. Criterion referencing provides objective data about material that all students in the class have had an equal opportunity to learn.

Objective tests may take a variety of forms. The most common are matching, true-false, multiple choice, and short-answer or completion forms.

Matching items provide both the question and response. Students have only to recognize the correct response for each item and draw a line to connect the two. Items appear in a column on one side of the paper and the responses in a different order on the other side. In terms of Bloom's taxonomy, matching items are an excellent way of measuring knowledge-level objectives that require students to recognize correct responses. An example of a matching quiz related to the astronomy unit might look like this:

Jupiter	Planet with rings and many moons
Earth	Planet closest to the sun
Mercury	Planet that is ⅗ water
Saturn	Largest planet

To construct fair matching items, each right-column response must be clearly identified with only one item on the left. In our astronomy test, for example, descriptions of the planets need to contain unambiguous elements so that only one matches each planet. If several responses are vaguely correct, the reliability and therefore the objectivity of the test decline.

True-false items are also knowledge-level items, consisting of a statement that students must recognize as either true or false. These items are difficult to write, as they must be factual and objective if they are to provide useful data. If items contain unsupported opinions or generalizations, the students must guess what the teacher intended.

For our astronomy unit, we might construct a quiz with statements such as these:

True	False	The sun orbits the Earth.
True	False	Venus is smaller than Jupiter.
True	False	Mars is closer to the sun than Neptune.

These items are reliable in that the correct responses are not likely to change in our lifetime. They are also valid because every item is an element directly related to our objective of teaching students about the physical characteristics of the solar system.

As examples of less reliable and less valid items, consider these:

True   False   Venus is a more interesting planet than Uranus.
True   False   The sun will never stop shining on the Earth.

Multiple-choice items also measure knowledge-level objectives because they call for the student to recognize a fact or idea. A multiple-choice item contains a question, problem, or unfinished statement followed by several responses. The directions tell the student to mark the one correct answer. While college admission tests may contain several near-right responses and students are expected to use reasoning to determine which one is best, classroom tests should probably be constructed with only one correct response. As in other objective measures, reliability and validity of each item must be considered.

To fit the astronomy unit, two valid and reliable items are these:

1. Which planet is known as the red planet?
    A.   Venus
    B.   Orion
    C.   Mars
    D.   Jupiter

2. It would take longest to travel from Earth to. . . .
    A.   Neptune
    B.   Mercury
    C.   Venus
    D.   Saturn

Short answer or *completion* items supply a question or an unfinished statement, and students are expected to supply a word, phrase, number, or symbol. These items are used primarily to test students' knowledge of specific facts and terminology. In our astronomy unit, two examples are these:

1. The planet Saturn has _____ rings around it.
2. Which planet has the most moons?

The advantage of the four types of objective items that make up most criterion-referenced tests is that they objectively measure students' knowledge of the basic content of a subject. They can be written to match directly the criteria of the teacher's objectives for the lessons. They are also relatively easy to correct, and the scores are easily recorded and can be averaged together to provide the basis for report card grades.

The disadvantage of such items is that they measure only students' understanding of basic knowledge-level content and skills. They do not provide information about what students comprehend, how they would apply the knowledge they have gained, what they would create, or how they analyze and evaluate the ideas they've learned.

MASTERY LEARNING

Some teachers prefer to use a strategy known as *mastery learning* to motivate students to learn a sequence of skills. In mastery learning, individual students work through a series of learning experiences at their own pace and demonstrate mastery as they complete each objective. The teacher uses the information gained on the tests to provide helpful feedback for reteaching rather than as a record of achievement. Summative evaluations occur only at the end of a unit of study, when students are expected to demonstrate mastery of a whole sequence or unit of learning. Grades of unit tests are recorded and become the basis for determining students' grades.

In the astronomy unit, the teacher may have written a number of outcome statements, such as these:

> After viewing the filmstrip on the solar system, the students will be able to match pictures of each planet with its name, with no more than one error.
>
> Students will be able to draw and label an illustration of the solar system with the sun and nine planets in their respective orbits, with 100% accuracy.

Together these two outcomes will inform the teacher whether students have learned the names, distinctive visual elements, and locations of the planets in the solar system. To measure whether students have mastered this content, the teacher simply carries out the tasks described in the objectives after students have had sufficient opportunity to learn the material. The teacher prepares a matching quiz with a column of nine names and another column of nine pictures of the planets. For those who do not achieve the criterion of eight correct answers, the teacher can provide a reteaching experience or require students to do additional reading on their own. They can be retested until they achieve the criterion.

On another occasion, the teacher distributes blank paper and asks students to draw and label the solar system. From these two objectives and others like them, the teacher can begin to answer the question, "How will I know what they have learned?" Also, the data gathered from this assessment system are more readily translated into letter grades than are the data from informal observations.

ESSAYS EVALUATED WITH RUBRIC GUIDELINES

Essays have the exact opposite advantages and disadvantages of criterion-referenced tests. They are subjective rather than objective. Two or more teachers rarely evaluate an essay the same way unless they are given specific criteria on which to base their ratings. Essays are also time-consuming to read and mark.

However, essays provide teachers with an excellent means of knowing what students comprehend, how they would apply their new learning, and how they analyze and evaluate the ideas and concepts. Essays also provide students with opportunities to be creative by asking them to synthesize a number of previously unrelated notions into an original expression of their own. Essays can answer the question, "How much more have they learned than I expected in this unit?"

To improve the way teachers rate essays, many school systems employ a rubric guide that specifies what an essay must contain and how it must appear on the page to earn a specific mark or grade. Teachers who use a rubric to guide their assessment of essays usually limit the topic of the essay with specific parameters and may even specify what must be included in the response. For example, in the astronomy unit, the teacher may want to assess whether students can describe the concept of outer space in their own words. This will provide information about how much students truly comprehend about the subject rather than what they simply remember. For example, a teacher may present students with these guidelines for writing their essay on the solar system:

> Write a two-paragraph essay in your own words comparing the earth's atmosphere with space. Tell why humans cannot live in outer space without life support. Use examples and provide evidence to support your ideas.

These guidelines are fairly explicit in terms of length and content. For these reasons, this form of essay is relatively objective. To make it even more likely that two or more teachers would look for similar elements when correcting the papers, school systems may provide teachers with *rubric evaluation* samples of student work, along with specific descriptions for measuring success on a particular essay topic.

Grade	Characteristics of Essay
A	Paragraphs are well-organized and contain at least six sentences. Facts are accurate and evidence is clearly given to support the student's viewpoints.
B	Paragraphs contain at least four sentences. Most facts are accurate. Examples are given to support ideas.
C	Paragraphs contain at least three sentences. Some facts are accurate, although one or more errors are present. One example is given.
D	Paper contains only one paragraph. Some facts are accurate, though no evidence or examples are given to support them.
F	Unconnected sentences contain few accurate facts. Many errors are stated. No examples given.

This format for essay evaluation is especially useful for assessing students' levels of comprehension on a topic. It also provides an opportunity for students to demonstrate their ability to analyze the topic, but limits the use of synthesis and evaluation. If students are provided with the rubric system before they begin writing, they are more likely to know what the teacher expects of them and thus be able to deliver it.

For other purposes, the *extended response essay* gives students more freedom to express ideas and opinions and to use synthesis-level thinking skills to transform knowledge into a creative new idea. In the astronomy unit the teacher may hope that students will gain a sense of responsibility for the Earth after studying its place in the universe. This affective goal for the unit may also be expressed as a series of problem-solving or expressive objectives. For example,

> At the end of the unit, students will write an essay titled "The Big Blue Marble," in which they express their own hopes and fears for the future of the Earth. The essays will be edited, rewritten, illustrated, and displayed for parents to view on parent's night.

This extended-response essay calls on students to integrate all that they have learned in this unit and combine it with previous learning from geography and social studies units. Their individual experiences and outside readings are likely to affect their responses as well. Objectivity in marking this essay is very low. It is quite likely that teachers will view the responses very differently from one another. Nevertheless, within a single classroom, a teacher can say or state a set of criteria or expectations that can lead students to write a successful essay. In this instance, as stated in the objective, students will have an opportunity to receive critical feedback and make corrections on their essays before the final products are displayed.

Despite the lack of objectivity of extended-response essays, there is good reason to include them in an educational program. They provide invaluable information about the creativity, values, philosophy, and maturity of students. Moreover, they encourage students to become more creative and give them practice in making difficult judgments. One of the most effective ways to provide students with the information they need to succeed is to provide them with the rubric descriptions before they write their essays. When students can see the criteria by which their work will be evaluated, they are able to meet the expectations with much greater degrees of success than when they try to guess what the teacher expects or wants from them.

ORAL REPORTS AND EXAMINATIONS

Like essays, *oral reports* can be restricted or unrestricted depending on the type of assessment the teacher wants to generate. To increase objectivity and communicate expectations to students, teachers can create rubric systems describing the length and format of the oral report as well as what must be included. Examples of *restricted* oral reports include book reports in which students are expected to describe the main characters, the setting, the plot, and their favorite part of the story. In a restricted oral examination, teachers may ask questions that students must answer within specified parameters. In the astronomy unit, an oral examination may be scheduled for a certain day. Students are told to prepare for it by reading material supplied by NASA on the U.S. space program. In the examination, teachers ask questions taken from the reading material, and students are expected to respond in their own words. For example,

> Tell how the astronauts prepared for weightlessness.
>
> Describe the food astronauts eat in space.

As teachers listen to the responses, they can judge whether the students' answers are right or wrong. They also can assess whether the students have a poor, average, or unusually good understanding of the ideas they speak about. The teacher's evaluation of the students' responses can be recorded in some form, to be shared with the student later.

Unrestricted oral reports allow students more opportunities to speak about matters of great interest and importance to them. They encourage students to use their imagination to generate synthesis-level responses or to be persuasive about a matter of opinion or judgment. For example,

Describe the space journey you'd like to take.

Tell what you think should be NASA's next big undertaking.

Debate is a form of oral examination that provides students with an opportunity to prepare to speak about a subject by learning a great deal of content and evidence for opinions before the event. During the debate, teachers can assess the students' energy and effort used in gathering information, as well as their understanding of the topic.

In evaluating oral presentations, teachers may write comments as they listen, or they may videotape the presentations so that they can evaluate them more comprehensively later. Students may be involved in self-evaluation of their own efforts as well. They can view the videotapes and discuss with the teacher what they did well and what they need to improve.

Designing Authentic Assessment Tasks

It is possible to construct assessment tasks that measure student performance in using higher-level thinking skills of analysis and evaluation, as well as critical thinking skills of observation and inference and problem-solving strategies such as the creation and testing of hypotheses. These tests can be constructed as paper-and-pencil exams, presenting a situation or dilemma and asking students to respond to it in various ways. Such a test may consist of a passage to be read that describes a problem or dilemma. Maps, charts, graphs, or other data might accompany the passage. The test items would then consist of questions that allow the student to observe, infer, formulate a hypothesis, design methods of testing the hypothesis, and speculate about the possible outcome.

Another common method of assessing student's authentic learning is to encourage them to do independent research on one aspect of a unit theme and create a product that shows what they have learned. This allows students to demonstrate their knowledge, comprehension, and all four of the higher-level thinking skills on a topic. This assessment technique is appropriate for every area of the curriculum. Students can do independent research or make an independent investigation in math, science, social studies, literature, music, or art. This method lends itself especially well to interdisciplinary units.

The strategy is for the teacher to introduce a unit or theme and provide some teacher-centered instruction on it at the outset. Readings may be assigned, and quizzes and worksheets may be used to assess the extent to which the student is developing a knowledge base about the topic. Essays or oral presentations may be assigned to assess whether students comprehend the main ideas and concepts of the topic. Finally, each student selects one aspect of the main topic on the basis of individual preference or interest and begins to research that subtopic independently. Each student decides on a final product that will demonstrate what has been learned and achieved during the independent study.

The kinds of products that students might create as a result of this type of investigation are limitless. Many teachers prefer to plan their evaluations of student accomplishment to correspond with Bloom's taxonomy. Specific student products are appropriate for learning objectives at all six levels. A sample of them can be found in Figure 11.1.

Teachers may evaluate these student products using a rubric checklist or rating scale. Very specific rubric systems may be prespecified so that students know exactly what their product must demonstrate to earn a high mark or positive evaluation from the teacher. Reflective teachers who wish to encourage critical thinking and reflectiveness among their students are also likely to involve the students in self-evaluation of their own products. When students evaluate their work critically, they are learning how to become more independent and responsible for revising and improving their work without an outside evaluator.

RUBRICS, CHECKLISTS, AND RATING SCALES

When teachers wish to assess students' products or presentations, they can tell the students their reactions in a conference or write comments on a piece of paper and give these comments to the students. These methods suffice for informing the students, in a general way, whether they have met the teacher's expectations in the product, and they may be adequate for evaluating an unrestricted product or presentation.

When the teacher has prespecified the criteria for a product or presentation and several important elements must be included, the teacher may choose to create a *rubric* or *checklist* to use for notation when listening, for example, to the speech. This is frequently done when the objective is for students to use effective speaking skills in a presentation. In preparing the students for the speech, the teacher will likely specify several important elements that the students should incorporate, such as maintaining eye contact with the audience, using appropriate volume to be heard by everyone in the room, and speaking rather than reading during the presentation. By preparing a simple checklist with these items on it, the teacher can quickly and accurately record whether each student used these skills in their presentations. To make the whole system even more valuable, when the teacher shares the rubrics with the students ahead of time, students are able to make much better judgments about what to study, what to include, or how to present the information they have learned.

Rubrics and checklists can record mastery of many basic skills in the primary grades. Each item on the checklist can correspond directly to a behavioral objective. Together the items on a checklist provide an overview of a sequence of objectives. Kindergarten teachers frequently employ checklists to record the letter recognition of each pupil, letter by letter. Primary teachers use checklists to record mastery of basic math operations. Intermediate and middle school teachers may use checklists to record whether students have demonstrated fundamental research skills. In our astronomy

Characteristics of Each Level	Products Associated with Each Level
Knowledge Level	**Knowledge Level**
Can recognize and recall specific terms, facts, and symbols.	Worksheet, Label a given diagram, Memorize poem or song, List, Quiz, Recognition of math symbols, Spelling bee, Response to flashcard.
Comprehension Level	**Comprehension Level**
Can understand the main idea of material heard, viewed, or read. Is able to interpret or summarize the ideas in own words.	Written paragraph or summary of main idea, Oral retelling of story, Use of math symbols and numbers in simple calculations, Report.
Application Level	**Application Level**
Is able to apply an abstract idea in a concrete situation, to solve a problem, or relate it to prior experiences.	Diagram, Map, Model, Illustration, Analogy, Mental problem solving, Action plan, Teaches others, Diorama, Costume, Diary, Journal.
Analysis Level	**Analysis Level**
Can break down a concept or idea into its constituent parts. Is able to identify relationships among elements, cause and effect, similarities and differences.	Graph, Survey, Chart, Diagram, Report showing cause and effect, differences and similarities, comparisons and contrasts.
Synthesis Level	**Synthesis Level**
Is able to put together elements in new and original ways. Creates patterns or structures that were not there before.	Artwork, Story, Play, Skit, Poetry, Invention, Song, Composition, Game, Collection, Hypothesis, Essay, Speech, Videotape, Film, Computer program.
Evaluation Level	**Evaluation Level**
Makes informed judgments about the value of ideas or materials. Uses standards and criteria to support opinions and views.	Debate, Discussion, Recommendation, Letter to editor, Court trial, Panel, Chart showing hierarchies, rank order, or priorities.

Figure 11.1   Student products related to Bloom's taxonomy

Note: Created by Judy Eby *from Taxonomy of Educational Objectives: Handbook I: Cognitive Domain* by B. S. Bloom et al. Copyright 1956, 1984 by Longman Publishing Group.

unit, for example, the teacher may combine a goal of developing research and study skills with the goal of content mastery. To record the accomplishment of these skills the teacher may use a checklist such as the one in Figure 11.2.

Checklists provide useful and efficient means of recording information about the accomplishments of individual students. They are also valuable during a student-teacher conference. Both teacher and student can quickly see what has been achieved and what still lies ahead. Checklists are also valuable when teachers confer with parents about the student's progress along a set of learning objectives.

Rating scales are used in circumstances similar to those of checklists. They provide additional information, however, in the form of a rating of how well the student achieved each element or skill on the list. Rating scales are useful in providing students with feedback that rates their performance on an objective. In the astronomy unit, for example, students' products may be turned in and evaluated by the teacher, using a rating scale of important elements. In many classrooms, teachers involve the student in their own evaluation of the product and the efforts expended in creating them. In Figure 11.3, a rating scale is structured so that both the student and the teacher rate the finished product.

A rubric system is similar to a checklist, but also employs detailed descriptions of the specific levels of mastery the teacher hopes students will attain. Student products are then compared to the levels of mastery described in the rubric system. In Figure 11.4, a rubric system is shown that allows the teacher to compare student products related to the astronomy research project against a set of very specific criteria. As has been suggested before, if students are given this rubric system prior to beginning the unit, they are empowered to make better choices about how to use their time, what to study, and how to present the material they have learned.

Many times, you will see rubrics with four levels of quality such as the one shown here. But, what do the Levels 4 through 1 mean? Are they the same as the grades A, B,

---

Name _____ Grade _____

This is a record of research and study skills demonstrated by this student. The teacher's initials and date indicate when the skill was successfully demonstrated.

Date	Initials	Skill Area
_____	_____	A. Located a book on astronomy in the card catalog
_____	_____	B. Located a book on astronomy on the library shelves
_____	_____	C. Used the table of contents to find a topic
_____	_____	D. Used the index to find a subtopic
_____	_____	E. Orally interpreted a graph or chart
_____	_____	F. Took notes on a chapter in a book on astronomy
_____	_____	G. Summarized the chapter from notes
_____	_____	H. Wrote the bibliography for the book

Figure 11.2 Astronomy unit checklist of research and study skills

Name _____ Grade _____

To the student: Please evaluate your own product, using the following scale:

    O = OUTSTANDING; one of my best efforts
    S = SATISFACTORY; I accomplished what I set out to do
    N = NEEDS IMPROVEMENT; I need to revise and improve this element

Student's Rating	Skill Area	Teacher's Rating
_____	Did adequate research and information gathering	_____
_____	Elements of the model are accurate in shape	_____
_____	Elements of the model are accurate in scale (except for orbits of planets)	_____
_____	Labeling is accurate and legible	_____
_____	Legend is accurate and legible	_____
_____	Model is visually interesting and pleasing	_____

Figure 11.3   Astronomy unit rating scale of the solar system model

C and D? Andrade (2000) observes, "Satisfactory labels are hard to come by, although it is obvious at a glance that a 4 is what everyone should try to achieve and a 1 is something to avoid. Some teachers indicate a cutoff point on the rubric, for instance, by drawing a box around the level that is considered acceptable" (p. 12).

How do you, as a classroom teacher, learn to create fair and useful rubrics for your classroom assignments? Andrade (2000) suggests that you look at other models of rubrics, but then involve your own students in the process. She envisions the teacher and students discussing the criteria together, listing the most important criteria, and then writing descriptions of the various levels of quality.

One method Andrade suggests for creating rubrics uses these four sentence stems: *Yes; Yes, but; No, but;* and *No.* For example, if the criterion is "Briefly summarize the plot of the story," the four levels might be the following:

Level 4—"**Yes,** I briefly summarized the plot."

Level 3—"**Yes,** I summarized the plot, **but** I also included some unnecessary details or left out key information."

Level 2—"**No,** I didn't summarize the plot, **but** I did include some details from the story."

Level 1—"**No,** I didn't summarize the plot." (Andrade, 2000, p. 14)

To the student: Read these criteria before you begin your research so that you will know how to earn the level you want to attain.

Turn in a 5–10 page booklet on the solar system. The booklet may contain a combination of words, pictures, graphs, and any other types of illustrations that show an understanding of the physical elements of the planets, moons, and sun that make up our solar system. The booklets will be evaluated according to the following criteria:

Level 4: The student clearly and completely identifies the important planets and moons of the solar system and shows how they are related to the sun and each other in size and space. There is a combination of verbal descriptions and visual illustrations that make the distinguishing features of each planet very evident. The writing is well organized, and references are given for sources of information. At least four references are provided.

Level 3: The student clearly identifies the planets and some of the most important moons of the solar system. Relationships of size and space are given, though they may be distorted in some cases. Verbal information is fairly well organized, and illustrations are useful in distinguishing among the planets. At least two references are given as sources of information.

Level 2: The student correctly names the nine planets and shows that they travel around the sun. Relationships among planets are not accurate. The booklet uses more pictures than words. Only one source of information is provided.

Level 1: The student incorrectly labels planets and shows little understanding of their relationship to the sun and to each other. Verbal information is given as captions for illustrations only. No source of information is given.

Figure 11.4   Rubric grading evaluation system for astronomy research project

LEARNING CONTRACTS

A learning contract is a device that can be thought of both as a teaching strategy and a means of assessment. The learning contract described in Chapter 10 lists several required activities and a number of options for the unit on settling the western United States. Teachers using this strategy meet with individual students to agree on a suitable number and type of optional activities. The activities on the contract then provide the structure for daily learning experiences. When the unit is complete, the contract is used as the basis for assessing what each student has accomplished. Just as in adult life, students are held accountable for meeting the terms of their contracts. If they succeed, they can expect a positive evaluation. If they have not met the terms of their contract, they can expect to have to explain why and describe what they will do to honor their contract.

Learning contracts can take several forms and can even be structured so that the student makes a contract to receive a certain grade for a specified amount of work. A point system can be employed to allow students to select from among options and earn the grade they desire. For example, in the astronomy unit, a learning contract with a built-in point system for earning a grade is shown in Figure 11.5.

Learning contracts also serve as the basis for recording accomplishments. In the sample learning contract in Figure 11.5, the parent is also required to sign the contract, agreeing to support the student's efforts. This strategy is an efficient way to communicate with parents about the goals and expectations of the class. Later, during parent-teacher conferences, the parent can see the work that was accomplished. If a student did not complete the contract, the parent can see what was left undone.

PORTFOLIOS OF STUDENT PRODUCTS

Portfolios are collections of work samples designed to illustrate a person's accomplishments in a talent area. Photographers collect portfolios of their best photos; artists collect their artwork; composers collect their compositions. Assessment portfolios are used to document what a student has achieved in school. To use this technique, teachers collect samples of each student's work and put them in a file folder with that student's name on it. Some teachers collect many types of work in a single portfolio; others have writing portfolios that contain only writing samples, math portfolios filled with worksheets and tests, and others for other subject areas.

It is important to understand that a collection of student work in a folder is not portfolio assessment. As an assessment tool, a portfolio contains a selection of work samples, anecdotal records, tests, and other materials that document the students' progress. The student's progress must be analyzed and summarized by the teacher and the student. There should be a statement of goals written jointly by the student and teacher. Students can select samples of work to be included in the portfolio and write brief explanations of the reason the item was selected and the progress it shows. Often there are summary sheets that document the students' growth.

Portfolio assessment allows students to demonstrate their content knowledge without being dependent on English fluency or reading ability. Portfolios allow the teacher and student to approach the anxiety-laden process of evaluation more comfortably because it celebrates progress rather than weaknesses.

Portfolios may be kept for a long or short time. Many teachers collect writing samples in the first week of school, then periodically throughout the school year. In some cases the teacher may assign a writing topic during the first week and then assign the same topic during the last week of school. When the two samples on the same topic are compared, the growth and development of the students' writing abilities is plain for everyone to see.

A short-term portfolio may be collected for the duration of a learning unit. For example, in the astronomy unit, all of the student's work, including quizzes, essays, pictures, and photos of the model solar system can be collected in a portfolio to document that student's accomplishment during the unit. If a contract was used during the unit, the contract will be included in the portfolio along with the work samples. In Case 11.1, Glenn Leto, a high school science teacher shares his experience on developing portfolios for short-term science units.

Astronomy Unit Learning Contract

I, _____ , a student in the fifth grade at Otis
School, do hereby contract to complete the following tasks during my investigation
of the solar system.

Furthermore, I agree to complete these tasks by _____ .

I understand that I am agreeing to earn _____ points, which will earn a
grade of _____ if my work is evaluated to be acceptable.
I understand that the point values listed below are the maximum number that can
be earned for each task and that fewer points may be awarded.

Points Needed to Earn Specific Grades

> 90 = A	> 80 = B	> 70 = C	> 60 = D	< 60 = F

_____	10 pts	Read Chapter 7 in the science text. Do exercises, pp. 145–146.
_____	10 pts	Matching quiz
_____	10 pts	True-false quiz
_____	10 pts	Multiple choice quiz
_____	10 pts	Short-answer quiz
_____	15 pts	Drawing of the solar system, labeled correctly
_____	20 pts	Model of the solar system, labeled and scaled to size
_____	10 pts	Essay on Earth's atmosphere and outer space
_____	10 pts	Essay on "The Big Blue Marble"
_____	05 pts	Per answer on NASA oral exam
_____	10 pts	Oral report on "A Space Journey I'd Like to Take"
_____	10 pts	Finished checklist on research skills

Signed this day _____ 20_____ at _____School.

_____   _____
        student signature   teacher signature

_____   _____
        parent signature   witness signature

Figure 11.5   Sample learning contract

Case 11.1 ⟳ The Homework Portfolio

Glenn K. Leto, Science Teacher
Barrington High School, Barrington, Illinois

Withitness

For me, the assessment and evaluation of written work is one of the least fulfilling and most tedious aspects of my job. Yet, I feel that reading and grading homework is an inescapable necessity for good teaching. Students learn through activity, and the creation of a written product has definite advantages.

Put Problem into Perspective

More importantly, written products can form a foundation for the development of review-resources that will be available days, weeks, and months later. So as I began my teaching career and for many years afterward, I assigned a wealth of work and spent what seemed like most of my waking hours grading it. As I gained experience, I realized that I also wanted to emphasize that assignments are steps along the pathway of learning; most assignments are learning tools rather than evaluation instruments. To this end, I wanted students to view each endeavor as part of a work in progress. I want my students to understand that the whole is more than the sum of its parts. With this in mind, I had my students accumulate their work for each unit in a notebook which was submitted at the end of each quarter.

Widen the Perspective

While this new approach lightened my load, it was not as well received by my students as I had anticipated, especially my higher ability students. Most students still viewed each assignment as an entity in itself, rather than as a part of an evolving whole. Ungraded work was considered busy-work; work that was only checked in must be unimportant. Most of my students still viewed every assignment as a test rather than as a tool. If they did the work, they wanted me to see it and acknowledge its value. Over time, I realized that the notebook grade was more a reward for neatness and organization than anything else. The notebook was simply a depository rather than evidence of an ongoing process.

With more experience, I more clearly delineated my needs. I wanted a more manageable system for assessing and evaluating written work; a system that was more integral to instruction rather than an adjunct to it. Such a system should:

1. emphasize that assignments are tools for learning, not another form of testing;
2. promote the accumulation and organization of written work to provide the basis for a review resource at the end of the semester and year;

3. communicate that each product has value and a place in the learning endeavor;
4. provide meaningful feedback, in a timely fashion;
5. focus on the holistic aspects, the big ideas, of a student's work;
6. recognize that people learn in a variety of ways; and
7. keep me from becoming a homework hostage trapped beneath a pile of papers.

Do Research and Invite Feedback

Colleagues offered various personal approaches for assessment and evaluation. While some approaches significantly reduced the amount of time grading papers, none appeared to achieve the goals I had in mind. It seemed that many teachers shared my desire for a better mouse trap, and a plethora of possibilities existed. Over a period of years, my participation in workshops and conference presentations increased my awareness of meta-cognition (thinking about thinking), multiple intelligences, and authentic assessment. Eventually, I grew more aware of the use of portfolio assessment. I say more aware because I first learned of portfolios some years earlier from a colleague who teaches drawing, where the portfolio has long been the basis of assessment. At that time, I felt that the concept of portfolio assessment was intriguing, but I did not see how it could be effectively applied to my classroom.

Redefine the Problem

Portfolio assessment has been a popular topic, but its application in the high school science classroom has been less widespread than in other disciplines. One of the better science portfolio assessment systems that I have encountered was developed by the State Collaborative on Assessment and Student Standards(SCASS). Portfolio assessment, as implemented in the SCASS program, accomplishes some of my goals. It focuses on the holistic nature of student work, and it certainly emphasizes that each assignment is a step in the overall learning process. A portfolio system promotes the accumulation and organization of a student's work, and it generally gives the student some degree of latitude and responsibility for selecting the portfolio's content.

While the portfolio concept spoke to me, this system of assessment had some shortcomings, in terms of my specific needs. The most significant problem was that these portfolio systems were meant to be summative devices. The typical portfolio reflects work over longer periods of study (a quarter, a semester, or a year) rather than a single two- to three-week unit.

Devise New Action Plan

Thus, my problem could be distilled down to my desire to refashion the long-term portfolio system into an assessment tool that I could apply to a typical two- to three-week unit of study. To this end, I introduced my students to my concept of the homework portfolio. The contents of a homework portfolio include the accumulated artifacts of the student's work over the course of the unit. I use the term artifacts because a student's work may take different forms and may include a variety of media. Typically, a portfolio's contents include:

> a title page;
>
> a table of contents;
>
> reports of laboratory investigations;
>
> written products that result from problem-based learning activities;
>
> other written assignments such as a study guide;
>
> a category I call Unassigned Work;
>
> a unit summary, which generally takes the form of a narrative; and
>
> extra credit.

The portfolio's Unassigned Work section is an attempt to encourage my students to develop personal techniques and strategies that enhance their learning. Credit is given for evidence of such techniques. Written notes, outlines, and concept maps are some of the more common elements of unassigned work, but the emphasis is on what works for each individual. Audio-notes, summary graphics, and even models are some of the other artifacts that have been included as unassigned work. Ultimately I want each student to come to the understanding that he or she has the primary responsibility for reaching their learning goal.

The Unit Summary section may be the most important part of the portfolio. This section requires the student to pull together the various unit concepts and activities into a meaningful whole. Through this summary, the student confronts the various assignments and concepts in the context of the big ideas and issues of the unit.

Predict Possible Outcomes

Although the portfolio is collected and evaluated at the end of the unit, students often need feedback on an ongoing basis. For example, lab work is best discussed immediately after finishing the investigation and report. Because I want to emphasize that assignments are tools for learning and not tests, discussion of some assignments can take place whenever appropriate. My expectation is that corrections should be made in the margins of the paper. I encourage students to make notes to themselves on the work as the discussion progresses. Of course, I make it clear that my eventual evaluation of the work will focus on their additions and corrections as well as the original effort. There is little doubt which students are prepared for the discussion and it is easy to record an appropriate grade for Daily Work and Preparation for anyone who is unprepared.

As a result of moving to homework portfolios, I believe that I am seeing a higher quality of product from my students. This improvement may, in part, be due to the longer block of time available to students to complete and polish their work before submission, but I think there is more to the explanation. In addition to accumulating the work of an entire unit, the student must interpret it when developing the summary. I think that as students become better trained in the process, they begin looking at each assignment—while doing it—as more than just an immediate task to fulfill. Although I do not think that most students are cognizant of the fact, I think they look more closely at each bit of work in terms of how it fits into the larger picture. They seem more likely to approach assignments as tools for learning rather than tests of their knowledge. While the homework portfolio may seem to be largely an issue of packaging, I think that this packaging contributes to the organization of thought associated with seeing the big picture. And after all, it's the big picture that we all strive to see.

Portfolios may be used at all grade levels and for any subject or course a student takes. When portfolios are meant to be used to document student accomplishment, they must be organized so that they reveal the development of a skill or the growing understanding of a set of ideas. To demonstrate growth and change, Wolf (1989) suggests collecting "biographies of works, a range of works and reflections" (p. 37).

The biography of a work consists of several drafts of a work, showing the student's initial conception of the project, the first attempts, and the final product. By collecting these items, the teacher can document the growth and development of the student. Wolf (1989) further recommends that after completing this collection, the teacher may ask the student to reexamine all the stages of the work and reflect on the process and the products from beginning to end. The student's reflection may be done in writing or captured on audiotape (and later transcribed onto paper) and should then be included in the portfolio itself. This self-evaluation process is valuable in helping the student develop metacognitive abilities that can be applied to future self-assessments in academic or real-life settings.

Wolf (1989) also suggests that teachers deliberately collect a range of works—meaning a diverse collection—consisting of journals, essays, poems, drawings, charts, graphs, letters, tests, and samples of daily work. When using the portfolios as a basis for a parent-teacher conference, this range allows the teacher to discuss and document many different aspects of the student's school accomplishments.

Primary teachers must take responsibility for collecting and filing all items in students' portfolios. At the upper grades, however, students may be asked to keep their own. The teacher may suggest items to be included, and the student may decide on others. At the end of a people and nature unit, for example, each student may have a portfolio containing the tests, lab reports, essays, creative writing, and charts created for the unit.

Portfolios of student work are an excellent way to communicate with parents about a student's accomplishments. When the parent and teacher look at the writing sample together, they can both understand the student's strengths and weaknesses at a glance. When a parent sees the signed contract and the completed work, both parent and teacher see the same evidence to support the resulting grades.

Some teachers, and even entire schools, schedule portfolio days at the end of the school year. Students select their best work of the year and prepare short presentations to talk about the work and what it represents in the way of effort and accomplishment.

Parents and community members are invited to the school to hear the students talk about their work and to ask questions of the students. In schools where portfolio days are a regular part of the school schedule, teachers make sure the students know about the presentation days in advance so that they have time to select their work and to write and practice their presentations. Teachers may also choose to assess the students' oral presentation skills as a part of the portfolio day.

VIDEOTAPE RECORDS

When the purpose of evaluation is to record the accomplishment of a student and allow later analysis and more comprehensive evaluation, a videotape is an excellent way to capture and store a variety of learning events. Speeches can be videotaped easily. So can dramas, skits, presentations, and displays of students products.

Videos are also excellent ways to communicate to parents the accomplishments of a student or the entire class. They allow all interested parties to view the final products or performances of a unit of study. Teachers can store on tape a whole year's worth of accomplishments.

Video recordings also provide teachers with data they need to evaluate their own plans. By reviewing a video of a classroom learning event, reflective teachers are able to gain new understandings about what students need from their learning environment to be successful.

GRADING COOPERATIVE GROUP PROJECTS AND PRODUCTS

Many of the assessment methods described in this chapter can be adapted for cooperative groups. Evaluation of cooperative group efforts should include an assessment of both a task that requires a group effort to complete and an assessment of individual efforts to ensure that each member of the group takes responsibility for doing personal reading and preparation.

As an illustration of how to adapt ordinary lessons and units into cooperative lessons and units, consider the astronomy unit. To adapt this unit for use by cooperative groups, each group can function as a study team with directions to assist one another in reading and preparing for the quizzes. Group scores can be computed and recorded for each quiz at the same time that individual scores are recorded.

The contract system works well with cooperative groups. When used in this way, there is one contract per group instead of per individual. Each group negotiates what they will accomplish together. Evaluations can include peer assessments, with members of the group providing critical feedback for one another.

Assessment of student accomplishment is a complex and multifaceted undertaking. There is no one best way to assess what students have learned or accomplished in school. Some methods work better than others at various grade levels. Some work better than others with different individuals. This chapter has provided you with a number of assessment methods so you can develop a repertoire of assessment devices to use as the basis for making judgments about the accomplishments of your students.

Reporting Student Accomplishments

Report cards. These two words are likely to elicit memories filled with anxiety and a variety of other conflicting emotions for most people.

In your many years of schooling, you have probably received more than 50 report cards. You probably viewed many with relief and happiness and proudly displayed them to your parents; others may have caused torment and disbelief. On occasion, you may have questioned the teacher's fairness or integrity; you may have questioned whether the teacher really got to know you or understood the effort you put into your work. Perhaps you have even approached a teacher and challenged the grade you received, showing evidence of why the assigned grade was unjustified.

Eight or nine weeks into your first school year, you will face the task of deciding on and recording report card grades for your students. Many first-year teachers consider the responsibility one of their most difficult challenges. Experienced teachers often report that the task doesn't get easier as the years pass. In fact, many reflective teachers find that the more they know about grades and children, the more difficult it is to sum up the work and efforts of a student in a single letter grade.

Reflective teachers struggle with many conflicting ideas, thoughts, and concerns when they confront existing evaluation systems. Systems using letter grades are likely to be based on the assumption that students vary in ability and acquire learning by passively receiving knowledge from the teacher. From this assumption, it is logical to conclude that students should be evaluated by determining what they have learned and how this compares to other students of the same age. Categorizing and rank ordering of students is the next step and is done by assigning letter grades to label their respective categories of ability. Teachers with this perspective can be overheard saying "John is an A student, and Sally is a C student."

Reflective, caring teachers are often uncomfortable with such statements. They recognize the complex mix of environmental, nutritional, genetic, and experiential factors that contribute to each student's success or lack of success in school. Moreover, according to their view of teaching and learning, it is the teachers' responsibility to diagnose their students' needs and then plan a series of learning experiences and the scaffolding each student needs to succeed. The competitive nature of letter grades contrasts sharply with this philosophy.

Due to the time-consuming nature of the task of correcting students' work and the complexities of the evaluation processes described previously, it is easy to see why school personnel have resorted to a form of shorthand to record and report student progress. Most teachers have too many students and too little time to hold discussions with each student's parents or to write extensive narratives of each student's learning on a regular basis. Schools use standardized shorthand methods known as *grades* and *test scores* to communicate with parents, future teachers, college admissions personnel, and future employers (Oakes & Lipton, 1990).

The practice of awarding letter grades as measures of individual achievement has been part of the U.S. educational scene for many decades. In the 1960s and '70s, personnel in some school districts attempted to replace conventional report cards with detailed anecdotal records, describing what each student had accomplished in each subject area during the course or term. But these attempts to change the prevailing evaluation system met with opposition from parents, who insisted on a return to the letter grade system with which they had grown up. Parents were not satisfied with a description of their own child's achievements. They wanted to know how their child compared with other students. They expressed concern that these records would not be accepted at the most prestigious colleges.

In response to these debates, school boards and administrators in most school districts arrived at a compromise. While they reestablished the letter-grade report cards for the intermediate and upper elementary grades, they retained the use of anecdotal report cards for the primary grades. This is the prevailing practice today. That means that if you are planning to teach at the primary grades (kindergarten through the second or third grades), you will be expected to write anecdotal report cards describing and documenting what each student in your classroom has learned. If you are planning to teach at the intermediate grades (second or third through sixth grade), you may be expected to compute letter grades every quarter for the students' report cards.

COMPUTATION OF GRADES

At the end of the Astronomy unit described earlier, the grades for all of the reports, tests and projects may be recorded in the teachers' gradebooks as shown in Figure 11.6.

Computation of the final grades for this curriculum unit involves a straightforward computation of an average grade by awarding numerical equivalents to each letter grade, adding the five items, and dividing the total score by 5. The average scores can

	Graded Objectives						Average Score	Report Card Grade
Name of Student	1	2	3	4	5			
Lisa	A	B	B	A	C			
	4 +	3 +	3 +	4 +	2	=	16/5 = 3.1	B
Peter	B	C	A	C	D			
	3 +	2 +	4 +	2 +	1	=	12/5 = 2.4	C+
Alejandro	B	A	A	B	A			
	3 +	4 +	4 +	3 +	4	=	18/5 = 3.6	A–

A = 4 points
B = 3
C = 2
D = 1
F = 0

Figure 11.6   Teacher's grade book

then be assigned a letter grade. After they are computed, the grades are recorded in the student's cumulative folder and on the report cards that are sent home to parents. Intermediate report cards are likely to use letter grades to sum up the student's achievement in each academic subject. Some report cards may also provide checklists of subskills beneath the letter grade as a means of explaining to parents how the letter grade was determined.

WRITING ANECDOTAL RECORDS

In most school districts, teachers are responsible for writing three or four report cards per year. These contain descriptions of each student's current level of accomplishment in each of the major areas of the curriculum, plus a summary of the student's work habits and social adjustment to school and peers. At the primary grades, report cards usually consist of either anecdotal records or checklists of skills rather than letter grades. Some school districts may use both. The advantage to this double format is that it allows teachers to describe and report their direct observations of a student's actual behaviors and accomplishments with sufficient detail so that parents understand the student's strengths and deficiencies. This is especially useful for such skill areas as listening, speaking, writing, study habits, social skills, and interests (Gronlund & Linn, 1990).

When a concern about a student arises, the teacher's daily observations of the student's work habits or social interactions can be important sources of data to help parents or other school personnel understand the student's particular needs and strengths. These observations may be augmented by the use of written anecdotal records of what the teacher observes. For example, if a student comes to school late, appears tired, and has difficulty sitting still, the teacher may want to document these observations by keeping a short anecdotal record for a week, recording how late the student is every morning and describing episodes of falling asleep or inattentiveness. When this written record is shown to the parents, it is more likely to enlist their cooperation with the teacher in seeking answers to the problem than if the teacher simply reports orally that the student is "always late and too tired to work."

To be used to their best advantage, anecdotal records should be limited to observations of specific skills, social problems, or behavioral concerns. If a teacher sets out to record every behavior and event in a student's school day, the process will become too tiring and difficult to be feasible. Instead, when a student is exhibiting a particular behavior or deficiency in a skill area, the teacher can focus on daily descriptions of that one area and produce a useful document.

The major limitation or disadvantage of the anecdotal record is teachers' tendency to project their own value judgments into the description of a student's behavior or accomplishment. This is due, in part, to the tendency to observe what fits one's preconceived notions. "For example, they will tend to notice more desirable qualities in those pupils they like best and more undesirable qualities in those they like least" (Gronlund & Linn, 1990, p. 380). The recommended way to avoid this tendency is to keep descriptions of observed incidents separate from your interpretation. First, state exactly what happened in nonjudgmental words. Then, if you wish to add your interpretation of the event, do so in a separate paragraph and label it as such (Gronlund & Linn, 1990).

In general, a single observation is seldom as meaningful as a series of events in understanding a student's behavior. Therefore, anecdotal records should contain brief descriptions of related incidents over time to provide a reliable picture of a student's behavior.

INVOLVING STUDENTS IN EVALUATION PROCEDURES

For reflective teachers, the natural extension of the teaching process is the interactive evaluation process that encourages students to become active evaluators of their own efforts and products. The current writing programs organized around periodic student-teacher conferences and the grouping of students who edit one another's work are excellent examples of this type of evaluation. In classrooms that feature such writing programs, the teacher's role in evaluation is to confer with the students about their current writing projects and to ask questions that engage them in analyzing what they have written.

Teachers may use open-ended questions designed to gather information on what the student has intended to do in a piece of writing. When the teacher has a sufficient understanding of the student's goal, the teacher and student may begin to zero in on ways to improve the quality of the writing so that it more nearly matches the student's purpose. This may mean correcting the mechanics of the writing so that it can be understood by others, or it may mean guiding the student to rethink the way a passage is written and to consider new ways of stating the ideas.

The editing groups used in such writing programs encourage students to learn how to listen to and respect the work their peers are creating. Students in a group, typically, each read aloud from a current piece of writing and then answer questions about the content from the other students in the group. Through this type of interactive evaluation, students may be learning how to work cooperatively, accept critical feedback, and write better at the same time.

This interactive evaluation system can be used in other parts of the curriculum as well. "What did you learn?" should form the core of the classroom evaluation. The more often this question is asked, the easier it is for students to identify and receive the help they need. It is a question children can learn to ask themselves (Oakes & Lipton, 1990, p. 132).

Providing students with self-evaluation checklists or rating scales assists them in learning more specific types of questions about their own progress and achievement. Checklists and rating scales that ask the student to evaluate specific outcomes may be developed for any learning activity, especially a unit of study that takes place over several weeks. Teacher evaluations may be entered on the same form to allow students and their parents to compare the student's self-evaluation with the teacher's assessment of the student's accomplishments. For example, in Figure 11.7, students are allowed to assess themselves after completing a research unit on leadership.

Interactive evaluation procedures are designed to breed success and enhance students' metacognitive capacities. They are as much a part of the *learning process* as they are a part of the assessment process. In fact, the long-term goals of most caring, reflective teachers are likely to emphasize the development of independence, self-responsibility, self-discipline, and self-evaluation as important affective goals of education. These goals are achieved through the development of metacognitive processes as children learn to understand how to succeed in any learning environment.

Leadership Unit

Student/Teacher Evaluation

Name of student_____ **Grade**_____ **Date**_____

Leader selected for research _____

The student completes the left side of this evaluation and then the teacher will complete the right side. Afterward, student and teacher discuss the accomplishments made by the student, decide on areas that need to be improved, and plan goals for future learning experiences.

O = Outstanding   S = Satisfactory   N = Needs Improvement

Student Evaluation: **Teacher Evaluation:**

____   I completed the readings and assignments for this unit on time.   ____

____   I showed responsibility by bringing appropriate materials to class.   ____

____   I showed growth in my planning, decision-making, and organizational skills.   ____

____   I have gained skills in doing research and taking notes to gather information.   ____

____   I used a variety of relevant and challenging resources to learn about my subject. ____

____   I improved my ability to speak in public.   ____

____   I gained confidence in my ability to speak in public.   ____

____   I gained independence in working on my own to achieve a goal.   ____

____   I am able to evaluate my own accomplishments and identify what   ____
       I need to improve with accuracy and honesty.

The most important thing I learned in this unit was:

Regarding my work in this unit, I am most proud of:

Figure 11.7   Interactive student/teacher evaluation for a leadership unit

Reflective Actions for Your Professional Portfolio
Your Design for an Interactive Portfolio Assessment System

Withitness: Observe a Portfolio Assessment System

Visit a classroom in which the teacher uses an interactive portfolio assessment system. What system does this teacher use for recording grades? Are there elements of this system that seem useful to you? Do the students appear to understand the teacher's grading policies and expectations? What would you do to improve their understanding?

Put Grades into Perspective

Did you get good grades in elementary school? Do you believe that the grades you received were an accurate reflection of your effort and achievement? How will you determine grades in your classroom? If you choose not to use letter grades, what will you use instead to report student progress?

Widen Your Perspective

If you have a choice, would you use letter grades or anecdotal records in your teaching? What place will portfolios have in your classroom?

Do Research and Invite Feedback

Read more about portfolio assessment. Research the topic on the World Wide Web. Visit classrooms to observe the systems other teachers use to collect student work in portfolios.

Redefine the Issue of Assessment

After you read more about assessment and visit teachers using a variety of assessment systems, how has your thinking changed? What is your new frame on the issue?

Create an Interactive Assessment System

For the unit plan you are working on, plan an interactive student-teacher evaluation system that encourages students to use metacognitive processes to assess their own performance. Create a contract, checklist, or rating scale that students and teachers can use to look at the students' positive achievements as well as providing realistic and useful information about what students need to improve.

Predict Possible Outcomes

Share your assessment plan with other prospective teachers. Get feedback from them on how clear and understandable your system is likely to be with students. Then try using the system with one student. Ask the student to tell you what is needed to make the plan clear, useful, and fair.

References

Andrade, H. (2000). What do we mean by results? Using rubrics to promote thinking and learning. *Educational Leadership, 57*(5), 11–14.

Gronlund, N., & Linn, R. (1990). *Measurement and evaluation in teaching.* Upper Saddle River, NJ: Merrill/Prentice Hall.

Guskey, T. (1994). Making the grade: What benefits students? *Educational Leadership, 52*(2), 14–19.

Marzano, R., Pickering, D., & McTighe, J. (1993). *Assessing student outcomes.* Alexandria, VA: Association for Supervision and Curriculum Development.

Oakes, J., & Lipton, M. (1990). *Making the best of schools.* New Haven, CT: Yale University Press.

Wolf, D. (1989). Portfolio assessment: Sampling student work. *Educational Leadership, 46*(7), 35–39.

chapter 12

REFLECTIVE TEACHERS AND the SCHOOL COMMUNITY

The teacher's role in the school community becomes more complex each day. Most school districts are undergoing some form of reform or systemic change that calls on teachers to take more responsibility for decision making beyond their own classrooms. School reform can be compared to piloting an airplane and conducting a major overhaul while in flight. While attempting to maintain a stable environment for students and faculty, many schools are overhauling their curriculum, schedules, student evaluation systems, and administrative relationships.

The motivation for many of these changes appears to be a shift in what people see as the basic purpose of schools. When reforms appear to be succeeding, teachers share in the glory. When reforms appear to be failing to meet their objectives, principals, teachers, and other staff must respond by working harder and longer hours to accomplish the many complex tasks needed to turn things around. They must also be able to reduce a natural tendency to become defensive upon hearing criticism. Instead, teachers must be able to examine what it is the community wants them to accomplish and communicate to the community what they view as important. This process is likely to generate conflict. It is probably unavoidable, and may perhaps be necessary to induce change. But reflective teachers are not afraid of conflict. They recognize that conflict is part of any important change, and they are willing to use their reflective action skills to perceive the needs of all members of the school community.

Two-Way Communication with Parents

At the beginning of Chapter 4, Lori Shoults described the many thoughts, feelings, and decisions she faced on her first day of teaching. In the week before that first day, Ms. Shoults spent a lot of time in her classroom setting up bulletin boards and learning centers. As she worked that week, many of her new students and their parents who had come to the school for registration stopped by her classroom to see the "new teacher." Some stood outside her door looking in quietly until she approached them and introduced herself. Others came into the room and looked around, exclaiming over the brightly decorated walls. The children were all interested in trying to discern whether the new teacher was "nice" and whether they thought they would be happy in her class.

Their visits, before the first day of school had even arrived, alerted Ms. Shoults to the fact that she had more than the needs of 28 students to consider. She realized that she had to use withitness and concern for their parents' needs as well.

Some parents of primary children may be especially reluctant to see the beginning of school because, for them, it marks an end to an important phase in their lives. For five years, they have had complete jurisdiction over the lives of their children. Now they recognize that the teacher may have almost as much influence over their children as they have. I have observed the parent of a first grader, for example, standing outside the school after dropping off the child, saying tearfully, "But we've had lunch together every day of his life."

For the majority of parents, many of whom work outside of the home and whose children have gone to day care centers and preschools, this leavetaking may not be so abrupt, but it is still a significant event in their own lives, as well as those of their children. Many parents feel a strong interest in, and responsibility for, determining whether this particular classroom is a healthy and welcoming environment for their children. For this reason, parents of primary schoolchildren are likely to come to school, on one pretext or another, in the first days of school, just to see for themselves that their children are in good hands.

Beginning teachers may feel somewhat overwhelmed by these visits. All of their available energy has gone into planning the curriculum, moving furniture, decorating the classroom, and meeting and becoming acquainted with other teachers in the school. When a parent suddenly shows up, unannounced, it can be unsettling, especially if the parent wants to ask questions when the students are present. When this occurs, it is necessary for the teacher to suggest politely but assertively, another time for this impromptu conference: "I'm sorry, Mrs. Jones, but all of my attention is needed in the class right now. Would you prefer to talk about this after school or tomorrow morning at 8:15?"

On many occasions throughout the school year, the teacher is expected to communicate with parents either singly or in large groups. In addition, many classroom teachers invite parents to become involved in the life of the classroom. Some students come from single-parent families, blended families in which divorced parents have remarried and have children with previous and current spouses, foster parents, and guardians. Teachers meet students who do not have the same last names as their parents. Teachers must recognize that the home lives they have experienced may be different from those of their students. When *parents* are mentioned in this chapter, the term is meant to refer to the people who are being contacted or are meeting with the teacher on behalf of a particular child.

FALL OPEN HOUSE

When parents come to visit the classroom early in the year, one method of addressing their concerns is to suggest that they will be able to have many of their questions answered within a few weeks at the annual fall open house (sometimes called *Back to School Night*). This event is planned especially for that purpose in many school districts.

The fall open house usually takes place on an evening in late September. To prepare for the event, teachers are asked to be ready to describe their goals for the year and give an overall picture of the school's curriculum at that grade level. The event usually begins in the school auditorium or other large meeting room, where the principal welcomes everyone to the school and describes the important events that the entire school has planned for the coming year. The teachers, counselors, other administrators, and sometimes the president of the parent–teacher organization are introduced. Special attention is given to introducing new teachers on the faculty. At the conclusion of this general meeting, the teachers are released to go to their classrooms and make themselves ready for the open house. After a few minutes, the visitors are dismissed from the general meeting to find their children's classrooms.

When the parents assemble in the classroom, the teacher makes a short presentation to the group, describing what is planned for the year. A time for questions and answers of interest to the group is also likely. Because most school districts intend the fall open house to be a time for general discussions of goals and curriculum, there is no planned opportunity for individual parents to ask teachers for specific information about their child's achievement or behavior. If parents approach the teacher and begin to discuss personal concerns, it is expected that the teacher will suggest an alternate time and place for an individual conference.

PARENT–TEACHER CONFERENCES

Conferences between individual parents and teachers vary greatly in purpose. Some are primarily used for diagnosing a problem or concern, and others are set up to report to the parents about a child's progress in school. Diagnostic conferences were described in Chapter 3, but are discussed briefly in this context as well because they are such valuable means of evaluation.

If either the teacher or the parent has a serious concern about a child, one or the other may arrange a conference in the first weeks of school. When teachers, for example, observe unusually aggressive, passive, depressed, or antisocial behavior in a child, they are wise to call home immediately and set up a conference right away to gain information about the nature of the child's problems. This is especially true when a child's behavior disrupts other students in the class.

Setting up a conference sends an important signal to a student who is exhibiting unusual or unacceptable behavior. It tells the student that the teacher has withitness and is going to take action to correct the problem rather than let it go. It allows the teacher to seek information about the underlying reasons for the observed behavior. In a conference of this type, it is recommended that the student attend with the parents to gain a better understanding of the adults' views of the behavior.

When the conference takes place, the teacher should describe the behavior and, if possible, supplement the oral description with written anecdotal reports of examples of the behavior. The teacher should express concern about the behavior and then ask both the student and the parents to explain why it is occurring.

"Students usually cannot explain fully why they act as they do, and teachers should not expect them to be able to do this. If the students had such insight, they probably would not be behaving symptomatically in the first place. Instead, the hope is that clues or helpful information will emerge from the discussion" (Good & Brophy, 1987, p. 293).

When the parents discuss their own views of the child's problem, the teacher may gain significant insight by learning about the home environment. For example, the parents may agree that they have observed the same behavior at home and that it seems to be related to a crisis the family is dealing with, such as a death, divorce, drugs, lost job, or move. When the teacher, the child, and the parents confront this matter together, they can begin to put together a workable plan to help support the student during this difficult period and, at the same time, help the child gain awareness about the effects of the behavior on others.

Conferences don't always result in such harmonious cooperation. Parents may not present much useful information. On occasion, they may become very defensive or resentful of the suggestion that their child's behavior is unacceptable. In their family, this behavior may be okay. For example, a fifth-grade teacher was alarmed to see a boy walk into her class on the first day of school wearing a T-shirt that read, "Born to Raise Hell!" True to the message on the shirt, the child fought with other children at least once a day. When the parents were called in for a conference and the teacher described this behavior to them, the father replied, "So what? I tell my kids not to let anyone get the best of them." From the words and the father's tone of voice, the teacher learned that fighting was an acceptable behavior in that family. No happy resolution was discovered in this conference, but it did give the teacher some additional insight into the source and the depth of the boy's difficulties in social interactions with his peers.

At times, a teacher may need to involve others in the conference. Counselors may need to be present to suggest alternative ways of dealing with problems. If the teacher, parents, and counselor cannot effectively address a problem with the student, additional professional help may need to be offered to the parents. At times, parents admit that they cannot even handle their child at home.

Conferences designed for reporting on student progress rather than for diagnostic purposes usually take place in the late fall to coincide with the end of the first marking period and the first report card. In many districts, the parents are asked to come to the school for a conference with the teacher shortly after report cards are sent home. This gives the parents an opportunity to look at the report card and think about the questions and concerns they may want to raise at the conference. Some school districts require parents to come to the school to pick up the child's report card and have a conference with the teacher. In this case, the teacher explains the grades and observations to the parent as the parent views the report card for the first time. This second strategy is used primarily to make sure that parents do attend the conference.

Report card conferences are generally 15 to 30 minutes in length. They may be offered during the day and at night so that parents who work during the day may choose a night conference. Usually one or two school days are used for the fall conferences. In some school districts, the entire process is repeated in the spring. In the elementary school, a schedule of 30 conferences over a period of one or two days is a very tiring experience for most teachers, who may find that conference days are more exhausting than regular teaching days. This is due primarily to the tension caused by the teachers' recognition that they are responsible for the smooth flow of conversation and information. When this feeling of responsibility is multiplied by a factor of 30 or more in a few short days, it is easy to see how draining it can be.

To minimize the tension, it is extremely important that teachers plan each conference carefully. Before the event, reflective teachers often write a page of notes about each student, highlighting the accomplishments and the matters of concern that the teacher wants to discuss with the parents. It is important for the teacher to identify the child correctly in the conference. Teachers have mentioned embarrassing moments when parents have a puzzled look on their faces only to discover that the teacher was talking about another student and not their child.

In addition to planning what you want to say about each child, it is a good idea to make a plan for how you will conduct your conferences. The primary purpose of report card conferences is for you to inform the parents about the child's progress in your class. But the conference is also designed to elicit information from the parents that may help you to help the child. The parents may also have concerns that they wish to discuss. To accomplish all of these things in 20 minutes is difficult. You must act as the timekeeper and allot a reasonable amount of time to each purpose. The parent will not be concerned about going overtime, but you will because you will be aware that the next set of parents is waiting outside the door for their appointment with you.

Gronlund and Linn (1990) suggest considering the following elements when you plan your conferences:

1. Make plans for each conference. For each child, make a list of the points you want to cover and the questions you want to ask.
2. Begin the conference in a positive manner. Making a positive statement about the child, such as, "Betty really enjoys helping others," or "Derek is an expert on dinosaurs," is likely to create a cooperative and friendly atmosphere.
3. Present the student's strong points before describing areas needing improvement. Present samples of work and focus on what the child can do and what he or she still has to learn.
4. Encourage parents to participate and share information. You must be willing to listen as well as talk. They may have questions and concerns about the school and about their child's behavior that need to be brought into the open before constructive, cooperative action can take place.
5. Plan a course of action cooperatively. Guide the discussion toward a series of steps that can be taken by the teacher and the parents to assist the child. At the end of the conference, review these steps with the parents.
6. End the conference with a positive comment. Thank the parents for coming and say something positive about the student, such as, "Erik has a good sense of humor and I enjoy having him in my class."

The regularly scheduled report card conferences may be the only time you meet with the parents of most of your students. For others—those whose behavior or learning problems are quite serious—you will need to continue to contact the parents by telephone or in follow-up conferences to monitor whether the cooperative plan of action is being implemented and what effects it is having.

Effective two-way communication with parents is essential for assisting students with severe problems. In working with children whose behavior interferes with their learning in school, an excellent resource for both teachers and parents is Rimm's (1986) *The Underachievement Syndrome: Causes and Cures.* This book describes many of the most feared behavior problems that teachers must face: hyperactivity, passiveness, perfectionism, rebellion, bullying, and manipulative behaviors. Rimm believes these behaviors cause children to achieve much less than they are capable of in school. In her studies of underachievement, Rimm has discovered that children learned most of these behaviors in response to some elements of their home environment. Changing the behavior takes a concerted effort by the parents to isolate the causes and create new procedures to help children learn healthier, more productive behavior patterns that can lead to success.

Often it is the teacher who spots the self-defeating behavior. Parents have been living with the child for so long that they may not see that the child's behavior is unusual, and they may not be able to recognize how it affects the child's school achievement. Some examples of home situations that may lead to underachievement include the following:

The Overwelcome Child

Although it has long been recognized that an unwelcome or rejected child is likely to have problems in life, it is also likely that excessive attention can cause achievement and emotional problems. When parents overprotect and overindulge, the child may develop a pattern of not taking initiative and of waiting for others to do his or her bidding.

Early Health Problems

When children are born with allergies, birth defects, or other disabilities and parents respond by investing themselves almost totally in the child's well-being, a set of behaviors similar to those of the overwelcome child can develop.

Particular Sibling Combinations

Birth order and sibling rivalry affect all children, but some combinations may be particularly damaging to a child's achievement. A student who is the sibling of a child with severe health problems or who is considered to be extremely gifted may feel left out or inadequate in comparison to the sibling. This can lead to the development of attention getting behavior patterns, such as clowning or mischief-making, that may prevent the child from achieving fully.

Specific Marital Problems

A single parent may develop a very close relationship with the child as a result of seeing the child as the only purpose for living. The parent may treat the child more like a spouse or a partner than a child, thus giving the child too much power. The child may learn to expect power and may not be willing to give it up to conform to the requirements of school (Rimm, 1995, pp. 24–32).

These are only four of many possible situations that can cause children to develop behaviors that may prevent them from achieving well in school. When a teacher spots a child who is exhibiting overly dependent or overly aggressive behaviors, it is important to confer with the child's parents, to report the problem, and to learn how the behavior first developed and how the parents are responding to it. The first step toward a positive behavior change is for the teacher to describe and give examples of the behavior and its effects on the child's achievement. The parents may deny that the behavior exists or that it is serious, but if the teacher can establish a cooperative dialogue with the parents, it may lead to new insights for all of them.

If parents do acknowledge the behavior, the next step is to describe the changes you are going to make at school to support the development of new, more positive behavior patterns and to suggest modifications that the parents may make at home. Together with the parents, set some reasonable goals for the child in terms of both behaviors and grades. Discuss methods of helping the child reach these goals, and agree on a plan that fits the child and the situation.

Rimm cautions that children will not change their behavior just because the adults in their lives want them to do so. The child must want to break the underachieving patterns and substitute them for behaviors that lead to success. Both the teacher and the parents must also confer with the child, describing the behaviors and their effects in words the child can understand and accept. When the teacher, parent, and child all have the same goal and are working together on a plan of action tailored to fit the needs of the child, it is quite possible that the child will succeed.

Independent contracts are also useful support systems for helping children change behavior. A contract can specify work the child is to with deadlines and expectations for success. It can also be used to specify behavioral expectations. When the teacher negotiates the contract with the child ahead of time, the child has an intrinsic incentive to complete it—after all, the child helped to create it and decide what would be required. A sense of ownership is likely to increase the likelihood of the contract being fulfilled (see Figure 12.1).

The teacher may employ additional extrinsic incentives if these seem useful in a given circumstance. It is most often recommended that students receive a reward that supports academics. For example, a student could earn points toward additional time at a learning activity or game. The major point is that the reward is something a student really would like to receive. Some things a teacher thinks would be rewarding are not rewarding to students. The types of rewards would vary by grade level.

Daily Evaluation Form

Student name _____   Teacher name _____   Date _____

Assignments completed: _____ All   _____ Most   _____ Less than half

Classroom effort: _____ Excellent   _____ Satisfactory
                           _____ Fair   _____ Unsatisfactory

Behavior   _____ Excellent   _____ Satisfactory
                           _____ Fair   _____ Unsatisfactory

Comments and missing assignments:

_____

_____

_____

_____

Thank you very much for your help.

Figure 12.1   Daily evaluation form

This type of plan may be created as a result of a successful parent–teacher conference, a visit by the teacher to the student's home, or by telephone, followed by written documents specifying what the teacher expects, what the parents agree to take responsibility for, and what the student agrees to do to earn the agreed-on incentive.

For example, if the teacher observes that a student is not turning in homework, the teacher may call the student's parents and ask for a conference at school or suggest that the teacher come to visit the home to discuss the matter. Alerting the parents to this concern is likely to result in a discussion of probable causes. The parents may or may not accept the teacher's perceptions of the problem and its negative consequences for their child's achievement. After a frank discussion of conditions at home that may support or interfere with the student doing homework, the parents may come to recognize that the major cause might be the fact that the child and the family watch a great deal of television, beginning right after school and continuing up to bedtime. If the parents express a willingness to do their part to help change the child's behavior, then together they can draft an agreement or contract, specifying when the student will do homework and when he or she can watch television. It is a good idea for the teacher to follow up on this type of agreement by sending the parents daily reports specifying whether the homework is actually being turned in. These daily reports are likely to help everyone remember the commitment they have made. Later, when the student appears to have learned the new pattern of behavior and is more consistent about turning in homework, the reports can be sent home weekly instead of daily (see Figure 12.2).

When the student is beginning to show more responsibility and independence, the teacher may choose to involve the student in writing a study plan contract such as the one in Figure 12.3. This contract describes the goal and how the student plans to accomplish it. It may specify a reward or positive consequence that the student wants to earn when the goal is reached.

One final caution about conducting parent–teacher conferences: Occasionally, participants in the conference may reveal a family problem that is unusual and extremely serious. The students or parents may describe extreme poverty, desertion, or physical or sexual abuse to a teacher as a desperate attempt to get help. The classroom teacher is well-advised not to try to deal with such problems alone. If this happens to you, ask the parent to allow you to discuss this matter with the school's social services personnel and immediately contact the principal, school psychologist, social worker, and other members of the crisis team to assist in the matter.

THROUGH THE EYES OF PARENTS

When parents send their children to school, they have many hopes and fears for their children's future. They want to be able to trust the school to create a safe, stable, nurturing environment for their students. They want their students' developing sense of self to be enhanced and their individual talents to be appreciated. But many parents feel left out of the decision-making process of their children's schools. If teachers describe their goals or programs using educational jargon unfamiliar to the parents, they may be reluctant to attend conferences or meetings at the school.

Weekly Evaluation Form

Name_____   Grade _____   Date _____

Week of_____

Subject	Behavior	Effort	Grade this week (optional)	Grade to date (optional)	Teacher initials
1.					
2.					
3.					
4.					
5.					
6.					
7.					
8.					
9.					

Comments and missing assignments:

_____

_____

_____

_____

Please use the same rating for effort, behavior, and achievement:

A–Excellent   B–Above average   C–Average   D–Below average   F–Failing

Figure 12.2   Weekly evaluation form

When parents are involved in establishing the school's vision statement, or invited to participate on advisory groups, they may contribute many valuable ideas. In Jefferson County, Colorado, a school created a parent-teacher focus group to provide teachers with feedback on how to increase student self-esteem. At first, teachers were reluctant to have the parent observers visit their classrooms. But team members worked collaboratively to design a set of guidelines for the observations and agreed to provide teachers with copies of their observation notes after each visit. A parent-teacher retreat was held to build trust and clarify roles and expectations. After

---

Sample Study Plan Contract

Richard, his mom, his dad, and Mrs. Norbert agree that Richard will spend at least one hour each day, five days a week, studying and doing his homework independently at his desk in his room. He will do this before he watches TV and there will be no radio, stereo, or TV on in his room during study time. After his work is complete, his dad will review his materials. At the end of the week, if all work is complete in class and homework has been handed in on time, Richard will receive ten points, which may be saved toward a bicycle. Each point is worth one dollar toward the price of the bike. Richard may also receive extra credit points for doing special projects. Richard's mom and dad will not remind him to study, and he will take the initiative independently. If Richard has not completed his homework, he will bring all his books home on Friday and Richard will not be allowed any weekend activities until he completes all missing work.

Richard
Dad
Mom
Mrs. Norbert

Figure 12.3   Sample study plan contract

observing classrooms and playgrounds, the parent observers worked with faculty to develop a statement of their beliefs about how the schools could enhance students' self-esteem. Their statement of beliefs includes the following:

Provide experiences that allow for individual differences

Provide opportunities to express creativity

View mistakes as learning opportunities

Provide a safe/clean learning environment (Meadows, 1993, p. 32)

While these recommendations were not new to the faculty, they were helpful in clarifying what the community wanted and expected from their school. From the team effort, both teachers and parents had a better understanding of the complexity of education.

In some communities, parents take a very active role in governance. Parents serve as members of school boards or advisory groups that work closely with the school administrators to make the important decisions about school funding and hiring and firing or personnel. On occasion, some parents have very strong views about a single issue and may try to influence school boards or administrators to provide a certain program or modify an existing program to coincide with the parents' values or philosophy. When this occurs, opinions can be strongly stated and conflict is likely to arise among parent factions and faculty. For the beginning teacher, it is important to try to learn as much about the values of a school community before submitting an application for employment or accepting a teaching contract. If your own values and philosophy differ greatly from that of the majority of the school governance teams, then you are unlikely to feel at home teaching in that school district.

TEACHING AND LEARNING IN A MULTICULTURAL COMMUNITY

When the language, culture, and values of the parents match those of the teachers in the child's school, communication is likely to be relatively clear and agreements relatively simple to achieve. When the culture of the child's home differs significantly from the culture of the teacher, the teacher must be especially willing to listen as well as talk during parent-teacher conferences.

Before the *Brown v. Board of Education* Supreme Court decision in 1954, children who were racially different from the "white majority" were often segregated in separate (and inferior) schools. Since that time, federal mandates have required school systems to integrate both the student bodies and the faculties of their schools. But federal laws have not been able to mitigate the subtler forms of racism that still exist in some educational settings.

Although the United States is known as a nation of immigrants, a melting pot of cultures, the traditionally accepted cultural norm has mirrored the philosophy of the white Anglo-Saxon majority. Other cultures have been known as minority cultures. The prevailing belief is that children from minority cultures must be taught the language and habits of the majority. Researchers have found that "to the extent that the home culture's practices and values are not acknowledged or incorporated by the school, parents may find that they are not able to support children in their academic pursuits even when it is their fervent wish to do so" (Florio-Ruane, 1989, p. 169).

Reflective teachers are aware that their own values and expectations may vary considerably from those of the families in their school community. But rather than assume that the children and their parents should be taught to mimic the language, behavior, and norms of the teacher's own culture, reflective teachers strive to gain a better understanding of the various cultures that make up the school community and to celebrate these differences by incorporating them into the curriculum.

In parent-teacher conferences, the reflective teacher is likely to ask with great interest about the home environment and the parents' cultural values as a means of better understanding the various cultures and conveying respect to the parents. When parents sense this respect from the teacher, they are more likely to return it and to believe that the teacher shares their own concerns for their child. The teacher may need to be especially encouraging to parents of other cultures, urging them to share their own concerns and ask questions. People from many cultures were raised not to ask questions of teachers and may be very reluctant to do so. But if the teacher encourages them to ask questions or make suggestions for the child's benefit, they may feel comfortable enough to do so. This two-way communication and mutual understanding can lead to a more productive arrangement to work together in supporting the child's achievement at home and at school.

The needs of children and their parents who have emigrated to the United States are especially important, as First (1988) found when she interviewed them:

> Immigrant children and adolescents, many of whom have survived wars, political oppression, and economic deprivation, find that their problems are not over when they enter American schools. Confronted with hatred, prejudice, and violence in U.S. schools, many newcomers are left asking what they have done to deserve such treatment. One Vietnamese student spoke for many when he said, "I like school here. But I wish there would be more friendships among immigrants and American students." (p. 210)

A Spanish-speaking child revealed the following:

> "I came upon a world unknown to me, a language I did not understand, and a school administration which made ugly faces at me every time I spoke Spanish. Many teachers referred to us as animals. Believe me, maintaining a half-decent image of yourself wasn't an easy thing. . . . I had enough strength of character to withstand the many school personnel who tried to destroy my motivation. But many of my classmates didn't make it." (First, 1988, p. 210)

The classroom teacher must demonstrate a willingness to assist culturally different children and their parents as they make the difficult transition from one land to another. One of the best ways to accomplish this is to show sensitivity and respect for the various cultures of all the children in the class. Each year, the teacher may plan a special unit of study on the contribution of the cultures represented by the class members. Parents can be invited to participate in the learning experience by visiting the classroom and sharing with children the crafts and food of their countries. They can teach the children the songs and games of their homelands. First (1988) believes that when teachers involve the parents in their children's education, they send a powerful message that the school cares about them.

However, a teacher should not feel offended if the parent does not want to be involved. This could be viewed as lack of interest. However, in some cultures parents have been taught that the school is responsible for their youngster's education, and they should not be involved in the process on the school campus.

VISITS TO STUDENTS' HOMES

When teachers care sufficiently about understanding the particular home and cultural environments that surround their students, one way to seek information is to visit the children and their families in their homes. Teachers may do this by sending home a newsletter early in the year, announcing that the teacher would enjoy meeting the parents and seeing the children in their homes, and that invitations to do so will be gladly received. This allows the parents to invite the teacher when it is a good time for them.

The visit will probably take place after school or during the evening meal. No agendas need to be established for such a visit; in fact, doing so would be counterproductive.

The visit is not a structured parent–teacher conference at all. It is simply an opportunity for the teacher to understand more fully the conditions in which the child lives. As the teacher shares the family's meal, looks at their photographs, and hears some of their family stories, it greatly enhances the feelings of the child and the parents that they are respected members of the school community.

On occasion, it may become necessary for school personnel to make a more structured visit with an agenda. This may occur if a child is having extremely serious problems and is referred for special services and a psychological evaluation. In that case, the school social worker or psychologist may visit the home to determine what factor in the home environment may be causing the child's problems.

NEWSLETTERS AND NOTES

Many elementary teachers communicate with parents by sending home handwritten notes describing a particular behavior or accomplishment of their child. In some classrooms, a note from the teacher signifies only bad news that is sent home when the teacher wants to describe an incident or pattern of misbehavior, a poor test result, or excessive tardiness. More recently, many reflective teachers have considered how to use the note home to encourage good behavior and reward achievement. Many teachers now send home notes describing a student's special accomplishment, improvement in classwork, or act of friendliness or generosity.

To ensure that all children benefit from this system, the teacher may send a note of good news home with a certain number of children per week until every child has had one. Others prefer not to use a schedule, but send a note whenever they observe a child doing something especially well. Without a schedule, however, it is important that teachers be careful not to favor some children over others.

In some classrooms, teachers prepare and send home classroom newsletters describing the important events planned for that week or month. The newsletter may contain items describing completed projects and new ones just getting underway. In the newsletter, the teacher can request parent volunteers for various projects and write notes of appreciation to parents who have recently helped out in some way.

In primary classrooms, the teacher generally takes full responsibility for creating the newsletter. But in intermediate and upper elementary classrooms, many teachers allow students to help write the items. They may use a computer program designed for creating newspaperlike formats. In this case, the production of the newsletter becomes more than just a method of communicating with parents. It becomes an enriching learning experience as well.

PARENT SUPPORT OF EDUCATIONAL ACTIVITIES

If teachers can communicate the classroom goals for that year of school and can supply parents with regular newsletters or other reports of student progress, this increases the likelihood that the parents will support the school's educational goals at home.

Parents can support their child's education and increase the chances for his or her success in school if they understand what they can do to help and are capable of giving that help at home. Teachers vary considerably in what they ask parents to do to support their children's education. The variation seems to reflect the different expectations teachers have about what parents are capable of and willing to do. Some teachers ask parents to read aloud to their children or allow the child to read aloud to them. To support this request, many teachers are willing to lend school books and other materials to parents to use at home.

Other teachers ask parents to take their children to the library. Many also suggest that parents ask their children what they did that day in school and discuss it with them. When asked for suggested activities and games that can be used at home to support the class' educational goals, most teachers attempt to provide parents with a list of ideas.

Most parents welcome the opportunity to support their children in school-related activities. Teachers who regularly report to parents on classroom events and ask parents to participate by doing parallel activities in the home are likely to develop very productive two-way relationships with parents that can increase the child's self-esteem and achievement and, at the same time, add to the teacher's understanding of the student's home environment.

TELEPHONE CALLS

The telephone provides an important link between school and home. Teachers often call students' homes for the same reasons as they write notes. Some use a telephone call to report a child's misbehavior and poor achievement and to enlist the support and assistance of parents in correcting the problems. Other teachers try to call home to report both positive and negative news. They may make their first call to report a problem or concern and follow up several days later with a second telephone call to report that the student is making progress in solving the problem.

Teachers are often on the receiving end of telephone calls from students' parents as well. Parents may call to clarify something about an assignment or an announcement that they cannot understand from their child's description. If parents hear confusing stories about something that happened during the school day, they may call the teacher to find out what really occurred. Responding to these promptly and in an open and informative manner promotes a positive pattern of communication between home and school.

Occasionally parents call in anger or frustration. They may disagree with the contents of the curriculum, the way a test was graded, or the way a classroom incident was handled. The teacher receiving one of these calls may easily become defensive and angry as well. Dealing effectively with these calls takes mature, well-developed communication skills. It is difficult, but very important, to listen empathetically to what the parent says. Even when the instinctive reaction of most teachers is to break into the parent's statements and present their own side of the situation, it is more productive if the teacher's initial responses encourage the parent to describe the problem in more detail and express personal feelings.

After the parent has had an opportunity to fully describe the reason for the telephone call, the teacher's side of the story can be presented in a quiet, nonthreatening, and nondefensive voice. In a situation such as this, the teacher has the responsibility for attempting to resolve the conflict and creating a mutually acceptable solution.

For example, suppose a fight occurs in the classroom during the day and John is punched in the face by Dean, a much stronger boy. Because his lip is bleeding, the teacher sends John to the nurse. She then talks to Dean to try to find out what prompted the fight. Dean claims he was provoked by John's name calling, and many children in the class support that claim. When John returns from the nurse, the teacher tells him that both he and Dean will have to stay in during recess for fighting. John seethes with anger for the rest of the day.

After school, the teacher is called to the telephone to find John's very angry parent on the other end. "Why did you keep my son in for recess when he got hit by that bully? And why didn't you call me immediately when he got hit? Did you know he was bleeding? I'm going to come in right now and talk to your principal about this matter, and you will be sorry you treated my son this way!"

The instinctive reaction for most teachers is to jump in and explain after the first few words are spoken. If the parent continues to question the teacher's judgment, the teacher may soon feel as angry as the parent does. But reflective teachers recognize that there will be days like this in the classroom with 30 students and one adult. They will try to keep their feelings in control and say something to soothe the parent's hurt pride and upset feelings.

"I'm glad you called, Mrs. Jones. I can understand how you feel. Tell me how John's lip is now." This type of comment will help the teacher gather information and gain time to formulate a good response. Not all such problems can be readily resolved. Perhaps the teacher and the parent will continue to have different points of view no matter how much they discuss it. If this is the case, it is necessary to acknowledge it and end the conversation with a comment such as, "I recognize how you feel about this situation. I'm sorry John got hurt today, and I'll do my best to see that he is not involved in any more fights this year."

The key point of this section is expressed in the phrase "reflective teachers recognize that there will be days like this." Every school year has days like these. Values clash and feelings are hurt. The beginning teacher may be shocked the first time this happens and overreact by feeling angry, guilty, or defensive. If possible, when incidents such as these occur in your classroom, remember that every teacher experiences conflict. Conflict is unavoidable in this career, and the first step in learning how to handle it is learning to expect and accept it as part of the job.

SPRING OPEN HOUSE AND OTHER SPECIAL EVENTS

In the fall, the purpose of most conferences and open house events is to allow parents and teachers to get to know each other, communicate their goals for their children (students), and make plans for accomplishing these goals. As the year goes by, the focus of most meetings between parents and teachers is for the teacher to demonstrate to the parents how these goals are being met.

Many classroom teachers invite parents frequently, perhaps as often as once a month, to attend exhibits, plays, assemblies, or other occasions for students to display what they are learning and what they have accomplished. Some of these events may be schoolwide assemblies, such as Thanksgiving plays, concerts, and feasts; winter pageants; midwinter cultural fairs; and spring open houses in which collections of student work are displayed throughout the school.

Individual teachers may also invite their students' parents to school to view the performances or an exhibit of products resulting from a unit of study. These events are usually highly prized by students and parents, and are an excellent way for the teacher to interact and communicate continually with the parents.

Consider, though, how some parents might feel if they attend a spring open house and find that their own child's work is not displayed. In some competitive classrooms, teachers tend to display only the papers with "100%" written across the top. For those children who rarely get perfect papers, this can be a discouraging experience; for their parents, it is likely to be equally discouraging. If classroom displays include examples of students' work, it is important to display the best works of every student in approximately equal numbers.

To avoid creating a competitive environment, you may want to display students' work inside their portfolios on their desks so that each parent can view the work done by his or her own child alone. General classroom displays can consist of group projects and murals so that every child and parent can take equal pride in the classroom.

Community Involvement in Classroom Activities

PARENTS AS VOLUNTEERS

Parents volunteer to do many things in schools to benefit their own children and the larger community. Many parents enjoy being members of an all-school organization known as the *Parent Teacher Association (PTA)* or *Parent Teacher Organization (PTO)*. These organizations have regularly scheduled meetings and yearly fundraising events to serve the needs of the school. In most cases, parents do the greatest part of the work on the committees, although teachers are usually represented as well.

Many elementary schools encourage parents to volunteer their time during the school day to assist teachers in educational or extracurricular programs. Parents can serve as coaches, assistant coaches, or referees for some sports events such as all-school field day events. They often serve as helpers on class field trips, accompanying the class on the bus ride and throughout the day. Usually, teachers ask each adult to be responsible for a small group of children during the trip, reducing the adult:child ratio from 28:1 down to 4:1 or 5:1.

In the classroom, many primary teachers invite parent volunteers to serve as assistants in the reading and language arts program. A parent can work with one small group while the teacher works with another, or with the rest of the class. In this way, parents can serve many important functions. They can read aloud to a group of children or listen to an individual or a small group of children read aloud to them. Parents can write the words as a child dictates a story or can edit a piece of writing done by a child. Parents can listen to book reports and keep records of the number and type of books each child has read.

With the advent of computers in the classroom, many teachers appreciate having parents who are knowledgeable about computers volunteer to work with groups of children as they learn to operate a computer or to monitor students' progress as they work with tutorial or problem-solving computer programs.

During individualized mathematics or spelling programs, or those structured on a mastery learning model, parents can serve as assistants who correct formative tests and provide feedback to students. They can also help to organize the large amounts of paperwork, filing, and record keeping that often accompany individualized instructional programs.

Having parents volunteer to work in your classroom has many benefits, and often you will find knowledgeable and experienced parents who enjoy this type of work. Many parents have interrupted their own careers to raise children and look forward to having a regular volunteer job.

Not all teachers, however, enjoy having parent volunteers in their classrooms. Some teachers are reluctant to have parents view the ups and downs that occur in any school day. Other teachers are not comfortable with parent volunteers because the teacher must be ready with activities and materials whenever the parent arrives. For some teachers, this is a burden that outweighs the benefit of having the extra help. It is true that working with parent volunteers means greater responsibility for the teacher who must manage the other adults as well as the students in the class.

Whether you wish to use parents as volunteers in your classroom is one of those issues that you will need to reflect on, considering the benefits against the costs. One of the best ways to gather information about the efficacy of this practice in your classroom is to try it out with one subject area and a knowledgeable, experienced parent volunteer to see if it is a system you want to employ.

To increase the likelihood that the practice will work in your room, you and the parent volunteer should discuss in advance what you expect the parent to do and agree on the times the parent will visit. Usually parents do only routine tasks or monitor students as they work on a program planned by you and your colleagues. When these matters are clarified, you will probably find the volunteer effort to be very productive, allowing you to reduce the amount of time you spend on routine tasks.

COMMUNITY RESOURCES

Parents with special interests, abilities, careers, and accomplishments can also enrich your program by visiting to speak to the class about their specialties. A unit on community helpers can certainly benefit from visits by parents who are nurses, police officers, fire fighters, and others who perform community services. Parents who are manufacturers or waste haulers can provide their input during a unit on ecology. When the class is studying economics, parents who work as merchants can describe the theory of supply and demand to the class.

During the first parent–teacher conference in the fall, you may be able to discover what talents your students' parents possess and create a community resource file to draw on throughout the year. In some schools, these files are kept schoolwide and parents in the file are happy to come to any classroom in the school to share their knowledge and experience with the children. The file may also contain names of adults in the community who are not parents of children attending the school but who are willing to visit as a service to the community.

Some schools seek financial contributions from the community to fund music, art, or other enrichment programs that have been eliminated from their school budgets. Booster clubs are often formed by parents and other community members raise money to support sports teams, the arts or technological programs that require expensive equipment.

Some districts have established an educational foundation that is administered by an administrator. People in the community donate money to the foundation and teachers apply for grants to be used within their department or classroom. If your school does not have such a foundation it might be worthwhile to encourage one.

Getting a foundation started can be an arduous task. A wall of donors prominently displayed at a conspicuous place within the school with plaques indicating the range of support for donating families is an effective procedure for encouraging funding. Auctions and other enjoyable pastimes may be occasions for bringing together families from the school community for a fun evening as well as fund-raising.

Occasionally, parents may approach a teacher and offer to pay for something or contribute something of value to the class. A parent who works in a scientific or technological field may approach a high-school science teacher, for example, and say, "I would like to donate a used cathode ray oscilloscope or a used computer to the department. Can you use one?" It is very hard to turn down this type of request when you may need the equipment and there are no funds available from other sources. It is important that you check with your administration before accepting an offer of this type or before making an appeal for funding at an open house or parent conference.

There could be confusion about whether money or gifts have been exchanged for grades. To reduce this fear for yourself and for the administration, send a letter to each parent stating that in the past some parents have approached you to donate certain items or money, and therefore, you would like to inform all parents about the procedures to be followed for classroom donations. Items of value or donations of money should be sent to the school office with a letter stating which department should receive the money. The teacher is not to be informed who donated the money or equipment. A ledger should be kept with all receipts so at any time during the year appropriate personnel can check how much money was collected and what was purchased. An administrator should be asked to oversee the fund. This procedure standardizes all gift giving practices for your class or department so that everyone is protected.

CHARACTER EDUCATION PROGRAMS

The interaction between home and school becomes more complex and controversial when the school's objective changes from supporting the child's academic development to supporting the child's moral development. Nevertheless, schools in the 21st century are likely to be at the center of a growing concern about the need for greater emphasis on moral education. This concern grows out of an awareness that schools must take more responsibility for countering the influence of drugs, violence on television and other media, the fragmentation of the family, and the publicity about questionable ethical practices in business and industry (ASCD, 1988).

A panel of educators met in the summer of 1988 to discuss the schools' role in teaching values. The educators agreed that due to the enormous temptations and distractions facing children today, schools must take an active role in teaching children about the nature of right and wrong. Although the panel recognized that the increasing social, religious, and ethnic diversity of the schools makes it difficult to agree on one set of values, a few common themes appear in almost every culture. The panel recommends that schools develop community-supported programs centering on at least these four themes: *justice, altruism, diligence,* and *respect for human dignity.*

Lickona (1988) recommends that each school recruit local parents to serve on a school-parent support group to: (1) arrive at a consensus of the moral values most important to that community and (2) write a moral education curriculum that will be taught at school and in the home at the same time (p. 36).

Mary Ellen Saterlie (1988), a school administrator in Baltimore, illustrates how such a parent-school partnership can be formed and what it can produce. She describes the Baltimore public schools' experience, in which school administrators created a community task force to participate in an open dialogue on community values. They purposely invited people with very different religious and political beliefs to serve on the task force. After extensive reading and debate, the task force was able to agree on a "common core" of values appropriate for a democratic and pluralistic society. They are the following:

> compassion, courtesy, critical inquiry, due process, equality of opportunity, freedom of thought and action, honesty, human worth and dignity, integrity, justice, knowledge, loyalty, objectivity, order, patriotism, rational consent, reasoned argument, respect for others' rights, responsible citizenship, rule of law, self-respect, tolerance and truth. (pp. 46–47)

After identifying these community-acknowledged values, the task force wrote outcome statements for development of these moral values. The board of education then discussed and ratified their report. The PTA developed a brochure on the values education program and distributed it to all parents in the system.

The method used to implement this program allowed each of the 148 schools in the district to appoint its own values committee, which was encouraged to select certain of the task force-identified values to emphasize in its own school projects. This encouraged a creative response from most schools. Some addressed additional values such as computer ethics or academic honesty, as well as those identified by the task force. The Baltimore model linked parents, schools, and the community in a unified examination of moral and ethical issues to "strengthen the character of our students, which in turn will contribute to strengthening our free society" (Saterlie, 1988, p. 47).

As a beginning teacher, you may find that your school district is taking similar measures, and you may wish to become an active part of the task force that identifies the moral values of your community and creates school programs to educate students in these values. If you find that your school district has not yet considered such a challenge, perhaps you can be the one who initiates the idea. Reflective individuals who are committed to upholding the moral values of the community can serve as important role models for the students they teach.

Teachers Mentoring and Coaching One Another

In recent history, the school principal was responsible for observing and evaluating teachers' classroom performance. The top-down hierarchy implied that only administrators could and should supervise teachers and make recommendations about improving their performance.

Currently, there is a growing consensus that teachers' growth and development is enhanced when they think of themselves as members of professional communities whose members take responsibility for teaching each other, learning together, and focusing on the successes and challenges of educating their students (Shaps, Watson, & Lewis, 1996). The idea of belonging to a community changes the way teachers think about their own learning. It tends to break the pattern of isolation that individual teachers used to experience when they went into their classrooms and closed their doors to the outside world. In supportive communities, teachers support one other, share teaching strategies, try out new ways of teaching, ask for and receive feedback, that leads them to be able to redesign their curriculum and methods of instruction. Teachers in professional communities learn how to reflect on their abilities and gain confidence for changing their practice to better meet their student's needs (Lieberman, 1995).

Being part of a teaching community encourages the type of reflective action in teaching that we have recommended throughout this book. When teachers seek out other, more experienced teachers to discuss their classroom dilemmas and ask for feedback, they are demonstrating their willingness to reflect on their own practice in an effort to improve it.

In many school systems today teachers are sharing their own perspectives with each other as part of the evaluation process. Experienced classroom teachers, sometimes called *coaches* or *mentor teachers*, observe less-experienced teachers as they work with children in their classrooms. Afterward, the two teachers discuss the observed classroom events. This practice allows the mentor teacher to provide critical feedback and to share personal knowledge with colleagues. It also encourages the beginning teachers to reflect on what they do, the effects of their actions and decisions, and ways to improve their teaching.

In Watsonville, California, teachers in two schools created a program called Professional Partnerships to decrease isolation and build collegial support systems. In this program, two teachers selected each other on a voluntary basis to become teaching partners. They observed one another's classrooms each month for a minimum of 30 minutes each visit. The partners meet prior to each observation to define the focus of the lesson and then discuss the visit afterwards. Quarterly, the partners meet with the principal and two additional teachers in the school, who serve as facilitators. Here are how two of the teacher partners described the project:

> My partner is coming to visit so I don't let things slide. My area of interest is improving the quality of student interactions. But I've also improved management, groupings, and materials because everything surrounding the lesson affected what I wanted to have happen.
>
> The postconferences give me a chance to talk about the details of the lesson that I couldn't pay attention to while I was teaching. My partner always gives me new ideas. I feel very supported, and I'm making changes (Stobbe, 1993, p. 41).

Teachers are also actively involved in selecting the type of staff development they need to accomplish the goals they've established for themselves. When teachers get interested in a new curriculum such as the whole language approach, or mathematics programs that emphasize problem solving, they are likely to propose conferences they'd like to attend and arrange to bring in consultants knowledgeable about the new methods.

Another powerful new result of being part of a professional community of teachers is the increase in the role of the teacher as a researcher. Asking questions of one another and generating ideas often leads teachers to investigate areas of concern. Informally, and quite naturally, they often begin doing active research to improve their own instructional practices. When they learn something valuable about their own efforts, they are increasingly taking the role of collaborating with other educators to communicate what they have found. To share the results of their investigations, many teachers are writing about their experiences and describing the investigations they've made. They submit their papers to journals and take part as presenters in local and regional conferences.

INTERACTING WITH COLLEAGUES IN CREATING PROFESSIONAL PORTFOLIOS

Beginning teachers are frequently interested in creating professional portfolios as a means of demonstrating their knowledge, awareness of issues, ability to communicate and reflectiveness on the important issues of K–12 education. Many school systems engage experienced teachers as mentor coaches and ask beginning teachers to create professional portfolios that document their accomplishments and strengths. Judy has worked with beginning teachers as a mentor coach and finds that the most valuable aspect of creating the professional portfolio is not the product itself, but the growth that occurs during the process of selecting what to include, reflecting on each document and work sample and talking with other colleagues and the mentor coach about the experiences that resulted in each document or page of the portfolio.

In this text, we have encouraged the creation of a professional portfolio, and have offered specific suggestions of what might be included. We also highly recommend that you view your portfolio as a work-in-progress, changing it weekly or monthly as new ideas or accomplishments occur. We also heartily recommend that you share your portfolio with other trusted colleagues and look at theirs. The ideas you will gain from one another will enable you to make your portfolio more and more interesting and useful as a means of communicating your strengths.

We hope that you have a mentor coach when you begin teaching, and that your mentor will assist you in collecting artifacts and documents for your portfolio. A mentor can be asked to photograph your classroom while you are teaching, so that you can include the photos in your portfolio. You may also ask your mentor to videotape you while you present your first unit or teach with manipulatives or lead a lively discussion. These videos are wonderful additions to your portfolio.

If there are no mentor coaches in your district during your first year of teaching, just find one for yourself. In the first few weeks of teaching, listen and watch for the teachers that have the most in common with your philosophy or curriculum orientation. Approach one and ask the teacher to serve as your informal mentor. The teacher is likely to be delighted with this invitation, as it offers both of you the opportunity to grow and learn. You will learn from the experience of your chosen coach, and the mentor will learn what's new from you. We hope that you will share this book with your coach and work on the professional portfolio pages together.

THE POWERFUL INFLUENCE A TEACHER CAN MAKE

At the center of all of this change is the teacher, and the growing power, responsibility, and respect the teacher has earned. Porter and Brophy (1988) report that since the early 1970s there has been a surge of activity in research on teaching. Much of it has been predicated on a deceptively simple thesis: Effective school learning requires good teaching, and *good teachers* are those who exercise good judgment in constructing the education of their students (p. 74). In our words, as we describe in Chapter 1 of this text, we believe that good teachers are *relational teachers*. They may have their own hopes and expectations when they enter the profession, but they choose to use withitness and reflective thinking to put the needs of their students above their own. Not satisfied with their own self-perceptions, they consciously seek out respected colleagues to ask for feedback on their actions and plans. We hope that we have made our case in this text that there is a strong, undeniable link between *reflective* and *effective* teachers.

As we discussed in Chapter 2, research shows that the most effective teachers are good classroom managers. This management skill grows directly out of reflective, relational, and democratic leadership from the first day of school. As shown in Chapter 3, the role of the teacher includes the responsibility for making accurate assessments of students' needs. Students from all cultures, ethnic groups and economic conditions can thrive in the classroom of a caring and relational teacher, who uses formal and informal sources of information as a means of ensuring that all students in the class can achieve success.

Throughout the research on effective teaching and effective schools the attribute of *teacher clarity* surfaces again and again. "Effective teachers are clear about what they intend to accomplish through their instruction, and they keep these goals in mind both in designing instruction and in communicating its purposes to the students" (Porter & Brophy, 1988, p. 81). Clarity of goal setting requires the reflective planning practices described in Chapter 4.

It is also becoming apparent that it is very effective to combine or integrate subjects into multidisciplinary units of study, as described in Chapters 5 and 6. Rather than being textbook technicians, reflective teachers prefer to create their own learning experiences either individually or with teammates. They frequently focus on interesting themes or topics in which students use and develop their reading, writing, and research skills as they gain new knowledge about a variety of subjects.

Another common element identified throughout the literature on effective teaching is that effective teachers create learning experiences in which students are not simply passive recipients of fact-based knowledge; instead, they teach their students how to use many *cognitive processes*, how to organize information in new ways, and how to solve problems for themselves. It takes a reflective, relational teacher to recognize and select the appropriate teaching strategies that will engage students in active learning, as described in Chapters 7, 8, 9, and 10.

Reflective teachers are eager to use a variety of assessment techniques, such as those described in Chapter 11, rather than rely on one objective method. This is an especially effective practice because it allows students with a variety of learning styles to demonstrate their accomplishments and succeed. Effective practitioners are also talented at providing students with useful, timely, and detailed *critical feedback* so that students know what is expected and what they must do to succeed. But we now know that simply being a good evaluator is not enough; the most effective teachers are those who cause their students to take an active role in the evaluation of their own learning by teaching them how to apply *metacognitive strategies* to become independent and self-reliant, able to monitor and regulate their own learning.

In addition to their responsibilities to their students, effective teachers are able to communicate well with the parents and other members of the school community to support the moral development of students as we've described in this chapter and in Chapter 2.

The teacher's role in the educational community is changing. Teaching shows considerable promise of becoming a highly respected profession in the United States during the 21st century. This is largely due to the efforts of reflective teachers who are asking the important questions about how they can improve classroom events and children's lives. Alone or in collaboration, relational teachers are seeking out new alternatives and selecting the ones they believe might improve their teaching. They are taking responsibility for evaluating their classroom practices by gathering data from their own observations and from the current research and knowledge base on teaching and learning. They are disseminating what works for them in faculty meetings, workshops, conferences, and articles in professional journals. The result is a new emphasis on inquiry, reflection, and building a knowledge base about the most successful and effective practices that create a stimulating and healthy learning community.

A single teacher can exert a powerful influence on the community and has the potential to literally change the lives of students in perceptible ways. Chaos theory in physics tells us that only slight changes to the initial conditions of two identical dynamical systems will result in two completely different outcomes as time proceeds. The classic example is a pinball machine where the pinballs are as identical as we can possibly make them. No matter how precisely we try to produce the same initial conditions for each release and operate each flipper the same way as our ball cascades down our slight incline, minute variations along the way will result in different scores and different paths for each ball. No two games are identical.

Our teaching influences others just like the pinball machine, as we "touch" each student's life. A teacher's acts of kindness or courage take on huge proportions months or even years down the road. What each individual does today to improve the lives of the next generation is the most lasting contribution any of us can make.

⊃ Reflective Actions for Your Professional Portfolio
Your Reflections on Your Role in the School Community

Use Withitness: Observe a Faculty Meeting

Arrange to visit a faculty meeting or another decision-making body at a school you are visiting. How are decisions made? Do teachers work as colleagues to propose programs or solve problems? Does the administrator respect the ideas of the faculty? Visualize yourself as a member of this faculty. What responsibilities would you be willing to assume?

Put School/Community Relations into Perspective

Throughout this text we have used the term *relational* about interpersonal interactions among teachers and students. How does this term correspond to the interactions among colleagues, administrators and teachers? What type of relationships do you envision for yourself and your colleagues?

Widen Your Perspective

Are you a person who is comfortable or uncomfortable with decision-making power? If you work in a school district that encourages teachers to take responsibility for many important decisions, will you welcome this as an opportunity or look on it as a burden? Would you prefer to make decisions about your own classroom independently, or would you rather share the power and the responsibility with your teammates?

Do Research and Invite Feedback

Ask several experienced teachers to tell you stories of their interactions with other faculty members at their schools. If there are mentor teachers at the schools you visit, talk with them about the way teachers coach one another in that setting. What are the advantages of having teachers visit one another's classrooms to offer support and suggestions? What are the possible disadvantages or fears related to these visits? In your view, how can these fears or disadvantages be minimized?

Redefine Your View of Collegial Relationships

You may have learned from your discussions with colleagues that it is difficult or impossible for teachers to please every student, every colleague or every administrator. Whenever a controversial issue arises in a school community, your point of view will be welcomed by some, but not all, of your colleagues on the faculty. If you accept that condition, how can you present your opinions to others on your faculty who may have very different opinions from yours?

Create an Action Plan

Choose an educational issue or dilemma that you are observing in schools you visit. Create an action plan to approach this problem that you would propose to your colleagues if you were a full-time faculty member at the school. Include a method to gather information from a variety of people who make up the school community.

Predict Possible Outcomes

Show your action plan to an experienced teacher. Get feedback on how to improve your plan or make it more realistic. What will you do if other teachers are reluctant to discuss your plan? What will you do if they think your issue is of little interest or value? What will you do if they disagree with you? Revise your plan and include it in your portfolio.

References

Association of Supervision and Curriculum Development (ASCD). (1988). Moral education in the life of the school. *Educational Leadership, 45*(8), 4–8.

First, J. (1988). Immigrant students in U.S. public schools: Challenges with solutions. *Phi Delta Kappan, 70*(3), 205–210.

Florio-Ruane, S. (1989). Social organization of classes and schools. In M. Reynolds (Ed.), *Knowledge base for beginning teachers* (pp. 163–172). Oxford: Pergamon.

Good, T., & Brophy, J., (1987). *Looking in classrooms* (4th ed.). New York: Harper & Row.

Gronlund, N., & Linn, R. (1990). *Measurement and evaluation in teaching.* Upper Saddle River, NJ: Merrill/Prentice Hall.

Lickona, T. (1988). How parents and schools can work together to raise moral children. *Educational Leadership, 45*(8), 36–38.

Lieberman, A. (1995). Practices that support teacher development: Transforming conceptions of professional learning. *Phi Delta Kappan, 76,* 591–596.

Meadows, B. (1993). Through the eyes of parents. *Educational Leadership, 51*(2), 31–34.

Porter, A., & Brophy, J. (1988). Synthesis of research on good teaching. *Educational Leadership, 45*(4), 74–85.

Rimm, S. (1995). *Why bright kids get poor grades.* New York: Crown.

Saterlie, M. (1988). Developing a community consensus for teaching values. *Educational Leadership, 45*(8), 44–47.

Shaps, E., Watson, M., & Lewis, C. (1996). A sense of community is key to effectiveness in fostering character education. *Journal of Staff Development, 17*(2), 42–47.

Stobbe, C. (1993). Professional partnerships. *Educational Leadership, 51*(2), 40–41.

name index

subject index

authors' biographies

Elliot Eisner described the role of an *educational connoiseur* in his book *Educational Imagination*. "The major distinction between connoisseurship and criticism is this: connoisseurship is the art of appreciation, criticism is the art of disclosure." He goes on to say that experience counts in the development of connoisseurship. "To develop connoisseurship one must have a desire to perceive subtleties, to become a student of human behavior, to focus one's perception." (1985, p. 220). We'd like to believe that this book was written by two very enthusiastic educational connoisseurs.

Judy Eby began teaching in 1960, and has been a classroom teacher, a gifted program coordinator, a teacher educator (De Paul University, University of San Diego, and San Diego State University), and a mentor teacher in the Beginning Teacher Support Academy with the San Diego Unified School District. Now retired, she still enthusiastically pursues her role as a connoiseur of best educational practices. She actively searches out and researches best practices, and shares her experiences and perceptions with other educators. She offers her experience to school districts as an educational consultant, specializing in the development of reflective action and professional portfolios for teachers.

She also volunteers in children's literacy programs on both sides of the San Diego-Tijuana border. Her most treasured project is the Tecolote Centro de Comunidad, a children's center in Tijuana, where she has created and runs a children's library for the community. She also participates in before and after school programs on both sides of the border.

Because Judy knows that teacher educators deserve to have the ideas of someone currently immersed in teacher education, she invited Adrienne Herrell, a children's literacy specialist, and Jim Hicks, a high school physics teacher, to co-author this book.

Adrienne Herrell received her Ph.D. from Florida State University in early childhood education/early literacy. She currently teaches early literacy, literacy for English language learners and reading/language arts assessment classes in the elementary credential and reading/language arts master's programs at California State University, Fresno.

She is author, or co-author of three other books published by Merrill/Prentice Hall: *Camcorder in the Classroom* (1997) with Joel P. Fowler, *Fifty Strategies for Teaching English Language Learners* (2000), and *Fifty Strategies for Assessing and Increasing Reading Comprehension* (in press) with Michael Jordan. Adrienne taught for 23 years in public school in Florida but considers raising five sons to be her most valuable life experience.

Jim Hicks, an award-winning educator, has been teaching physics at Barrington High School, District 220, Barrington, IL for 35 years. He received a master's degree in physics from Purdue University in 1970 and in a Ph.D. in science education from Northwestern University in 1978. He has taught part time at the University of Illinois at Champaign-Urbana, University of Illinois at Chicago, and McHenry County College in Crystal Lake, IL.

His numerous educator awards include the Radio Shack Tandy Scholar Award as a top secondary educator in America in 1999; Instructional Innovation in Mathematics and Science Award from Business Week in 1992; Most Outstanding Physics Teacher, State of Illinois, awarded by the American Association of Physics Illinois chapter in 1991; and the Kohl Education International Foundation Award for exemplary teaching in 1985. The Omni Society of Lake County, IL presented Jim with an International Youth Mentor award in 1998. He and Chris Chiaverinas of New Trier High School, District 203 in Winnetka, Illinois, were the subject of two documentaries: *Rock and Roll Physics,* produced and directed by Kurtis Productions of Chicago, and *Amusement Park Physics*, produced by Beyond 2000, an Australian based television production company.

Jim and his wife, Fran, live in Crystal Lake, IL. They have six children. "The perfect teacher, mother, and friend" is how he describes Fran, a middle-school science teacher who has offered her own reflective action in Chapter 10.